Humanization of Arms Control

Despite clear legal rules and political commitments, no significant progress has been made in nuclear disarmament for two decades. New ideas and strategies are therefore necessary. The author explores an alternative approach to arms control focusing on the human dimension rather than on States' security: "humanization" of arms control!

The book explores the preparatory work on arms control treaties and in particular the role of civil society. It analyzes the positive experiences of the movements against chemical weapons, anti-personnel mines, and cluster munitions, as well as the recent conclusion of the Arms Trade Treaty. The author examines the question of whether civil society will be able to replicate the success strategies that have been used, in particular, in the field of anti-personnel mines (Ottawa Convention) and cluster munitions (Oslo Convention) in the nuclear weapons field. He also explores the contribution of those treaties to the protection of the human being, and their implementation by NGOs, the European Court of Human Rights and the International Criminal Court.

The book also explains the effects of weapons, especially nuclear weapons, on human beings, the environment, and global development, thereby focusing on vulnerable groups, such as indigenous peoples, women, and children. It takes a broad approach to human rights, including economic, social, and cultural rights. The author concludes that the use of nuclear weapons is illegal under international humanitarian and human rights law and, moreover, constitutes international crimes under the Rome Statute of the International Criminal Court.

In his general conclusions, the author makes concrete proposals for the progress toward a world without nuclear weapons.

Daniel Rietiker (PhD) is a senior lawyer at the European Court of Human Rights and teaches international law and human rights at Suffolk University Law School (Boston, MA) and Lausanne University (Switzerland).

Routledge Research in the Law of Armed Conflict

Available titles in this series include:

Islamic Law and the Law of Armed Conflict
The Armed Conflict in Pakistan
Niaz Shah

Cluster Munitions and International Law
Disarmament with a Human Face?
Alexander Breitegger

Accountability for Violations of International Humanitarian Law
Essays in Honour of Tim McCormack
Jadranka Petrovic

Humanization of Arms Control
Paving the Way for a World Free of Nuclear Weapons
Daniel Rietiker

Forthcoming titles in this series include:

International Law and Drone Strikes in Pakistan
The Legal and Socio-Political Aspects
Sikander Ahmed Shah

Islam and Warfare
Context and Compatibility with International Law
Onder Bakircioglu

The Concept of Military Objectives in International Law and Targeting Practice
Agnieszka Jachec-Neale

Cosmopolitan Ethics and Law on Autonomous Weapons in Modern Warfare
Ozlem Ulgen

Humanization of Arms Control

Paving the Way for a World Free of Nuclear Weapons

Daniel Rietiker

Routledge
Taylor & Francis Group
LONDON AND NEW YORK

First published 2018 by Routledge

2 Park Square, Milton Park, Abingdon, Oxfordshire OX14 4RN
52 Vanderbilt Avenue, New York, NY 10017

Routledge is an imprint of the Taylor & Francis Group, an informa business

First issued in paperback 2019

British Library Cataloguing in Publication Data
A catalogue record for this book is available from the British Library

Library of Congress Cataloging in Publication Data
Names: Rietiker, Daniel, author.
Title: Humanization of arms control : paving the way for a world free of nuclear weapons / Daniel Rietiker.
Description: Abingdon, Oxon ; New York, NY : Routledge, 2017. | Series: Routledge research in the law of armed conflict | Includes bibliographical references and index.
Identifiers: LCCN 2017002096| ISBN 9781138225428 (hbk) | ISBN 9781315399706 (ebk)
Subjects: LCSH: Nuclear disarmament. | Nuclear weapons (International law)
Classification: LCC KZ5665 .R54 2017 | DDC 327.1/747—dc23
LC record available at https://lccn.loc.gov/2017002096

ISBN: 978-1-138-22542-8 (hbk)
ISBN: 978-0-367-26701-8 (pbk)

Typeset in Galliard
by Keystroke, Neville Lodge, Tettenhall, Wolverhampton

To Yulia, with much love and gratitude for her patience,
and to Wolfgang, our sunshine!

Contents

Table of Cases

African Commission on Human and Peoples' Rights

Committee on Economic, Social and Cultural Rights

Committee on the Elimination of Discrimination against Women

Committee on the Rights of the Child

European Court of Human Rights

Human Rights Committee

Inter-American Commission of Human Rights

Inter-American Court of Human Rights

International Court of Justice

International Tribunal for Rwanda

International Criminal Tribunal for the former Yugoslavia

Permanent Court of International Justice

Arbitration

Japan

Abbreviations

ACA	Arms Control Association
ACHPR	African Charter on Human and Peoples' Rights
ACHR	American Convention on Human Rights
AComHPR	African Commission on Human and Peoples' Rights
ADRDM	American Declaration on the Rights and Duties of Man
AFS	American Federation of Scientists
ASEAN	Association of Southeast Asian Nations
ATT	Arms Trade Treaty
BWC	Biological Weapons Convention
CCD	Conference of the Committee on Disarmament
CCW	Convention on Certain Conventional Weapons
CD	Conference on Disarmament
CEDAW	Convention on the Elimination of All Forms of Discrimination Against Women
CESCR	Committee on Economic, Social and Cultural Rights
CIA	Central Intelligence Agency
CMC	Cluster Munitions Coalition
CPPNM	Convention on the Physical Protection of Nuclear Material
CRC	Committee on the Rights of the Child
CRPD	Convention on the Rights of Persons with Disabilities
CTBT	Comprehensive Test Ban Treaty
CWC	Chemical Weapons Convention
DPI	Department of Public Information
DPRK	Democratic People's Republic of Korea
DRIP	Declaration on the Rights of Indigenous Peoples
ECCC	Extraordinary Chambers in the Courts of Cambodia
ECHR	European Convention on Human Rights
ECOSOC	United Nations Economic and Social Council
ECtHR	European Court of Human Rights
EMP	Electro-Magnetic Pulse
ERW	Explosive Remnants of War
FARC	Revolutionary Armed Forced of Colombia
FRY	Former Federal Republic of Yugoslavia

HI	Handicap International
HRC	Human Rights Committee
HSP	Harvard Sussex Program on Chemical and Biological Weapons
HRW	Human Rights Watch
IAComHR	Inter-American Commission of Human Rights
IACtHR	Inter-American Court of Human Rights
IAEA	International Atomic Energy Agency
IALANA	International Association of Lawyers Against Nuclear Arms
ICAN	International Campaign to Abolish Nuclear Weapons
ICBL	International Campaign to Ban Landmines
ICC	International Criminal Court
ICCPR	International Covenant on Civil and Political Rights
ICEAFRD	International Convention on the Elimination of All Forms of Racial Discrimination
ICESCR	International Covenant on Economic, Social and Cultural Rights
ICJ	International Court of Justice
ICRC	International Committee of the Red Cross
ICTR	International Criminal Tribunal for Rwanda
ICTY	International Criminal Tribunal for the former Yugoslavia
ILC	International Law Commission
ILO	International Labour Organization
INESAP	International Network of Engineers and Scientists
IPB	International Peace Bureau
IPPNW	International Physicians for the Prevention of Nuclear War
ISIL	Islamic State in Iraq and the Levant
ISIS	Islamic State
IUPAC	International Union for Pure and Applied Chemistry
KFOR	Kosovo Force
KGB	Committee of State Security of the former Soviet Union
LSN	Landmine Survivors Network
MDG	Millennium Development Goals
NAM	Non-Aligned Movement
NATO	North Atlantic Treaty Organization
NEA	Nuclear Energy Agency (within the Organisation for Economic Co-Operation and Development (OECD))
NGO	Non-Governmental Organization
NNWS	Non-Nuclear Weapon State
NPT	Treaty on the Non-Proliferation of Nuclear Weapons
NPT PrepCom	Preparatory Committee of the Treaty on the Non-Proliferation of Nuclear Weapons
NSS	Nuclear Security Summit
NWFZ	Nuclear-Weapons-Free Zone
NWS	Nuclear Weapon State
OCHA	Office for the Coordination of Humanitarian Affairs

OEWG	Open-Ended Working Group
OPANAL	Agency for the Prohibition of Nuclear Weapons in Latin America
OPCW	Organization for the Prohibition of Chemical Weapons
PCIJ	Permanent Court of International Justice
PGA	Parliamentarians for Global Action
PNET	Peaceful Nuclear Explosions Treaty
PNND	Parliamentarians for Nuclear Non-Proliferation and Disarmament
PTBT	Partial Test Ban Treaty
PTS	Provisional Technical Secretariat of the Preparatory Commission of the OPCW
SAB	Scientific Advisory Board
SALW	Small Arms and Light Weapons
SCSL	Special Court for Sierra Leone
SDG	Sustainable Development Goals
SDI	Strategic Defense Initiative
SIPRI	Stockholm International Peace Research Institute
STL	Special Tribunal for Lebanon
SVK	Army of Serbian Krajina
TNT	Trinitrotoluene
TTBT	Threshold Test Ban Treaty
UDHR	Universal Declaration of Human Rights
UNCRC	United Nations Convention on the Rights of the Child
UNDP	United Nations Development Program
UNGA	United Nations General Assembly
UNICEF	United Nations International Children's Emergency Fund
UNIDIR	United Nations Institute for Disarmament Research
UNMIK	United Nations Interim Administration in Kosovo
UNSC	United Nations Security Council
UNSCEAR	United Nations Scientific Committee on the Effects of Atomic Radiation
UNSG	United Nations Secretary-General
USSR	Union of Soviet Socialist Republics
UXO	Unexploded Ordnance
VCLT	Vienna Convention on the Law of Treaties
VJ	Yugoslav Army
WFC	World Future Council
WFP	World Food Program
WHO	World Health Organization
WMD	Weapons of Mass Destruction
YWCA	Young Women's Christian Association

Acknowledgments

I conducted the main research for the present study at the Human Rights Program (HRP) at Harvard Law School (Cambridge, MA, United States of America) during a fellowship in 2014. I would like to thank the HRP for having received me so warmly. The eight months spent in Cambridge count among the best and most exciting ones of my life.

Special thanks go to Gerald Neuman and Tyler Giannini, Co-Directors of the HRP, who, in spite of their busy schedules, always had time to discuss human rights issues with me. I am also extremely grateful to Mindy Roseman, who coordinated and received the new visiting fellows. Moreover, I want to thank Bonnie Docherty (senior clinical instructor HRP) with whom I shared my passion for international humanitarian law and arms control, and my co-fellow Jure Vidmar (University of Maastricht) for all the stimulating discussions on international law we had in Cambridge, MA.

During my fellowship at Cambridge, I also had the opportunity to follow lectures and events at the Harvard Kennedy School of Government (HKS). Special thanks go to Kathryn Sikkink for involving me in her courses and the events organized at the Carr Center for Human Rights at HKS, which gave me further ideas for the present book. I also express my gratitude to "Managing the Atom" (MTA) at HKS, in particular to its former associate Sven-Eric Fikenscher, for the open door and the stimulating discussions.

Furthermore, I want to thank John Burroughs, from Lawyers Committee for Nuclear Policy (LCNP), and Alyn Ware, internationally recognized peace and disarmament educator and campaigner, for the many valuable discussions we had (and still have) regarding nuclear disarmament. I also express my sincere gratitude to Dr. Nurlan Zhanabilov, renowned Kazakh legal expert, thanks to whom Olzhas Suleimenov, Kazakh poet and leader of the "Nevada-Semipalatinsk" movement, kindly agreed to write a foreword to the present book.

Special thanks also go to the staff of the different libraries that facilitated so greatly my research, namely the library of the Harvard Law School (HLS), the libraries of the IUHEID (Geneva) and the ISDC (Lausanne), as well as the library of the European Court of Human Rights. As far as the latter is concerned, Geneviève Woods and Alain Heisserer deserve to be mentioned in particular.

I also want to thank my former boss, Michael O'Boyle, former deputy Registrar of the ECtHR, for his support in the application for the fellowship at HLS, and my dear colleagues, James Brannan and Kresimir Kamber, for their friendship and their concrete proposals on the text and the publication of my study.

But particularly sincere thanks are due to Lucius Caflisch, former judge of the ECtHR and former member of the ILC, for having supported me over the years and, above all, for his careful reading of the entire manuscript and his numerous appreciated comments and proposals. No one else invested more time and patience than him in the present book. I feel very privileged.

Finally, I owe special thanks to my wife, Yulia, and our son, Wolfgang, who was born during the preparation of the present book. Without the patience, and moral and technical (IT) support of my wife, my work would not have been completed yet. Therefore, my book is dedicated to her and Wolfgang.

Foreword

(Translation from Russian)

This book is a significant contribution to one of the biggest challenges faced by the world today: nuclear weapons. Very often, such studies have concentrated on the interests and security of the States, which are merely abstract values. The author, however, has chosen a very original approach to the topic: instead of insisting on the States' priorities and viewpoints, he places the individual at the center of the debate – humanization of arms control. He describes, in many details and based on past experience (Hiroshima, Nagasaki, Chernobyl, Fukushima, and nuclear testing on the Marshall Islands), the concrete destruction and disruption that the use of nuclear weapons causes among societies, families, innocent children, and women. He then concludes very convincingly that such a use amounts to a total denial of humanitarian law and the human rights of the victims. Nuclear explosions cause radiation, nuclear fallout, death, and cancer. Therefore, the author takes into account a broad range of human rights, in particular the right to life, but also very modern rights such as the right to health, the right to a healthy environment, and the right to water. For weighty reasons, he focuses on particularly exposed groups, such as children, women, and indigenous peoples. History shows and science confirms that those groups suffer more than others from war, nuclear disasters, and radiation.

I am personally very grateful to the author that he did not forget one of the saddest chapters of human existence, namely the testing of nuclear weapons. My country, Kazakhstan, was one of the places where hundreds of nuclear weapons have been exploded, with devastating consequences for the local population and the natural environment. The book describes the suffering of some of the indigenous peoples of this world, but the author also gives hope by describing how a peaceful, popular movement (Nevada-Semipalatinsk), under capable leadership, can change the course of history. Only thanks to the courage of the Kazakh people, the Semipalatinsk nuclear test site was closed and a test moratorium announced by President Gorbachov in 1991. Today, Kazakhstan is part of a region completely free of nuclear weapons. For this reason, my country serves as an example for many others.

This book goes far beyond an ordinary law book. It should be read by everybody who cares about the human being, our planet, and our children.

Olzhas Suleimenov

Kazakh poet, and leader of the "Nevada-Semipalatinsk" movement, thanks to which the former USSR pronounced a moratorium on nuclear testing.

(Russian original)

Книга Даниэля Ритикера представляет собой значительный вклад в обсуждение одной из самых больших проблем, с которыми сегодня сталкивается мир: ядерное оружие. Очень часто такие исследования были сосредоточены на интересах самих государств и их безопасности, которые являются просто абстрактными ценностями. Автор выбрал, однако, весьма оригинальный подход к теме: вместо того, чтобы настаивать на приоритетах и точках зрения государств, он ставит человека в центре дебатов - гуманизация контроля над вооружением. Он детально описывает на основе реальных событий (Хиросима, Нагасаки, Чернобыль, Фукусима, ядерные испытания на Маршалловых островах) конкретные разрушения и нарушения, которые вызывает применение ядерного оружия у людей, семьей, невинных детей и женщин. Затем автор приходит к весьма убедительному выводу, что такое использование приводит к полному отрицанию гуманитарного права и прав человека жертв таких испытаний. Ядерные взрывы вызывают радиоактивный фон, радиоактивные осадки, смерть и рак. Таким образом, автор обращает внимание на широкий круг прав человека, как на право на жизнь, так и на довольно современные права, такие как право на здоровье, право на благоприятную окружающую среду и право на воду. Вполне обоснованно он делает акцент на особо уязвимых группах населения, таких как дети, женщины, а также малые коренные народы. История показывает, а наука подтверждает, что эти группы больше других страдают от войны, ядерных катастроф и радиации.

Я лично очень благодарен автору, что он не забыл одну из самых печальных глав человеческой истории, а именно испытания ядерного оружия. Моя страна, Казахстан, была одним из тех мест, где были взорваны сотни единиц ядерного оружия, повлекшие разрушительные последствия для местного населения и окружающей среды. Книга описывает страдания некоторых малых коренных народов, но при этом автор также дает и надежду, показывая, как мирное общественное движение (Невада-Семипалатинск) под умелым руководством может изменить ход истории. Только благодаря мужеству казахского народа, Семипалатинский ядерный полигон был закрыт и в 1991 году президентом Горбачевым был объявлен мораторий на ядерные испытания. Сегодня Казахстан-часть региона полностью свободного от ядерного оружия. По этой причине, моя страна является примером для многих других.

Эта книга выходит далеко за рамки обычной юридической литературы. Она должна быть прочитана всеми, кому небезразлична судьба человечества, нашей планеты и наших детей.

Олжас Сулейменов

казахский поэт, и лидер движения «Невада-Семипалатинск», Благодаря которому СССР наложил мораторий на ядерные испытания.

General introduction

Member States of the United Nations have made significant progress on important global issues, such as climate change and Sustainable Development Goals (SDGs).[1] Regarding nuclear disarmament, however, the record is very poor. Despite considerable bilateral reductions between Russia and the United States since the Cold War peaks, there still remain 16 000 nuclear weapons worldwide, sometimes on a high state of alert, ready to be used within a few minutes.[2] Moreover, the stockpiles of certain States having reached a certain age, modernization of nuclear weapons will necessitate a large amount of resources in the near future.[3] It is expected that States will spend US $1 trillion on nuclear weapons globally in the next ten years.[4] By comparison, the annual UN core budget is only US $5.1 billion – that is, 5 percent of the annual global nuclear weapons budget.[5] In addition, even though nuclear testing has become rare in recent years, it is still very much a reality.[6] Moreover, given the current international climate, certain States have not ceased to rely on their own nuclear weapons or on nuclear protection guaranteed by other States.[7]

1 P. Lewis, B. Unal, and S. Aghlani, "Nuclear Disarmament: The Missing Link in Multilateralism," Chatham House, October 2016, p. 3, https://www.chathamhouse.org/publication/nuclear-disarmament-missing-link-multilateralism (accessed February 28, 2017).

2 International Peace Bureau (IPB), Parliamentarians for Nuclear Nonproliferation and Disarmament, and World Future Council, "Move the Nuclear Weapons Money: A Handbook for Civil Society and Legislators," 2016, p. 2, https://www.worldfuturecouncil.org/time-move-nuclear-weapons-money-new-resource-launched-parliamentary-event-geneva/ (accessed February 28, 2017).

3 See, for instance, D. Cook, "An Insider's View of Nuclear Weapons Modernization," *Arms Control Today*, October 2016, pp. 14–18.

4 IPB et al., "Move the Nuclear Weapons Money," p. 2.

5 *Ibid.*, p. 1.

6 The Democratic People's Republic of Korea has conducted five nuclear tests since 2006, the two last ones on January 6, 2016 and September 9, 2016; https://www.ctbto.org/the-treaty/developments-after-1996/2016-sept-dprk-announced-nuclear-test/ (accessed March 1, 2017). Moreover, former US Defense Secretary William Perry declared to *Arms Control Today* that he had information according to which Russia might also conduct new tests in the future (*Arms Control Today*, January/February 2016, p. 24).

7 See, for a recent example, K. Reif, "NATO Highlights Role of Nuclear Weapons," *Arms Control Today*, September 2016, pp. 5–6, 5.

What are the reasons for the deficit in nuclear disarmament? Is it due to an insufficient or unclear legal landscape? On the contrary, the 1968 Treaty on the Non-Proliferation of Nuclear Weapons (NPT) obliges all the States Parties, under its Article VI, to "pursue negotiations in good faith on effective measures relating to cessation of the nuclear arms race at an early date and to nuclear disarmament, and on a treaty on general and complete disarmament under strict and effective international control." Moreover, the International Court of Justice (ICJ), in its 1996 Advisory Opinion on the *Legality of the Threat or Use of Nuclear Weapons*, confirmed that "there exists an obligation to pursue in good faith and bring to a conclusion negotiations leading to nuclear disarmament in all its aspects under strict and effective international control."[8] It flows from this citation that the duty to obtain the precise result of nuclear disarmament is imposed on all States, whether or not they have ratified the NPT.

In other words, the law regarding nuclear disarmament is crystal clear in itself, but its implementation is lagging behind. As an example, in Prague in April 2009, President Barack Obama called for action to seek the peace and security of a world without nuclear weapons.[9] His ambitions were rewarded by the Nobel Peace Prize in 2009, but his voice was ultimately not echoed by concrete measures due to, inter alia, the political environment in the United States during his second term of office.

Despite those clear legal duties and political commitments, it is generally agreed upon today that no significant progress has been made in the field of nuclear disarmament for two decades. This point of view was explicitly recognized by the UN General Assembly (UNGA) in October 2016:

> The General Assembly . . . Mindful of the absence of concrete outcomes of multilateral nuclear disarmament negotiations within the United Nations framework for two decades . . .[10]

Indeed, the last major "success" that could be celebrated in the Conference on Disarmament (CD) was the conclusion, in September 1996, of the Comprehensive Test Ban Treaty (CTBT), which, due to its very undemocratic entry-into-force clause and despite its more than 180 ratifications, has still not come into force.[11] Moreover, for nearly two decades, the CD has failed to agree to begin talks on the long-sought ban on fissile material production, as well as on other disarmament

8 ICJ Reports 1996, p. 226, Operative paragraph 2 F.

9 D. G. Kimball, "The Debate over Banning the Bomb," *Arms Control Today*, October 2016, p. 3; for the speech, see http://www.acronym.org.uk/old/building-security/reducing-arsenals-incl-start/president-obama-speech-nuclear-disarmament (accessed March 8, 2017).

10 UNGA, UN Doc. A/C.1/71/L.41, October 14, 2016, "Taking forward multilateral nuclear disarmament negotiations."

11 This volume, Chapter 5, section B.

proposals, mostly as a result of the blocking strategies of a handful of States insisting on the consensus principle.[12]

In light of the foregoing, new ideas and strategies and "out-of-the-box" thinking seem indispensable. The present study explores an alternative approach to arms control that focuses on the human dimension of arms control treaties rather than on considerations of States' security: "humanization" of arms control. This approach is currently being promoted by civil society and numerous non-nuclear weapon States (NNWS) which aim to view nuclear weapons through a humanitarian lens. A series of international conferences were convened in 2013 and 2014[13] as a reaction to the failure of the nuclear weapon States (NWS) to eliminate their stocks of nuclear weapons, as stipulated in Article VI NPT. It was also a focal topic at the 2015 NPT Review Conference.

The debates about this new approach have really taken off only at the beginning of the present decade, and where exactly this new movement will lead is still quite open to date. While its supporters hold high hopes, others believe that it has little chance of stimulating the slow-moving course of the nuclear arms control negotiations. Based on the recent positive experience of the movements against anti-personnel mines (Ottawa Convention) and cluster munitions (Oslo Conventions), civil society is pushing toward negotiations for a new treaty banning nuclear weapons, or at least banning their use. Just before this study was concluded, the United Nations General Assembly (UNGA) adopted Resolution L.41,[14] calling for negotiations for the conclusion of a new treaty banning nuclear weapons, to start in 2017. It is not excluded that such a treaty has much in common with the Ottawa and Oslo Conventions, both deeply inspired by considerations of humanity.

In light of the foregoing, it is legitimate to hope that a new chapter of humanization of arms control will be written soon, this one being in the field of nuclear weapons. The present analysis is intended to advance and contribute to this ongoing debate.

Part I of this study is devoted to recent arms control treaties on non-nuclear weapons which aim to eliminate entire categories of weapons, namely chemical weapons, anti-personnel mines, and cluster munitions. It also examines the Arms Trade Treaty (ATT), the conclusion of which in 2013 can be considered one of the greatest successes recently achieved by the international community in this field and which provides a particularly good example of an international instrument combining arms control aspects with the protection of human beings. The human dimension of these treaties is analyzed based on the following criteria: First, the preparatory history of the treaties, with special regard to the role of civil society (Chapter 2); second, the substantive contribution of these treaties to the

12 Kimball, "The Debate over Banning the Bomb," p. 3.

13 Oslo Conference (March 4–5, 2013), Nayarit (February 13–14, 2014), and Vienna (December 8–9, 2014).

14 October 27, 2016.

protection of the individual (Chapter 3); and, third, their implementation and verification by human rights actors and institutions, in particular relevant NGOs and the European Court of Human Rights in conjunction with the Committee of Ministers of the Council of Europe (Chapter 4). Attention will also be paid to the potential role of the International Criminal Court regarding these treaties.

Part II analyzes whether the humanistic approach, which places the individual at the center of the debate, can also be used in connection with instruments restricting or prohibiting nuclear weapons. Traditionally, these weapons have been considered as crucial for States' security. By the same token, nuclear weapons proponents admit that these weapons are a particularly serious threat to the life and health of human beings and to the natural environment. While anti-personnel mines or remnants of cluster munitions cause injuries and loss of human life every day, the nuclear catastrophes in Chernobyl (1986) and, more recently, in Fukushima (2011) illustrate the potential devastation that the use of a nuclear weapon could cause; and one should not forget the indescribable and long-term suffering caused by the use of atomic bombs in Hiroshima and Nagasaki in August 1945, which killed over 100 000 civilians within the first two months, not to mention the thousands of victims who died later as a result of radiation. Part II will examine the devastating effects of the use of nuclear weapons on human beings. Moreover, past testing of nuclear weapons gives an idea of the harm that could be caused by the use of modern nuclear weapons "in real life," and certain conclusions on their lawfulness under international law can possibly be drawn.

The structure of Part II follows closely that of Part I. Contrary to the treaties dealing with non-nuclear weapons (Part I), where bans on the use of the relevant weapons already exist, such a global ban has not yet been agreed upon in the field of nuclear weapons. Therefore, Chapter 7 in Part II will focus on the legality of the use of nuclear weapons. That assessment will be made separately for the legality under humanitarian law (section B) and human rights law (section C), the latter aspect not having received the attention it deserves in legal writing so far. Finally, section D will examine the impact on human beings of other activities, such as development, manufacture, production, acquisition, and possession and threat of use of nuclear weapons.

The most important conclusions emerging from the present study will be summarized and assessed in the General Conclusions. It will also be examined whether the human-centered approach that paved the way for the successful adoption, inter alia, of the Ottawa and Oslo Conventions, as well as the ATT, can be used as a model for a new treaty outlawing nuclear weapons. A few concrete proposals for progress toward a world without nuclear weapons will be made.

Part I

Humanization of arms control treaties dealing with non-nuclear weapons

1 Introductory remarks*

A. SCOPE OF PART I

Part I of the present study focuses on the following treaties:

Convention on the Prohibition of the Development, Production, Stockpiling and Use of Chemical Weapons and on Their Destruction, January 13, 1993 (hereafter "CWC");

Convention on the Prohibition of the Use, Stockpiling, Production and Transfer of Anti-Personnel Mines and on Their Destruction, September 18, 1997 (hereafter "Ottawa Convention"); and

Convention on Cluster Munitions, May 30, 2008 (hereafter "Oslo Convention").

Several reasons support this choice. First, all three treaties were adopted after the Cold War ended and are therefore perceived as modern instruments concluded in a spirit of cooperation rather than of simply coexistence. Second, these treaties can be considered effective, although the Oslo Convention entered into force too recently to be fully assessed. In any event, they are intended to be models for future treaties. Third, the goal of Article I of all three treaties is to abolish entire categories of weapons through a comprehensive list of prohibitions (e.g., development, production, acquisition, stockpiling, transfer) and a positive obligation to destroy the weapons in question. By the same token, States Parties agree to refrain from using the targeted weapons. Finally, these instruments clearly aim at achieving universal ratification and pursue the vision of a world free from the dangers of those weapons.

Arms Trade Treaty, April 2, 2013 (hereafter "ATT")

The ATT, adopted on April 2, 2013, is a particularly illustrative example of the close link between arms control and human rights. It prohibits, inter alia, the exportation of conventional weapons to States that could use them to commit serious violations of humanitarian or human rights law (see Article 7 ATT).

* The views expressed in this study are the author's personal ones and do not necessarily reflect those of the ECtHR.

The special attention given to the ATT in the present study is also justified by the fact that it is fairly new and relatively unexplored by legal writers.

For these reasons, it is these four treaties that are examined in Part I. This does not mean that other arms control treaties that aspire to establish a significant protection of the individual are disregarded. The CWC negotiations were closely linked to the conclusion of the Convention on the Prohibition of the Development, Production and Stockpiling of Bacteriological (Biological) and Toxin Weapons and on Their Destruction (BWC of April 10, 1972), the first arms control treaty aimed at eliminating an entire category of weapons. Moreover, the use of certain gases had already been banned by the Protocol for the Prohibition of the Use in War of Asphyxiating, Poisonous or Other Gases, and of Bacteriological Methods of Warfare (hereafter "Geneva Protocol") signed in Geneva on June 17, 1925 and inspired by the use of toxic gases in World War I. The negotiations on the CWC will be viewed together with efforts to ban biological weapons.

Furthermore, there is some overlap between the Ottawa and Oslo Conventions and the Convention on Prohibitions or Restrictions on the Use of Certain Conventional Weapons Which May Be Deemed to Be Excessively Injurious or to Have Indiscriminate Effects (CCW of October 10, 1980), and in particular its Protocols on the Prohibitions or Restrictions on the Use of Mines, Booby-Traps and Other Devices (Protocol II) and on Explosive Remnants of War (ERW) (Protocol V). The relationship between these protocols – considered instruments of international humanitarian law because they restrict only the actual use of the weapons dealt with – and the Ottawa and Oslo Conventions will be explained to the extent necessary for developing the main concepts in this study.

The proposed human-centered approach to arms control treaties has been facilitated, from the author's point of view, by certain recent developments in the international legal order. The first development consists in the blurring of the boundaries of the law applicable in peacetime and that regarding armed conflict as a result of modern, asymmetric warfare and, therefore, concerns the structure of the international legal order more generally. The second development relates to the notions of security and development, which have expanded to encompass concerns for the well-being of human beings ("human security" and "human development"). These recent developments are explored in the following preliminary section.

B. RECENT DEVELOPMENTS IN THE INTERNATIONAL LEGAL ORDER FAVORING THE CONCLUSION OF THE TREATIES EXAMINED IN PART I

1. Permeability of the borders between the law applicable in peacetime and in armed conflict

In order to place the subsequent developments concerning the human dimension of treaties introduced into their contemporary legal framework, it is appropriate, first, to recall the traditional domains of international law applicable to the instruments analyzed here and, second, to examine whether these well-established categories can be maintained.

The CWC and the Ottawa and Oslo Conventions are, above all, arms control treaties. The content of the ATT is mixed, but does include arms control features. The "immediate neighbors" in this field are the other two categories that deal with international peace and security, namely, the international humanitarian law of armed conflicts, *jus in bello*, and *jus ad bellum*, which provide for principles governing the legality of the use of force in international law. The body of law established by these three disciplines is sometimes called "law of military security."[1] Even though their scope is not identical, there is a close link between them. Indeed, when defining the law applicable to the use or threat of nuclear weapons, the International Court of Justice (ICJ) summarized this link in the following terms in its 1996 Advisory Opinion:

> In the light of the foregoing the Court concludes that the most directly relevant applicable law governing the question of which it was seized, is that relating to the use of force enshrined in the United Nations Charter and the law applicable in armed conflict which regulates the conduct of hostilities, together with any specific treaties on nuclear weapons that the Court might determine to be relevant.[2]

In light of this quotation, it may be recalled that, traditionally, *jus ad bellum* aims at avoiding war and, in the event of a failure of this goal, *jus in bello* limits the horrors of armed conflict for the combatants as well as for the civilian population.[3] From this author's point of view, these two categories are nevertheless not the only law relevant for the question of arms control, in particular because the dichotomy between the legal norms applicable during peace time and war has become increasingly blurred.[4] In parallel, a deeper interdependence between the fields of human rights and humanitarian law can be observed as a consequence.[5]

1 E. P. J. Myjer, "The Law of Arms Control, Military Security and the Issues: An Introduction," in E. P. J. Myjer (ed.), *Issues of Arms Control Law and the Chemical Weapons Convention, Obligation Inter Se and Supervisory Mechanism*, The Hague, Boston, and London, 2001, pp. 1–10, 1, 4–7.

2 Advisory Opinion on the *Legality of the Use or Threat of Nuclear Weapons*, ICJ Reports 1996, § 34.

3 G. Den Dekker, *The Law of Arms Control – International Supervision and Enforcement*, The Hague, Boston, and London, 2001, p. 45.

4 See, for instance, L. Boisson de Chazournes and P. Sands, "Introduction," in L. Boisson de Chazournes and P. Sands (eds.), *International Law, the International Court of Justice and Nuclear Weapons*, Cambridge, 1999, pp. 1–24, 13.

5 The relationship between humanitarian law and human rights law has been extensively examined; see, for instance, R. Provost, *International Human Rights and Humanitarian Law*, Cambridge, 2002; J. K. Kleffner, "Scope of Application of International Humanitarian Law," in D. Fleck (ed.), *The Handbook of International Humanitarian Law*, 3rd edn., Oxford, 2013, pp. 43–78, 71–78. Regarding the Oslo Convention, see J. Corsi, "Towards Peace through

Several elements attest the fading of borders between the legal categories after World War II: First, the Genocide Convention of 1948 prohibits that crime under all circumstances, "whether committed in time of peace or in time of war."[6] In the same year, the International Court of Justice held, in the *Corfu Channel* case, that the obligations of the Albanian authorities to prevent the British warships from hitting the mines were based

> not on the Hague Convention of 1907, No. VII, which is applicable in time of war, but on certain general and well-recognized principles, namely: elementary considerations of humanity, even more exacting in peace than in war; the principle of the freedom of maritime communication; and every State's obligation not to allow knowingly its territory to be used for acts contrary to the rights of other States.[7]

In the 1950s, UN bodies gradually started recognizing that human rights do play a role in armed conflict. As an example, the UNGA invoked human rights as early as in the context of the 1953 Korean conflict and the 1956 events in Hungary.[8] The UN Security Council (UNSC) made reference to "essential and inalienable human rights" that "should be respected even during the vicissitudes of war" when referring to the territories occupied by Israel after the Six-Day War of 1967.[9] The first Resolution of the 1968 Teheran International Conference on Human Rights was entitled "Respect and Enforcement of Human Rights in the Occupied Territories" and called on Israel to apply both the Universal Declaration of Human Rights and the Geneva Conventions in the occupied Palestinian territories. A further resolution entitled "Respect for Human Rights in Armed Conflict" asserted that "even during the periods of armed conflicts, humanitarian principles must prevail."[10]

The Teheran Conference was followed by the 1974–1977 Diplomatic Conference negotiating the two Additional Protocols to the 1949 Geneva

Legal Innovation: The Process and the Promise of the 2008 Cluster Munitions Convention," *Harvard Human Rights Journal*, vol. 22, 2009, pp. 145–157, 145 et seq.

6 Article 1 of the Convention reads as follows: "The Contracting Parties confirm that genocide, whether committed in time of peace or in time of war, is a crime under international law which they undertake to prevent and to punish."

7 ICJ Reports 1949, p. 22.

8 UNGA Resolution 804 (VII), UN Doc. A804/VIII, December 3, 1953, on the treatment of captured soldiers and civilians in Korea by North Korean and Chinese forces, as well as UNGA Resolution 1312 (XIII), UN Doc. A38/49, December 12, 1958 concerning Hungary.

9 UNGA Resolution 237, UN Doc. A237/1967, June 14, 1967.

10 Final Act of the International Conference on Human Rights, UN Doc. A/Conf.32/41 (April 22–May 13, 1968). See also the Report on Respect for Human Rights in Armed Conflict, UN Doc. A/7729, November 20, 1969, in particular Chapter 3, §§ 20–29, annex 1, UN Doc. A/8052, September 18, 1970, and UNGA Resolution 2675 (XXV), Principles for the Protection of Civilian Populations in Armed Conflict, UN Doc. A/8028Basic, December 9, 1970.

Conventions. The influence of human rights law on this process is apparent in the text of the two Protocols, both of them including guarantees "borrowed" from human rights law and thereby acknowledging implicitly the applicability of human rights law in armed conflict, as argued by some.[11] Most significantly, the ICJ acknowledged the continuing applicability of the right to life (Article 6 of the 1966 International Covenant on Civil and Political Rights, ICCPR) in time of warfare. The Court observed, however, that the test of what amounts to an arbitrary deprivation of life, by the use of a certain type of weapon, for instance, has to be determined by the applicable *lex specialis*, that is the law governing armed conflict.[12] Even though this straightforward *renvoi* to humanitarian law seems too simplistic today and has been criticized by certain authors,[13] the Court thereby confirmed, nevertheless, the relevance of human rights law to the question of nuclear weapons and the continuity of the application of human rights treaties in times of armed conflict.[14] The question will be discussed in Part II of the present study on treaties dealing with nuclear weapons.[15]

Moreover, from the 1990s on, the international community has witnessed a multiplication of non-international conflicts that are often fought out in the territory of "failed States." This category of conflicts "benefits" from the absence of governmental structures and from a legal, military, and political vacuum, and is moreover characterized by so-called asymmetric warfare.[16] Under these circumstances, the distinction between the norms applicable in international and non-international armed conflicts has lost much of its significance.[17]

For all these reasons, it is proposed to depart here from the idea that international law constitutes a "series of watertight compartments" and to adopt a broader,

11 C. Droege, "The Interplay between International Humanitarian Law and International Human Rights Law in Situations of Armed Conflict," *Israel Law Review*, vol. 40, 2007, pp. 310–355, 316.

12 Advisory Opinion on the *Legality of the Threat or Use of Nuclear Weapons*, ICJ Reports 1996, § 25.

13 See, for instance, V. Gowlland-Debbas, "The Right to Life and Genocide: The Court and an International Public Policy," in L. Boisson de Chazournes and P. Sands (eds.), *International Law, the International Court of Justice and Nuclear Weapons*, Cambridge, 1999, pp. 315–337, 319 and 325.

14 See also the Advisory Opinion on the *Legal Consequences of the Construction of a Wall in the Occupied Palestinian Territory*, ICJ Reports 2004, § 136.

15 This volume, Chapter 7, section C.1.b).

16 See, for instance, A. Hinds, "The Arms Race and Human Rights," *International Journal of Human Rights*, vol. 1, 1997, pp. 26–40, 26; P. W. Kahn, "Imagining Warfare," *European Journal of International Law*, vol. 24, no. 1, pp. 199–226; R. Geiss, "Asymmetric Conflict Structures," *International Review of the Red Cross*, vol. 864, December 2006, pp. 757–777; T. Pfanner, "David gegen Goliath oder asymmetrische Kriegsführung," *Humanitäres Völkerrecht*, vol. 3, 2005, pp. 165–176; and I. Herrmann and D. Palmieri, "Les nouveaux conflits: une modernité archaïque?" *International Review of the Red Cross*, vol. 849, March 2003, pp. 23–44.

17 Hinds, "The Arms Race," p. 26.

more global approach to the international legal order.[18] Such a view has, inter alia, been expressed in the report of a study group of the International Law Commission (ILC) led by Martti Koskenniemi on the phenomenon of the fragmentation of international law, in which it is argued that characterizations such as "human rights law," "environmental law," or "trade law" are "arbitrary labels" without normative value per se.[19]

2. A new approach to international security: "Human security" as a linkage between security and human rights

The tendency to perceive international law as a single unit, rather than as a fragmented legal order, also affects the notion of international security. "Security" may be defined as a state of affairs devoid of danger or threat.[20] The notion of "security" is connected with the concept of "peace and security," placed at the heart of the current UN system of collective security.[21]

From a contemporary point of view, security is no longer understood as being related exclusively to the "public" interest of the States, but as depending also on the well-being and the "private" interests of the individual.[22] A change in the definition of security is probably justified even more when considering the human rights abuses and violations frequently committed in the name of State security and interest.[23] It is generally recognized that the concept of human security was introduced by the 1994 Human Development Report submitted by the UN Development Programme (UNDP).[24] In this report, UNDP stressed the shift in the concept of security "from security through armaments to security through sustainable human development."[25]

An abstract definition of human security is probably neither possible,[26] nor necessary or useful, but this new approach aims at placing the individual at the

18 Ch. Greenwood, "*Jus Ad Bellum* and *Jus in Bello* in the Nuclear Weapons Advisory Opinion," in L. Boisson de Chazournes and P. Sands (eds.), *International Law, the International Court of Justice and Nuclear Weapons*, Cambridge, 1999, pp. 247–266, 252.

19 "Fragmentation of International Law: Difficulties Arising from the Diversification and Expansion of International Law," Report of the Study Group of the International Law Commission Finalized by Martti Koskenniemi, A/CN.4/L.682, April 13, 2006, §§ 21 and 254.

20 G. Giacca, "Article 1, Object and Purpose," in S. Casey-Maslen, A. Clapham, G. Giacca, and S. Parker, *The Arms Trade Treaty: A Commentary*, Oxford, 2016, pp. 41–57, 52.

21 See, in particular, Article 1 § 1, Articles 11, 24, 33 § 1, 36 § 1, and 39 of the UN Charter.

22 See, in this sense, A. A. Cançado Trindade, *International Law for Humankind: Towards a New Jus Gentium*, 2nd edn., Leiden and Boston, 2013, p. 403. See also S. Ogata and J. Cels, "Human Security – Protecting and Empowering the People," *Global Governance – A Review of Multilateralism and International Organizations*, vol. 9, 2003, pp. 273–282, in particular pp. 274 et seq.

23 Cançado Trindade, *International Law for Humankind*, p. 403, n. 11.

24 UNDP, *Human Development Report*, 1994, published by Oxford University Press, 1994.

25 *Ibid.*, § 24.

26 M. Zambelli, "Putting People at the Centre of the International Agenda: The Human Security Approach," *Die Friedenswarte*, vol. 77, 2002, pp. 173–186, in particular 176 and 182.

center of the international security debate. In 2010, the UN Secretary-General (UNSG) submitted a Report on Human Security where human security is broadly defined, encompassing "freedom from fear, freedom from want and freedom to live in dignity."[27] That broad definition was later confirmed in UNGA Resolution 66/290, underlining moreover the interlinkage between peace, development, and human rights.[28]

In other words, whereas the traditional notion of security focused on threats against the State, the concept of human security uses individual safety and well-being as yardsticks.[29] From our point of view, Cançado Trindade expresses this idea very clearly when he says:

> . . . the central concern is no longer with State properly, but rather, and more appropriately, with human beings, "within and across State borders," thus replacing the old State-centric approach of the matter by an anthropocentric one.[30]

The law of arms control is sensitive to this new approach, in particular during armed conflicts or in the immediate aftermath of hostilities, when the civilian population and society are particularly vulnerable.[31] In such situations, the elimination of the "legacies" of the war, for instance the fight against anti-personnel landmines, unexploded remnants of war, or cluster munitions play a prominent role.[32] But the concept is also relevant in the field of arms trade. The UN Charter recognizes the link between the regulation of arms transfers, on the one hand, and the maintenance of peace and security, on the other, in particular through Article 26 of the UN Charter, which is mentioned explicitly in the second preambular paragraph of the ATT and regularly confirmed by subsequent practice within the United Nations.[33]

Without denying the vagueness of the definition of this notion and the uncertainties surrounding it, it may be asserted that human security stands for the idea of taking into consideration the needs and interests of the human being and that it avoids reducing the notion of security to mere State interests.

27 UNGA, "Human Security, Report of the Secretary-General," March 8, 2010, UN Doc. A/64/701, § 4.

28 UN Doc. A/RES/66/290, "Follow-up to paragraph 143 on human security of the 2005 World Summit Outcome," October 25, 2012, § 3 c).

29 Giacca, "Article 1, Object and Purpose," p. 52.

30 Cançado Trindade, *International Law for Humankind*, p. 403, referring to Ogata and Cels, "Human Security," pp. 274 et seq.

31 See, for instance, D. Garcia, *Disarmament Diplomacy and Human Security: Regimes, Norms and Moral Progress in International Relations*, New York, 2012.

32 In this sense Zambelli, "Putting People at the Centre," p. 185; and J. Borrie, "Rethinking Multilateral Negotiations: Disarmament as Humanitarian Action," in J. Borrie and Martin Randin (eds.), *Alternative Approaches in Multilateral Decision Making, Disarmament as Humanitarian Action*, UNIDIR, Geneva 2005, pp. 7–37, 23–27.

33 Giacca, "Article 1, Object and Purpose," p. 52.

This approach goes hand in hand with a procedural aspect that is no longer restricted to inter-State negotiations and takes into account the voices of other actors, such as international organizations and civil society, in particular NGOs engaged in the struggle for the rights of the victims of human rights abuses or of certain types of weapons.[34]

Another element attesting to the growing interaction between security issues and human rights, in the sense of human security, is the fact that the UNSC, the organization's principal organ for the maintenance of international peace and security, has increasingly had to deal with situations where the actual threat against international peace and security was a consequence of serious violations of humanitarian law and human rights, especially during and after non-international armed conflicts.[35] The link between the two aspects is mentioned in the preamble of the Rome Statute establishing the International Criminal Court (ICC):

> *The States Parties to this Statute* . . .
> *Mindful* that during this century millions of children, women and men have been victims of unimaginable atrocities that deeply shock the conscience of humanity,
> *Recognizing* that such grave crimes threaten the peace, security and well-being of the world . . .[36]

To sum up, it may be claimed that the purposes of security, on the one hand, and the protection of the human being, on the other, should no longer be considered as contradictory, but as complementary and mutually strengthening each other. It will be shown throughout Part I of the present study that the CWC, the Ottawa and Oslo Conventions, as well as the ATT, are instruments which fit very well into this new legal environment. As far as the ATT is concerned, the reference in the treaty's second preambular paragraph to the principle of the least diversion of the world's human and economic resources,[37] within the meaning of Article 26 of the UN Charter, suggests that the notion of "security" should encompass a broad range of issues affecting human well-being of a socio-economic nature, including development and sustainability.[38]

34 In this sense Borrie, "Rethinking Multilateral Negotiations," pp. 23–27.

35 See, for instance, Resolution 2000(2011) concerning Ivory Coast, 2002(2011) concerning Somalia, 2003(2011) concerning Sudan, or 2005(2011) concerning Sierra Leone, as well as Resolution 1325(2000) on women, peace and security, and Resolution 1612(2005) on children in armed conflict. See also D. P. Forsythe, "The UN Security Council and Human Rights: State Sovereignty and Human Dignity," *International Policy Analysis*, Friedrich Ebert Stiftung, May 2012, http://library.fes.de/pdf-files/iez/09069.pdf (accessed February 14, 2017).

36 Paragraphs 2 and 3 of the preamble to the Rome Statute (emphasis in the original).

37 Second preambular paragraph to the ATT: "*The States Parties to this Treaty* . . . *Recalling* Article 26 of the Charter of the United Nations which seeks to promote the establishment and maintenance of international peace and security with the least diversion for armaments of the world's human and economic resources" (emphasis in the original).

38 Giacca, "Article 1, Object and Purpose," pp. 52–53.

This brings us to another field, closely linked to security, where the focus on the needs and the well-being of human beings has also been emphasized more recently, i.e. the domain of development.

3. A new approach to development: "Human development"

In parallel with the shift from national to human security, the notion of development underwent a similar change, by the drifting away from the earlier, traditional idea of development that concentrated on development *of* the people, to a notion of development *by* the people.[39] Since the end of the Cold War, the concepts of security and peace have sought to integrate a broader vision of social development.[40] A statement of the UNSC presidency made in 1992 summarizes this approach in the following terms:

> The absence of war and military conflicts among States does not in itself ensure international peace and security. The non-military sources of instability in the economic, social, humanitarian and economical fields have become threats to peace and security. The United Nations membership as a whole, working through the appropriate bodies, needs to give the highest priority to the solution of these matters.[41]

The most important aspect of human development lies in the placement of the human being, and the individual participation in this process, at the center of the politico-economic changes.[42] The aim is no longer an abstract concept of development in terms of gross domestic product (GDP), etc., but a sustainable human development based on the people's empowerment and the strengthening of democracy and human rights.[43]

In June 2012, Rio de Janeiro hosted the UN Conference on Sustainable Development. The outcome of this conference is summarized in Resolution 66/288 adopted by the UNGA on July 27, 2012, entitled "The Future We Want". This resolution fully confirms the tendency to place the people at the center of the development debate:

> We recognize that people are at the centre of sustainable development and, in this regard, we strive for a world that is just, equitable and inclusive, and we commit to work together to promote sustained and inclusive economic growth, social development and environmental protection and thereby to benefit all.[44]

39 UNDP, *Human Development Report*, New York and Oxford, 1993, p. 3.
40 Giacca, "Article 1, Object and Purpose," p. 52.
41 UN Security Council Presidential Note, UN Doc. S/23500, January 31, 1992, p. 3.
42 Cançado Trindade, *International Law for Humankind*, pp. 362 et seq.
43 *Ibid.*
44 Paragraph 6.

Many studies explain the impact of violence and armed conflict on socio-economic development.[45] These explanations help to establish the contours of the cost factors of armed violence and the relationship with the general phenomenon of violence.[46] The UN Programme of Action on Small Arms and Light Weapons is noteworthy in this context, stating that the "excessive accumulation and uncontrolled spread" of small arms and light weapons have "a wide range of humanitarian and socio-economic consequences and pose a serious threat to peace, reconciliation, safety, security, stability and sustainable development."[47] At the UN Sustainable Development Summit held in New York on September 25, 2015, the United Nations adopted its Sustainable Development Goals (SDGs) which replaced its Millennium Development Goals (MDGs) at the end of 2015.[48] SDG 16 aims, until 2030, to "promote peaceful and inclusive societies for sustainable development, provide access to justice for all and build effective, accountable and inclusive institutions at all levels." It includes the specific target of "significantly reduc[ing] all forms of violence and related death rates everywhere."[49]

This new approach to development will play a significant role in the assessment of anti-personnel mines and cluster munitions, as well as in the arms trade.

45 See, for instance, World Bank, "World Development Report 2011: Conflict, Security, and Development," *World Bank Publications*, 2011; or Geneva Declaration on Armed Violence and Development, "Global Burden of Armed Violence 2011," http://www.genevadeclaration.org/measurability/global-burden-of-armed-violence/global-burden-of-armed-violence-2011.html (accessed February 14, 2017).

46 Giacca, "Article 1, Object and Purpose," p. 54, with other references.

47 United Nations, "Programme of Action to Prevent, Combat and Eradicate the Illicit Trade in Small Arms and Light Weapons in All Its Aspects," 2001, UN Doc. A/CONF.192/15, p. 7, I, § 2.

48 Giacca, "Article 1, Object and Purpose," p. 54.

49 SDG 16: Promote just, peaceful and inclusive societies, https://sustainabledevelopment.un.org/?menu=1300 (accessed February 14, 2017).

2 The preparatory history of the relevant treaties, and in particular the role played by civil society

A. GENESIS OF THE CWC

Chemical warfare and disarmament have a long history. From time immemorial, the use of poison has been considered treacherous and, therefore, incompatible with good behavior and customs in time of war.[1] The large-scale use of poisonous gas in World War I – despite the guarantees stemming in particular from the Hague Convention IV of 1907[2] – led to the conclusion of the Geneva Protocol in 1925.[3] This Protocol has been violated on several occasions, in particular during the wars in Ethiopia in the 1930s, in Yemen in the 1960s, and in Iran in the 1980s.[4]

After World Wars I and II, the prevailing view was that the possession of chemical and bacteriological (biological) weapons should be prohibited simultaneously.[5] In the 1960s, however, the situation changed and a two-step approach advanced by Western countries was followed.[6] The main reason for doing so was the different perception of the military value of the two categories of weapons.[7] Chemical weapons were supposed to be of a certain military

1 J. Goldblat, "The 1993 Chemical Weapons Convention: A Significant Step in the Process of Multilateral Disarmament," in D. Bardonnet (ed.), *The Convention on the Prohibition and Elimination of Chemical Weapons: A Breakthrough in Multilateral Disarmament*, Workshop, The Hague, November 24–26, 1994, Dordrecht, Boston, and London, 1995, pp. 15–25, 15. See also, for an overview of the *travaux préparatoires*, J. P. Robinson, "The Negotiations on the Chemical Weapons Convention: A Historical Overview," in M. Bothe, N. Ronzitti, and A. Rosas (eds.), *The New Chemical Weapons Convention – Implementation and Prospects*, The Hague, 1998, pp. 17–36.

2 According to the Organization for Prohibition of Chemical Weapons (OPCW), the use of chemical weapons during World War I resulted in more than 100 000 fatalities and 1 million casualties: OPCW, "Genesis and Historical Development," http://www.opcw.org/chemical-weapons-convention/genesis-and-historical-development/ (accessed February 14, 2017).

3 Goldblat, "The 1993 CWC," p. 15.

4 *Ibid.*, pp. 15–16.

5 *Ibid.*, p. 16.

6 *Ibid.*

7 *Ibid.*; see also B. Docherty, "Ending Civilian Suffering: The Purpose, Provisions, and Promise of Humanitarian Disarmament Law," *Austrian Review of International and European Law*,

importance, compared to biological weapons that were perceived as instruments of terror rather than as means of warfare. They were seen as unpredictable and having little value in combat, unlike chemical weapons that seemed more controllable and had already been used massively in combat.[8] Moreover, the verification of compliance was considered to be easier in the case of biological weapons.[9]

When the large-scale use of herbicides and irritants in Vietnam caused growing concern about this means of warfare, efforts for a comprehensive prohibition of chemical weapons were stepped up.[10] A report on chemical and bacteriological weapons was prepared by the UNSG following a request made by the UNGA in 1968.[11] Once the Soviet Union and the United States had concluded a bilateral agreement, in August 1971,[12] the Conference of the Committee on Disarmament (CCD) drafted a Convention on the Prohibition of the Development, Production and Stockpiling of Bacteriological (Biological) Weapons and on their Destruction (BWC) and found agreement in 1971.[13] This instrument was finally signed in 1972, and States recognized, in Article IX, that they had to take further steps toward an agreement prohibiting chemical weapons and providing for their destruction.

Once the work on the BWC was successfully completed, discussion focused on a complete ban of chemical weapons.[14] Discussions proceeded on two tracks: bilaterally between the United States and the Soviet Union, and multilaterally, because several States or groups of States had presented draft conventions.[15] Nevertheless, more than 20 years elapsed after the adoption of the BWC before consensus could be reached on the CWC, in particular owing to the reluctance of certain great powers to divest themselves of chemical weapons.[16] As late as 1990, the United States and the Soviet Union, the States with the largest stockpiles of chemical weapons, still insisted on keeping a certain amount of these weapons and

vol. 15, 2010, pp. 7–44, 13, expressing the view that the international community decided to deal with biological weapons first because they raised fewer political challenges.

8 Goldblat, "The 1993 CWC," p. 16.

9 See, in this sense, OPCW, "Genesis and Historical Development." See also Robinson, "Negotiations on the CWC," pp. 18–22.

10 W. Krutzsch, "The Preamble to the Chemical Weapons Convention," in W. Krutzsch, E. Myjer, and R. Trapp (eds.), *The Chemical Weapons Convention – A Commentary*, Oxford, 2014, pp. 51–57, 55 et seq.

11 "Chemical Weapons and Bacteriological (Biological) Weapons and the Effects of Their Possible Use."

12 Robinson, "Negotiations on the CWC," p. 23.

13 W. Krutzsch, E. Myjer, and R. Trapp, "The Chemical Weapons Convention – Objectives, Principles and Implementation Practice," in Krutzsch et al. (eds.), *The CWC – A Commentary*, pp. 3–16, 5.

14 Official negotiations started in the Conference on Disarmament in 1984 (Docherty, "Ending Civilian Suffering," p. 13).

15 Docherty, "Ending Civilian Suffering," p. 13.

16 Goldblat, "The 1993 CWC," p. 16.

on retaining the right to use them.[17] Only in 1991 did the two superpowers retreat from their positions and announce their willingness to commit themselves to the destruction of all chemical weapon stocks and production facilities.[18] It is probable that they considered chemical weapons no longer indispensable for their defense purposes, whereas further proliferation of these weapons among other States might have jeopardized their security.[19] The main obstacle to a global agreement was thereby removed and the CWC was opened for signature in Paris on January 13, 1993.[20]

When analyzing the genesis of the CWC, one can argue that even though the motivation of the major military powers for the conclusion of this instrument was, at the final stage of the process, probably strategic rather than humanitarian, insofar as they considered proliferation of these weapons to be a growing threat to their security,[21] the human suffering caused by the use of chemical weapons, as demonstrated, inter alia, in March 1988 by the massacres perpetrated in the Kurdish village of Halabja, killing approximatively 5 000 persons, and whose images shocked the whole international community long before the era of internet and social media, was another powerful factor for the conclusion of the CWC only a few years later.[22]

Regarding the involvement of civil society in the process toward the adoption of the CWC, it can be recalled that NGOs have actively supported the negotiations that finally led to the adoption of this instrument in 1993.[23] Between 1970 and 1972, the Stockholm International Peace Research Institute (SIPRI) had already hosted an East-West expert workshop that studied the possibilities of verifying whether States refrained from producing nerve agents.[24] Since 1974, the international Pugwash movement has organized events to discuss policy and legal as well as technical aspects of chemical weapons disarmament.[25] The Pugwash Chemical Warfare Study Group ("Pugwash Study Group") was active between 1974 and 1992 and focused on the theme of verification and the design of on-site industry inspections and challenge inspections.[26] Thanks to its informal nature,

17 *Ibid.*
18 *Ibid.*, p. 17.
19 Docherty, "Ending Civilian Suffering," p. 20; and Goldblat, "The 1993 CWC," p. 17. See also R. J. Mathews and T. L. H. McCormack, "The Influence of Humanitarian Principles in the Negotiations of Arms Control Treaties," *International Review of the Red Cross*, vol. 81, no. 834, 1999, pp. 331–352, in particular p. 331.
20 Goldblat, "The 1993 CWC," p. 17.
21 Docherty, "Ending Civilian Suffering," p. 20.
22 See, in this sense, the Association for Diplomatic Studies and Training, "The Birth of the Chemical Weapons Convention (and the OPCW)," http://adst.org/2013/09/the-birth-of-the-chemical-weapons-convention-and-the-opcw/ (accessed February 14, 2017).
23 Krutzsch et al., "The CWC," p. 13.
24 *Ibid.*
25 *Ibid.*
26 C. McLeish and M. Lak, "The Role of Civil Society and Industrial Non-State Actors in Relation to the Chemical Weapons Convention," in Krutzsch et al. (eds.), *The CWC – A*

that group became a forum where scientists and experts could meet and discuss issues of significance for the future treaty.[27]

B. GENESIS OF THE OTTAWA AND OSLO CONVENTIONS

1. The Ottawa Process

Sometimes failures turn out to be the starting point for unexpected developments and produce spectacular results. The preparatory history of the Ottawa Convention is such a case.

It actually had been hoped that the use of anti-personnel mines would be restricted by Additional Protocol I to the Geneva Conventions of 1949, but in the absence of agreement, it was decided to recommend to the UNGA the convening of a conference under UN auspices to negotiate a separate legal instrument.[28] Such a conference was held in 1979 and 1980 and, on October 10, 1980, the CCW was adopted, an "umbrella" treaty consisting of only ten articles,[29] to which three Protocols were annexed at the moment of its conclusion: the Protocol on Non-Detectable Fragments (Protocol I); the Protocol on Prohibitions or Restrictions on the Use of Mines, Booby-Traps and Other Devices (Protocol II); and the Protocol on Prohibitions or Restrictions on the Use of Incendiary Weapons (Protocol III).[30]

The CCW and its protocols, heavily restricted in scope, did not produce an important reaction in the international community and only few States acceded

Commentary, pp. 37–48, 39. Between 1974 and 1992, a total of 312 people from 38 countries, including the Soviet Union, Europe, and the United States, attended these meetings, participating in their personal capacities. See also J. P. Robinson, "The Impact of Pugwash on the Debates over Chemical and Biological Weapons," *Annals of the New York Academy of Science*, no. 866, 1998, pp. 224–252.

27 The Pugwash movement was described as "a perfect type of global public policy network. It gathers individuals from different sectors – natural and social scientists, public policy-makers and private actors and individuals acting in their own names – who do not represent their own organization or countries. The entry selection criteria are based on the qualifications of the actors . . . and Pugwash pays attention to balanced representation." (E. Tuerlings and J. P. Robinson, "A Trisectoral Analysis of the Chemical Weapons Convention," in W. Reinicke and F. Deng (eds.), *Critical Choices: The United Nations, Networks and the Future of Global Governance*, International Development Research Centre, Ottawa, 1999, p. 26, cited by McLeish and Lak, "The Role of Civil Society," p. 39).

28 S. Maslen, *Commentaries on Arms Control Treaties*, vol. 1: *The Convention on the Prohibition of the Use, Stockpiling, Production, and Transfer of Anti-Personnel Mines and on their Destruction*, 2nd edn., Oxford/New York, 2005, p. 16.

29 *Ibid.*

30 The idea of such a structure came from the Mexican Delegation and was aimed at enhancing the flexibility in the negotiations of future weapons (Maslen, *Commentaries on Arms Control Treaties*, vol. 1, p. 17). In order to adhere to the CCW, the States had to accept at least two Protocols (Article 4 § 3).

to them.[31] In parallel, anti-personnel mines had become a serious threat to life and limb in States which were engaged in armed conflicts, such as Afghanistan, Angola, and Cambodia. War surgeons working, inter alia, for the International Committee of the Red Cross (ICRC), an organization with a long experience and expertise in humanitarian aide and law,[32] faced large numbers of traumatic amputations resulting from individuals stepping on anti-personnel mines and were not used to and skilled in dealing with such injuries.[33] The ICRC became more engaged in the issue also at a legal as well as political level, mainly under the influence of its recently created Medical Division. It convened several expert meetings in 1993 and 1994, gathering lawyers, mine-clearance experts, surgeons, military experts, and NGOs to discuss the various aspects of the landmine problem.[34] In October 1992, six NGOs, which would later form the steering committee of the "International Campaign to Ban Landmines" (ICBL), met in New York to plan a coordinated civil society campaign against these weapons.[35]

In parallel, in February 1993, France submitted a request to the UNSG to convene a Review Conference of the CCW in order to strengthen, inter alia, the provisions dealing with verification and compliance. This request was promptly accepted and a group of governmental experts was established in order to prepare the meeting.[36] But progress in the review process of the CCW was slow and difficult, in particular as a result of the self-imposed consensus principle.[37] Only on May 3, 1996, on the last day of the third session, consensus was reached and the Amended Protocol II (Protocol on Prohibitions or Restrictions on the Use of Mines, Booby-Traps and Other Devices) could be adopted.[38]

But the new instrument was far from prohibiting these weapons across the board and was limited to certain types of use of these weapons, thus following the CCW's humanitarian-law logic. It lacked, in particular, basic verification mechanisms.[39] As a whole, the Amended Protocol was disappointing and remained far behind expectations, not only in the eyes of civil society but also in those of certain governments participating in the negotiations.[40]

31 Maslen, *Commentaries on Arms Control Treaties*, vol. 1, p. 18.
32 *Ibid.*, pp. 19 et seq. Technically speaking, the ICRC is an association within the meaning of Articles 60 et seq. of the Swiss Civil Code.
33 Maslen, *Commentaries on Arms Control Treaties*, vol. 1, p. 18.
34 In April 1993, for instance, the ICRC convened the "Montreux Symposium" and, in 1994, it organized a meeting of military experts to discuss the military value of these weapons (Maslen, *Commentaries on Arms Control Treaties*, vol. 1, pp. 19 et seq.).
35 These NGOs were Handicap International, Human Rights Watch, Medico International, Mines Advisory Group, Physicians for Human Rights, and the Vietnam Veterans of America Foundation.
36 UNGA Resolution 48/79, §§ 5–7.
37 Maslen, *Commentaries on Arms Control Treaties*, vol. 1, p. 21.
38 Protocol II as amended on May 3, 1996. It entered into force on December 3, 1998.
39 J. M. Lavieille, *Droit international du désarmement et de la maîtrise des armements*, Paris and Montreal, 1997, pp. 296 et seq.
40 Maslen, *Commentaries on Arms Control Treaties*, vol. 1, pp. 22 et seq. For the ICRC, the restrictions on the use of anti-personnel mines were "woefully inadequate," adding that

Even more shocking for civil society gathering during the second session of the CCW Review Conference in Geneva at the beginning of 1996 was the fact that the needs of the victims of these weapons – for the majority non-combatants – were largely disregarded by the Conference. Persons mutilated by mines, who had travelled long distances in order to make their voices heard in Vienna and Geneva, felt completely unheard and neglected.[41]

It was at that moment that a development took place, outside of the traditional disarmament machinery, whose dynamism and effectiveness were unprecedented and surprised all the actors in the field of arms control, a branch of international law which had so far rather been known for the slowness of its procedures,[42] in particular as a result of the above-mentioned consensus principle.[43] The phenomenon that would later be known as "Ottawa Process" is generally considered to have taken off at a Conference held in Ottawa on October 3–5, 1996 and its final declaration adopted on October 5, 1996,[44] urging the international community to negotiate a legally binding instrument prohibiting the use, stockpiling, production, and transfer of anti-personnel mines.[45] The campaign of civil society in favor of such an instrument was quickly supported by a "core group" of friendly States, bringing together like-minded governments.[46] Furthermore, the Ottawa Conference was followed by a series of other conferences in 1997, the first one held in Vienna (February 12–14, 1997) and the last one again in Ottawa (December 3–4, 1997), during and between which many drafts of the future convention were prepared, circulated, and discussed.[47] A total of 121 States signed

the Protocol alone was "unlikely to significantly reduce the level of civilian landmine casualties." (Statement of Eric Roethlisberger, Vice-President of the ICRC, at the closing session of the First Review Conference of the CCW, May 3, 1996.)

41 J. White, "Landmine Survivors Speak Out," *Disarmament Forum*, 1999, pp. 7–18, 9.

42 B. Gautam-Ott, *The Legality of Landmines and International Law*, PhD, Geneva, 2004, p. 83. This author stresses that it took the Conference of Disarmament (CD) 25 years of negotiations to adopt the CWC.

43 See, for more details about the difficulties that the CD has been encountering for many years, V. Martin Randin and J. Borrie, "A Comparison between Arms Control and Other Multilateral Negotiation Processes," in J. Borrie and V. Martin Randin (eds.), *Alternative Approaches in Multilateral Decision Making, Disarmament as Humanitarian Action*, UNIDIR, Geneva, 2005, pp. 67–129, in particular 86–91.

44 *International Strategy Conference: Towards a Global Ban on Anti-Personnel Mines (the Ottawa Conference)*, held on October 3–5, 1996.

45 See preamble to the Ottawa Convention, § 9. Gautam-Ott, *The Legality of Landmines*, p. 81, describes the Ottawa Process in the following terms: "in the middle of the carnage caused by mines, a flower grew: the Ottawa Process." See, for another commentary, Z. Lachowski, "The Ban on Anti-Personnel Mines," *SIPRI Yearbook*, 1998, pp. 546–558.

46 The exact membership of this group is subject to some debate, but it is supposed to include, initially, Austria, Belgium, Canada, Ireland, Mexico, the Netherlands, Norway, the Philippines, South Africa, and Switzerland (Maslen, *Commentaries on Arms Control Treaties*, vol. 1, p. 27).

47 See, for an overview, Maslen, *Commentaries on Arms Control Treaties*, vol. 1, pp. 26–44.

the treaty at the second Conference held in Ottawa.[48] In other words, only 14 months after the first meeting in Ottawa, the conclusion of an international treaty prohibiting these weapons in absolute terms could be celebrated. The Convention entered into force on March 1, 1999, six months after the deposit of the 40th instrument of ratification.[49]

It is obvious that the key driving force behind the Ottawa Process was civil society. Two organizations deserve to be mentioned in particular. The first was the "Landmine Survivors Network" (LSN), which revealed itself to be the universal defender of the victims of mines and the most significant organization to offer concrete assistance to one of the most vulnerable groups of persons worldwide.[50] The activities and efforts deployed by the International Campaign to Ban Landmines (ICBL), a coalition of numerous NGOs,[51] with a view to successfully negotiating and concluding the Ottawa Convention, were considered so important that it was decided to mention them expressly in the preamble of the treaty. This is probably the first time in the history of international treaty-making that the involvement of an NGO is expressly recognized in the instrument negotiated. The relevant paragraph of the preamble of the Ottawa Convention reads as follows:

> *The States Parties . . .*
>
> *Stressing* the role of public conscience in furthering the principles of humanity as evidenced by the call for a total ban of anti-personnel mines and recognizing the efforts to that end undertaken by the International Red Cross and Red Crescent Movement, the International Campaign to Ban Landmines and numerous other non-governmental organizations around the world . . .[52]

It follows from this passage that a crucial role in the Ottawa Process was also played by the ICRC, in particular by its medical staff, namely, the surgeons working in war zones and having been confronted with the rather new challenge of victims of mine explosions. Finally, it should not be forgotten to mention that the Ottawa Process has been made possible, or at least facilitated, by the support of certain States, in particular Canada, which pursued the goal of the elimination of anti-personnel mines not for strategic reasons, but rather on humanitarian grounds.[53]

48 The Prime Minister of Canada, Jean Chrétien, described this achievement as "without precedent or parallel in either international disarmament or international humanitarian law" (Maslen, *Commentaries on Arms Control Treaties*, vol. 1, p. 44).

49 Article 17 § 1 of the Ottawa Convention.

50 White, "Landmine Survivors Speak Out," p. 10.

51 See, for a detailed description of the role played by ICBL in the Ottawa Process, K. R. Rutherford, *Disarming States: The International Movement to Ban Landmines*, Praeger Security International, 2011. The author is a victim of an accident caused by a mine.

52 Preamble, § 8 (emphasis in the original).

53 See, for the role of Canada in the Ottawa Process that was praised by many States, Maslen, *Commentaries on Arms Control Treaties*, vol. 1, p. 44, and Gautam-Ott, *The Legality of Landmines*, pp. 85–87.

The Ottawa Process, which led to the adoption of a treaty on a total ban of anti-personnel mines in record time,[54] served later as a template for an instrument prohibiting cluster munitions.

2. The Oslo Process

The idea of eliminating cluster munitions is not new. Concerns about the impact of these weapons on civilians, along with other weapons such as napalm, emerged in the late 1960s on account of their massive use in Southeast Asia.[55] As a result, during the negotiations of the 1977 Additional Protocols to the Geneva Conventions, it was proposed to include such weapons. Once it had been decided not to include provisions on specific weapons in the Protocols, certain States advocated their inclusion into the CCW, but this did not happen either.[56] Moreover, despite the similarities in effects of anti-personnel mines and unexploded cluster sub-munitions, the latter did not fall within the purview of the Ottawa Convention.[57] For these reasons, cluster munitions remained "unfinished business" until the 1990s.[58]

From 2000 on, the ICRC urged the States to refrain from using these weapons and to start negotiating a legally binding instrument for their total ban.[59] In a proposal addressed to the First Meeting of the Preparatory Committee for the 2001 Review Conference on the CCW, the ICRC called for the negotiation of a new instrument on ERW enshrining the principle that the users of failed munitions should be responsible for their clearance or at least assist clearance by the affected State.[60] Such a new instrument should also contain a prohibition of the use of cluster munitions in densely inhabited areas.[61] This call has to be seen as a reaction,

54 Rutherford, *Disarming States*, p. 122, argues that the Ottawa Convention is the fastest multilateral global arms control treaty having entered into force in the twentieth century.

55 V. Wiebe, J. Borrie, and D. Smyth, "Introduction," in G. Nystuen and S. Casey-Maslen (eds.), *The Convention on Cluster Munitions, A Commentary*, Oxford, 2010, pp. 1–36, 4 and 11. See also A. Breitegger, *Cluster Munitions and International Law: Disarmament with a Human Face*, London and New York, 2012, p. 134.

56 J. Corsi, "Towards Peace through Legal Innovation: The Process and the Promise of the 2008 Cluster Munitions Convention," *Harvard Human Rights Journal*, vol. 22, 2009, pp. 145–157, pp. 147 et seq. In 1974, a group of countries led by Sweden called for the prohibition of a number of anti-personnel weapons, including "cluster warheads," a proposition which was subsequently discussed during the negotiations that resulted in the adoption of the Additional Protocols to the Geneva Conventions, as well as in those of the CCW (Wiebe et al., "Introduction," p. 12).

57 Breitegger, *Cluster Munitions and International Law*, p. 135.

58 *Ibid.*

59 J. Kellenberger, "Foreword," in *Convention on Cluster Munitions*, Geneva, 2008, p. 5, http://www.icrc.org/eng/assets/files/other/icrc_002_0961.pdf (accessed February 15, 2017).

60 Breitegger, *Cluster Munitions and International Law*, p. 135.

61 *Ibid.*

in particular, to NATO's air campaign against the Federal Republic of Yugoslavia over the province of Kosovo in 1999, during which 1 765 cluster bombs containing 295 000 sub-munitions were dropped.[62] But, in spite of concerns expressed by the ICRC and other humanitarian organizations, the States Parties to the CCW still saw no need to take up the issue at that moment.[63]

In 2001 and 2002, momentum grew in favor of a new treaty on clearance of ERW, on the sharing of information to facilitate clearance and risk education, and on the warning of civilians.[64] At the end of 2002, States Parties to the CCW endorsed the negotiation of a protocol dealing with risk reduction of ERW, including the question of whether negotiations could also deal with measures to improve the reliability of munitions.[65] Over the following years, efforts on the humanitarian concerns relating to cluster munitions were embedded into the broader category of ERW that came to an end in November 2003 through the adoption of Protocol V to the CCW.[66]

In November 2003, taking the Ottawa Convention as an example, certain NGOs, mostly those involved in the movement leading to the ban on anti-personnel mines, decided to create a coalition fighting for the total abolition of cluster munitions – the "Cluster Munitions Coalition" (CMC).[67] The creation of a global network to address the humanitarian dimensions of cluster munitions had been decided during a conference on ERW hosted by the Irish Government in collaboration with Pax Christi Ireland, just after the 2003 Iraq invasion by US and UK troops.[68] This consortium favored the idea of an immediate moratorium on the use of cluster munitions, an acknowledgment of States' responsibility for the explosive remnants of war caused by the use of cluster munitions, and a commitment to provide resources to victims affected by them.[69] Moreover, certain States Parties to the CCW expressed frustration about the inefficiency of the negotiations within the different Review Conferences for the CCW which should have made it possible to adopt a protocol prohibiting the use of cluster munitions, after Protocol V had already been adopted in 2003, but without addressing the specific problems caused by cluster munitions.[70]

62 Wiebe et al., "Introduction," p. 10; see also Human Rights Watch (HRW), "Ticking Time Bombs: NATO's Use of Cluster Munitions in Yugoslavia," vol. 11, no. 6 (D), June 1999, https://www.hrw.org/reports/1999/nato2/ (accessed February 15, 2017).
63 Wiebe et al., "Introduction," p. 10.
64 Breitegger, *Cluster Munitions and International Law*, p. 135.
65 *Ibid.*, pp. 135–136.
66 *Ibid.*, p. 136.
67 Corsi, "Towards Peace through Legal Innovation," p. 149.
68 Breitegger, *Cluster Munitions and International Law*, p. 136.
69 HRW and Landmine Action, "Banning Cluster Munitions, Government Policy and Practice," *Mines Action Canada*, Canada, May 2009, p. 2.
70 See, for a commentary of Protocol V, L. Maresca, "A New Protocol on Explosive Remnants of War: The History and Negotiation of Protocol V to the 1980 Convention on Certain Conventional Weapons," *International Review of the Red Cross*, vol. 86, no. 856, December 2004, pp. 815–835.

In 2006, in view of the upcoming Third Review Conference to the CCW, the CMC emphasized that the time had come for the CCW to start negotiating a treaty prohibiting cluster munitions, otherwise the taking of further steps outside this forum would be considered.[71] At the Third Review Conference held in November 2006, former UNSG, Kofi Annan, called for a "freeze" on the use of cluster munitions in populated areas and for the destruction of "inaccurate and unreliable" types of such munitions.[72] Another factor triggered momentum for a new treaty banning cluster munitions, namely the numerous civil deaths and injuries caused by cluster munitions used massively by Israel and Hezbollah in the 2006 armed conflict.[73] This conflict added an element of urgency to the cause and provided civil society with another opportunity to gather and present concrete evidence of the humanitarian consequences of the use of cluster munitions and to mobilize the media to stigmatize these weapons.[74]

In spite of all these efforts and positive circumstances, it was certainly not surprising that the Third Review Conference refused to embark on negotiations for a new treaty on cluster munitions.[75] After a proposition by the Swedish delegation had been blocked, certain States decided to turn their backs on this arena and pursue their efforts outside the traditional disarmament channels.[76] In February 2007, on a Norwegian initiative,[77] an irreversible process aiming at the elimination of this category of weapons, later referred to as the "Oslo Process," was launched. A core group of States was built up to support Norway and the civil society, which turned out to be very similar to that formed in the Ottawa Process, consisting of Austria, Ireland, Mexico, New Zealand, Norway, Peru, and the Holy See.[78]

71 Breitegger, *Cluster Munitions and International Law*, p. 136.

72 UNGA, Message to the Third Review Conference of the Convention on Certain Conventional Weapons, November 7, 2006.

73 During the 2006 armed conflict in Lebanon, Hezbollah reportedly fired more than 100 Type-81 122mm cluster munition rockets into northern Israel; see HRW, "Civilians under Assault: Hezbollah's Rocket Attacks on Israel in the 2006 War," vol. 19, no. 3(E), August 2007, pp. 44–48, https://www.hrw.org/reports/2007/iopt0807/iopt0807webwcover.pdf (accessed February 15, 2017). See also B. Docherty, "Breaking New Ground: The Convention on Cluster Munitions and the Evolution of International Humanitarian Law," *Human Rights Quarterly*, vol. 31, 2009, pp. 934–963, 939; and K. Hulme, "The 2008 Cluster Munitions Convention: Stepping outside the CCW Framework (Again)," *International and Comparative Law Quarterly*, vol. 58, 2009, pp. 219–227, 221, who refers to a report of Handicap International, published in May 2007, "Circle of Impact: The Fatal Footprint of Cluster Munitions on People and Communities."

74 Breitegger, *Cluster Munitions and International Law*, pp. 136–137.

75 *Ibid.*, p. 137.

76 Corsi, "Towards Peace through Legal Innovation," p. 149.

77 Already in June 2006, Norway declared a national moratorium on the use of its stockpile of artillery-delivered cluster munitions until further testing (Wiebe et al., "Introduction," p. 14).

78 Wiebe et al., "Introduction," pp. 17 et seq.

Negotiations formally started at the Oslo Conference on Cluster Munitions (February 22–23, 2007) and were opened to all States that would agree to the immediate signature of a treaty banning cluster munitions, as well as to representatives of civil society.[79] In the beginning of the Oslo Conference, Norway stated that the objective was to agree on a plan for developing and implementing a new instrument of international humanitarian law that would address *all* the unacceptable aspects of cluster munitions by 2008. It underlined the humanitarian character of the process, which should be all-inclusive and embrace States, humanitarian actors, civil society, and the United Nations.[80] The Conference produced a document called the "Oslo Declaration" in which the States undertook, inter alia, "to conclude by 2008 a legally binding international instrument that will prohibit the use, production, transfer and stockpiling of cluster munitions that cause unacceptable harm to civilians."[81]

After international conferences had been held in Lima, Vienna, and Wellington, accompanied and reinforced by regional meetings in Africa, Asia, Europe, and Latin America,[82] the Convention on Cluster Munitions could finally be signed in Dublin on May 30, 2008, only 15 months after formal negotiations had started in Oslo, in the framework of a diplomatic conference that was attended by more than 100 States.[83] It entered into force on August 1, 2010, six months after the deposition of the 30th instrument of ratification.[84]

As had already been done in its "mother" treaty, the Oslo Convention recognizes the efforts made by the ICRC, the CMC, and other NGOs for the adoption of a legally binding instrument banning this category of weapons.[85]

C. GENESIS OF THE ATT

International efforts to control transboundary arms trade can be traced back to the end of the nineteenth century, in particular to the Brussels Act of 1890, designed to combat slave trade and to regulate the transfer of arms to colonial territories.[86]

79 Kellenberger, "Foreword," p. 5.

80 Norway, Opening Statement by Foreign Minister Jonas Gahr Støre, Oslo Conference on Cluster Munitions, February 22, 2007, http://www.clusterconvention.org/files/2012/12/NorwayOpening-Statement.pdf (accessed February 15, 2017).

81 Declaration, Oslo Conference on Cluster Munitions, February 22–23, 2007, http://www.clusterconvention.org/files/2012/11/Oslo-Declaration-final-23-February-2007.pdf (accessed February 15, 2017).

82 See, for an overview, Wiebe et al., "Introduction," pp. 21–36.

83 *Ibid.*

84 Article 17 § 1 of the Oslo Convention.

85 Preamble, § 17.

86 K. Krause and M. K. MacDonald, "Regulating Arms Sales through World War II," in R. D. Burns (ed.), *Encyclopedia of Arms Control and Disarmament*, vol. 2, New York, 1993, pp. 707 et seq., 712.

Other measures were taken,[87] but significant efforts toward the regulation of the international trade in conventional arms appeared only after the Cold War.[88] The invasion of Kuwait by Iraq was tragic proof of the potential consequences of an unregulated international arms trade.[89] In 1991, the five permanent members of the UNSC adopted the "P5 Guidelines for Conventional Arms Transfers" and,[90] in the same year, the UNGA adopted a resolution establishing the UN Register of Conventional Arms (UN Register) with the aim of promoting transparency in conventional weapons trade.[91] Another non-binding instrument pursuing the same purpose was the 1995 Wassenaar Arrangement on Export Controls for Conventional Arms and Dual-Use Goods and Technologies, Guidelines and Procedures, Including the Initial Elements.[92]

In 1999, a study of the ICRC concluded that the uncontrolled proliferation of arms and ammunition facilitates violations of international humanitarian law, leads to high levels of insecurity, and contributes to prolonging armed conflicts.[93] At the same time, the United Nations started targeting the issues of small arms and light weapons (SALW) that led to the adoption of a Programme of Action at the "UN Conference on the Illicit Traffic in Small Arms and Light Weapons in All Its Aspects" in 2001.[94] At the European level, a Code of Conduct of Arms Exports (EU Code) was adopted in 1998, aimed at preventing arms exports that might prolong armed conflicts or be used to violate human rights.[95]

It is certainly not exaggerating to say that certain of these precursors to the 2013 ATT – in particular the EU Code and the UN Programme of Action – are

87 See also the 1919 St. Germain Convention for the Control of the Trade in Arms and Ammunition and the 1925 Geneva Traffic Convention, which both never entered into force (M. Bromley, N. Cooper, and P. Holtom, "The UN Arms Trade Treaty: Arms Export Controls, the Human Security Agenda and the Lessons of History," *International Affairs*, vol. 88, 2012, pp. 1029–1048, 1032 et seq.

88 M. Brandes, "'All's Well that Ends Well' or 'Much Ado About Nothing'?: A Commentary on the Arms Trade Treaty," *Goettingen Journal of International Law*, vol. 5, 2013, pp. 399–429, http://www.gojil.eu/issues/52/52_article_brandes.pdf (accessed February 15, 2017).

89 *Ibid.*, pp. 403 et seq.

90 United Nations, "Guidelines for Conventional Arms Transfers," October 18, 1991.

91 UNGA Resolution 46/36 L, UN Doc. A/RES/46/36L, 9 December 1991.

92 The arrangement was updated in 2001, 2003, 2004, 2007, and 2011; see, for more information, http://www.wassenaar.org/.

93 ICRC, "Arms Availability and the Situation of Civilians in Armed Conflict," Geneva, 1999, https://www.icrc.org/eng/assets/files/other/icrc_002_0734_arms_availability.pdf (accessed February 15, 2017).

94 UN Conference on the Illicit Trade in Small Arms and Light Weapons in All Its Aspects, Programme of Action to Prevent, Combat and Eradicate the Illicit Trade in Small Arms and Light Weapons in all its Aspects, UN Doc. A/CONF.192/15, July 20, 2001, 7 (Programme of Action).

95 Bromley et al., "The UN Arms Trade Treaty," p. 1036. The EU Code was replaced in 2008 by the "EU Common Position Defining Common Rules Governing Control of Exports of Military Technology and Equipment" (*ibid.*, pp. 1036 and 1040).

largely attributable to successful campaigning by civil society.[96] This is *a fortiori* true for the ATT, which constitutes one of the most tangible examples of a treaty originating from the idea of human security, as described above.[97] It emerged from a campaign of civil society initiated by the Nobel Peace Laureates' International Code of Conduct on Arms Transfers, published in 1997, and led by the former Costa Rican President Oscar Arias Sánchez.[98] In support of the Code, the Nobel Laureates had this to say:

> The international community can no longer ignore the repercussion of irresponsible arms transfers. Indiscriminate weapons sales foster political instability and human rights violations, prolong violent conflicts, and weaken diplomatic efforts to resolve differences peacefully. Arms transfers often take place under a cloud of secrecy . . . Our children urgently need schools and health centres, not machine guns and fighter planes. Our children also need to be protected from violence . . .[99]

In 2001, this Code became the Framework Convention on International Arms Trade. That instrument did not go as far as the Code,[100] limiting itself to codify States' existing international obligations.[101]

From 2001 onward, the campaign, inspired in particular by the successful campaign of civil society in favor of the prohibition of anti-personnel mines, changed their objective from that of a framework convention to that of a treaty.[102] In October 2003, Amnesty International, Oxfam, and the International Action Network on Small Arms launched the "Control Arms" campaign, which has to date gathered support for the ATT from over 1 million people worldwide.[103] This campaign was led by a network of national and international NGOs from more than 100 States, thus reaching more easily a large audience and able to provide efficient and rapid analytical, legal, and technical support to interested governments.[104] It urged the international community to start negotiations

96 *Ibid.*, pp. 1036–1038; and Brandes, "All's Well that Ends Well," p. 404.

97 See this volume, Chapter 1, section B.2.

98 Bromley et al., "The UN Arms Trade Treaty," p. 1038; and Brandes, "All's Well that Ends Well," pp. 404 et seq. The Code is reproduced in UN doc. A/54/766-S/2000/146, February 24, 2000.

99 Reproduced in S. Casey-Maslen, "Introduction," in S. Casey-Maslen, A. Clapham, G. Giacca, and S. Parker, *The Arms Trade Treaty: A Commentary*, Oxford, 2016, pp. 1–13, 8.

100 Brandes, "All's Well that Ends Well," p. 405.

101 Casey-Maslen, "Introduction," p. 8.

102 Bromley et al., "The UN Arms Trade Treaty," p. 1039.

103 See, for more information, Control Arms campaign, http://controlarms.org/en/about-controlarms/ (accessed March 8, 2017).

104 R. Isbister and K. Tricot O'Farrell, "Lessons Learned: How NGOs Contributed to the ATT Success," *saferworld*, June 4, 2013, http://www.saferworld.org.uk/news-and-views/comment/97-lessons-learned-how-ngos-contributed-to-the-att-success (accessed February

with a view to adopting a legally binding treaty that would: first, require States to abstain from authorizing arms transfers that could have a negative humanitarian impact or be diverted to unauthorized end-users or to the illicit arms trade; and, second, aim at a comprehensive instrument in terms of activities and scope, covering conventional arms, ammunitions, military equipment, and technology.[105]

The "Control Arms" campaigners persuaded a considerable number of States to support and promote their idea of a strong and maximalist ATT. Early supporters of the initiative included States in sub-Saharan Africa, Latin America, and the Caribbean. Finland was an early European supporter and the United Kingdom the first permanent member of the UNSC to support the ATT process.[106] In October 2005, the EU Council expressed support for the ATT initiative,[107] observing that the campaign was compatible with existing EU commitments enshrined in the 1998 EU Code mentioned above.

In 2006, Australia, Costa Rica, Finland, Japan, Kenya, and the United Kingdom circulated a draft resolution entitled "Towards an Arms Trade Treaty" among the members of the UNGA First Committee, and requested the UNSG to "seek the views of Member States on the feasibility, scope and draft parameters for a comprehensive, legally binding instrument establishing common international standards for the import, export and transfer of conventional arms."[108] In the same year, pursuant to Resolution 61/89, whose adoption could only be achieved thanks to the lobbying of engaged NGOs,[109] the UNGA recognized that "the absence of common international standards on the import, export and transfer of conventional arms" constituted a "contributory factor to conflict, the displacement of people, crime and terrorism."[110] In 2007, more than 100 States submitted their views to the UNSG. In 2008 and 2009, discussions were conducted in the UN Group of Governmental Experts and Open-Ended Working Groups, where

15, 2017). See, for the long list of member organizations, its homepage: http://controlarms.org/en/ (accessed February 15, 2017).

105 Bromley et al., "The UN Arms Trade Treaty," p. 1039. See also S. Lorthois Louembet, "Vers un traité international réglementant les transferts d'armes classiques en 2012," *Revue générale de droit international public*, vol. 114, 2010, pp. 723–746, in particular 736–739.

106 *Ibid.*

107 Council of the European Union, EU Council Conclusions on an International Treaty on the Arms Trade, 2678th General Affairs Council Meeting, Luxembourg, October 3, 2005.

108 "United Nations Conference Aimed at Strengthening Global Effort Against Illicit Small Arms Trade Ends Without Agreement on Final Document," UN Press Release, UN Doc. DC/3037, July 7, 2006. The resolution was co-sponsored by 77 States and 153 voted in favor, with only the United States voting against (UNGA Resolution 61/89, "Towards an Arms Trade Treaty: Establishing Common International Standards for the Import, Export and Transfer of Conventional Arms," September 11, 2006).

109 Lorthois Louembet, "Vers un traité international," p. 736.

110 Resolution 61/89, adopted on December 6, 2006, by 153 votes to 1 (United States), with 24 abstentions, para. 9 of the preamble.

submissions of States were considered.[111] In December 2009, despite various differences among States on the ATT issue, the UNGA adopted Resolution 64/48 by 151 votes, calling for a conference on the ATT in 2012. That conference was to be charged with the task of elaborating "a legally binding instrument on the highest possible common international standards for the transfer of conventional arms."[112]

Five weeks of Preparatory Committee meetings took place in 2010–2012 in order to prepare for the conference.[113] During this phase, influential States manifested their support for the ATT. Writing an article entitled "Why This Arms Trade Treaty Is Essential," the Ministers for Foreign Affairs of France, Germany, and the United Kingdom, and the Minister for Trade of Sweden, asserted that each year millions of people around the world suffered directly or indirectly as a result of poor regulation of the arms trade and illicit trafficking of arms.[114] On account of the consensus principle, the First Conference collapsed, several States, including the major suppliers of conventional weapons such as the United States and Russia, rejecting the proposed draft convention on July 27, 2012.[115]

On December 24, 2012, the UNGA nevertheless voted to convene a final UN Conference on the ATT in 2013 under the same rules of procedure.[116] That conference did not reach consensus due to the negative votes of Syria, North Korea, and Iran,[117] but a group of over 100 States decided to submit the draft ATT for a vote to the UNGA. On April 2, 2013, an overwhelming majority of 154 States voted in favor of the treaty, only Syria, North Korea, and Iran rejecting it and 23 States abstaining.[118] The ATT was therefore adopted and opened for signature on June 3, 2013.[119] On September 25, 2014, a group of eight States – Argentina, the Bahamas, Bosnia-Herzegovina, the Czech Republic, Portugal, Saint Lucia, Senegal, and Uruguay – deposited their instruments of ratification, bringing the total number of ratifications to 53. On December 24, 2014, 90 days

111 Bromley et al., "The UN Arms Trade Treaty," p. 1040. See, for more details, Geneva Academy of International Law and Human Rights, "The Arms Trade Treaty (2013)," *Academy Briefing*, no. 3, June 2013, p. 5, http://www.snis.ch/system/files/academy_briefing_3_2013_arms_trade_treaty.pdf (accessed February 15, 2017).

112 UNGA Resolution 64/48, "The Arms Trade Treaty," § 4. Only Zimbabwe opposed the resolution and 20 States abstained.

113 Bromley et al., "The UN Arms Trade Treaty," p. 1040.

114 W. Hague, L. Fabius, G. Westerwelle, and E. Björling, "Why This Arms Trade Treaty Is Essential," *The Guardian*, July 2, 2012.

115 Brandes, "All's Well that Ends Well," p. 405; Geneva Academy, "The Arms Trade Treaty (2013)," p. 5. NGOs had warned against the dangers of the consensus principle (Isbister and Tricot O'Farrell, "Lessons Learned").

116 UNGA Resolution 67/234 A, UN Doc. A/RES/67/234 A.

117 See, for more details, Geneva Academy, "The Arms Trade Treaty (2013)," pp. 5 et seq.

118 Brandes, "All's Well that Ends Well," p. 406. For the detailed record of the vote, see Geneva Academy, "The Arms Trade Treaty (2013)," p. 6, n. 14.

119 Casey-Maslen, "Introduction," p. 12.

after the 50th ratification,[120] the ATT entered into force. Former UNSG Ban Ki-moon underlined in a statement that "[f]rom now on, the States Parties to this important treaty will have a legal obligation to apply the highest common standards to their international transfers of weapons and ammunition."[121]

The preamble of the ATT highlights the reasons for the treaty's adoption. Among those reasons, the human, social, and economic effects and the costs caused by the uncontrolled spread of conventional weapons are particularly important, as it transpires from the following preambular paragraph:

> *The States Parties to this Treaty,*
>
> . . .
>
> *Recognizing* the security, social, economic and humanitarian consequences of the illicit and unregulated trade in conventional weapons . . .[122]

Perhaps the main reason for pressing for the ATT was the fact that the illicit and unregulated transfer of conventional arms encourages and enables breaches of human rights and leads to serious violations of humanitarian law and to the destabilization of countries or entire regions.[123] Other paragraphs of the preamble confirm this idea. They will be mentioned in the next chapter, which examines the substantive contribution of the treaties analyzed here to the protection of human beings.

D. CONCLUSIONS TO THE CHAPTER

To sum up this Chapter, it can be recalled that the CWC has been negotiated along more traditional inter-State channels and has been inspired significantly by security concerns. Therefore, the influence of considerations of humanity and the contribution of civil society are perhaps less conspicuous than in the case of the ATT or the Ottawa and Oslo Conventions. It has nevertheless been observed that certain events, in particular the Halabja massacres in 1988, have triggered public awareness and, therefore, favored the call for a legally binding instrument outlawing these weapons. Moreover, civil society has played a significant role in the process leading to the conclusion of the CWC in 1993.

As far as the Ottawa and Oslo Processes are concerned, these phenomena can be best summarized in seven points: First, it is obvious that the partisans of

120 Article 22 § 1 ATT.

121 "Statement by the Secretary-General on the Entry into Force of the Arms Trade Treaty," UNSG Ban Ki-moon, UN Headquarters, December 23, 2014, https://www.un.org/sg/en/content/sg/statement/2014-12-23/statement-secretary-general-entry-force-arms-trade-treaty (accessed February 15, 2017).

122 Paragraph 9 of the preamble (emphasis in the original).

123 Geneva Academy, "The Arms Trade Treaty (2013)," p. 11.

these two treaties had a clear and rather simple goal in mind, namely, the ban of anti-personnel mines and cluster munitions. A straightforward but comprehensive ban seemed more appropriate and effective than restricting certain uses of certain weapons only, as does for instance the 1980 CCW.[124] Second, the conclusion of these treaties has undeniably been favored by humanitarian motivations, in particular the numerous innocent victims, including children and women, caused by anti-personnel mines and cluster munitions until very long after the end of the actual combat actions. Third, these humanitarian concerns were put on the international agenda by civil society which, very efficiently, alerted the international community by drawing its attention to the useless loss of human lives and the intolerable sufferings of the civil population in recent or current conflicts. Civil society thereby turned the problems of anti-personnel mines and cluster munitions from a strictly military and strategic problem into an urgent humanitarian concern.[125] Fourth, an essential role was played by medical personnel who were confronted by the grave and particular injuries caused by anti-personnel mines and cluster munitions. As a result, it is in particular thanks to the involvement and the strategy of NGOs, building their cases around certain events and situations, that these two treaties could be adopted quickly and enter into force only months after their conclusion.

Fifth, the activities of civil society were supported by a group of like-minded States whose interest in the ban of certain weapons was genuinely humanitarian rather than political. Sixth, another key aspect of the Ottawa and Oslo Processes was the involvement of the victims, who directed the attention of the international community to the danger and the disastrous humanitarian impact of the weapons concerned. The recognition of the special needs of the victims also left its traces in the texts of the treaties, shown by their preambular paragraphs:

> *The States Parties . . .*
> *Wishing* to do their utmost in providing assistance for the care and rehabilitation, including the social and economic reintegration of mine victims . . .[126]

The question of assistance to the victims of anti-personnel mines and cluster munitions will be discussed in more detail in the following Chapter, which deals with the substantive contribution of these treaties to the protection of human beings.[127] Lastly, it can be recalled that the developments described took place

124 Rutherford, *Disarming States*, p. 129.

125 *Ibid.*, p. 123.

126 Paragraph 3 of the preamble. See also, for similar paragraphs, the preamble of the Convention on Cluster Munitions (emphasis in the original).

127 See Chapter 3, section A.3.b). See also, concerning the Ottawa Process and similar phenomena, K. Sikkink, "Transnational Advocacy Networks and the Social Construction of Legal Norms," in Y. Dezalay and B. G. Garth (eds.), *Global Prescriptions, The Production, Exportation, and Importation of a New Legal Orthodoxy*, Ann Arbor, 2002, pp. 37–64.

outside the traditional disarmament mechanisms which had been deadlocked for a long time.[128]

Similar conclusions can be drawn for the ATT. This treaty, too, was inspired by humanitarian concerns, as appears clearly from its preambular paragraphs. Moreover, the conclusion of that instrument has rightly been considered the "culmination" of almost 20 years of campaigning efforts by civil society in favor of the regulation of the international trade in conventional arms.[129] A broad and well-organized network of many NGOs was also the driving force behind the ATT, namely, the "Control Arms" campaign. As has already been observed in connection with the Ottawa and Oslo Processes, the successful adoption of the relevant treaties was pushed forward by civil society, but significantly backed up by certain key governments. Given the idea of an ATT having been launched by NGOs and some smaller States, it was surely the announcement of UK support of the ATT that gave the campaign a decisive boost. Once this momentum had been established, the EU Member States and many African and Latin American States followed this trend.[130]

128 According to Martin Randin and Borrie, "A Comparison," p. 67, the Conference on Disarmament, whose last tangible result was the adoption of the CTBT in 1996 (not yet entered into force), has been deadlocked since 1999. See also P. McCarthy, "Deconstructing Disarmament: The Challenge of Making the Disarmament and Arms Control Machinery Responsive to the Humanitarian Imperative," in J. Borrie and V. Martin Randin (eds.), *Alternative Approaches in Multilateral Decision Making, Disarmament as Humanitarian Action*, UNIDIR, Geneva 2005, pp. 51–66.

129 Isbister and Tricot O'Farrell, "Lessons Learned."

130 *Ibid.*

3 The contribution of the relevant treaties to the protection of the human being

A. PROHIBITION OF "USING" THE RELEVANT WEAPONS IMPOSED BY THE CWC, AND THE OTTAWA AND OSLO CONVENTIONS

1. Introduction

This Chapter will examine the contribution of arms control treaties to human welfare. It will be suggested that the obligation not to use these weapons under any circumstances is the key duty prescribed. The other treaty obligations – not to develop, produce, acquire, stockpile, or transfer these weapons – are, from this author's point of view, intended to create a world free of these weapons and, therefore, an impossibility of using them.

The impact of the prohibition of use of these weapons on human beings is two-fold: First, it follows the logic of humanitarian law by obliging States to refrain from such use as a means of warfare. The UNSC's condemnation of the use of chemical weapons against the Syrian population underlines the dramatic humanitarian impact of these weapons and the need for a truly universal ban.[1] Second, through the extension of the prohibition of such use to all circumstances, the treaties also protect the human being in times of peace. Both aspects will be examined hereafter.

2. Prohibition of using the relevant weapons in light of humanitarian law

a) General clause prohibiting use of the relevant weapons (Article I of the Conventions)

The essence of each of these three treaties is expressed in their general clauses. (General obligations).[2] Articles I of the CWC, and the Ottawa and Oslo

1 See, in particular, UNSC Resolution 2118(2013) of September 27, 2013 and Resolution 2209(2015) of March 6, 2015.

2 The title of Article I of the Oslo Convention is "General obligations and scope of application." This type of clause is particularly valuable for the identification of the object of a treaty (J. Klabbers, "Strange Bedfellows: The 'Interim Obligations' and the 1993 Chemical Weapons Convention," in E. P. J. Myjer (ed.), *Issues of Arms Control Law and the Chemical Weapons*

Conventions impose on the States Parties a prohibition of using the relevant weapons. The CWC, for example, expresses this duty in the following terms: "Each State Party undertakes never under any circumstances . . . b) to use chemical weapons."[3]

The fact that the Ottawa and Oslo Conventions mention the prohibition of using these weapons right at the beginning of their text, confirms what has already been suggested with regard to the *travaux préparatoires*, namely, that the aspect of human protection is particularly significant in these treaties. The use of chemical weapons against innocent civilians is probably, from a humanitarian point of view, the most shocking breach within the framework of the CWC. In Resolution 2118(2013) of September 27, 2013, the UNSC declared itself "deeply outraged by the *use* of chemical weapons . . . condemning the killing of civilians that resulted from it . . ."[4]

The prohibition of using chemical weapons, antipersonnel mines, and cluster munitions, deriving from the relevant treaties, follows the logic of humanitarian law, the application of which is linked to the existence of an international or non-international armed conflict. In particular, the absolute ban on using anti-personnel mines and cluster munitions is a significant contribution to the protection of the combatants and civilian populations in times of armed conflict, especially on account of the indiscriminate nature of these weapons (further detailed below).[5]

The stringent language used in Article I of the treaties ("never under any circumstances") also suggests that the obligation not to use such weapons does not apply only in relation to other States Parties, but also to other States, as well as *vis-à-vis* non-State actors and the civilian population. This principle was confirmed by the UNSC in its Resolution 2118(2013) of September 27, 2013 concerning the situation in Syria, where the Council held that: "*[t]he Security Council* . . . *Condemns* in the strongest terms *any use* of chemical weapons in the Syrian Arab Republic . . . in violation of international law."[6]

Convention – Obligations Inter Se and Supervisory Mechanism, The Hague, Boston, and London, 2001, pp. 11–29, 22; see also the ICJ in the case on the *Application of the Convention on the Prevention and Punishment of the Crime of Genocide (Bosnia and Herzegovina v. Serbia and Montenegro)*, Judgment, ICJ Reports 2007, §§ 162 and 165).

3 Article I § 1(b).

4 Paragraph 8 of the preamble (emphasis added); see also Annex I to Resolution 2118 (2013), paragraph 3: "The Executive Council, Noting the 'Report on the Alleged Use of Chemical Weapons in the Ghouta area of Damascus on 21 August 2013 (S/2013/553, dated 16 September 2013),' prepared by the United Nations Mission to Investigate Allegations of the Use of Chemical Weapons in the Syrian Arab Republic . . . which concludes that 'chemical weapons have been used in the ongoing conflict between the parties in the Syrian Arab Republic, also against civilians, including children, on a relatively large scale.'"

5 See this volume, Chapter 3, section A.2.c).bb).

6 Operative paragraph 2 (emphasis added). See also paragraph 8 of the preamble: "*The Security Council* . . . stressing that those responsible for *any use* of chemical weapons must be held accountable" (second emphasis added). See also Annex I to Resolution 2118 (2013), containing the OPCW Executive Council Decision on the destruction of Syrian chemical

This complete absence of reciprocity shows that the present instruments considerably differ from traditional humanitarian law treaties which apply only "between two or more of the High Contracting Parties."[7] The UNSC, in Resolution 2118(2013), goes even further by demanding "non-State actors not develop, acquire, manufacture, possess, transport, transfer, or use nuclear, chemical or biological weapons and their means of delivery . . ."[8]

b) Relevance of the Geneva Protocol and the Biological Weapons Convention (BWC) in the CWC

The prohibition of using chemical weapons as a means of warfare enshrined in Article I of the CWC is closely linked to the 1925 Geneva Protocol, the adoption of which, as stated above,[9] was clearly motivated by humanitarian concerns.[10] Already in 1918, the ICRC had referred to these weapons as a "barbaric" innovation.[11]

The number of references to the Geneva Protocol and the BVWC in the preamble of the CWC is significant:

> *Recalling* that the General Assembly of the United Nations has repeatedly condemned all actions contrary to the principles and objectives of the Protocol for the Prohibition of the Use in War of Asphyxiating, Poisonous or Other Gases, and of Bacteriological Methods of Warfare, signed at Geneva on 17 June 1925 (the Geneva Protocol of 1925),[12]
>
> *Recognizing* that this Convention reaffirms principles and objectives of and obligations assumed under the Geneva Protocol of 1925, and the Convention on the Prohibition of the Development, Production and Stockpiling of Bacteriological (Biological) and Toxin Weapons and on their

weapons, paragraph 2: "The Executive Council . . . Recalling also that the Third Review Conference (RC-3/3*, 19 April 2013) expressed 'deep concern that chemical weapons may have been used in the Syrian Arab Republic and underlined that *use of chemical weapons by anyone under any circumstances* would be reprehensible and completely contrary to the legal norms'" (emphasis added).

7 See, inter alia, common Article 2 § 1 of the 1949 Geneva Conventions.

8 Operative paragraph 19; see also paragraph 5 of the preamble.

9 This volume, Chapter 2, section A.

10 B. Docherty, "Ending Civilian Suffering: The Purpose, Provisions, and Promise of Humanitarian Disarmament Law," *Austrian Review of International and European Law*, vol. 15, 2010, pp. 7–44, 20.

11 R. J. Mathews and T. L. H. McCormack, "The Influence of Humanitarian Principles in the Negotiations of Arms Control Treaties," *International Review of the Red Cross*, vol. 81, no. 834, 1999, pp. 331–352, 331.

12 Paragraph 3 of the preamble (emphasis in the original).

> Destruction signed at London, Moscow and Washington, on 10 April 1972[13] . . .
>
> *Determined* for the sake of all mankind, to exclude completely the possibility of the use of chemical weapons, through the implementation of the provisions of this Convention, thereby complementing the obligations assumed under the Geneva Protocol of 1925[14] . . .
>
> *Recognizing* the prohibition, embodied in the pertinent agreement and relevant principles of international law, of the use of herbicides as a method of warfare . . .[15]

The references to the Geneva Protocol in the preamble of the CWC emphasize the importance of the ban on the use of chemical weapons as a means of warfare. The preamble to the Protocol states that the "use in war of asphyxiating, poisonous or other gases, and of all analogous liquids materials or devices, has been justly condemned by the general opinion of the civilized word . . ."[16] Since the international community had had to face grave breaches of this precept on several occasions,[17] there was a strong desire for creating a comprehensive rule outlawing such weapons completely.[18] The drafters of the 1972 BWC were well aware of the contribution of the Geneva Protocol to humanity in general and to the humanization of warfare in particular, as shown in the preamble of the BWC:

> *The States Parties to this Convention*
>
> . . . *conscious* also of the contribution which the said Protocol has already made, and continues to make, to mitigating the horrors of war . . .[19]

Moreover, insofar as the CWC, in its preamble, refers to the "principles" of the Protocol, it expresses the view that the obligations deriving from it are today binding on all States on the basis of rules of customary international law prohibiting the use of such gases in international and non-international armed conflict.[20]

13 Paragraph 4 of the preamble (emphasis in the original).
14 Paragraph 6 of the preamble (emphasis in the original).
15 Paragraph 7 of the preamble (emphasis in the original).
16 Paragraph 1 of the Preamble to the 1925 Geneva Protocol.
17 There is a long list of UN resolutions calling on all States for strict observance of the principles and objectives of the Geneva Protocol. The earliest to mention is UNGA Resolution 2162 B (XXI) of December 5, 1966. See also UNSC Resolution 2118 (2013) in the context of the adoption of measures to eliminate Syria's chemical weapons program. Of special interest is also UNGA Resolution 2603 A (XXIV) of December 16, 1969 confirming, inter alia, the customary nature of the Geneva Protocol.
18 W. Krutzsch, "The Preamble to the Chemical Weapons Convention," in W. Krutzsch, E. Myjer, and R. Trapp, *The Chemical Weapons Convention – A Commentary*, Oxford, 2014, pp. 51–57, 53.
19 Paragraph 2 of the preamble to the BWC (emphasis in the original).
20 See the comprehensive Study of the ICRC on Customary International Humanitarian Law, whose Rule 74 states explicitly: "The use of chemical weapons is prohibited" (J.-M. Henckaerts and L. Doswald-Beck, *Customary International Humanitarian Law*, vol. I: *Rules*,

Regarding international armed conflicts, this was clearly confirmed by the European Court of Human Rights (ECtHR) in *Van Anraat v. the Netherlands*, where the applicant challenged the Dutch tribunals' conclusion that the prohibition of using gases enshrined in the Geneva Protocol was of a customary nature.[21] Van Anraat was a businessman who had been convicted by Dutch courts for having supplied mustard gas (thiodiglycol) to the Iraqi Government between April 1984 and August 1988.[22] Mustard gas is known to have been used by the Iraqi military against Iranian armed forces and civilians during the Iran–Iraq War (1980–1988) and in attacks against the Kurdish population of northern Iraq, including Halabja.[23] The ECtHR, which had to deal with the alleged illegality of Van Anraat's conviction, expressed the following opinion:

> The Court thus finds that at the time when the applicant supplied thiodiglycol to the Government of Iraq a norm of customary international law existed prohibiting the use of mustard gas as a weapon of war in an international conflict.[24]

The link between the CWC and the 1925 Geneva Protocol is moreover confirmed by Article XIII of the CWC, which indicates that "[n]othing in this Convention shall be interpreted as in any way limiting or detracting from the obligation assumed by any State under the [Geneva] Protocol," as well as by Article XVI § 3 of the CWC, according to which the withdrawal of a State Party from the Convention "shall not in any way affect the duty of States to continue fulfilling the obligations assumed under any relevant rules of international law, particularly the Geneva Protocol of 1925."[25]

Cambridge, 2005, p. 259). See also the ICTY in the *Tadić* case, where it held that "there undisputedly emerged a general consensus in the international community on the principle that the use of [chemical] weapons is also prohibited in internal armed conflicts" (*The Prosecutor v. Duško Tadić a.k.a. "Dule,"* Decision on the Defence Motion for Interlocutory Appeal on Jurisdiction, Appeals Chamber, October 2, 1995, Case No. IT-94-1-AR72, § 499).

21 *Van Anraat v. the Netherlands* (dec.), no. 65389/09, July 6, 2010.

22 *Ibid.*, § 3.

23 *Ibid.*, § 5.

24 *Ibid.*, § 92. It is suggested here that the aim of a customary international rule prohibiting the use of asphyxiating, poisonous, and other gases was already expressed in the preamble of the Geneva Protocol: "To the end that this prohibition shall be universally accepted as a part of international law, binding alike the conscience and the practice of nations" (paragraph 3). It is not exaggerated to recognize in this paragraph the two elements that, in their conjuncture, generate customary international law, namely the *opinio juris* and State practice.

25 See, for a comment, N. Ronzitti, "Relations between the Chemical Weapons Convention and Other Relevant International Norms," in D. Bardonnet (ed.), *The Convention on the Prohibition and Elimination of Chemical Weapons: A Breakthrough in Multilateral Disarmament*, Workshop, The Hague, November 24–26, 1994, Dordrecht, Boston, and London, 1995, pp. 167–185. See also D. Rietiker, *Le régime juridique des traités de maîtrise des armements: Plaidoyer pour l'unité de l'ordre juridique international*, Bern and Brussels, pp. 277–281.

An important question that also touches upon the relationship between the CWC and the Geneva Protocol is whether reservations that had commonly been inserted in the Geneva Protocol and according to which the use of the prohibited gases was legal when made in response to an attack launched by the same means (so-called "reservation of reciprocity") remain valid and in force after the ratification of the CWC by a reserving State Party.[26] It is suggested here that the ratification of the CWC would render void this kind of reservation.[27] This not only follows from the absolute formulation ("never under any circumstances")[28] of the prohibition of use contained in Article I § 1 of the CWC, one of the core duties of the States Parties, but also derives from its Article XXII that allows no reservation.[29]

Finally, the preamble of the CWC, quoted above, suggests that the CWC is not only closely related to the Geneva Protocol, but also to the BCW. As mentioned in the section on the preparatory history of the treaties, the adoption of the CWC in 1993 was only the last step in a sequence of actions between the adoption of the Geneva Protocol (1925) and that of the BWC (1972). Considered together, they form a broad framework banning chemical and bacteriological (biological) warfare and, therefore, free humanity from that threat. It is obvious that, from a normative point of view, the CWC is highly inspired by the BWC, guided by the aspiration of eliminating an entire category of weapons and complementing the Geneva Protocol, by imposing on the States Parties the duty "never in any circumstances, to develop, produce, stockpile or otherwise acquire or retain" such weapons.[30] The ratio underlying this instrument is the protection of the human being too, as witnesses the following paragraphs of its preamble:

> *The States Parties to this Convention . . .*
>
> *Determined*, for the sake of all mankind, to exclude completely the possibility of bacteriological (biological) agents and toxins being used as weapons,

26 For the definition of "reservation" and the applicable law, see Articles 2 § 1(d) and 19–23 of the Vienna Convention on the Law of Treaties (VCLT). See, for a discussion of this type of reservation, S. Oeter, "Methods and Means of Combat," in D. Fleck (ed.), *The Handbook of International Humanitarian Law*, 3rd edn., Oxford, 2013, pp. 115–228, 163 et seq.

27 See, in this sense, Krutzsch, "The Preamble to the CWC," p. 54.

28 The clear wording excludes any justification for such activities, whether for self-defense in the case of attack with such weapons or in other exceptional circumstances. It covers all intents and purposes for such activities, independent of the nature of the armed conflict, whether international or non-international, whether the parties involved have recognized each other or not, or whether the weapons are used in a civil strife (W. Krutzsch, "Article I: General Obligations," in Krutzsch et al., *The Chemical Weapons Convention – A Commentary*, Oxford, 2014, pp. 61–72, 64).

29 Article XXII adds, in harmony with Article 19(c) VCLT, that the annexes of the CWC shall not be subject to reservations that are incompatible with its object and purpose.

30 See, in this sense, Krutzsch, "Article I: General Obligations," p. 63.

> *Convinced* that such use would be repugnant to the conscience of mankind and that no effort should be spared to minimize this risk . . .[31]

In light of the adoption of the CWC in 1993, it is fair to say that the States Parties to the BWC have lived up to their undertaking enshrined in its Article IX to hold negotiations with a view to reaching (early) agreement on such an instrument.[32]

c) Relevance of the principles of humanitarian law in the Ottawa and Oslo Conventions

aa) Introductory observations

When applied to a situation of armed conflict, the ban on the use of anti-personnel mines and cluster munitions pursues the respect of the core principles of humanitarian law. Both the Ottawa and the Oslo Conventions contain the following clause in their preamble:

> *The States Parties . . .*
>
> *Basing themselves* on the principle of international humanitarian law that the right of the parties to an armed conflict *to choose methods or means of warfare is not unlimited*, on the *principle that prohibits the employment in armed conflicts of weapons, projectiles and materials and methods of warfare of a nature to cause superfluous injury or unnecessary suffering* and on the principle that a *distinction must be made between civilians and combatants* . . .[33]

Humanitarian law sets certain essential limitations to the way of waging war. In its Advisory Opinion of July 8, 1996 on the *Legality of the Threat or Use of Nuclear Weapons*, the ICJ made it clear that these fundamental rules are to be observed by all States whether or not they have ratified the conventions containing them, since they constitute "intransgressible principles of international customary law."[34]

The most relevant of these principles will be detailed in the present subdivision. A more recent principle, prohibiting the use of methods and means of warfare

31 Emphasis in the original.

32 Krutzsch, "The Preamble to the CWC," p. 54. This objective is also reflected in paragraph 5 of the preamble to the CWC.

33 Paragraph 11 of the preamble to the Ottawa Convention (first emphasis in the original, subsequent added). See, for a similar clause, also the last paragraph of the preamble to the Oslo Convention.

34 ICJ Reports 1996, § 79. In its judgment in the *Corfu Channel* case of April 9, 1949 (ICJ Reports 1949, p. 22), the Court referred to "elementary considerations of humanity." See also J.-L. Blondel, "The Meaning of the Word 'Humanitarian' in Relation to the Fundamental Principles of the Red Cross and Red Crescent," *International Review of the Red Cross*, no. 273, November–December 1989, pp. 507–515.

that would cause serious damage to the natural environment, shall only be mentioned here. That prohibition is contained in Article 35 § 3 of Additional Protocol I to the Geneva Conventions: "It is prohibited to employ methods or means of warfare which are intended, or may be expected, to cause widespread, long-term and severe damage to the natural environment."[35] Even though this principle is certainly relevant for anti-personnel mines and unexploded submunitions that make agricultural areas unusable for cultivation and remain dangerous to the local population, the high threshold of application may in practice be difficult to reach.[36]

bb) Principle of distinction

The principles of humanitarian law impose, first of all, the drawing of a distinction between combatants and military targets, on the one hand, and non-combatants (civilians) and civilian objects, on the other. Today, the principle of distinction is found in Article 48 (Basic rule) of Additional Protocol I to the 1949 Geneva Conventions:

> In order to ensure respect for and protection of the civilian population and civilian objects, the Parties to the conflict shall at all times distinguish between the civilian population and combatants and between civilian objects and military objectives and accordingly shall direct their operations only against military objectives.

This principle prohibits indiscriminate warfare and constitutes the core of a central idea of humanitarian law, namely that of the protection of the civilian population against the effects of armed conflict.[37] As far as the use of weapons in international armed conflict is concerned, the prohibition of inherently indiscriminate methods and means of warfare was codified in Article 51 § 4 of Additional Protocol I, which provides that: "Indiscriminate attacks are prohibited. Indiscriminate attacks are . . . b) those which employ a method or means of combat which cannot be directed at a specific military objective."[38] It is generally accepted today that customary international law prohibits the use of indiscriminate weapons both in

35 The principle is further specified in its Article 55 of the First Protocol (Protection of the natural environment).

36 A. Breitegger, *Cluster Munitions and International Law: Disarmament with a Human Face*, London and New York, 2012, pp. 50–51.

37 S. Maslen, *A View from the Vanishing Point, Anti-Personnel Mines on the Battlefield under International Humanitarian Law*, PhD thesis submitted to Tilburg University, The Netherlands, 2000, p. 137.

38 See also the ICJ in its Advisory Opinion on the *Legality of the Threat or Use of Nuclear Weapons*, ICJ Reports, § 78: "States must never make civilians the object of attack and must consequently never use weapons that are incapable of distinguishing between civilian and military targets."

international and in non-international armed conflicts in spite of the fact that efforts to include such a prohibition in Additional Protocol I to the Geneva Conventions failed.[39] The fact that the ICRC Study of Customary International Humanitarian Law states this principle in its Rule 1 attests to its importance.[40]

Any weapon whose guidance system is so rudimentary or unreliable that there is no way of knowing where it will impact is inherently indiscriminate and therefore prohibited under international law.[41] But even weapons that are not inherently indiscriminate may still be used indiscriminately, in particular when aimed at targets from a distance going beyond their effective operational range.[42] Finally, certain weapons are said to be more prone to indiscriminate use than others. According to Stuart Casey-Maslen, this is the reason why the international community has concluded the Ottawa and Oslo Conventions.[43] As regards cluster munitions, the distribution of their explosive force and their effect of fragmentation over a wide area are technical characteristics that were first identified as problematic.[44] The risk to civilians from the use of these weapons was also a concern throughout the Oslo Process, and it was argued that any cluster munition not prohibited by the future treaty should at least be subject to an explicit prohibition of use in populated areas.[45] The allegation that cluster munitions have in the past also (but rather exceptionally) been used against military targets does not make them automatically compatible with the principle of distinction. The Judgment of the Trial Chamber of the International Criminal Tribunal for Yugoslavia (ICTY) in the case of *Milan Martić* of June 12, 2007 dealt with the firing of cluster munitions against Zagreb in 1995. It will be discussed further in the section on implementation of treaties by the ICC.[46]

Alexander Breitegger highlights another problem related to these weapons, namely the post-conflict legacy of unexploded sub-munitions that would fit the

39 See, in this sense, the ICTY in the case of *Prosecutor v. Tadíc*, Case No. IT-94-1-AR72, Appeal on Jurisdiction, October 2, 1995, § 127.

40 Rule 1 reads as follows: "The parties to the conflict must at all times distinguish between civilians and combatants. Attacks may only be directed against combatants. Attacks must not be directed against civilians" (Henckaerts and Doswald-Beck, *Customary International Humanitarian Law*, p. 3).

41 S. Casey-Maslen, "The Use of Nuclear Weapons under Rules Governing the Conduct of Hostilities," in G. Nystuen, S. Casey-Maslen, and A. Golden Bersagel (eds.), *Nuclear Weapons Under International Law*, Cambridge, 2014, pp. 91–127, 99 et seq., giving the examples of "long-range" rockets or missiles.

42 *Ibid.*, p. 100.

43 *Ibid.* According to ICBL and ICRC, only a complete ban of anti-personnel mines would effectively counter the indiscriminate effects of these weapons and their long-lasting impairments of civilians (Oeter, "Methods and Means of Combat," p. 135).

44 T. Nash, "Preamble (2nd Paragraph)," in G. Nystuen and S. Casey-Maslen (eds.), *The Convention on Cluster Munitions: A Commentary*, Oxford and New York, 2010, pp. 45–50, 47.

45 *Ibid.*, p. 48.

46 See Chapter 4, this volume, section D.2.

description of an uncontrollable weapon, especially uncontrollable in time. The reason for this lies in the fact that sub-munitions duds, which usually remain on the ground in large numbers due to excessive failure rates, may kill and maim any person, whether military or civilian, for years after hostilities have ended.[47] An even greater humanitarian evil, in this respect, are anti-personnel mines specially designed to explode with delay, sometimes long after the armed conflict.[48]

cc) Principle according to which the choice of methods and means of warfare are not unlimited and the prohibition of inflicting unnecessary suffering

Another cornerstone of humanitarian law mentioned in the preamble of the Ottawa and Oslo Conventions is the principle according to which States' choices of methods and means of warfare are not unlimited.[49] This principle is closely linked to the prohibition of causing unnecessary suffering to combatants.[50] A contemporary version of the two principles is enshrined in Article 35 of Additional Protocol I to the Geneva Conventions, applicable in international armed conflicts:

> 1. In any armed conflict, the right of the Parties to the conflict to choose methods or means of warfare is not unlimited.
> 2. It is prohibited to employ weapons, projectiles and material and methods of warfare of a nature to cause superfluous injury or unnecessary suffering . . .[51]

It is generally recognised that the obligation not to use weapons causing superfluous injury or unnecessary suffering is part of customary international law, at

47 Breitegger, *Cluster Munitions and International Law*, pp. 44–45.

48 *Ibid.*, p. 46.

49 The rule is generally regarded as being of customary international law applicable to all States (ICJ, Advisory Opinion on the *Legality of the Threat or Use of Nuclear Weapons*, ICJ Reports 1996, § 77).

50 The ICRC, in its Study of Customary International Humanitarian Law, gives a list of weapons that have been cited in practice as having caused unnecessary suffering "if used in certain or all contexts" (Rule 70): Lances or spears with a barbed head, serrated-edged bayonets, expanding bullets, explosive bullets, poison and poisoned weapons, including projectiles smeared with substances that inflame wounds, biological and chemical weapons, weapons that primarily injure by fragments not detectable by X-ray, including projectiles filled with broken glass, certain booby-traps, anti-personnel landmines, torpedoes without self-destruction mechanisms, incendiary weapons, blinding laser weapons, and nuclear weapons (Henckaerts and Doswald-Beck, *Customary International Humanitarian Law*, pp. 243–244).

51 This principle goes at least back to the nineteenth century. See already the 1868 Declaration of Saint Petersburg, https://www.icrc.org/applic/ihl/ihl.nsf/Article.xsp?action=openDocument&documentId=568842C2B90F4A29C12563CD0051547C (accessed February 16, 2017). See, for the historical development of this rule up to the 1977 Additional Protocol I, S. O'Connor, "Nuclear Weapons and the Unnecessary Suffering Rule," in G. Nystuen, S. Casey-Maslen, and A. Golden Bersagel (eds.), *Nuclear Weapons under International Law*, Cambridge, 2014, pp. 128–147, 128–132.

least in international armed conflict.[52] Contrary to the principle of distinction, it is meant to protect the combatants and other personnel taking part in hostilities, rather than civilians.[53] It is aimed at ensuring that, in the course of a lawful combat operation, army members limit their conduct to legitimately injuring or killing their enemy combatants, without causing sufferings that go beyond what is strictly necessary.[54]

As far as anti-personnel mines are concerned, the former President of the ICRC, Cornelio Sommaruga, enquired publicly whether blast anti-personnel mines were not of a nature to cause superfluous injury or unnecessary suffering:

> If a person steps on a buried anti-personnel mines, his or her foot or leg is blown off. The force of the blast drives earth, grass, the vaporized mine case and portions of the victim's shoe and foot upwards into the tissues of the other leg, buttocks, genitals, arms and sometimes the eyes . . . If the wounded person gets to hospital and if the hospital has the necessary facilities and expertise (both of which are rare in mine affected countries) he or she will require several operations, will stay in hospital four weeks at least and will require a safe blood transfusion . . . Likewise, fragmentation mines, which can propel hundreds of metal fragments into a person at waist height, are designed to inflict very severe wounds. "Very severe" means tearing the person apart, or, for the one who triggers the mine, death . . . Would not most people, including soldiers, describe the effects of mines described above as superfluous and excessive to the military need?[55]

Moreover, it has been observed in 1997 by a field doctor of ICRC that "buried" or "point detonating" anti-personnel mines cause specific and severe injury resulting in permanent disability and that the treatment of these kinds of injuries requires, on average, twice as many operations and four times as many blood transfusions as injuries from other weapons.[56] It is generally suggested that, legally

52 Advisory Opinion on the *Legality of the Threat or Use of Nuclear Weapons*, ICJ Reports 1996, §§ 78 et seq. According to Henckaerts and Doswald-Beck, *Customary International Humanitarian Law*, pp. 237, 239–240, this rule applies also in non-international armed conflicts.

53 According to O'Connor, "Nuclear Weapons," p. 133, the unnecessary suffering rule was also at the core of the 1925 Geneva Protocol, the BWC as well as the CWC, even though the use of the weapons banned under these treaties would also breach the distinction rule.

54 B. M. Carnahan, "Unnecessary Suffering, The Red Cross and Tactical Laser Weapons," *Loyola of Los Angeles International and Comparative Law Journal*, vol. 18, September 1996, pp. 705–732, 711 et seq. See also A. Cassese, "Weapons Causing Unnecessary Suffering: Are They Prohibited?" *Rivista di Diritto Internazionale*, vol. LVIII, 1975, pp. 12–42.

55 C. Sommaruga, "Does the Nature of Mine Injuries Also Justify a Total Ban?" in United Nations, *Landmines*, 1.4, September 1996, p. 11.

56 R. M. Coupland, "Abhorrent Weapons and 'Superfluous Injury or Unnecessary Suffering': From Field Surgery to Law," *British Medical Journal*, vol. 315, November 29, 1997, pp. 1450–1452.

speaking, weapons that are specifically designed to cause traumatic amputations of, at least, the foot and lower leg cause more suffering than is strictly necessary to render soldiers unable to fight (*hors de combat*). Indeed, it is hard to see what military purpose is served by deliberately inflicting life-long disability on the combatants when wounding them less severely would be sufficient to remove them from the battle.[57] In this context, it is relevant to mention that revised Protocol II to the CCW deals with mines, booby-traps, and other devices.[58] Its Article 3 § 3 reads: "It is prohibited in all circumstances to use any mine, booby-trap or other device which is designed or of a nature to cause superfluous injury or unnecessary suffering."[59] Basically the same humanitarian problems are caused by cluster munitions. Protocol V to the 1980 Convention deals with ERW. Unlike the previous four protocols, this one does not regulate or prohibit a particular weapon, but addresses the question of the impact of unexploded ordnance in the aftermath of armed conflict and also applies to unexploded sub-munitions.[60]

dd) Principle of proportionality

It has been argued that the prohibition of inflicting superfluous injury or unnecessary suffering is linked to the principle of military necessity and to considerations of humanity or, more generally, the underlying principle of proportionality in warfare.[61] That principle involves the balancing of the advantages to be expected from a military attack against its humanitarian consequences.[62] It can also be considered as a form of the prohibition of indiscriminate attack, explained above.[63] Article 51 § 5 of the 1977 Protocol I is formulated as follows:

> Among others, the following types of attacks are to be considered as indiscriminate: . . . b) an attack which may be expected to cause incidental loss of civilian life, injury to civilians, damage to civilian objects, or a combination thereof, which would be excessive in relation to the concrete and direct military advantage anticipated.

57 Maslen, *A View from the Vanishing Point*, p. 162.

58 See also paragraph 3 of the preamble to this treaty.

59 According to the ICRC, anti-personnel mines are weapons that are generally considered to cause unnecessary suffering (Henckaerts and Doswald-Beck, *Customary International Humanitarian Law*, p. 244).

60 Breitegger, *Cluster Munitions and International Law*, pp. 58–59. Unlike the Oslo Convention, Protocol V does not address the problems of inaccuracy and wide dispersal pattern of the explosive sub-munitions at the time of use (*ibid.*, p. 59).

61 See, for instance, E. Cannizzaro, "Contextualizing Proportionality: *Jus Ad Bellum* and *Jus In Bello* in the Libanese War," *International Review of the Red Cross*, no. 864, December 2006, pp. 779–792.

62 See, for instance, A. P. V. Rogers, *Law on the Battlefield*, Manchester, 1996, p. 14, referring to F. Krüger-Spengel, "Le concept de proportionalité dans le droit de la guerre," *Military Law and Law of War Review*, 1980, pp. 175–204, 179.

63 Breitegger, *Cluster Munitions and International Law*, p. 48.

Today this rule is considered part of customary international law, also in non-international armed conflict.[64] As an example, manifestly disproportionate collateral damage caused to reach operational objectives will generally result in the attack being considered an act of illegal and indiscriminate warfare.[65] It is necessary to proceed to a balancing exercise taking into consideration the broader picture, including, on the one hand, the impact of the weapon on the individual, its socio-economic impact, and its impact on the environment and, on the other, its military utility and the question of whether alternatives to this type of weapon exist in the given circumstances.[66] Proportionality has to be assessed *ex ante*, at the moment of the attack, comparing potential (civilian) losses to the potential military advantage, and not *post facto*, on the basis of a comparison of the human suffering caused in reality and the military advantage gained.[67]

It is generally agreed that the low military value of anti-personnel mines is largely outweighed by their high humanitarian costs.[68] The problems caused to society by the use of anti-personnel mines are well described in the preamble of the Ottawa Convention:

> Determined to put an end to the suffering and casualties caused by anti-personnel mines, that kill or maim hundreds of people every week, mostly innocent and defenseless civilians and especially children, obstruct economic development and reconstruction, inhibit the repatriation of refugees and internally displaced persons, and have other severe consequences for years after emplacement . . .[69]

As far as cluster munitions are concerned, legal problems may arise with regard to the post-conflict legacy of unexploded sub-munitions, namely, the potential killing and maiming of civilians, the denial of access to agricultural and grazing lands, and the impossibility of the return of refugees or internally displaced people.[70] Moreover, the inaccuracy and wide dispersal of sub-munitions in strikes may create problems under the proportionality rule in populated areas. By contrast, the use in isolated, inhabited areas may not necessarily run against the rule of proportionality.[71]

64 See also the ICRC Study of Customary International Humanitarian Law, Rule 14: "Launching an attack which may be expected to cause incidental loss of civilian life, injury to civilians, damage to civilian objects, or a combination thereto, which would be excessive in relation to the concrete and direct military advantage anticipated, is prohibited" (Henckaerts and Doswald-Beck, *Customary International Humanitarian Law*, p. 46).

65 See, for more details, Oeter, "Methods and Means of Combat," pp. 34–38.

66 See, regarding anti-personnel mines, Maslen, *A View from the Vanishing Point*, pp. 144–151.

67 Breitegger, *Cluster Munitions and International Law*, p. 48, with further references.

68 Maslen, *A View from the Vanishing Point*, p. 152.

69 Paragraph 1 of the Preamble.

70 Breitegger, *Cluster Munitions and International Law*, p. 49, with further references.

71 *Ibid.*, pp. 48–49.

ee) Martens Clause

The relevance of humanitarian law for the Ottawa and Oslo Conventions is furthermore highlighted by the insertion of a contemporary version of the so-called "Martens Clause" in both treaties. This clause reads as follows:

> *The States Parties to this Convention . . .*
> *Reaffirming* that in cases not covered by this Convention or by other international agreements, civilians and combatants remain under the protection and authority of the principles of international law, derived from established custom, from the principles of humanity and from the dictates of public conscience.[72]

The Martens Clause is named after the Russian jurist Fedor Fedorovitch Martens, who was instrumental in drafting it and who ensured its adoption.[73] It first appeared in the Preamble to the 1899 Hague Convention IV and is now codified in Article 1 § 2 of Additional Protocol I to the Geneva Conventions (General principles and scope of application):

> In cases not covered by this Protocol or by other international agreements, civilians and combatants remain under the protection and authority of the principles of international law derived from established custom, from the principles of humanity and from the dictates of public conscience.[74]

In its Advisory Opinion on the *Legality of the Threat or Use of Nuclear Weapons*, the ICJ explicitly referred to this clause, as did the International Criminal Tribunal for Rwanda (ICTR) in a case before it.[75] According to the ICJ, the Martens Clause had "proved to be an effective means of addressing the rapid evolution of military

72 Paragraph 11 of the preamble to the Oslo Convention and, for a similar clause, paragraph 8 to the preamble of the Ottawa Convention (emphasis in the original).

73 Maslen, *Commentaries on Arms Control Treaties*, vol. 1, p. 62. The clause is based on paragraph 3 of the Declaration of June 20, 1899 read by Martens who chaired then, as Russian delegate, the 11th meeting of the Second Committee of the Second Commission on the occasion of the First Hague Peace Conference of 1899 (S. Miyazaki, "The Martens Clause and International Humanitarian Law," in C. Swinarski (ed.), *Studies and Essays on International Humanitarian Law and Red Cross Principles in Honour of Jean Pictet*, The Hague and Geneva, 1984, pp. 433–444, 434).

74 Moreover, the clause was also inserted in the denunciation clauses of the four Geneva Conventions. See, for instance, Article 63 of the First Geneva Convention: "The denunciation . . . shall in no way impair the obligations which the Parties to the conflict shall remain bound to fulfil by virtue of the principles of the law of nations, as they result from the usages established among civilized peoples, from the laws of humanity and the dictates of the public conscience."

75 ICJ Reports 1996, §§ 78, 84, and 87; and ICTY, *Prosecutor v. Jean-Paul Akayesu*, Judgment of September 2, 1998 (ICTR-96-4-T), § 566.

technology."[76] While its exact meaning is uncertain,[77] it is nevertheless conceded that the clause applies to both international and internal armed conflicts,[78] which is compatible with its insertion into the preambles of the Ottawa and Oslo Conventions.[79] Stuart Casey-Maslen suggests that the aims of the clause are, first, to show that the absence of applicable law on a certain behavior at a certain time does not mean that there are no legal constraints,[80] and, second, that States are duty-bound to assess the legality of the use of weaponry that is not already regulated by existing humanitarian law.[81] In his view, the successful conclusion of the Ottawa and Oslo Conventions can be attributed largely to the "laws of humanity" and "dictates of public conscience."[82]

3. Prohibition of using the relevant weapons in light of human rights law

a) Prohibition of using these weapons "never under any circumstances" in the CWC and the Ottawa and Oslo Conventions

Insofar as the States Parties undertake, in accordance with Article I of these Conventions, "never under any circumstances" to use these weapons, their duties go even further and are not limited to an armed conflict, contrary to what is the case, for instance, for the 1925 Geneva Protocol or the Geneva Conventions and the Additional Protocols thereto.[83] In other words, the instruments examined in the present study also apply in peacetime and in situations where it is uncertain

76 ICJ Reports 1996, § 78.

77 R. Ticehurst, "The Martens Clause and the Laws of Armed Conflict," *International Review of the Red Cross*, March–April 1997, no. 317, Geneva, pp. 125–134, 126. See also, for a discussion of the different opinions, Maslen, *Commentaries on Arms Control Treaties*, vol. 1, pp. 167–169.

78 See paragraph 4 of the preamble of the 1977 Additional Protocol II: "Recalling that, in cases not covered by the law in force, the human person remains under the protection of the principles of humanity and the dictates of the public conscience."

79 According to Miyazaki, "The Martens Clause," pp. 439–441, given the absence of extensive legal regulation, the Martens Clause turns out to be even more relevant in internal armed conflicts.

80 Casey-Maslen, *Commentaries on Arms Control Treaties*, vol. 1, p. 168.

81 *Ibid.* See also in this regard Article 36 (New weapons) of the 1977 Additional Protocol II.

82 *Ibid.*, pp. 168 et seq. The following statement made by the President of the First CCW Review Conference is noteworthy in this regard: "In a setting which excluded a number of major mine-using and mine-producing countries, some hundred States were able to translate their understanding of the 'dictates of public conscience' in the words of the Martens Clause, into a treaty text banning anti-personnel landmines" (L. Maresca and S. Maslen (eds.), *The Banning of Anti-Personnel Landmines: The Work of the International Committee of the Red Cross (1955–1999)*, Cambridge, 2000, p. xxiv).

83 See also the CCW, which also only applies in international armed conflict and, since 2001, for those States who adhered to this amendment, also in non-international armed conflicts.

whether the threshold of an armed conflict has been met. This element may present a crucial advantage, since the distinction between situations of armed conflict and peace, as a result of modern, asymmetric warfare, has become blurred.[84]

In light of the foregoing, the general clauses imposing on States Parties the duty "never" to use these weapons "under any circumstances" act as an effective tool for the protection of the rights of people affected by such use. Regarding the human rights aspects of the three treaties analyzed here, the picture that will be drawn shows a similar pattern, already observed in the subdivision devoted to the *travaux préparatoires* to the treaties,[85] namely, that the concerns for the protection of the human being have played a more prominent role in the Ottawa and Oslo Conventions than in the CWC. It is certainly not exaggerated to claim that the two treaties adopt human rights language and logic in several respects.

b) The human-rights aspects of the Ottawa and Oslo Conventions

aa) Relevance of human rights law for the civilian population exposed to anti-personnel mines and cluster munitions

In modern armed conflict, the main victims of such weapons are civilians, through death, injury, displacement, and the loss of both livelihood and property.[86] Since 1999, the UNSG has provided regular, comprehensive reports on the protection of civilians in armed conflict, including recommendations for improvement, many of which have been subsequently endorsed by the UNSC.[87] The Ottawa and Oslo Conventions are sensitive to the protection of particularly vulnerable groups of persons in times of armed conflict and in their aftermath. The relevant paragraphs of the preamble of the Oslo Convention, for example, read as follows:

> *The States Parties to this Convention . . .*
>
> *Deeply concerned* that civilian populations and individual civilians continue to bear the brunt of armed conflict,[88]
>
> *Determined* to put an end for all time to the suffering and casualties caused by cluster munitions at the time of their use, when they fail to function as intended or when they are abandoned,[89]
>
> . . .

84 As explained above, this volume, Chapter 1, section B.1.

85 See this volume, Chapter 2.

86 Nystuen and Casey-Maslen, *The Convention on Cluster Munitions*, p. 44.

87 See UNSC Resolutions 1265 (1999), 1296 (2000), 1674 (2006), and 1738 (2006). The negative effects of cluster munitions on civilian populations were specifically recognized, for the first time, by the UNSG in his 2007 report to the UNSC (Report of the Secretary-General on the protection of civilians in armed conflict, UN Doc. S/2007/643, October 28, 2007, §§ 61 et seq.).

88 Paragraph 1 of the preamble to the Oslo Convention (emphasis in the original).

89 Paragraph 2 of the preamble (emphasis in the original).

> *Determined* also to ensure the full realisation of the rights of all cluster munition victims and *recognizing* their inherent dignity.[90]

Whereas humanitarian law only applies during armed conflict, Part II of the present study, devoted to treaties dealing with nuclear weapons will address in more detail the question of whether and to what extent exactly human rights law applies during armed conflict. For the purposes of the present Chapter, it is sufficient to mention that human rights treaties generally remain applicable during armed conflict. Different categories of human rights might come into play as regards the use of anti-personnel mines and cluster munitions. First, it is obvious that the explosion of a mine or a cluster munition in the hands or under the feet of an innocent civilian infringes above all his right to life, protected, in particular, by Article 6 ICCPR, Article 2 of the European Convention on Human Rights (ECHR), or Article 4 of the American Convention on Human Rights (ACHR). Breitegger suggests that, in the case of sub-munition contamination of a State Party's territory, the right to life would impose on the State the positive obligation to take preventive operational measures to protect the lives of people under its jurisdiction, in particular technical measures of marking and clearance of unexploded sub-munitions, in order to prevent the killing and maiming of individuals.[91] Moreover, it would be incumbent on the State to provide information to those being put at risk by cluster munitions remnants.[92] These aspects have in fact been dealt with by the ECtHR in the context of anti-personnel mines. These cases will be explained in more detail in the section on the role of the ECtHR and the Committee of Ministers of the Council of Europe in the implementation of the Ottawa Convention.[93] Moreover, such explosions might also violate the right to physical and moral integrity guaranteed, inter alia, by Article 8 ECHR (Right to respect for private and family life).[94]

In addition, the notion of "human dignity," addressed in the sixth preambular paragraph of the Oslo Convention, quoted above, is an example of language borrowed from the human rights context, in particular from the 1948 Universal Declaration of Human Rights (UDHR), whose first Article characterizes this concept as "foundation of freedom, justice and peace in the world."[95] As victims

90 Paragraph 6 of the preamble (emphasis in the original).

91 Breitegger, *Cluster Munitions and International Law*, p. 99.

92 *Ibid.*

93 See this volume, Chapter 4, section C.2.

94 See, for instance, the judgment of the ECtHR in the case of *El-Masri v. FYR of Macedonia* [GC], no. 39630/09, December 13, 2012, § 248: "According to the Court's case-law, the notion of 'private life' is a broad one and is not susceptible to exhaustive definition; it may, depending on the circumstances, cover the moral and physical integrity of the person . . ." See also *Glor v. Switzerland*, no. 13444/04, April 30, 2009, § 52.

95 The first paragraph of the preamble to the Universal Declaration of Human Rights, adopted by the UNGA in Resolution 217 A (III) of December 10, 1948, reads as follows: "Whereas recognition of the inherent dignity and of the equal and inalienable rights of all members of the human family is the foundation of freedom, justice and peace in the word." See also Article 1 of that Declaration: "All human beings are born free and equal in dignity and rights."

of mines or cluster munitions often suffer considerable physical and mental harm and frequently face huge challenges in their daily lives, frequently resulting in social and economic marginalization or exclusion, the clauses inserted in the Oslo Convention are valid reminders of their inherent human rights and dignity.[96]

The preamble of both treaties reiterates furthermore what has already been mentioned above, namely that anti-personnel mines and cluster munitions are particularly harmful to civilian populations not only because of their indiscriminate impact when used as intended, but also as a result of the high rate of unexploded or abandoned weapons. Some risk of leaving behind unexploded remnants of war is inherent in all explosive weapons,[97] but cluster munitions have been found to represent a particularly severe threat, due to larger numbers of sub-munitions deployed, the complexity of their delivery, their small size, the sensitivity of their fusing systems, and the density of contamination.[98] The comprehensive ban on these weapons, if implemented seriously, strongly contributes to minimize the harm to civilians after the end of the hostilities.[99]

Reconstruction after an armed conflict can take long periods of time, owing in particular to the often costly and time-consuming clearance operations. Therefore, the third preambular paragraph of the Oslo Convention focuses on the negative long-term consequences of cluster munitions remnants:[100]

> *The States Parties to this Convention* . . .
>
> *Concerned* that cluster munition remnants kill or maim civilians, including women and children, obstruct economic and social development, including through the loss of livelihood, impede post-conflict rehabilitation and reconstruction, delay or prevent the return of refugees and internally displaced persons, can negatively impact on national and international peace-building and humanitarian assistance efforts, and have other severe consequences that can persist for many years after use . . .[101]

96 Nystuen and Casey-Maslen, *The Convention on Cluster Munitions*, p. 56.

97 Therefore, a specific protocol to the 1980 CCW was adopted on November 23, 2003 (Protocol V on Explosive Remnants of War).

98 Nystuen and Casey-Maslen, *The Convention on Cluster Munitions*, p. 48.

99 See, e.g., Opening statement by Jakob Kellenberger, President of the ICRC, Dublin Diplomatic Conference, May 19, 2008. Problems of unexploded ordnance from cluster munitions have been specifically identified, inter alia, in Cambodia, the Lao People's Democratic Republic (Laos), and Vietnam following US bombardment during the Vietnam War, in the former Yugoslavia and in particular in Kosovo following the NATO bombardment in 1999, in Afghanistan during the US attack in 2001–2002, in Iraq in the Gulf War in 1991 and in the invasion in 2003, as well as in Lebanon in 2006 (Nystuen and Casey-Maslen, *The Convention on Cluster Munitions*, p. 49).

100 Nystuen and Casey-Maslen, *The Convention on Cluster Munitions*, pp. 50 et seq.

101 See, for a similar clause, paragraph 1 of the preamble to the Ottawa Convention.

The impact of cluster-munition remnants on innocent civilians was one of the principal factors motivating States when adopting the Oslo Convention.[102] Apart from death and injury, their presence causes long-term "area denial" as a consequence of the fear of unexploded sub-munitions that prevents or dissuades people from returning to their homes, land, and places of work.[103] In other words, not only the explosion of cluster munitions hitting the home of civilians constitutes a breach of the right to property, but also the mere presence of a minefield that renders useless an agricultural area and, therefore, leads to a *de facto* expropriation.[104]

It would nonetheless be too narrow to confine this effect of remnants of war to the individual right to property. The problem has to be seen in a broader context, taking into account concerns for security, peace-building, reconstruction, and the right to development. Transitional periods in the aftermath of armed conflict, when people are deprived of adequate food and health services, employment, stability, and safe environment, are ideal examples for the relevance of the concepts of human security and human development, dealt with above.[105] The Ottawa and Oslo Conventions obviously fit well into this logic.

Finally, the contamination of water installations, such as sanitarian or irrigation canals, and agricultural and pastoral land with sub-munition duds makes these areas useless. This is incompatible with the enjoyment of basic aspects of the right to health, guaranteed in particular by Article 7 of the International Covenant on Economic, Social and Cultural Rights (ICESCR). Vital elements at stake in the context of non-exploded sub-munitions may be the obligation to ensure access to essential food, basic shelter, housing, and sanitation, or to provide an adequate supply of safe and potable water, all considered non-derogable rights.[106]

bb) Victim-centered approach to anti-personnel mines and cluster munitions

The Ottawa and Oslo Conventions definitively take on features of human rights treaties when they refer to "victims" of anti-personnel and cluster munitions. The Ottawa Convention is the first disarmament treaty to impose humanitarian duties

102 Nystuen and Casey-Maslen, *The Convention on Cluster Munitions*, p. 50, no. 46, referring to two reports of Handicap International Belgium that showed that a very high proportion of recorded casualties from cluster munitions were civilians.

103 Nystuen and Casey-Maslen, *The Convention on Cluster Munitions*, pp. 50 et seq.

104 The right to property is guaranteed, inter alia, by Article 17 of the Universal Declaration of Human Rights and, on a regional level, by Article 1 of Protocol I to the ECHR, Article 21 ACHR, and Article 14 of the African Charter on Human and Peoples' Rights.

105 See this volume, Chapter 1, sections B.2) and B.3).

106 Breitegger, *Cluster Munitions and International Law*, p. 101.

of victim assistance,[107] even if it is still somehow cautious in employing the term "victim," referring to it only three times, most prominently in its preamble:

> *The States Parties . . .*
> *Wishing* to do their utmost in providing assistance for the care and rehabilitation, including the social and economic reintegration of mine victims . . .[108]

Even more significant is the protection of and assistance to "victims" in the Oslo Convention, adopted more than a decade later. It is not exaggerated to affirm that the concerns for the victims of cluster munitions have been one of the major driving forces behind the treaty.[109] The aim was to guarantee assistance that is provided efficiently, with dignity, without discrimination, and taking into account the specific needs of the affected persons.[110] The place taken by the protection of the rights of the victims is striking, and the preamble alone devotes five paragraphs to this aspect, including one referring explicitly to the Convention on the Rights of Persons with Disabilities (CRPD). The relevant paragraphs read as follows:

> *The States Parties to the Convention,*
> . . .
> *Determined* also to ensure the full realisation of the rights of all cluster munition victims and *recognising* their inherent dignity,
> *Resolved* to do their utmost in providing assistance to cluster munition victims, including medical care, rehabilitation and psychological support, as well as providing for their social and economic inclusion,
> *Recognising* the need to provide age- and gender-sensitive assistance to cluster munition victims and to address the special needs of vulnerable groups,
> *Bearing in mind* the Convention on the Rights of Persons with Disabilities which, *inter alia*, requires that States Parties to that Convention undertake to ensure and promote the full realisation of all human rights and fundamental freedoms of all persons with disabilities without discrimination of any kind on the basis of disability,

107 *Ibid.*, p. 103.

108 Paragraph 3 of the preamble (emphasis in the original). See, for a commentary on this clause, Maslen, *Commentaries on Arms Control Treaties*, vol. 1, pp. 57 et seq. The Ottawa Convention moreover refers to the expression "victim" in paragraphs 3 and 7(e) of Article 6 (International cooperation and assistance); see Maslen, *Commentaries on Arms Control Treaties*, vol. 1, pp. 194–199, and pp. 206 et seq.

109 See, in this respect, K. Hulme, "The 2008 Cluster Munitions Convention: Stepping outside the CCW Framework (Again)," *The International and Comparative Law Quarterly*, vol. 58, 2009, pp. 219–227, 224.

110 D. Rietiker, "Entre sécurité et protection de l'individu: la Convention sur les armes à sous-munitions comme dernier exemple d'un nouveau type de traité – et un modèle pour l'avenir?" *Journal du droit international*, vol. 139, no. 4/2012, pp. 1295–1322, 1309.

> *Mindful* of the need to coordinate adequately efforts undertaken in various fora to address the rights and needs of victims of various types of weapons, and *resolved* to avoid discrimination among victims of various types of weapons . . .[111]

In Article 2 § 1, the Oslo Convention provides for a definition of the term "victim" that, interestingly, includes not only persons who have been killed or injured physically, but also those who have suffered "psychological injury, economic loss, social marginalization or substantial impairment of the realization of their rights" caused by cluster munitions, as well as their families and communities. This definition is broad and includes social and economic rights of the victims, as "collective rights."[112] Social marginalization is a frequent factor of victimization, insofar as disability leads in many societies to social stigmatization of the individual.[113] Moreover, by using the expression "all human rights," the preamble also clarifies that victimization does not depend on the legal status of the affected persons, but covers all persons who have suffered harm, regardless of their status in society, including migrants, refugees, and internally displaced persons.[114]

The Oslo Convention clearly takes a "rights-based" approach to victim assistance.[115] By emphasizing the "realization" of rights, in the preamble and in Article 2 § 1, this Convention follows another feature of human rights instruments, namely, the need for a teleological interpretation, aiming at the protection of concrete and effective rights and freedoms of victims.[116] For instance, while in democratic societies everyone has the right to vote in elections, it might actually be very difficult for a cluster munition victim to participate in the vote as a consequence of his injury, for instance the loss of eyesight, or because the risk of unexploded cluster munitions makes it difficult to access a voting station.[117]

111 Paragraphs 6–10 of the preamble (emphasis in the original).

112 Corsi, "Towards Peace through Legal Innovation," pp. 153 et seq.; E. David, "La Convention de 2008 sur les armes à sous-munitions," *Revue générale de droit international public*, vol. 113, 2009, pp. 785–806, 801 ; T. Di Ruzza, "The Convention on Cluster Munitions: Towards a Balance between Humanitarian and Military Considerations?" *Revue du droit militaire et du droit de la guerre*, vol. 47, 2008, pp. 405–448, 430.

113 B. Docherty, L. Maresca, R. Moyes, and M. Reiterer, "Article 2," in Nystuen and Casey-Maslen, *The Convention on Cluster Munitions*, pp. 144–245, 158.

114 Nystuen and Casey-Maslen, *The Convention on Cluster Munitions*, p. 55; and Docherty et al., "Article 2," pp. 157 et seq.

115 Nystuen and Casey-Maslen, *The Convention on Cluster Munitions*, p. 55; and Docherty et al., "Article 2," p. 357.

116 See, for instance, the approach adopted by the ECtHR in the case of *Emonet and Others v. Switzerland*, no. 39051/03, § 77, December 13, 2007, where it expressed this principle as follows: "It should be remembered that the aim of the Convention is to guarantee not rights that are theoretical or illusory but rights that are practical and effective (see, *mutatis mutandis*, *Artico v. Italy*, Judgment of 13 May 1980, Series A no. 37, p. 16, § 33) . . ."

117 Docherty et al., "Article 2," p. 158.

cc) Gender- and age-sensitive approach to "victims"

Groups of persons particularly exposed to anti-personnel mines and cluster munitions are mentioned in the preambles of both the Ottawa and Oslo Conventions, namely children, women, refugees, and internally displaced persons.[118] These are society's most fragile members in times of war and in the aftermath of a conflict that can last many years. Some of their rights are protected in separate international treaties, such as the 1989 UN Convention on the Rights of the Child (UNCRC), which contains its own provisions for the protection of children from the effects of armed conflict. Certain rights of women are addressed by the Convention on the Elimination of All Forms of Discrimination against Women (CEDAW), which does not deal, however, with violence against women as such.[119]

In its first paragraph, Article 5 of the Oslo Convention deals with the special vulnerability of children and women in situations of war by referring to "age- and gender-sensitive" assistance:

> Each State Party with respect to cluster munition victims in areas under its jurisdiction or control shall, in accordance with applicable international humanitarian and human rights law, adequately provide age- and gender-sensitive assistance, including medical care, rehabilitation and psychological support, as well as provide for their social and economic inclusion . . .[120]

Handicap International (HI) has observed that more than 80 percent of cluster munition victims are male, while almost 30 percent are young boys.[121] Some

118 See S. Maslen, "The 1996 Landmines Protocol for Refugees and the Internally Displaced," *International Journal of Refugee Law*, vol. 8, 1996, pp. 383–396; and S. Beauchamp, *Explosive Remnants of War and the Protection of Human Beings under Public International Law*, Geneva, 2008, pp. 335–354.

119 For the time being, certain instruments have been concluded on a regional level; see in particular the Inter-American Convention on the Prevention, Punishment and Eradication of Violence against Women (Belem Convention, September 6, 1994), the Protocol to the African Charter on Human and Peoples' Rights on the Rights of Women in Africa (Maputo Protocol, July 11, 2003), and the Council of Europe Convention on Preventing and Combating Violence against Women and Domestic Violence (Istanbul Convention, May 11, 2011).

120 See, for more details, Hulme, "The 2008 Cluster Munitions Convention," pp. 224 et seq.; and Di Ruzza, "The Convention on Cluster Munitions," p. 431. In a report entitled "Key Developments since May 2005," the *Landmine and Cluster Munition Monitor* reported that a survey by the Ministry of Labor and Social Affairs and the International Rescue Committee found an estimated 84 percent unemployment rate among people with disabilities (information taken from the judgment of the ECtHR in the case of *S.H.H. v. United Kingdom*, no. 60367/10, January 29, 2013, § 50).

121 Handicap International (HI), "Circle of Impact – the Fatal Footprint of Cluster Munitions on People and Communities," Brussels, 2007, http://reliefweb.int/sites/reliefweb.int/files/resources/948D323F9A5BA883852572DF00674624-HI_ClusterMunitions_2007.pdf (accessed February 16, 2017).

40 percent of cluster munition casualties concern children.[122] According to the ICRC, the effects of cluster munition incidents are netherless often worse for women and children. For example, a disability might render women unmarriageable in certain societies.[123] Moreover, it is often women who have to deal with the consequences of war. In the absence of the man, who is frequently the breadwinner, women have to ensure the family's day-to-day survival.[124] They often have to travel long distances to find water, food, firewood, medicine, and other basic necessities, thereby exposing themselves to risks to their physical safety.[125] After an armed conflict, women may play a key role in rebuilding communities.[126] For all these reasons, they are particularly vulnerable to landmines and failed cluster munitions, which continue to cause injury and death long after the end of hostilities.

Children are among those who are most at risk due to their tampering with unexploded sub-munitions. This risk has a heavy impact on their enjoyment of rights protected by the UNCRC, in particular of the right to life (Article 6), which imposes the positive duty to ensure the survival and development of the child.[127] Moreover, Breitegger suggests that the presence of unexploded sub-munitions also heavily compromises the obligation to diminish child mortality and to ensure the provision of necessary assistance and health care to all children (Article 24 UNCRC).[128] Finally, according to Article 39 UNCRC, States Parties shall take all appropriate measures to promote the physical and psychological recovery and social reintegration of child victims of armed conflict. Significant progress in providing assistance to victims, not only to children but in general, has been achieved with the adoption of the Ottawa and Oslo Conventions,[129] the latter relying explicitly on the CRPD, as explained in the section below.

dd) Relevance of the Convention on the Rights of Persons with Disabilities (CRPD)

To what extent the Oslo Convention resembles a human rights instrument is finally shown by another aspect. In fact, the Convention urges the States Parties

122 Women International League for Peace and Freedom (WILPF), "Cluster Munitions and Gender – It Takes More than a Ban," 2008, http://reliefweb.int/sites/reliefweb.int/files/resources/C9A349A5ED559761C125751D0037C209-wilpf_nov08.pdf (accessed February 16, 2017).

123 M. Reiterer, "Preamble (8th Paragraph)," in Nystuen and Casey-Maslen, *The Convention on Cluster Munitions*, pp. 57–58, 57.

124 ICRC, "Women Protected under International Humanitarian Law, Overview," October 29, 2010, http://www.icrc.org/eng/war-and-law/protected-persons/women/overview-women-protected.htm (accessed February 16, 2017).

125 *Ibid.*

126 *Ibid.*

127 Breitegger, *Cluster Munitions and International Law*, p. 102.

128 *Ibid.*

129 *Ibid.*, p. 103.

not only to take all appropriate measures to eliminate discrimination on the basis of disabilities,[130] but also to ensure that no discrimination occurs among victims – of cluster munitions, other weapons, or yet other causes – and that differences in treatment shall be based only on medical, rehabilitative, psychological, or socio-economic needs.[131] Clauses of non-discrimination are nowadays included in all major human rights instruments.[132]

Furthermore, the preamble of the Oslo Convention explicitly refers to applicable rules of human rights law.[133] For obvious reasons, the CRPD, mentioned in paragraph 9 of its preamble, plays an essential role here. As mentioned above in Chapter 2, section B.2, the CRPD had been adopted only some two months before the Oslo Process took off in February 2007 and served as an important source of inspiration for the Convention's provisions on the assistance to and protection of victims.[134] Its purpose was to ensure and promote the full realization of all human rights and fundamental freedoms of all persons with disabilities, without discrimination of any kind on the basis of disabilities, and to promote respect for their inherent dignity.[135] The adoption of the CRPD was the result of the realization that the issue of people with disabilities is a human rights concern rather than one of purely medical or social welfare.[136] The CRPD also highlights the need for an enhanced protection of children and women with disabilities.[137]

Furthermore, the CRPD stresses the need for special protection of persons with disabilities in situations of armed conflict, which is naturally a very relevant issue for victims of cluster munitions and anti-personnel mines who, after having been injured by the explosion of such a weapon, often continue to live in an environment of hostility and humanitarian emergency.[138] Furthermore, most of the ongoing armed conflicts and most of the explosions of these weapons occur in developing

130 Paragraph 9 of the preamble.

131 Paragraph 10 of the preamble (see for a commentary, Nystuen and Casey-Maslen, *The Convention on Cluster Munitions*, pp. 59–61) and Article 5 § 2(e). The latter provision clarifies that, for example, an occupying power is required to provide medical care to civilians in an area and, at the same time, not to discriminate in the provision of this treatment and ensure that the sole consideration is a medical one (M. Reiterer and T. Leibowitz, "Article 5," in Nystuen and Casey-Maslen, *The Convention on Cluster Munitions*, pp. 328–372, 371 et seq).

132 See, in particular, Article 26 ICCPR, Article 3 ICESCR, Article 5 CRPD, and, on a regional level, Article 14 ECHR and Article 24 ACHR.

133 In order to be "applicable," a norm has *a priori* to be ratified by the State Party concerned or being of customary nature (Reiterer and Leibowitz, "Article 5," p. 359).

134 Nystuen and Casey-Maslen, *The Convention on Cluster Munitions*, p. 58.

135 See Article 1 § 1, combined with Article 3 CRPD.

136 Breitegger, *Cluster Munitions and International Law*, p. 108.

137 Article 6 (Women with disabilities) and Article 7 (Children with disabilities); see also the preamble, paragraphs (q) and (r).

138 See, in particular Article 11 (Situations of risk and humanitarian emergencies).

countries. The CRPD highlights the particular difficulties and requirements of persons with disabilities living in conditions of poverty.[139]

The following paragraphs of the Report of the Afghanistan Independent Human Rights Commission on the Situation of Economic and Social Rights in Afghanistan adequately reflect the difficult situation of persons with disabilities in post-conflict situations:[140]

> Persons with disabilities are among the most vulnerable segments of population and the government has taken no measures to enable their full participation in society and to ensure their access to social and educational services . . . Thirty years of war in Afghanistan had unfavourable effects and one of these is the rise in the number of persons with disabilities. The Afghan conflict not only physically incapacitated people, but it also had negative implications for the psyche of Afghan public . . . Handicap International estimates that there are 800,000 persons with severe disabilities, however, according to the national disability survey in Afghanistan, out of 25 million Afghan people, 747,500 to 867,100 people have severe disabilities, 17% of which are persons with war disability and 6.8% are victims of mines and other unexploded ordnance (UXO). On an average basis, for every five families, there is a person with a disability . . . Approximately 70% of persons with disabilities aged over 15 are jobless. Disability has had a direct and strong correlation with the rising trend of unemployment . . .[141]

In the context of victims of mine and cluster munition explosions, it is finally noteworthy to mention the provisions on health and rehabilitation contained in Articles 25 and 26 of the CRPD. This instrument also emphasizes the need for assistance provided in a gender-sensitive, health-related, and non-discriminatory manner,[142] as well as the aim of social reinsertion of victims in their own communities, including in rural areas.[143]

139 See, in particular, paragraph (t) of the preamble (emphasis in the original): "*The States Parties* . . . *Highlighting* the fact that the majority of persons with disabilities live in conditions of poverty, and in this regard recognizing the critical need to address the negative impact of poverty on persons with disabilities." See, regarding the right to development in the context of disability rights, M. A. Stein, "Disability Human Rights," *California Law Review*, vol. 95, 2007, pp. 75–121, in particular 94–98.

140 Report of November/December 2009, IV, Qaws 1388.

141 Quotations taken from the judgment of the ECtHR in the case of *S.H.H. v. United Kingdom*, no. 60367/10, January 29, 2013, § 47.

142 Article 25 § 1 CPRD.

143 See, in particular, Articles 25(c) and 26 § 1(b) CPRD.

B. THE OTHER LEGAL DUTIES (ARMS CONTROL, NON-PROLIFERATION, AND DISARMAMENT OBLIGATIONS) UNDER THE CWC AND THE OTTAWA AND OSLO CONVENTIONS

Apart from the obligation not to use these weapons, and in order to achieve their total elimination, the three treaties examined in this Chapter contain provisions that can be referred to as arms control, non-proliferation, and disarmament obligations. Four observations shall be made in this context:

First, the States Parties undertake to refrain from developing, producing, otherwise requiring, stockpiling, retaining, or transferring the weapons concerned.[144] It is worth mentioning that the obligation not to transfer these weapons is formulated in an absolute manner, including, as is the case for the prohibition of use, States Parties, non-States Parties, and non-State actors ("directly or indirectly . . . to anyone"). In Resolution 2188(2013) concerning the war in Syria, the UNSC has stated that the "proliferation of chemical weapons . . . constitutes a threat to international peace and security."[145] In this resolution, the UNSC further decided that Syria shall declare and give up all her remaining chemical weapons in order to be destroyed under the supervision of the OPCW. The Council had already asserted in its Resolution 1540 of April 28, 2004 that the spread of weapons of mass destruction (WMD) constituted a threat to international peace and security,[146] emphasizing explicitly "its support for the multilateral treaties whose aim is to eliminate or prevent the proliferation of nuclear, chemical or biological weapons and the importance for all States parties to these treaties to implement them fully in order to promote international stability."[147]

Second, the States Parties agree not to assist, encourage, or induce anyone, in any way, to engage in any activity prohibited under the treaties.[148] The language of these provisions shows that these duties are also imposed on States Parties absolutely and allow for no exception.

Third, the treaties impose on the States Parties the "positive" obligation to destroy or to ensure the destruction of the weapons banned, whether stockpiled or deployed in the field.[149] As far as the CWC is concerned, this duty comprises the destruction of all chemical weapons production facilities for which a State Party might be responsible.[150]

144 Articles 1 § 1(b) of the Ottawa and Oslo Conventions and Article I § 1(a) of the CWC.
145 Paragraph 3 of the preamble.
146 Paragraph 1 of the preamble.
147 Paragraph 5 of the preamble.
148 Articles 1 § 1(c) of the Ottawa and Oslo Conventions and Article I § 1(d) of the CWC.
149 Article 1 § 2, combined with Article 4 (Destruction of stockpiled anti-personnel mines) and 5 (Destruction of anti-personnel mines in mined areas) of the Ottawa Convention; Articles 3 (Storage and stockpile destruction) and 4 (Clearance and destruction of cluster munition remnants and risk reduction education) of the Oslo Convention, and Article I §§ 2 and 3, combined with Article IV of the CWC.
150 Article I § 4, combined with Article V of the CWC.

Fourth, in its Article 21, the Oslo Convention contains interesting innovations. Paragraphs 1 and 2 read as follows:

> *Relations with States not Party to this Convention*
>
> 1. Each State Party shall encourage States not party to this Convention to ratify, accept, approve or accede to this Convention, with the goal of attracting the adherence of all States to this Convention.
> 2. Each State Party shall notify the governments of all States not party to this Convention, referred to in paragraph 3 of this Article, of its obligations under this Convention, shall promote the norms it establishes and shall make its best efforts to discourage States not party to this Convention from using cluster munitions.
>
> . . .

The first paragraph of Article 21 imposes a positive duty on States Parties to encourage other States to join the treaty with a view to achieving its universality.[151] From this author's point of view, this obligation is comparable with the obligation of the States Parties under common Article 1 of the 1949 Geneva Convention "to respect and to ensure respect for the present Convention in all circumstances." The rule in question is part of customary international law.[152] The unconditional obligation enshrined in common Article 1 of the Geneva Conventions does not depend on reciprocity, applies in peacetime, and is applicable to international armed conflicts covered by the Geneva Conventions and Additional Protocol I thereto, as well as to the duties in non-international armed conflicts embodied in common Article 3 of the Geneva Conventions, spelled out in more detail in Additional Protocol II.[153] Moreover, Article 21 § 1 is a clear indication that the Oslo Convention, as well as the other treaties analyzed in the present study, are of an *erga omnes* nature, concluded in the interest of the entire international community.[154] Paragraph 2 pursues the same objective.

151 Docherty, "Ending Civilian Suffering," p. 955, and Rietiker, "Entre sécurité et protection de l'individu," p. 1311.

152 ICJ, *Case concerning Military and Paramilitary Activities in and against Nicaragua (Nicaragua v. United States)*, Judgment (Merits), June 27, 1986, ICJ Reports 1986, § 220.

153 S. Vöneky, "Implementation and Enforcement of International Humanitarian Law," in D. Fleck (ed.), *The Handbook of Humanitarian Law*, 3rd edn., Oxford, 2013, pp. 647–700, 650.

154 *Ibid.* See, for this notion, the ICJ in the case of *Barcelona Traction, Light and Power Company, Ltd, Judgment*, ICJ Reports 1970, p. 3, § 33: ". . . an essential distinction should be drawn between the obligations of a State towards the international community as a whole, and those arising *vis-à-vis* another State in the field of diplomatic protection. By their very nature, the former are the concern of all States. In view of the importance of the rights involved, all States can be held to have a legal interest in their protection; they are obligations *erga omnes.*"

In light of the foregoing, it is obvious that the duties in the field of arms control, non-proliferation, and disarmament spelled out in the CWC and in the Ottawa and Oslo Conventions, if respected, will render impossible the "use" of the weapons prohibited and, therefore, contribute to the protection of human beings during and after armed conflict.

C. THE ATT

1. *Raison d'être* of the ATT

The ATT is the most recent example of an international instrument combining arms control with the protection of the human being. Its potential relevance for the rights of the human being can hardly be overstated. First, before the conclusion of the ATT in 2013, no common and binding international rules had been put in place to control the international trade in conventional arms in spite of the awareness of the effect of that trade.[155] Second, SALW account for the majority of civil casualties in modern conflicts. Without there being any knowledge of how many such arms exist in the world, the number is considered to be in the hundreds of millions.[156] Each year, half a million people are killed through the use of SALW, mostly civilians.[157] Therefore, former UNSG Kofi Annan rightly pointed out that small arms could well be described as "weapons of mass destruction:"

> The death toll from small arms dwarfs that of all other weapons systems – and in most years greatly exceeds the toll of the atomic bombs that devastated Hiroshima and Nagasaki. In terms of the carnage they cause, small arms, indeed, could well be described as "weapons of mass destruction." Yet there is still no global non-proliferation regime to limit their spread, as there is for chemical, biological and nuclear weapons.[158]

155 M. Brandes, "'All's Well that Ends Well' or 'Much Ado About Nothing'?: A Commentary on the Arms Trade Treaty," *Goettingen Journal of International Law*, vol. 5, 2013, pp. 399–429, p. 401, http://www.gojil.eu/issues/52/52_article_brandes.pdf (accessed February 15, 2017). In 1986, the ICJ reiterated that "in international law there are no rules, other than such rules as may be accepted by the State concerned, by treaty or otherwise, whereby the level of armaments of a sovereign State can be limited, and this principle is valid for all States without exception" (ICJ, *Case Concerning Military and Paramilitary Activities in and Against Nicaragua (Nicaragua v. United Nations States of America)*, Judgment (Merits), June 27, 1986, § 269).

156 In a report of 2007, "Small Arms Survey" suggested that 875 million firearms alone were in circulation, of which 650 million were in the hands of civilians (Small Arms Survey, *Small Arms Survey 2007: Guns and the City*, Cambridge, 2007, p. 39).

157 UNSG, "Small Arms Report of the Secretary-General," UN Doc. S/2002/1053, September 20, 2002, § 4: "Of the estimated 4 million war-related deaths during the 1990s, 90 percent of those killed were civilians, and 80 percent of those were women and children, mostly victims of the misuse of small arms and light weapons."

158 UNSG, "We the Peoples: The Role of the United Nations in the 21st Century," 2000, p. 52.

Standing between different branches of international law, the ATT is difficult to situate and might best be described as being of a *sui generis* nature. Its main goal is to prevent States Parties from exporting certain weapons to other States, where they might be used to either commit crimes or serious violations of humanitarian or human rights law, above all against an innocent civilian population. This idea is reflected in several paragraphs of the ATT's preamble, one of which asserts "that civilians, particularly women and children, account for the vast majority of those adversely affected by armed conflict and armed violence."[159] The term "armed violence" implies that the ATT covers situations outside the strictly defined categories of (international and non-international) armed conflict.[160] Moreover, the above passage confirms what has already been said in the Chapter dealing with anti-personnel mines and cluster munitions, namely, that women and children suffer the most from the consequences of armed violence and conflict and, therefore, from the uncontrolled availability of weapons. Moreover, due to the light weight of modern small arms, in particular of assault rifles, minors are increasingly used as soldiers by both government armed forces and non-state armed groups.[161] The preambles to the Ottawa and Oslo Conventions mention the special attention to be paid to the needs of the victims of armed conflicts,[162] as does a similar clause inserted into the preamble of the ATT: "*Recognizing* also the challenges faced by victims of armed conflict and their need for adequate care, rehabilitation and social and economic inclusion."[163]

Rather unique for an international treaty is the fact that the ATT's preamble contains a section on principles of international law. Even though the preamble of a treaty does not in general contain provisions binding on the States Parties, its

159 Paragraph 10; for a similar formulation, see UNSC Resolution 1325 on Women, Peace and Security (adopted on October 31, 2010), paragraph 4 of the preamble : ". . . civilians, particularly women and children, account for the vast majority of those adversely affected by armed conflict, including as refugees and internally displaced persons, and increasingly are targeted by combatants and armed elements."

160 Geneva Academy of International Law and Human Rights, "The Arms Trade Treaty (2013)," *Academy Briefing*, no. 3, June 2013, p. 11, http://www.snis.ch/system/files/academy_briefing_3_2013_arms_trade_treaty.pdf (accessed February 15, 2017) and S. Casey-Maslen, "Preamble," in S. Casey-Maslen, A. Clapham, G. Giacca, and S. Parker, *The Arms Trade Treaty: A Commentary*, Oxford, 2016, pp. 17–32, 27.

161 See, in this sense, UN Study on the Impact of Armed Conflict on Children, UN Doc. A/51/306, August 26, 1996, § 27: "Involving children as soldiers has been made easier by the proliferation of inexpensive light weapons. Previously, the more dangerous weapons were either heavy or complex, but these guns are so light that children can use them and so simple that they can be stripped and reassembled by a child of 10."

162 Paragraph 3 of the preamble to the Ottawa Convention and paragraph 7 of that to the Oslo Convention.

163 Paragraph 11 (emphasis in the original). Norway, supported by other States, tried in vain to include a substantive provision that would encourage States Parties to the ATT to support care, rehabilitation, and reintegration of victims of armed conflict and violence (Casey-Maslen, "Preamble," p. 29; Geneva Academy, "The Arms Trade Treaty (2013)," p. 12).

principles might reflect customary international law.[164] Paragraph 5 of the principles is particularly pertinent for the present study:

> Respecting and ensuring respect for international humanitarian law in accordance with, inter alia, the Geneva Conventions of 1949, and respecting and ensuring respect for human rights in accordance with, inter alia, the Charter of the United Nations and the Universal Declaration of Human Rights.[165]

This paragraph was certainly inspired by common Article 1 of the four Geneva Conventions and Additional Protocol I thereto, according to which the parties to a conflict "undertake to respect and ensure respect for the present Convention in all circumstances," as explained earlier.[166] It is obvious that the delivery of weapons to a State that violates humanitarian law, with clear knowledge of the situation, is hardly compatible with the duty to respect and ensure respect for the Geneva Conventions and their Additional Protocols.[167]

The obligation to respect human rights is sometimes formulated as a general obligation preceding the operative provisions of human rights treaties.[168] This duty entails the (positive) obligation to prevent human rights violations, even outside of the jurisdiction of the State Party.[169] States thus have to refrain from providing other States with weapons if they know that they could be used to commit human rights violations, regardless of whether the receiving State is or is not bound by the relevant human rights instruments.[170]

Only rarely does an international treaty define its own "object and purpose"[171] – perhaps one of the most important[172], but also one of the most mysterious

164 Geneva Academy, "The Arms Trade Treaty (2013)," p. 13.

165 Paragraph 5 of the principles; see for a commentary, S. Casey-Maslen, "The Principles," in Casey-Maslen et al., *The Arms Trade Treaty: A Commentary*, pp. 33–40, 37–38.

166 See this Chapter, section B.

167 See also the position of the ICRC: "To ensure that violations of humanitarian law are not facilitated by unregulated access to arms and ammunition, arms transfer decisions should include a consideration of whether the recipient is likely to respect this law" (ICRC, "Arms Transfer Decisions, Applying International Humanitarian Law Criteria," *Practical Guide*, Geneva, June 2007, p. 3, https://www.icrc.org/eng/assets/files/other/icrc_002_0916.pdf (accessed February 16, 2017).

168 See, for instance, Article 1 of the ECHR (Obligation to respect human rights): "The High Contracting Parties shall secure to everyone within their jurisdiction the rights and freedoms defined in Section I of this Convention." See, for a similar provision, Article 1 of the American Convention on Human Rights.

169 See, for more details on extraterritoriality of human rights treaties, this volume, Chapter 7, section C.1.c).

170 Geneva Academy, "The Arms Trade Treaty (2013)," p. 15.

171 G. Giacca, "Article 1, Object and Purpose," in Casey-Maslen et al., *The Arms Trade Treaty: A Commentary*, p. 45.

172 The object and purpose is relevant, inter alia, regarding Article 18 VCLT (Obligation not to defeat the object and purpose of a treaty prior to its entry into force), Article 19 VCLT

concepts of treaty law.[173] This is exactly what the ATT does, however, Article 1 of which defines its object and purpose in the following terms:

> *Article 1 (Object and purpose)*:
> The object of the Treaty is to
>
> a) Establish the highest possible common international standards for regulating or improving the regulation of the international trade in conventional arms;
> b) Prevent and eradicate the illicit trade in conventional arms and prevent their diversion;
>
> For the purpose of:
>
> c) Contributing to international and regional peace, security and stability;
> d) Reducing human suffering;
> e) Promoting cooperation, transparency and responsible action by States Parties in the international trade in conventional arms, thereby building confidence among States Parties.

The second purpose, aiming at "reducing human suffering" (letter d), is particularly relevant for this study. It is additional evidence for the high relevance of the ATT for the protection of human beings. While neither that treaty nor public international law in general defines the notion of human suffering, the latter would certainly reach beyond physical wounding to include psychological and emotional impairment, as well as elements of a socio-economic nature.[174]

2. Contribution to the protection of the human being through absolute prohibitions of transfers of arms that might be used to commit certain international crimes (Article 6 ATT)

Article 6 can be considered to be a core provision of the ATT on which the States' views were particularly divided during the preparation of the treaty.[175] It prohibits any transfer of conventional arms, or of their ammunition/munitions, parts, or

(Formulation of reservations), Article 31 VCLT (General rule of interpretation), Article 41 VCLT (Agreements to modify multilateral treaties between certain of the parties only), Article 58 VCLT (Suspension of the operation of a multilateral treaty by agreement between certain of the parties only), and Article 60 VCLT (Termination or suspension of the operation of a treaty as a consequence of its breach).

173 See, in this sense, I. Buffard and K. Zemanek, "The Object and Purpose of a Treaty: An Enigma?" *Austrian Review of International & European Law*, vol. 3, 1998, pp. 311–343.

174 Giacca, "Article 1, Object and Purpose," p. 53.

175 Brandes, "All's Well that Ends Well," p. 409; and Geneva Academy, "The Arms Trade Treaty (2013)," p. 23. S. Casey-Maslen and G. Giacca refer to the "heart" of the treaty ("Article 6, Prohibitions," in Casey-Maslen et al., *The Arms Trade Treaty: A Commentary*, pp. 177–192, 178).

components, if such a transfer would violate a State Party's obligations under an arms embargo imposed by the UNSC or obligations of States Parties in respect of other treaties, or if the State Party "has knowledge at the time of authorization" that the arms or other items would be used to commit crimes under international law. Paragraph 3 of Article 6 ATT reads as follows:

> A State Party shall not authorize any transfer of conventional arms covered under Article 2 (1) or of items covered under Article 3 or Article 4, if it has knowledge at the time of authorization that the arms or items would be used in the commission of genocide, crimes against humanity, grave breaches of the Geneva Conventions of 1949, attacks directed against civilian objects or civilians protected as such, or other war crimes as defined by international agreements to which it is a Party.

How, in concrete terms, would the prevention of international crimes contribute to the protection of human rights? The added value of the ATT lies exactly there, namely, in the prevention of assistance to the commission of these crimes through prohibiting the transfer of means and instruments capable of facilitating their realization. In addition, it is worth recalling that the ICC has jurisdiction in respect of genocide, crimes against humanity, war crimes, and the crime of aggression.[176] It transpires from the definitions of these crimes in the Court's Statute that,[177] apart from the crime of aggression, the victims of these crimes are generally human beings, that is, civilians suffering from the atrocities of armed conflict. The same logic applies to the ATT. Considering the fact that the said crimes correspond to those enumerated in Article 6 § 3 of the ATT, there is an obvious link between the prevention of crimes and the protection of human beings in this treaty, too.

3. Contribution to the protection of the human being through export assessments (Article 7 ATT)

a) Relevance of the ATT for the respect of international humanitarian law

Article 7 is another key provision of the ATT.[178] It stipulates that, if an export is not prohibited under Article 6, an exporting State Party, before deciding whether or not to authorize the export of certain conventional arms or items, has to assess the risk that the export concerned could undermine peace and security

176 Article 5 of the Rome Statute.

177 Articles 6–9 of the Rome Statute (see, for the questions of impunity and deterrence, W. A. Schabas, *The International Criminal Court: A Commentary on the Rome Statute*, Oxford and New York, 2010, pp. 43 et seq.).

178 Geneva Academy, "The Arms Trade Treaty (2013)," p. 26.

or be used to commit or facilitate a serious violation of international humanitarian law or human rights law, or acts constituting terrorism or a transnational organized crime.

Among those identified under Article 7 ATT, the risk that the export concerned would be used to commit or facilitate serious violations of international humanitarian law is one of the most relevant aspects for the purpose of the present study. The scope of the notion of "serious violation of international humanitarian law" is broader than that of Article 6 § 3 ATT, since it is not limited to "war crimes as defined by international agreements" ratified by the States Parties.[179] It corresponds basically to the notion of war crimes.[180] According to the ICRC,[181] serious violations of international humanitarian law are:

- grave breaches as specified under the four Geneva Conventions;[182]
- grave breaches as specified under Additional Protocol I to the Geneva Conventions;[183]
- serious violations of common Article 3 to the Geneva Conventions;
- war crimes as specified under Article 8 of the Rome Statute; and
- other war crimes in international and non-international armed conflicts under customary law.[184]

In both international and non-international armed conflicts, key violations would include: deliberate attacks on the civilian population; attacks that fail to distinguish between military objectives and civilians and civilian objects (indiscriminate attacks); attacks that would cause harm to civilians or civilian objects that is excessive in relation to the expected concrete and direct military advantage

179 *Ibid.*, p. 27; and A. Clapham, "Article 7, Export and Export Assessment," in Casey-Maslen et al., *The Arms Trade Treaty: A Commentary*, pp. 244–285, 257.
180 See ICRC, "Protecting Civilians and Humanitarian Action through the Arms Trade Treaty," Geneva, 2013, p. 4, https://www.icrc.org/eng/assets/files/publications/icrc-002-4069.pdf (accessed February 16, 2017).
181 Statement of the ICRC to the UN Diplomatic Conference on the Arms Trade Treaty, New York, July 12, 2012. See also ICRC, "What Are 'Serious Violations of International Humanitarian Law'?" *Explanatory Note*, Geneva, 2012, https://www.icrc.org/eng/assets/files/2012/att-what-are-serious-violations-of-ihl-icrc.pdf (accessed February 16, 2017).
182 Articles 50, 51, 130, and 147 of the four Geneva Conventions, respectively.
183 Articles 11 and 85.
184 In non-international armed conflict, this could include: using prohibited weapons, launching an indiscriminate attack resulting in death or injury to civilians, or an attack in the knowledge that it will cause excessive incidental civilian loss, injury, or damage (or a combination thereof), making non-defended localities and demilitarized zones the object of attack, using human shields, slavery, collective punishment, using starvation of civilians as a method of warfare by depriving them of objects indispensable to their survival, including impeding relief supplies (Henckaerts and Doswald-Beck, *Customary International Humanitarian Law*, p. 599).

(disproportionate attacks); and violence against detainees, irrespective of whether they are civilians or captured combatants.[185]

b) Relevance of the ATT for the respect of human rights law

Under Article 7 § 1(b)(ii) ATT, States Parties also have to establish whether arms or items could be used to commit or facilitate a "serious violation" of international human rights law. The seriousness of a human rights violation within the meaning of Article 7 § 1 ATT is difficult to define.[186] For practical reasons, the present study limits itself to the following observations.

The qualifying expression "serious" refers to either the gravity of the violation or the type of human right at stake.[187] As far as the second aspect is concerned, it seems undisputed that acts or omissions that affect the enjoyment of rights considered of *jus cogens* nature amount to serious violations of human rights. Even though the precise scope of that notion is not entirely clear, it can be asserted that the right to life, the prohibition of torture, inhuman and degrading treatment or punishment, and the prohibition of slavery, as well as the prohibition of retroactive criminal measures, belong to this category.[188] Under the relevant international human rights instruments, these rights are generally considered non-derogable.[189]

It is argued, however, that the expression "serious violation of human rights law" within the meaning of Article 7 § 1 ATT can also be applied to fundamental human rights that are not of *jus cogens* nature. Such rights include, for example, the right to liberty and security, the freedom of expression, the right to peaceful assembly, the freedom of movement, or the prohibition of discrimination.[190] But, in order to fall within the scope of Article 7 ATT, these rights must be breached seriously enough in order to cross a certain threshold.[191] Finally, conventional arms transfers are not only relevant for civil and political rights, but can also endanger the enjoyment of social, economic, and cultural rights.[192] As a result, the assessment of what constitutes a serious violation of human rights law must also, in order to be comprehensive, take into consideration these rights.

185 Geneva Academy, "The Arms Trade Treaty (2013)," p. 27; in this sense, see also Clapham, "Article 7, Export and Export Assessment," p. 257.

186 *Ibid.*

187 Clapham, "Article 7, Export and Export Assessment," p. 260.

188 Geneva Academy, "What Amounts to 'a Serious Violation of International Human Rights Law'?", *Academy Briefing*, no. 6, August 2014, p. 6, https://www.sipri.org/sites/default/files/research/disarmament/dualuse/pdf-archive-att/pdfs/20140800_ga_what-amounts-to-a-serious-violation-of-international-human-rights-law.pdf (accessed February 16, 2017).

189 See, in particular, Article 4 § 2 ICCPR, Article 27 IACHR, and Article 15 ECHR, the last allowing derogations to the right to life for lawful acts of war.

190 Geneva Academy, "The Arms Trade Treaty (2013)," p. 28; and *ibid.*, "What Amounts to 'a Serious Violation'?", p. 5.

191 Clapham, "Article 7, Export and Export Assessment," p. 260.

192 Geneva Academy, "What Amounts to 'a Serious Violation'?", p. 6, with further references.

c) Need for a gender- and age-sensitive assessment of human rights violations (Article 7 § 4 ATT)

A violation of a right that, as such, does not *a priori* seem very significant might entail serious consequences in the specific circumstances of a given case, in particular when a group of vulnerable persons is targeted.[193] In this regard, it is worth noting that Article 7 § 4 ATT indicates that the exporting State Party, in making its assessment, "shall take into account the risk of the conventional arms . . . being used to commit or facilitate serious acts of gender-based violence or serious acts of violence against women and children." This provision has to be read in light of paragraph 10 of the preamble to the ATT, mentioned above, which explicitly refers to women and children as being particularly affected by armed conflict and violence.[194]

The 1993 Vienna Declaration and Programme of Action stated that "the human rights of women and of the girl-child are an inalienable, integral and indivisible part of universal human rights."[195] Article 1 of the 1993 UN Declaration on the Elimination of Violence against Women defines "violence against women" in the following terms:

> For the purposes of this Declaration, the term "violence against women" means any act of gender-based violence that results in, or is likely to result in, physical, sexual or psychological harm or suffering to women, including threats of such acts, coercion or arbitrary deprivation of liberty, whether occurring in public or in private life.[196]

Within the meaning of the 1995 Beijing Declaration and Platform of Action, acts of violence against women include breaches of human rights of women in situations of armed conflict, in particular murder, systematic rape, sexual slavery, and forced pregnancy.[197] According to the 1994 Inter-American Convention on the Prevention, Punishment and Eradication of Violence Against Women, violence against women "shall be understood as any act or conduct, based on gender, which causes death or physical, sexual or psychological harm or suffering to women, whether in the public or the private sphere."[198] The prohibition of rape

193 See, for instance, the ECtHR in the case of *El-Masri v. "The Former Yugoslav Republic of Macedonia"* [GC], no. 39630/09, December 13, 2012, § 196, *Ireland v. United Kingdom*, January 18, 1978, § 162, Series A no. 25, and *Jalloh v. Germany* [GC], no. 54810/00, § 67, ECHR 2006-IX.

194 See this volume, Chapter 3, section C.1.

195 Vienna Declaration and Programme of Action, adopted by the World Conference on Human Rights in Vienna on June 25, 1993, § 18.

196 The same formulation is contained in the 1995 Beijing Declaration and Platform of Action, § 113.

197 *Ibid.*

198 Article 1 of the Inter-American Convention on the Prevention, Punishment and Eradication of Violence Against Women, adopted at Belem do Para, Brazil, on September 6, 1994.

and other forms of sexual violence is absolute in situations of armed conflict, as it is in peacetime.[199] According to State practice, this is a rule of customary law applicable in both international and non-international armed conflicts.[200] In its Resolution 1325 (2000) on Women, Peace and Security, the UNSC called on all parties to armed conflicts to take special measures to protect women and girls from gender-based violence, in particular rape and other forms of sexual abuse, and all other forms of violence in armed conflict.[201]

The Committee on the Rights of the Child (CRC) has referred to "serious violations" in many respects, including violence against children at home and at work or when they live on the streets,[202] the use of children as human shields or sexual slaves, or when they are victims of mass rapes.[203] The Committee on Economic, Social and Cultural Rights (CESCR) expressed itself to be "deeply concerned" by the infringement of the right to education caused by the attacks, of military personnel and settlers, on school children and educational facilities in the occupied Palestinian territories.[204] The Inter-American Court of Human Rights (IACtHR) has judged that the special vulnerability of children made violations particularly serious,[205] concluding that States are under a special duty to protect and assist children.[206]

Children who are victims or perpetrators of armed violence have been the object of a number of UNSC resolutions, including Resolution 1612 (2005), which establishes a UN-led monitoring and reporting mechanism informing

See also the Convention on Preventing and Combating Violence Against Women and Domestic Violence, concluded within the Council of Europe and opened for signature in Istanbul on May 11, 2011, entry into force on August 1, 2014 (so-called "Istanbul Convention"). It applies in times of peace and armed conflict (Article 2 § 3).

199 Casey-Maslen, "Article 7, Export and Export Assessment," p. 283.

200 Henckaerts and Doswald-Beck, *Customary International Humanitarian Law*, pp. 323–327 (Rule 93 of the ICRC Customary International Humanitarian Law Study).

201 UNSC Resolution 1325 (2000) on women, peace and security, § 10, https://documents-dds-ny.un.org/doc/UNDOC/GEN/N00/720/18/PDF/N0072018.pdf?OpenElement (accessed March 8, 2017).

202 CRC, Concluding Observations: Guatemala, UN Doc. CRC/C/15/Add.154, July 9, 2001, §§ 30 et seq.

203 CRC, Concluding Observations (OP-CAC): DRC, UN Doc. CRC/C/OPAC/COD/CO/1, February 3, 2012, § 8, http://www.crin.org/docs/CRC-C-OPAC-COD-CO-1-1.pdf (accessed February 16, 2017).

204 CESCR, Report of Israel (Third Periodic Report/List of Issues and Written Replies), UN Doc. E/C.12/ISR/Q/3/Add.1, § 35.

205 See, for instance, IACtHR, *Villagran-Morales v. Guatemala*, Judgment, November 19, 1999, Series C, No. 63 (1999), § 146, concerning "Street Children." See also *Gomez Paquiyauri v. Peru*, Judgment, July 8, 2004, Series C, No. 110, § 162, and *Bulacio v. Argentina*, Judgment, September 18, 2003, Series C, No. 100, § 133.

206 See, for instance, *Dilcia Oliven Yean and Violeta Bosico Cofi v. Dominican Republic*, Judgment, September 8, 2005, § 134. See, for a similar case, ECtHR, *Opuz v. Turkey*, no. 33401/02, June 9, 2009; and for a leading case dealing with trafficking in women, ECtHR, *Rantsev v. Cyprus and Russia*, no. 25965/04, January 7, 2010.

on "grave violations" against children in armed conflict.[207] As observed above, the lighter weight of modern small arms, particularly assault rifles, facilitates and encourages engagement of minors as fighters by government forces and non-state actors.[208] Finally, a particularly disturbing phenomenon receiving public attention more recently is the growing use of children as suicide bombers, especially by the "Islamic State" (ISIS).[209]

But women and children are not the only groups deserving special attention under Article 7 ATT. Based on the Geneva Academy of International Humanitarian Law and Human Rights' study on the notion of "serious violation of human rights law," analyzing the practice of relevant international bodies, at least the following vulnerable groups can be identified as deserving special care: minorities, including political ones,[210] people living in poverty, in particular in rural areas,[211] elderly and sick people, and persons with disabilities,[212] as well as prisoners and detained persons.[213]

The vulnerability of these groups has been confirmed repeatedly by international practice and by case law. For instance, as far as people living in rural areas are concerned, the IACtHR, considering the impact on the lives of villagers of the theft of their livestock and the destruction of their houses, concluded that there had been significant infringements of the right to property.[214] The Court ruled that the damage suffered by the people who lost their livestock from which they earned their living was "especially severe," since it caused the loss of the villagers' main source of income and food. It added that the way in which the livestock was stolen, with the explicit or implicit collaboration of members of the armed forces, increased the villagers' feelings of impotence and vulnerability.[215] As far as the villagers' houses were concerned, the Court found that their destruction not only caused the loss of material possessions, but destroyed the social frame of reference of the inhabitants, some of whom had lived there all their lives. The villagers

207 July 26, 2005, UN Doc. S/RES/1612 (2005).

208 See UN Study on the Impact of Armed Conflict on Children, UN Doc. A/51/306, August 26, 1996, § 27, http://www.un.org/documents/ga/docs/51/plenary/a51-306.htm (accessed February 16, 2017).

209 See, inter alia, Action on Armed Violence (AOAV), "Rise in Child Suicide Bombings – International Community Must Take Action," London, October 9, 2015, http://counteriedreport.co.uk/news/rise-in-child-suicide-bombings-international-community-must-take-action (accessed February 16, 2017).

210 Geneva Academy, "What Amounts to 'a Serious Violation'?", p. 5.

211 "Serious" violations could be the failure by States to address poverty and inadequate living standards, forced evictions, and pillage in situations of armed conflicts (*ibid.*).

212 Generally amount to "serious" violations: Attacks on hospitals and health facilities and, more generally, failure to respect the right to health, and discrimination (*ibid.*).

213 Generally considered to be "serious" violations: Failure by States to provide conditions of detention that meet international norms, slave and forced labour, and discrimination (*ibid.*).

214 IACtHR, *Ituango Massacres v. Colombia*, Judgment, July 1, 2006, Series C, No. 148, § 178.

215 *Ibid.*

thus lost their basic living conditions. Therefore, the Court concluded that a "particularly serious violation" of the right to property had occurred.[216]

D. CONCLUSIONS

To sum up the Chapter devoted to the substantive contribution made by the examined arms control treaties to the well-being of individuals, it will be recalled that the general clauses enshrined in Articles I of the CWC and the Ottawa and Olso Conventions reflect the core duties imposed on the States Parties.

The positive impact on individuals that these treaties might have is obvious in light of the duty to refrain from using these weapons. This impact is double: First, in the logic of humanitarian law, as it obliges the States Parties to refrain from using these weapons as a means of warfare. The condemnation, by the UNSC, of the repeated use of chemical weapons against the civilian population in Syria underlines the dramatic humanitarian impact of these weapons and the need for a truly universal ban. Second, by extending the prohibition of using such weapons in all circumstances, the treaties also protect human beings in peacetime.

While the core obligation is the duty not to use the prohibited weapons, the arms control, non-proliferation, and disarmament obligations can be considered as aiming at a definitive exclusion forever and, therefore, at achieving a world free of this threat. Therefore, and in light of the principle that a treaty has to be read as a whole,[217] these duties are also relevant for the protection of the human being. An interesting innovation is brought by Article 21 of the Oslo Convention, imposing on the States Parties a positive duty to encourage other States to join the treaty with a view to achieving universality.

Furthermore, the long and detailed preambles to the three treaties reflect the human spirit that was behind their adoption. This is, moreover, confirmed by certain articles in the operative part of the instruments. In the CWC, the idea of the protection of the human being is less obvious than in the Ottawa and Oslo Conventions, but it nevertheless reiterates the close link between itself and the 1925 Geneva Protocol and underlines, therefore, the importance of the ban on

216 *Ibid.*, §§ 181–183, and 192, which reads as follows: "192. The Court has considered that, in this case, the violation of the right to property was particularly serious, since the homes of the inhabitants of El Aro were burnt down . . . In view of the foregoing findings and the evolution of international human rights law on this issue, the Court considers it necessary to make some additional observations on the inviolability of the home and privacy, from the perspective of Article 11(2) of the Convention".

217 See, for instance, M. Villiger, *Commentary on the 1969 Convention on the Law of Treaties*, Leiden and Boston 2009, p. 427. As far as the ECHR is concerned, see, for instance, the ECtHR in the case of *Stec v. United Kingdom* (GC), § 48, ECHR 2006-V, or the much earlier case of *Klass v. Germany*, Series A no. 28 (1978), § 68: "The Convention is to be read as a whole and therefore, as the Commission indicated in its report, any interpretation of Article 13 must be in harmony with the logic of the Convention . . ."

the use of chemical weapons as a means of warfare with a view to protecting the individual during armed conflicts. Banning the use of chemical weapons in an absolute manner, the CWC directly contributes to these goals.

The Ottawa Convention and, even more so, the Oslo Convention go considerably further in the protection of the individual. On the one hand, their preambles recall the key principles which have to be respected in armed conflicts and contain the Martens Clause. It has been demonstrated that the use of anti-personnel mines and cluster munitions would hardly be compatible with these principles. On the other hand, they take up what has been said in the introduction of this Chapter, namely, that modern warfare causes enormous suffering to the civilian population, in particular women and children. Weapons such as anti-personnel landmines and cluster munitions put an enhanced risk to life and property long after the end of actual hostilities. The ban on these weapons has therefore a direct positive bearing on the enjoyment of their rights by these groups.

In this regard, the Ottawa and Oslo Conventions take inspiration from human rights treaties, by singling out particularly vulnerable groups, such as women and children, as well refugees and internally displaced persons, following the trend which exists in the field of international human rights law, where a considerable number of treaties have been adopted protecting of these groups. Moreover, once an explosion of an anti-personnel mine or a cluster munition occurs, these treaties take a victim-based approach by placing the dignity and the right to assistance of the injured persons at the center of attention. Here, again, the conventions are gender- and age-sensitive, without neglecting the principle of non-discrimination in the treatment of victims. It is obvious that, in this regard, the inspiration taken by the Oslo Convention from the CRPD, concluded shortly beforehand, reveals itself to be invaluable.

To sum up, the Ottawa and Oslo Conventions' purposes are twofold, namely, the reduction of the number of victims of the targeted weapons by banning them completely and, in the eventuality of explosions causing harm to human beings, to provide prompt, efficient, and individualized assistance to the victims.

According to former UNSG Ban Ki-moon, the adoption of the ATT was "a victory for the world's people" and "the culmination of long-held dreams and many years of effort."[218] The humanitarian spirit and *raison d'être* of the ATT already appears in its preamble, including the enumerated principles of humanitarian law, as well as in its object and purpose, in particular that of "reducing human suffering." Moreover, the contribution of the ATT to the protection of the human being is obvious and relies mainly on two legal techniques: on the one hand, through the absolute prohibitions of transfers of arms that might be

218 UNSG, "Arms Trade Treaty Will Generate 'Much-Needed Momentum' for Other Global Disarmament, Non-Proliferation Efforts, Secretary-General Says," UN Press Release SG/SM/14919-DC/3426, April 2, 2013, http://www.un.org/press/en/2013/sgsm14919.doc.htm (accessed February 16, 2017).

used to commit international crimes, namely genocide, crimes against humanity, and war crimes, involving necessarily violations of basic human rights and of rules of humanitarian law; and, on the other, through export assessments by States Parties to exclude that the planned arms transfer contributes to serious violations of humanitarian law or human rights law. It has been suggested that a broad definition of "serious violation" is preferable, taking into account civil and political as well as economic, social, and cultural rights. Finally, the need for a gender- and age-sensitive assessment on the basis of Article 7 § 4 ATT, conducted with due regard to the special vulnerability of women, children, and other groups, has also been underscored.

In the first chapter, the involvement of civil society in the preparatory work to the treaties analyzed in the present study has been highlighted. It is likely that States are also able to rely on the cooperation and competence of NGOs in the implementation and verification of the duties deriving from these instruments. This aspect will be addressed in the next Chapter.

4 Implementation and verification of the relevant treaties by human rights actors and institutions

A. INTRODUCTORY REMARKS

The institutional support of a treaty, in particular the possibility of verification of the respect of the obligations imposed, is often considered instrumental for its effectiveness.[1] Therefore, certain conclusions concerning the human-related interests pursued by the relevant treaties can be expected from the following institutional analysis that covers actors whose role is generally to protect the human being or other values of public interest. This Chapter will focus on three types of actors, namely civil society (section B), the ECtHR in conjunction with the Committee of Ministers of the Council of Europe (section C), and the ICC (section D).

It is in general suggested that the strong institutional support on which arms control treaties can count is a characteristic for this category of treaties, contrary for instance to humanitarian law or human rights instruments.[2] This is probably true as far as instruments dealing with nuclear weapons are concerned, which will be detailed further in this Chapter.[3] However, not all arms control treaties, not even all those dealing with WMDs, benefit from a powerful institutional framework. It is a fact, for instance, that the States Parties to the BWC have for many years made vain efforts to establish a regime for the verification of the respect of the duties imposed by the treaty.[4] Moreover, treaties prohibiting or restricting

1 See, for the notion of verification, A. Poucet, "Arms Control and Non-Proliferation Treaties: An Ontology of Concepts and Characteristics," in R. Avenhaus, N. Kyriakopoulos, M. Richard, and G. Stein (eds.), *Verifying Treaty Compliance: Limiting Weapons of Mass Destruction and Monitoring Kyoto Protocol Provisions*, Berlin, 2006, pp. 41–60, 46; or R. Avenhaus and N. Kyriakopoulos, "Conceptual Framework," in Avenhaus et al., *Verifying Treaty Compliance*, pp. 13–37, 21–27.

2 See, in this sense, Poucet, "Arms Control and Non-Proliferation Treaties," pp. 41 et seq.; and D. Rietiker, *Le régime juridique des traités de maîtrise des armements: Plaidoyer pour l'unité de l'ordre juridique international*, Berne and Brussels, 2010, pp. 44 et seq.

3 See, in particular, the NPT, which benefits from the institutional support of the IAEA, as well as the 1996 CTBT (not yet in force) establishing an international organization.

4 J. E. Goodby, "A World without Nuclear Weapons: Fantasy or Necessity?" *SIPRI Yearbook 2010*, pp. 17–34, 25; and M. Kurosawa, "New Vision towards a World Free of Nuclear Weapons," *Osaka University Law Review*, vol. 55, 2008, pp. 1–14, 12.

the use of conventional weapons, in particular the CCW, do not at all benefit from a traditional control mechanism, and this places them closer to humanitarian law instruments, which are normally not backed up by a significant institutional framework.[5] Human rights instruments can today often rely on certain institutional structures, even though the power and scope of supervision of the relevant bodies vary considerably in practice.

The CWC has established its own international organization to administer its provisions, the OPCW, but it will be demonstrated that other actors also play a role in its implementation and verification. While the Ottawa and Oslo Conventions, in contrast, cannot rely on such a powerful institutional support, other actors fill this gap, as will be explained in this Chapter. The ATT is a rather recent instrument whose implementation and verification can only be fully assessed in years to come. The potential role played by human rights actors and institutions will nevertheless be addressed.

B. CIVIL SOCIETY

1. Implementation of the CWC: Civil society assisting the OPCW

In order to support the CWC institutionally, the States Parties established the OPCW with headquarters in The Hague (Netherlands). All States Parties to the CWC are also members of the OPCW.[6] The aim of the organization is to "achieve the object and purpose of this Convention, to ensure the implementation of its provision, including those for international verification of compliance with it, and to provide for consultation and cooperation among States Parties."[7] The OPCW consists of three main organs: the Conference of States Parties, the Executive Council, and the Technical Secretariat.[8] The organization and its staff enjoy privileges and immunities, which have proven particularly important during verification activities, such as those undertaken in Syria.[9]

5 This is the case, inter alia, with the four Geneva Conventions and their Protocols. The Fact-finding Commission, established under Article 90 of Additional Protocol I, has never been used so far. The precious activities and efforts of the ICRC deserve to be mentioned here, but they cannot be regarded as an implementation or verification mechanism in the literal sense.

6 Article VIII.A(2) of the CWC.

7 Article VIII.A(1) of the CWC.

8 Article VIII.A(4) of the CWC. The powers and activities of the three organs are described in more depth in Article VIII.B–D.

9 Article VIII.E and Part II, Section B, of the Verification Annex. See also Paragraph 9 of the UNSC's Resolution 2118(2013): "*Notes* that the Syrian Arab Republic is a party to the Convention on the Privileges and Immunities of the United Nations, *decides* that OPCW-designated personnel undertaking activities provided for in this resolution or the decision of the OPCW Executive Council of 27 September 2013 shall enjoy the privileges and immunities contained in the Verification Annex, Part II, Section B, of the Chemical Weapons Convention, and *calls* on the Syrian Arab Republic to conclude modalities agreements with the United Nations and the OPCW" (emphasis in the original).

As explained above,[10] the CWC was negotiated and adopted through relatively traditional channels, still following a Cold War logic, unlike, for instance, the Ottawa and Oslo Conventions. It was observed that civil society nevertheless played a role in the negotiation and adoption of the CWC, even though its support was more discrete than that given to the Ottawa and Oslo Conventions. In this Chapter, it will be shown that civil society is relevant, on different levels, in the implementation of the CWC.

Civil society has established discrete relationships with the OPCW, in particular the Preparatory Commission's Provisional Technical Secretariat (PTS) and the Technical Secretariat. Highly recognized and well-established supporters of the CWC, such as the Monterey Institute for International Studies and SIPRI (Sweden), were allowed to place interns in the organization.[11] Moreover, the "Harvard Sussex Program on Chemical and Biological Weapons" (HSP)[12] provided researchers ("HSP researcher in The Hague") who were given significant access to the organization and wrote a quarterly review on activities associated with the OPCW for publication in the "CBW Conventions Bulletin."[13] The fact that civil society representatives were allowed to report on the organization's activities enhanced its transparency considerably.[14]

Furthermore, civil society has taken on the role of technical "service providers" to help implement the treaty. Already after the adoption of the CWC in 1993, but pending its entry into force in 1997, the PTS and signatory States worked jointly on manuals and model acts to implement the CWC. They were assisted by NGOs active in this field, including the HSP, Pugwash, SIPRI, and Parliamentarians for Global Action, as well as scholars from various institutions and universities, such as The Hague Academy of International Law, DePaul University College of Law (Chicago, IL), and the University of Frankfurt (Germany).[15]

Certain non-governmental actors have remained instrumental after the entry into force of the CWC, for instance by preparing briefing materials for Review Conferences and meeting summaries of annual sessions of the Conference of States Parties.[16] These include the University of Surrey (UK), the semi-governmental

10 See this volume, Chapter 2, section A.

11 C. McLeish and M. Lak, "The Role of Civil Society and Industrial Non-State Actors in Relation to the Chemical Weapons Convention," in W. Krutzsch, E. Myjer, and R. Trapp (eds.), *The Chemical Weapons Convention – A Commentary*, Oxford, 2014, pp. 37–48, 39.

12 See http://www.sussex.ac.uk/Units/spru/hsp/ (accessed February 20, 2017).

13 See the CBW Convention Bulletin, The Harvard Sussex Program on Chemical and Biological Weapons, http://www.sussex.ac.uk/Units/spru/hsp/pdfbulletin.html (accessed February 20, 2017).

14 McLeish and Lak, "The Role of Civil Society," p. 39.

15 L. Tabassi and A. Dhavle, "Article VII: National Implementation Measures," in Krutzsch et al., *The CWC – A Commentary*, pp. 195–233, 212. See also B. Kellman and E. A. Tanzman, *Manual for National Implementation of the Chemical Weapons Convention*, Chicago IL, 2nd edn., International Criminal Justice and Weapons Control Center, 1998.

16 Krutzsch et al., *The CWC – A Commentary*, pp. 13 et seq.

Organization for Applied Scientific Research TNO (Netherlands),[17] specialized research institutes such as SIPRI, as well as some NGOs. As far as the latter are concerned, VERTIC (UK) deserves a particular mention. Its mission is to support the development, implementation, and effectiveness of international agreements and related regional and national initiatives, with particular attention to issues of monitoring, review, legislation, and verification.[18]

NGOs are moreover entitled to participate in some of the debates held in the Conference of States Parties or the periodical Review Conferences in accordance with Article VIII.B(22) of the CWC.[19] Rule 33 of the Conference of States Parties' Rules of Procedure provides that NGOs may be invited to plenary meetings under certain circumstances.[20] Once permission is granted, approved NGOs are authorized to attend open meetings of the plenary session, be issued with name tags, display literature at designed sites for distribution, and be provided, on request and with certain exceptions, with all the documents referred to in the annotated agenda distributed during the sessions.[21] The practice of holding open-forum side events during the conferences is another channel for civil society to express its views.[22]

The closest interaction with civil society, however, has occurred in the preparations for Review Conferences. For example, prior to all three Review Conferences, the International Union for Pure and Applied Chemistry (IUPAC), together with the OPCW and members of its Scientific Advisory Board (SAB), has convened international workshops to address the challenges and opportunities presented by technical change and development. These workshops brought together members of the SAB and government experts, as well as industrial and academic experts.[23] The Chemical Weapons Convention Coalition ("CWC Coalition") deserves particular mention as an independent international body whose mission consists of supporting the aims of the treaty, in particular its

17 *Organisatie voor Toegepast Natuurwetenschappelijk Onderzoek* (McLeish and Lak, "The Role of Civil Society," p. 40).

18 See http://www.vertic.org/pages/homepage.php (accessed February 20, 2017).

19 Such participation is not explicitly envisaged in the CWC, contrary to what is foreseen in the Ottawa Convention (Articles 11 § 4 and 12 § 3) and the Oslo Convention (Articles 11 § 2 and 12 § 3).

20 Rule 33 reads as follows: "Representatives of non-governmental organizations may be invited to attend the plenary meetings of the Conference in accordance with such rules as the Conference has approved."

21 McLeish and Lak, "The Role of Civil Society," p. 40.

22 *Ibid.*, p. 41.

23 *Ibid.* During the preparations for the Second Review Conference, the Chair of the Open-Ended Working Group offered NGOs and industry engagement opportunities of a more political nature, including an Industry Meeting (June 11, 2007) and an NGO Event (November 19, 2007), as well as invitations to submit written papers. Similarly, the OPCW working group preparing the Third Review Conference held a meeting with chemical industry representatives (September 24, 2012) and a meeting with representatives of NGOs (November 29, 2012) (*ibid.*).

universality and the promotion of the safe and timely destruction of all chemical weapons, involving a considerable number of NGOs, academia, experts, chemical industries, chemical associations, professional organizations, and other interested stakeholders, especially from developing countries and non-States Parties to the CWC.[24]

Civil society has also become instrumental in raising awareness of certain topics, dangers, or trends among a broader audience. An ongoing discussion within the OPCW and among States Parties is the issue of so-called "incapacitating chemical agents" or "non-legal weapons." Under Article II, subparagraph 9(d) of the CWC, "law enforcement including domestic riot control purposes" are considered "purposes not prohibited" under this instrument. Moreover, in accordance with Article I § 5 of the CWC, "each State Party undertakes not to use riot control agents as a method of warfare." In other words, riot control agents are as such permitted under the CWC in situations falling short of an armed conflict. In that context, a discussion has arisen on whether so-called "incapacitating chemical agents,"[25] which are toxic chemicals within the meaning of Article II § 2 of the CWC and incapacitate by causing sedation or unconsciousness of the victim for a certain period of time, can be used for law enforcement purposes. Expert opinions differ widely on this point.[26] Another uncertainty arises regarding the question of what is meant by "law enforcement" in the sense of Article II § 9(d) of the CWC. As a result, distinctions between law enforcement, counter-terrorism, counter-insurgency, and low-intensity warfare may get blurred.[27] At this stage, it can be pointed out that civil society is fearing that certain toxic chemicals are coming close to becoming normal law enforcement or peace-keeping tools.[28] Whereas little attention has so far been paid to this issue among States Parties and the OPCW, numerous NGOs have raised their voices, including the ICRC,[29] the HSP, the Pugwash Study Group on the Implementation of the Chemical and Biological Weapons Conventions, and the Federation of American Scientists'

24 McLeish and Lak, "The Role of Civil Society," p. 40. See, for more details, http://www.cwccoalition.org/ (accessed February 20, 2017).

25 There has been continued interest in certain countries in the development and use of certain toxic chemicals as weapons for law enforcement, described as "incapacitating chemical agents," "incapacitating agents," "knock-out gas," "calmatives," "pharmacological weapons," or "drugs as weapons"; see ICRC, "Toxic Chemicals as Weapons for Law Enforcement: A Threat to Life and International Law?", Synthesis prepared by the ICRC, in *"Incapacitating Chemical Weapons," Law Enforcement, Human Rights and Policy Perspectives*, Expert Meeting, Montreux, April 24–26, 2012, Report, pp. 151–160, 151, http://www.icrc.org/eng/assets/files/publications/icrc-002-4121.pdf (accessed February 20, 2017).

26 See, for a discussion, R. Trapp, "'Incapacitating Chemical Agents': Potential Policy Options," Background Paper, in *"Incapacitating Chemical Weapons,"* pp. 99–116, 99, with references.

27 Report of the Advisory Panel on Future Priorities of the Organization for the Prohibition of Chemical Weapons, published by the OPCW Director-General (Doc. S/951/2011, July 25, 2011), § 13.

28 Tabassi and Dhavle, "Article VII," p. 229.

29 See the proceedings of the Expert Meeting, held in Montreux, April 24–26, 2012.

Working Group on Chemical and Biological Weapons Control. More recently, the OPCW's SAB has made repeated efforts to place the issue on the agenda.[30] Worries about incapacitating chemicals were also raised in the context of *Finogenov and Others v. Russia* before the ECtHR, a case that will be discussed in more detail below.[31]

There is also increasing awareness of breaches of international law through the use of chemical weapons. As far as the current war in Syria and, in particular, the use of chemical weapons is concerned, Human Rights Watch (HRW), for instance, has produced a detailed report on the "Attacks on Ghouta," published on September 10, 2013, which documents two alleged chemical weapons attacks on the opposition-controlled suburbs of Eastern and Western Ghouta, in the early hours of August 21, 2013. HRW analyzed witness accounts of the rocket attacks, information on the likely source of the attacks, the physical remnants of the weapon systems used, and the medical symptoms exhibited by the victims as documented by medical staff. It came to the conclusion that the evidence concerning the type of rockets and launchers used strongly suggested that these were weapons systems exclusively in possession of, and used by, Syrian Government armed forces.[32] HRW also reported the use by Syrian forces of barrel bombs embedded with cylinders of chlorine gas, in Idlib in April 2014 as well as in March 2015.[33] Two doctors who treated victims of chemical attacks provided HRW with data that they had collected from medical centers in the Idlib Governorate on more than 20 additional attacks between March 16 and May 19, 2015, causing symptoms consistent with exposure to toxic chemicals.[34] They reported that the attacks during this period killed at least nine people and affected more than 520 others with symptoms consistent with exposure to chlorine.[35] To sum up, civil society has played a key role in the clarification of the circumstances of this human tragedy – a role that is closely related to the CWC.

In spite of the growing interaction between States Parties and the OPCW, on the one hand, and civil society and academia, on the other, there is awareness that cooperation could still be improved and intensified. The Third Review Conference held in The Hague in April 2013 explicitly recognized the need for an enhanced

30 OPCW CSP, "Report of the Scientific Advisory Board on Development in Science and Technology for the Third Special Session of the Conference of the States Parties to Review the Operation of the Convention," RC-3/DG.1 (October 29, 2012).

31 Below, section C.3.a).

32 To view the report, see http://www.hrw.org/reports/2013/09/10/attacks-ghouta-0 (accessed February 20, 2017).

33 Human Rights Watch (HRW), "Syria: New Chemical Attacks in Idlib, Security Council Should Urgently Determine Responsibility," June 3, 2015, https://www.hrw.org/news/2015/06/03/syria-new-chemical-attacks-idlib (accessed February 20, 2017).

34 *Ibid.*

35 *Ibid.*; see also HRW, "Syria: Chemicals Used in Idlib Attacks," April 13, 2015, https://www.hrw.org/news/2015/04/13/syria-chemicals-used-idlib-attacks (accessed February 20, 2017).

role to be played by civil society in achieving the goals of the Convention, encouraging the

> Secretariat and the States Parties to improve interaction with the chemical industry, the scientific community, academia, and civil society organizations engaged in issues relevant to the Convention, and the Secretariat and States Parties to develop a more open approach, in conformity with the Rules of Procedure of the policy-making organs with regard to such interaction.[36]

In addition, the idea of an increased consideration of victims of chemical weapons seems to be gaining support. In this respect, it is worth mentioning that, at its Sixteenth Session in 2011, the Conference of the States Parties adopted a decision on "The Establishment of the International Support Network for Victims of Chemical Weapons and the Establishment of a Voluntary Trust Fund for this Purpose."[37] In line with this decision, the Technical Secretariat has been requested to create links to appropriate sources of information relevant to the victims of chemical weapons, and to set up and administer a subpage on the OPCW official website containing information, inter alia, on the history of the use of chemical weapons from the victims' perspective and on NGOs mandated to provide assistance to victims of chemical weapons.[38] This initiative can be seen as an expression of the will of the States Parties to involve civil society more intensively in the activities of the OPCW.

2. The Ottawa and Oslo Conventions: Decisive role played by civil society

Contrary to the CWC, the Ottawa and Oslo Conventions lack traditional verification and implementation mechanisms. Within these treaties, international cooperation and assistance,[39] transparency measures,[40] the periodical Meetings of the States Parties, and the Review Conferences[41] replace, to a large extent, the absence of an institutional framework. The role of civil society in the implementation and verification of these treaties is instrumental, and this is probably best expressed in the broad articles dealing with international cooperation and assistance.[42] In fact, cooperation with and assistance from civil society is proposed

36 RC-3/3*, § 9.155 (n).
37 See https://www.opcw.org/special-sections/victims-of-chemical-weapons-network/ (accessed February 20, 2017).
38 *Ibid.*
39 Articles 6 of Ottawa and Oslo Conventions.
40 Articles 7 of Ottawa and Oslo Conventions.
41 Articles 11 and 12 of Ottawa and Oslo Conventions.
42 For instance, Article 6 § 3 of the Ottawa Convention reads as follows: "Each State Party in a position to do so shall provide assistance for the care and rehabilitation and social and economic reintegration of mine victims and for mine awareness programs. Such assistance

in various fields, such as assistance to mine victims and in mine awareness programs, for mine clearance or the elaboration of de-mining programs.[43]

First of all, the Ottawa and Oslo Conventions confer to the ICRC as well as to other relevant organizations a role in connection with the periodical Meetings of the States Parties and the Review Conferences. These organizations "may" be invited to attend meetings as observers, which gives them the right to attend the open debates, to communicate publicly their points of view, and to express their positions *vis-à-vis* the States Parties.[44]

Even more significant for the effectiveness of the Ottawa and Oslo Conventions than the participation of civil society in various meetings and conferences is the "Landmine and Cluster Munition Monitor," mentioned above, an initiative of the ICBL. A "core group" of five of its members (HI, the mine-clearance NGO Norwegian People's Aid, HRW, and the Canadian and Kenyan national Mine-Ban Campaigns) has assumed responsibility for the coordination of the initiative.[45] It provides monitoring and research on the humanitarian and developmental consequences of landmines, cluster munitions, and explosive remnants of war. The initiative has become the *de facto* monitoring regime of the treaty and, since the adoption of the Convention on Cluster Munitions in 2008, also for that instrument.[46]

The Landmine and Cluster Munition Monitor is best described and summarized in its own words:

> Landmine Monitor is an unprecedented initiative by the International Campaign to Ban Landmines (ICBL) to monitor implementation of and compliance with the 1997 Mine Ban Treaty, and more generally to assess the efforts of the international community to resolve the landmine crises. It is

may be provided, inter alia, through the United Nations system, international, regional or national organizations or institutions, the International Committee of the Red Cross, national Red Cross and Red Crescent societies and their International Federation, ***non governmental organizations***, or on a bilateral basis" (emphasis added). See also Article 6 § 7 of the Oslo Convention.

43 See, in particular, Article 6 §§ 3, 4, and 7 of the Ottawa Convention and Article 6 §§ 2, 7, and 11 of the Oslo Convention.

44 It derives from the text of Articles 11 § 4 and 12 § 3 of the Ottawa Convention and of Articles 11 § 3 and 12 § 3 of the Oslo Convention that the States Parties enjoy a broad discretion as to whom to invite.

45 M. Wareham, "The Role of Landmine Monitor in Promoting and Monitoring Compliance with the 1997 Anti-Personnel Mine Ban Convention," in J. Borrie and V. Randin (eds.), *Disarmament as Humanitarian Action: From Perspective to Practice*, UNIDIR, Geneva, 2006, pp. 79–108, p. 83.

46 The initiative formally changed its name from *Landmine Monitor* to ***Landmine and Cluster Munition Monitor*** in December 2009 to better reflect its increased reporting of cluster munition issues. See http://www.the-monitor.org/index.php/LM/About-Us/History (accessed February 20, 2017).

> the first time that non-governmental organizations are coming together in a co-ordinated, systematic and sustained way to monitor a humanitarian law or disarmament treaty, and to regularly document progress and problems. The main elements of the Landmine Monitor system are a global reporting network, a central database, and an annual report . . . It should be understood that Landmine Monitor is not a technical verification system or a formal inspection regime. It is an effort by civil society to hold governments accountable to the obligations that they have taken on with regard to anti-personnel mines; this is done through extensive collection, analysis and distribution of information that is publicly available.[47]

It follows from this description that the Monitor is particular insofar as it establishes, for the first time, a "civil-society-based reporting network for monitoring" compliance with an international convention.[48] It denounces alleged violations of the treaty, thereby often prompting reactions by the accused States.[49] But it is also unique as far as its internal structure and research methods are concerned. In fact, the information collated and published in its annual reports is provided by a global research network. The main task of local researchers is to document activities related to mines and cluster munitions, for instance on the use of these weapons, through collection, analysis, and distribution of public information such as media reports or interviews with a wide range of sources, including NGOs, diplomats, other officials, parliamentarians, media representatives, refugees, mine survivors, rebels, and local residents.[50]

One of the core duties of the States Parties under the Ottawa and Oslo Conventions relates to the "transparency measures" under Articles 7 which impose on those States the duty to submit annual reports on various aspects, such as the national implementation measures referred to in Article 8,[51] the number of all stockpiled or possessed weapons,[52] the location of mined or cluster-contaminated areas,[53] or the status of programs for the destruction of weapons.[54] Given the lack

47 "About Landmine Monitor," *Landmine Monitor Report 1999*.

48 This idea was first raised by the Canadian Foreign Minister, Lloyd Axworthy, during his visit to the NGO Forum running in parallel with the Oslo Diplomatic Conference (S. Maslen, *A View from the Vanishing Point, Anti-Personnel Mines on the Battlefield under International Humanitarian Law*, PhD thesis submitted to Tilburg University, the Netherlands, 2000, p. 123). See also K. R. Rutherford, *Disarming States: The International Movement to Ban Landmines*, Praeger Security International, 2011, pp. 131–134.

49 See, for instance, the *1999 Landmine Monitor Report*, which detected violations committed, inter alia, by Angola and Senegal. The latter immediately denied use, while the former claimed that its use was discriminate since it aimed at the protection of security targets only (Rutherford, *Disarming States*, p. 133).

50 Wareham, "The Role of Landmine Monitor," pp. 84 et seq.

51 Articles 7 § 1(a) of the Ottawa and Oslo Conventions.

52 Articles 7 § 1(b) of the Ottawa and Oslo Conventions.

53 Article 7 § 1(c) of the Ottawa Convention and Article 7 § 1(h) of the Oslo Convention.

54 Article 7 § 1(e) of the Ottawa Convention and Article 7 § 1(i) of the Oslo Convention.

of institutional verification mechanisms, such as those of the CWC, these obligations prove particularly significant in the Ottawa and Oslo Conventions. For obvious reasons, Articles 7 constitute the starting point for the Landmine and Cluster Munition Monitor's own reporting. On the other hand, it is suggested that ICBL and the Monitor have not only helped to ensure the timely submission of Article 7 reports, but have played a crucial role in improving the quality and quantity of the information provided by governments.[55] Moreover, ICBL campaigners and Monitor researchers sometimes review and comment on draft Article 7 reports provided by their governments before submission.[56] If the Monitor reaches the conclusion that a State Party is responsible for a serious violation of a duty flowing from the Ottawa or Oslo Conventions, it may invite the government concerned to submit observations before publication of the report.[57] Finally, the Monitor's scrutiny of Article 7 reports can reveal gaps and discrepancies, for instance on the numbers of mines that are reported as destroyed.[58]

Apart from the assistance that ICBL provides to States Parties when fulfilling their duty to submit Article 7 reports, and from the control it exercises over their duties under the Ottawa and Oslo Conventions,[59] it also provides guidelines on how States Parties are supposed to interpret certain notions contained in these treaties, promotes mine and cluster munitions clearance, and publishes information on States Parties that are not likely to meet their ten-year clearance deadlines or on those that have not even taken initial steps to establish a plan to meet their clearance deadlines.[60]

Another important area where ICBL has proven very useful is its documentation of survivor needs and the promotion of assistance to mine and cluster munitions victims. ICBL has raised awareness about needs and rights of survivors and has also enabled victims to request assistance and services that would meet their needs.[61] The Landmine and Cluster Munition Monitor has pointed to significant gaps regarding geographic coverage, affordability, and quality of available facilities, and to the lack of resources for implementing or maintaining victim assistance programs, including socio-economic reintegration of survivors.[62] In addition, it has been instrumental in estimating the global number of landmine and cluster munitions casualties, which is certainly one of the most visible and

55 Wareham, "The Role of Landmine Monitor," p. 87. It appears that the number of States Parties submitting their initial reports increased dramatically from 63 percent in 2001 to 96 percent by October 2005 (*Landmine Monitor Report 2005*).

56 *Ibid.*, p. 87.

57 *Ibid.*, p. 85.

58 *Ibid.*, p. 88, including the example of Ecuador and its declaration of 2000, according to which it intended to retain more than 170 000 mines for "training purposes."

59 See, for more details, Wareham, "The Role of Landmine Monitor," pp. 93–96.

60 Article 5 of the Ottawa Convention and Article 4 of the Oslo Convention. See, for more details, Wareham, "The Role of Landmine Monitor," pp. 96 et seq.

61 Wareham, "The Role of Landmine Monitor," p. 97.

62 *Ibid.*, p. 98.

significant tools to determine the impact of the treaties. By the same token, this activity enables donors and others to determine the needs of the victims and to make sure that the scarce resources are used most effectively.[63]

For all these reasons, the international community has largely acknowledged the essential role played by the Landmine Monitor in the implementation of the Ottawa Convention and, more broadly, as a humanitarian response to the global mines issue.[64] It has truly become "an annual citizen's companion to the [Ottawa and Oslo] Convention[s]."[65]

Finally, it is noteworthy that ICBL has closely followed the conflict in Ukraine as regards the use of cluster munitions and anti-personnel mines,[66] in cooperation with other organizations, in particular HRW, a co-founder and chair of ICBL.[67] HRW has been instrumental in investigating and informing about the use of cluster munitions in populated areas of Donetsk (Ukraine) in early October 2014. During a week-long investigation in eastern Ukraine, widespread use of these weapons in fighting between Ukrainian Government forces and pro-Russian rebels in more than a dozen urban and rural locations was reported. HRW argued that the use of cluster munitions in populated areas violated the laws of war due to the indiscriminate nature of the weapons and could amount to war crimes.[68] In a report published in March 2015, HRW stated that both Government and Russian-backed rebel forces had resorted repeatedly to cluster munitions in eastern Ukraine in January and February 2015, killing at least 13 civilians, including two or more children.[69] Moreover, in April 2015, HRW issued a "technical briefing note" on the use of landmines in the Ukraine conflict, alleging that anti-personnel mines were used on a limited and localized scale, including victimactivated booby-traps prohibited by the Ottawa Convention, ratified by Ukraine, but not by Russia.[70]

63 *Ibid.*

64 *Ibid.*, p. 84.

65 Statement by Hon. Lloyd Axworthy, Minister of Foreign Affairs of Canada to the First Meeting of States Parties to the 1997 Mine Ban Treaty, Maputo, Mozambique, May 3, 1999.

66 See, for instance, ICBL, "Troubling Reports of Landmines Seizures and Use in Eastern Ukraine," July 8, 2014, http://www.icbl.org/en-gb/news-and-events/news/2014/troubling-reports-of-landmine-seizures-and-use-in-eastern-ukraine.aspx (accessed February 20, 2017).

67 HRW, "Landmines in Ukraine," *Technical Briefing Note*, April 2015, https://www.hrw.org/sites/default/files/supporting_resources/lm_landmines_in_ukraine-technical_briefing_note_6april2015_final.pdf (accessed February 20, 2017).

68 HRW, "Ukraine: Widespread Use of Cluster Munitions," October 20, 2014, http://www.hrw.org/news/2014/10/20/ukraine-widespread-use-cluster-munitions (accessed February 20, 2017).

69 HRW, "Ukraine: More Civilians Killed in Cluster Munition Attacks," March 19, 2015, https://www.hrw.org/news/2015/03/19/ukraine-more-civilians-killed-cluster-munition-attacks (accessed February 20, 2017). See also HRW, "Cluster Munition Use in Ukraine," *Technical Briefing Note*, June 2015, https://www.hrw.org/sites/default/files/supporting_resources/ukraine_clusters_briefing_note_final.pdf (accessed March 1, 2017).

70 HRW, "Landmines in Ukraine," *Technical Briefing Note*.

HRW's activities in the field of cluster munitions and anti-personnel mines are comparable to those related to the use of chemical weapons in Syria. The fact that this organization – traditionally focusing on human rights – is increasingly active in arms control matters is another aspect attesting to the relevance of this kind of treaties for the protection of human beings and the growing linkage between these two domains of international law.

3. The ATT

The ATT has only entered into force recently, on December 24, 2014. Thus, the precise involvement of civil society in the implementation of this treaty is not easy to predict. Nevertheless, following the example of the Ottawa and Oslo Conventions, the engagement of NGOs is expected to be significant, considering the fact that certain organizations, in particular within the network of the "Control Arms" campaign, have already been instrumental in the establishment and implementation of control mechanisms for SALW prior to the entry into force of the ATT, mainly the EU Code of Conduct and the UN Programme of Action.[71] Therefore, it is certainly not by coincidence that the preamble of the ATT stresses the potential role of NGOs in this respect:

> *The States Parties to this Treaty* . . .
> *Recognizing* the voluntary and active role that civil society, including non-governmental organizations, and industry can play in raising awareness of the object and purpose of this Treaty, and in supporting its implementation . . .[72]

The ATT cannot count on an international organization backing it up from an institutional point of view, but its Article 14 contains the following general clause on implementation:

> Each State Party shall take appropriate measures to enforce national laws and regulations that implement the provisions of the treaty.[73]

This general clause leaves room for civil society assistance and partnership between NGOs and States Parties. The broadness of the mandate likely to be given to civil

71 See, in this sense, S. Bauer and M. Bromley, "Implementing the Arms Trade Treaty: Building on Available Guidelines and Assistance Activities," *SIPRI Background Paper*, May 2015, p. 5, http://books.sipri.org/files/misc/SIPRIBP1505.pdf (accessed February 20, 2017).

72 Paragraph 15 of the preamble.

73 See, for a brief comment, Geneva Academy of International Humanitarian Law and Human Rights, "The Arms Trade Treaty (2013)," *Academy Briefing*, no. 3, June 2013, http://www.snis.ch/system/files/academy_briefing_3_2013_arms_trade_treaty.pdf (accessed February 15, 2017), pp. 36 et seq.

society in the framework of the ATT is possibly best expressed in its Article 16, which is the provision on international assistance. Its paragraph 1 describes the large scope of assistance in the following terms:

> In implementing this Treaty, each State Party may seek assistance including legal or legislative assistance, institutional capacity-building, and technical, material or financial assistance.[74] Such assistance may include stockpile management, disarmament, demobilization and reintegration programmes, model legislation, and effective practices for implementation. Each State Party in a position to do so shall provide such assistance upon request.

The formulation "in a position to do so" is clearly inspired by the Ottawa and Oslo Conventions.[75] Moreover, like these two treaties, Article 16 § 2 ATT reiterates that any State Party is entitled to request, offer, or receive assistance through a variety of mechanisms, fora, or organizations, including NGOs:

> Each State Party may request, offer or receive assistance through, *inter alia*, the United Nations international, regional, subregional or national organizations, non-governmental organizations, or on a bilateral basis.

This reference to civil society constitutes another confirmation and recognition of the valuable contribution and expertise of NGOs in the area of arms trade.[76]

Article 14 ATT has to be read in close connection with Article 5 ATT, paragraph 1 of which contains more specific duties of implementation.[77] Paragraph 2 of Article 5, considered another core provision of the treaty,[78] requires States Parties to establish and maintain a national control system, including a national control list. This list will define which conventional arms are covered by the national control system in accordance with Article 2 and paragraph 3 of Article 5.[79]

74 For definitions such as "legal or legislative assistance" or "institutional capacity building," see Bauer and Bromley, "Implementing the Arms Trade Treaty," pp. 3 et seq.

75 Articles 6 of the Ottawa and Oslo Conventions. In addition, according to paragraph 3 of Article 16 ATT, States Parties are obliged to establish a voluntary trust fund to assist States Parties which require international assistance in the implementation of the ATT. Each State Party is encouraged, but not obliged, to contribute.

76 According to Bauer and Bromley, "Implementing the Arms Trade Treaty," p. 4, assistance activities could take a variety of forms, such as seminars, workshops, peer visits, practical exercises, and training. It could also use a wide range of tools, such as scenario-based tabletop exercises, staff exchanges, and working groups.

77 Article 5 § 1 reads as follows: "Each State Party shall implement this Treaty in a consistent, objective and non-discriminatory manner, bearing in mind the principles referred to in this Treaty."

78 Geneva Academy, "The Arms Trade Treaty," p. 22.

79 *Ibid.*

NGOs are also expected to offer training programs and capacity-building projects for interested circles, in particular governmental agents in charge of national arms transfer control, focusing, inter alia, on aspects of customs and border controls, as well as law enforcement.[80] As an example, SIPRI's "Dual-Use and Arms Trade Control Programme" provides technical expertise for capacity-building for licensing, customs, and prosecution services in different regions of the world.[81] Such activities have obviously direct and positive implications for the States' ability to implement their arms transfer controls.[82] In addition, certain organizations have shown considerable expertise in drafting model legislation or templates.[83]

Furthermore, civil society and academia have conducted assessments of national transfer control systems and, when identifying loopholes in licensing and enforcement practices and policies, provided technical assistance to close these gaps.[84] Moreover, the ICRC has as early as 2007 produced a handbook on how to apply principles of international humanitarian law in the decision-making process about arms transfers.[85] The study, conducted by the Geneva Academy of International Humanitarian Law and Human Rights, entitled "What amounts to 'a serious violation of international human rights law'?" and referred to above, goes in the same direction.[86]

Moreover, civil society might prove instrumental in assessing human rights situations in potential recipient States before a decision on arms transfer is taken, thereby assisting the competent national authorities in applying the relevant human rights and humanitarian law principles and standards to concrete situations. Information from organizations that have a long experience in working in the

80 P. Holtom and M. Bromley, "Implementing an Arms Trade Treaty: Mapping Assistance to Strengthen Arms Transfer Controls," *SIPRI Insights on Peace and Security*, no. 2012/2, July 2012, p. 11, http://books.sipri.org/files/insight/SIPRIInsight1202.pdf (accessed March 1, 2017).

81 SIPRI, Dual-Use and Arms Trade Control Programme; see, for more details, http://www.sipri.org/research/disarmament/dualuse (accessed February 20, 2017).

82 Holtom and Bromley, "Implementing an ATT," p. 11.

83 *Ibid.*, p. 10.

84 *Ibid.*, p. 11.

85 ICRC, "Arms Transfer Decisions, Applying International Humanitarian Law Criteria," *Practical Guide*, Geneva, June 2007, https://www.icrc.org/eng/assets/files/other/icrc_002_0916.pdf (accessed February 16, 2017).

86 *Academy Briefing*, no. 6, August 2014, https://www.sipri.org/sites/default/files/research/disarmament/dualuse/pdf-archive-att/pdfs/20140800_ga_what-amounts-to-a-serious-violation-of-international-human-rights-law.pdf (accessed February 16, 2017). See also Amnesty International, "How to Apply Human Rights Standards to Arms Transfer Decisions," October 2008, http://www.amnesty.org.uk/sites/default/files/how_to_apply_human_rights_standards_to_arms_transfer_decisions.pdf (accessed February 20, 2017). See also Oxfam International, "Practical Guide: Applying Sustainable Development to Arms-Transfer Decisions," *Oxfam International Technical Brief*, https://www.oxfam.org/sites/www.oxfam.org/files/tb-practical-guide-arms-trade-decisions-apr09.pdf (accessed February 20, 2017).

field, such as the ICRC or HRW, providing up-to-date country profiles or reports on human rights abuses worldwide, is expected to facilitate the decision on arms transfers.[87]

Article 13 ATT deals with the reporting obligations of the States Parties. Pursuant to its paragraph 1, States are required, on becoming parties to the ATT, to submit an initial report to the Secretariat, within one year, describing the measures taken by them with a view to implementing the treaty. The reports must include national laws, control lists, and other relevant regulations and administrative measures. Later on, States shall report on any relevant new measure when appropriate. Reports will be made available and distributed to the other States Parties by the Secretariat.[88] Moreover, paragraph 3 of Article 13 ATT requires States Parties to report on an annual basis on authorized or actual exports and imports of conventional arms covered by Article 2 § 1 ATT. These reports shall also be made available to the other States Parties. However, the States Parties may exclude "commercially sensitive or national security information" from their reports. This vague formulation suggests a broad discretion enjoyed by States Parties.[89]

In the same vein, certain NGOs and academic institutions have made available analyses, templates, and proposals for comprehensive and coherent reporting on treaty implementation and arms transfers.[90] The recent effort by the "Control Arms" campaign in assessing the States Parties' reporting policies is noteworthy in this regard. In 2015, it launched the first "ATT Monitor," entitled "State Positions and Practices concerning Reporting and the Arms Trade Treaty." The first edition of the ATT Monitor claimed to establish "a comprehensive interpretation of the standards, obligations and aspirations contained in the Treaty."[91] Judging from its name, the inspiration drawn from the Landmine and Cluster Munition Monitor, described above,[92] is obvious. Its purpose is to assess the record

87 Homepage of HRW: http://www.hrw.org/home (accessed February 20, 2017). Reliable information for the assessment of the risk of human rights or humanitarian law violations might also be gathered from the UN High Commissioner for Refugees, which provides the latest information on human rights situations of all Member States; see, for more details, http://www.unhcr.org/pages/49c3646c206.html (accessed February 20, 2017).

88 See also Article 13 § 2 ATT.

89 Geneva Academy, "The Arms Trade Treaty," p. 36; and M. Brandes, "'All's Well that Ends Well' or 'Much Ado About Nothing'?: A Commentary on the Arms Trade Treaty," *Goettingen Journal of International Law*, vol. 5, 2013, pp. 399–429, http://www.gojil.eu/issues/52/52_article_brandes.pdf (accessed February 15, 2017), p. 426.

90 See E. Kytömäki, P. Holtom, and M. Bromley, "Implementing the Arms Trade Treaty: Reporting International Arms Transfers," *UNIDIR Resources, Ideas for Peace and Security*, http://www.unidir.org/files/medias/pdfs/background-paper-implementing-the-arms-trade-treaty-reporting-international-arms-transfers-elli-kytoemaeki-paul-holtom-and-mark-bromley-eng-0-258.pdf (accessed February 20, 2017).

91 Control Arms, ATT Monitor Report 2015, August 2015, http://controlarms.org/en/att-monitor-report/ (accessed March 8, 2017).

92 See this volume, Chapter 4, section B.2.

and position on reporting for 130 States Parties and signatory States of the ATT when it came into force in December 2014.[93] It summarizes what those States have advocated as regards reporting during the negotiations of the ATT and shows which States have reported conventional arms imports or exports between 2009 and 2013.[94] It remains to be seen whether the ATT Monitor will take a place as important as that of the Landmine and Cluster Munition Monitor.

Finally, civil society is also involved on an institutional level. Article 17 ATT deals with the annual Conference of States Parties which, according to its paragraph 4, shall inter alia review the implementation of the treaty, including developments in the field of conventional arms,[95] consider and adopt recommendations regarding implementation and operation, promote universality,[96] discuss issues arising from the interpretation of the treaty and consider amendments to it,[97] as well as perform any other function consistent with the ATT.[98] Contrary to the Ottawa and Oslo Conventions,[99] Article 17 of the ATT does not explicitly mention civil society's participation in the annual Conference of States Parties, but this element was included in the Rules of Procedure at the first Conference held in 2015.[100] As regards "developments in the field of conventional arms," in particular, organizations such as the ICRC, "Control Arms" campaign, and "Article 36" have considerable know-how in humanitarian issues of weapon technology and, accordingly, are expected to play a significant role within the Conference of States Parties and its sub-organs.[101]

93 ATT Monitor Report 2015.
94 *Ibid.*, Introduction.
95 Subparagraph (a).
96 Subparagraph (b).
97 Subparagraphs (c) and (d).
98 Subparagraph (g).
99 Under the Ottawa (Article 11 § 4) and Oslo Conventions (Article 11 § 3), NGOs "may be invited to attend the meetings as observers in accordance with the agreed Rules of Procedure."
100 Rules 4 and 5 §§ 1 and 2. Civil society was also interested and engaged in the establishment and shaping of the Secretariat in accordance with Article 18 ATT; see, for instance, Control Arms, "Policy Guide for the Arms Trade Treaty 2012," p. 13, http://icip.gencat.cat/web/.content/continguts/centre_de_documentaci/dossiers_tem_tics/dossier_tca/documents/docs_previs_confediplomatica/arxius/control_arms_policy_guide-_english.pdf (accessed March 8, 2017); and S. Bauer, P. Beijer, and M. Bromley, "The Arms Trade Treaty: Challenges for the First Conference of States Parties," *SIPRI Insights on Peace and Security*, no. 2014/2, September 2014, pp. 5–7, http://books.sipri.org/files/insight/SIPRIInsight1402.pdf (accessed February 20, 2017).
101 According to its homepage, "Article 36" is a UK-based NGO working to prevent the unintended, unnecessary, or unacceptable harm caused by certain weapons. It undertakes research, policy, and advocacy, and promotes civil society partnerships to respond to harm caused by existing weapons and to build a stronger framework to prevent harm as weapons are used or developed in the future. Its name refers to Article 36 of Additional Protocol I to the Geneva Conventions that requires States to review new weapons, and means and methods of warfare. See, for more details, http://www.article36.org/about/ (accessed February 20, 2017).

4. Conclusions

In view of the foregoing observations, one may conclude that, today, civil society plays an essential role in supporting the OPCW in the implementation and verification of the CWC. Traditionally, disarmament was seen as a prerogative of sovereign States and, above all, as a question of national security. According to R. Trapp et al., this has changed, as NGOs are becoming partners of governments and of the OPCW in the implementation of the CWC; they represent the voice of reason, addressed to citizens, nations, and the world. Their views reflect the recognition of global values and rules, of which States are no longer the only guardians, and their contribution to accountability, global governance, and greater legitimacy is significant today.[102]

Regarding the Ottawa and Oslo Conventions, it can be asserted that NGOs have not only been instrumental in the establishment of these Conventions, as indicated above, but that they also play a decisive role in the implementation and verification of the duties deriving from these instruments. As a result, they largely fill the gap left by the lack of traditional control mechanisms. It is not exaggerated to claim that the implementation of these two treaties, to a large extent through independent NGOs, has deviated from "business as usual" in multilateral disarmament and arms control.[103] Implementation and verification by civil society, in particular thanks to ICBL and the Landmine and Cluster Munition Monitor, have proven essential in this new approach and ensure the effective realization of the objects and purposes of the treaties. Moreover, those annual reports have become essential reading for diplomats, practitioners, donors, and media representatives. Civil society has helped to bring to the international arms control and disarmament agenda humanitarian perspectives which differ from orthodox, national-security-focused approaches.[104]

The ATT is a relatively recent treaty. Therefore, a definitive assessment of the influence of civil society on its implementation and verification would be premature. It can nevertheless be expected, particularly in light of the significant role played by civil society in the negotiation and conclusion of this treaty, that the ATT will follow the examples of the Ottawa and Oslo Conventions where certain NGOs play a key role in the implementation of their provisions and the verification of the duties imposed. NGOs will intervene on various levels, including the assessment of human rights situations in States which potentially receive arms, thereby rendering relevant the expertise and field experience of traditional human rights organizations. Academic institutions such as SIPRI have already proven very valuable and are likely to continue their technical and legal input. It will also have to be seen whether the idea of the Landmines and Cluster Munitions

102 W. Krutzsch, E. Myjer, and R. Trapp, "The CWC – Objectives, Principles and Implementation Practice," in Krutzsch et al., *The CWC – A Commentary*, p. 14.

103 Wareham, "The Role of Landmine Monitor," p. 103.

104 *Ibid.*, p. 104.

Monitor, a very effective verification mechanism ran by civil society, is per se exportable to the ATT.

C. ROLE OF THE EUROPEAN COURT OF HUMAN RIGHTS (ECTHR) AND THE COMMITTEE OF MINISTERS OF THE COUNCIL OF EUROPE

1. The ECtHR and the execution of its final judgments under the supervision of the Committee of Ministers

What makes the ECHR regime so unique is the fact that the States Parties are not only obliged to "secure to everybody within their jurisdiction the rights and freedoms defined in Section 1" of the Convention in accordance with Article 1 (Obligation to respect human rights), but that they also "undertake to abide," within the meaning of Article 46 ECHR (Binding force and execution of judgment), by the final judgments of the Court in cases to which they are parties.[105] The implementation ("execution") of the judgments is, moreover, supervised by the Committee of Ministers, one of the principal organs of the Council of Europe.[106]

In the course of the deliberations of the Committee of Ministers, the question is generally raised whether the payment of just satisfaction under Article 41 ECHR is sufficient to redress the violation of the ECHR or whether the judgment of the Court calls for measures of individual and/or general nature, such as the modification of national legislation in order to avoid similar violations in the future.[107] During the procedure of execution of judgments, States are required to provide the Committee of Ministers with detailed, up-to-date information on possible legal and factual developments.[108]

105 D. Rietiker, "Strange Bedfellows? The Cross-Fertilization of Human Rights and Arms Control, The European Court of Human Rights on Cases Involving Chemical Weapons and Anti-Personnel Mines," *Cyprus Human Rights Law Review*, vol. 3, no. 2, 2014, pp. 130–159, 150.

106 Article 46 § 2 ECHR. These principles are well summarized in the case of *Verein gegen Tierfabriken v. Switzerland (no. 2)* [GC], no. 32772/02, § 84, June 30, 2009. See also X.-B. Ruedin, *L'exécution des arrêts de la Cour Européenne des Droits de l'Homme: Procédure, obligations des Etats, pratique et réforme,* Basel, Brussels, and Paris, 2009; T. Barkhuysen and M. Van Emmerik, "A Comparative View on the Execution of the Judgments of the European Court of Human Rights," in T. A. Christou and J. P. Raymond (eds.), *European Court of Human Rights, Remedies and Execution of Judgments,* British Institute of International and Comparative Law, 2005, pp. 1–23; and G. Ress, "The Effects of Decisions and Judgments of the European Court of Human Rights in the Domestic Legal Order," *Texas International Law Journal,* vol. 40, 2005, pp. 359–382.

107 *Verein gegen Tierfabriken v. Switzerland (no. 2)* [GC], no. 32772/02, § 85, June 30, 2009.

108 On May 10, 2006, at the 964th meeting of the Ministers' Deputies, the Committee of Ministers adopted "Rules for the supervision of the execution of judgments and of the terms of friendly settlements."

Even though the respondent State is in principle free to choose the means by which it will discharge its obligations under Article 46 § 1 ECHR, these means must be compatible with the conclusions set out in the Court's judgment (no obligation of means, but of result).[109] In order to facilitate the subsequent work of the Committee of Ministers and of the defending States, the Court has indicated in recent judgments what is expected from them in execution procedures.[110] The case of *İzci v. Turkey* concerning riot control, which will be discussed below, is an example of this new tendency.[111]

The subdivision that follows will demonstrate how and to what extent the execution of the ECtHR's judgments has some positive effect on the CWC and the Ottawa and Oslo Conventions. The role played in this context by the ECtHR, acting hand-in-hand with the Committee of Ministers of the Council of Europe, is somehow unexpected: traditionally, the fields of human rights and arms control have not had much in common.

2. Cases involving anti-personnel mines

a) Paşa and Erkan Erol v. Turkey

The applicants, Paşa Erol and his son Erkan, are Turkish nationals and live in Tunceli (Turkey).[112] In March 1995, Paşa Erol was informed that anti-personnel mines had been laid along one side of the premises of the Akdemir gendarmerie command in the district of Pertek (Tunceli). The zone in question was cordoned off with barbed wire at waist level and warning signs were placed at 20-meter intervals. In the following days, the local people were informed orally that the area, which they used for grazing, had been mined.[113]

On May 11, 1995 Erkan, then aged 9, was grazing his sheep. They strayed into the mined area and Erkan, together with other children aged between 7 and 13, followed the animals across the barbed-wire fence. Erkan tried to pick up a piece of metal, which turned out to be a mine, and he was wounded by the ensuing explosion.[114] Following the explosion, he was taken to a nearby hospital by military helicopter where he had his left leg amputated below the knee. Paşa Erol vainly brought administrative proceedings against the Ministry of the Interior, seeking

109 See *Scozzari and Giunta v. Italy* [GC], nos. 39221/98 and 41963/98, § 249, ECHR 2000-VIII; and *Lyons and Others v. United Kingdom* (dec.), no. 15227/03, ECHR 2003-IX.

110 See, for instance, *Öcalan v. Turkey*, no. 46221/99, § 210 *in fine*, ECHR 2005-IV; and *Popov v. Russia*, no. 26853/04, § 263, July 13, 2006. Sometimes, the Court found that the nature of the violation does not even leave any choice as to the measures to be taken (*Assanidze v. Georgia* [GC], no. 71503/01, § 202, ECHR 2004-II).

111 See below, section C.3.b).

112 Application no. 51358/99, lodged on September 7, 1999.

113 Legal summary of the Court (the judgment exists only in French), http://hudoc.echr.coe.int/sites/eng/pages/search.aspx#{"itemid":["002-2961"]} (accessed February 20, 2017).

114 *Ibid.*

compensation on account of insufficient safety measures around the military zone. The Supreme Administrative Court upheld the first instance's judgment on November 24, 1998.[115]

Before the ECtHR, the applicants complained that the authorities had failed to protect the right to life in allowing anti-personnel landmines to be laid without taking the necessary safety measures. They relied, in particular, on Article 2 (right to life), Article 6 § 1 (fair hearing), and Article 13 ECHR (effective remedy).

In its judgment of December 12, 2006, the Court noted, regarding Article 2 ECHR,[116] that the anti-personnel mines had been laid to protect the gendarmerie near the village. It further observed that the mined area had been pastureland where the villagers regularly went to feed their animals. Owing to the specific situation, the safety measures had been of particular importance and it had been the authorities' duty, in the absence of other means of protection provided by the regional gendarmerie, to take the measures needed to prevent innocent civilians from entering the area.[117] The Court observed that the minefield had been cordoned off by only two rows of barbed wire, which were too far apart from each other to ensure effective protection. Moreover, even though the local people had been told about the mines, their children could not be expected, in the natural environment and given the way of life in a very rural community where they were actively involved in day-to-day tasks, such as grazing animals, to have behaved in the same way as responsible adults would have done when faced with such dangers.[118]

In conclusion, the Court found it incomprehensible that a grazing area should have been mined and simply surrounded by two rows of barbed wire that were relatively distant from each other and clearly insufficient to prevent children from crossing over. It thus concluded that Turkey had not taken all the necessary measures to ensure protection from the risk of death or injury.[119]

Accordingly, there had been a violation of Article 2 in respect of Erkan Erol. The relevance of the ECHR and the Court for the implementation of the Ottawa Convention derives from the following reasoning, wherein the Court relied heavily on that Convention (non-official translation from French by the author):

115 *Ibid.*

116 Even though the force used by State has not led to a fatal outcome, the applicant could nevertheless rely on Article 2 ECHR insofar as the force had the potential to cause his death. See, in this sense, *Makaratzis v. Greece* [GC], no. 50385/99, December 20, 2004, § 49; and *İlhan v. Turkey* [GC], no. 22277/93, § 75, ECHR 2000-VII.

117 Legal summary, *op. cit.*

118 *Ibid.*

119 The Court referred, *mutatis mutandis*, to the cases of: *Osman v. United Kingdom*, October 28, 1998, Report 1998-VIII, p. 3159, § 116; and *Demiray v. Turkey*, no. 27308/95, § 46, ECHR 2000-XII.

> Article 1 of the Ottawa Convention on the Prohibition of the Use, Stockpiling, Production and Transfer of Anti-Personnel Mines and on their Destruction, signed on 18 September 1997, imposes on State Parties the duty to refrain from using anti-personnel mines and to destroy all anti-personnel mines or ensure their destruction within ten years of the date of the entry into force of the Convention after approval by the international authorities.[120]
>
> Turkey has been a Party to the Ottawa Convention since 28 March 2003, which entered into force [on behalf of Turkey] on 1st March 2004.[121]
>
> . . .
>
> The Court has observed from the outset that the anti-personnel mines were intended to protect the local gendarmerie situated near the village. Nevertheless, such mines represent a particular danger for young children and their use has been largely condemned by international opinion, which called for an international convention prohibiting their use, to which Turkey has been a Party since 2003.[122]

The reference to the Ottawa Convention in *Paşa and Erkan Erol v. Turkey* is useful because it confirms that the application of this treaty, unlike traditional humanitarian law, is not conditional on a state of armed conflict, but that the treaty is to apply also in peacetime or in situations of emergency or social unrest which do not meet the threshold of an "armed conflict" within the meaning of Articles 2 and 3 of the Geneva Conventions.[123] As indicated above,[124] it results from its Article I § 1 (General obligations) that the Ottawa Convention imposes its prohibitions in an absolute manner ("never under any circumstances").

The proceedings on the execution of the final judgment in *Paşa and Erkan Erol v. Turkey* were closed in 2011 by a final resolution of the Committee of Ministers.[125] Regarding general measures, the Appendix to the resolution reads as follows:

> *Resolution of the Committee of Ministers of 2011:*
>
> . . .
>
> II. General measures
>
> Turkey is a party to the Ottawa Convention, which came into force in Turkey on 1 March 2004. Under the text [sic] of the Convention, Turkey has the obligation to clear mined areas by 2014. Since 1996, a number of three-year moratoria have been put into place providing for prohibition of production, sale and transfer of anti-personnel landmines and systematic

120 Paragraph 17 of the judgment.
121 *Ibid.*
122 Paragraph 32.
123 Common Article 2 defines armed conflicts of an international nature and common Article 3 sets minimum standards for non-international armed conflicts.
124 Above, Chapter 3, section A.2.a).
125 CM/ResDH(2011)168, adopted on September 14, 2011.

mine clearance began in 1998. The government periodically informs the United Nations about the total number of anti-personnel mines destroyed and preparations for the destruction of remaining mines according to its obligations under the Ottawa Convention. A military installation was put into place in July 2007 for further mine clearance operations. This installation has been operational since 8 November 2007. Until 16 November 2009, 1 822 886 stockpiled anti-personnel mines were separated, selected and destroyed in the installation. The remaining stockpiled anti-personnel mines were planned to be destroyed by November 2010.

On 17 June 2009, the Law on the Destruction of the Anti-Personnel Land Mines on Syrian Border entered into force. In this connection, an area of 31 893 m^2 in Şanlıurfa, and an area of 38 500 m^2 in Kilis were demined.

Meanwhile, given that mine-clearance efforts under the Ottawa Convention are expected to continue until 2014, the Committee of Ministers has enquired about any additional measures taken or envisaged by the Turkish authorities to enhance safety measures. In response, the authorities indicated on 06/03/2008 that they had put in place additional measures to place clear and adequate signs around mined zones in line with international standards. Local authorities continuously issue warnings to inhabitants near such zones. Finally, an awareness project is under way in co-ordination with the Ministry of Education for training teachers, students and inhabitants of districts in order to issue warnings on risk of mines.

The judgment of the European Court was published and sent out to all the authorities concerned.

In view of the foregoing, it may be argued that the Committee of Ministers played a key role in implementing the Ottawa Convention and in verifying compliance with it.[126] For instance, several moratoria were put in place prohibiting the production, sale, and transfer of anti-personnel landmines, i.e. precisely enforcing the obligation imposed on Turkey by Article 1 § 1(b) of the Convention. Moreover, mine clearance and the destruction of stockpiles are ongoing in Turkey, as provided for in Article 1 § 2, 4, and 5 of the treaty.[127] For that purpose, Turkey has enacted national legislation as prescribed by Article 9.[128]

It also transpires from the above-mentioned Appendix to the Resolution that the Committee of Ministers urged Turkish authorities, on the basis of the Court's judgment, to enhance safety measures in respect of anti-personnel mines.[129] In reply, the Turkish authorities reported that they installed "danger" signs and

126 Rietiker, "Strange Bedfellows?", p. 153.

127 Article 1 § 2 reads as follows: "Each State Party undertakes to destroy or ensure the destruction of all anti-personnel mines in accordance with the provisions of this Convention." This paragraph refers to Articles 4 and 5.

128 Article 9 (National implementation measures).

129 Rietiker, "Strange Bedfellows?", p. 153.

issued warnings in order to alert the local residents, and in particular, the children in the affected regions. The Committee of Ministers, by adopting the resolution, has acknowledged these efforts, which can be regarded having been made to meet duties under Article 5 of the Ottawa Convention (Destruction of anti-personnel mines in mined areas).

b) Albekov and Others v. Russia

A similar case decided by the ECtHR involving human rights violations caused by the use of anti-personnel mines is *Albekov and Others v. Russia*.[130]

The applicants were three Russian nationals who lived in the Chechen Republic and whose relatives were killed in October 2000 by anti-personnel mines planted in a forest close to the village of Akhinchu-Barzoy. The applicants alleged that the mines were laid by military personnel and that one of the victims had failed to return after leaving to bring in his cattle. The other victims hit a mine during the search for their missing relatives.[131]

In its judgment of October 9, 2008, and as far as Article 2 ECHR (Right to life) is concerned, the ECtHR left open the question of who had laid the mines in the vicinity of Akhinchu-Barzoy. However, since the Government did not deny that the authorities had been aware that mines had been laid in the area, the Court found that the domestic authorities had been under a positive obligation to protect the residents from the risks involved. In view of the State's failure to endeavor to locate and deactivate the mines, to mark and seal off the mined area so as to prevent anybody from freely entering it, and to provide the villagers with comprehensive warnings concerning the mines laid in the vicinity of their village, the Court concluded that the State had failed to comply with its positive obligation under Article 2 of the Convention to protect the lives of the victims and that there had therefore been a violation of that provision.[132]

As far as the relevance of the Ottawa Convention in this case is concerned, the Court only observed that Russia was not a State Party to that instrument, without further relying on it in its reasoning.[133] The judgment demonstrates nevertheless that there is a link between the ECHR and anti-personnel mines, and it is not excluded that the Committee of Ministers will impose on Russia similar measures as it did on Turkey in the *Erol* case, thereby taking inspiration from the spirit and letter of the Ottawa Convention.

130 Application no. 68216/01, lodged on December 10, 2001.

131 See the press release of the Court: http://hudoc.echr.coe.int/sites/eng/pages/search.aspx#{"itemid":["003-2506013-2719278"]} (accessed February 20, 2017).

132 *Ibid.* The Court found moreover that the authorities had failed to carry out an effective criminal investigation into the deaths and injuries of the victims and that there had been a violation of Article 2 ECHR on this account also. The Court also found a violation of Article 13 ECHR (Right to an effective remedy).

133 Paragraph 66 of the judgment.

3. Cases involving chemicals

a) Finogenov v. Russia: Legality of "incapacitating chemical agents"

In the subdivision on implementation of arms control treaties by civil society, the problem of incapacitating chemical agents has been raised already. That the question is not only of academic nature and importance is illustrated by the fact that the ECtHR was confronted with such a situation. The tragic case of *Finogenov and Others v. Russia* has the hostage-taking in the Moscow "Dubrovka" Theatre (while performing the play "North East," *Норд-Ост*) as background.[134] In the evening of October 23, 2002, a group of armed terrorists belonging to the Chechen separatist movement took some 900 people hostage in that theatre. They called for the immediate withdrawal of Russian troops from the Chechen Republic. Negotiations were conducted in vain and several hostages were shot dead. In the morning of October 26, 2002, Russian security forces pumped an unknown narcotic gas into the theatre's main auditorium through the building's ventilation system. A few minutes later, when almost all the terrorists had lost consciousness under the influence of the gas, a special squad stormed the building and killed all of them. The hostages were then evacuated from the building and transported to hospitals in ambulances or city buses. However, some 125 of them died on the spot, during transportation or in hospital. A criminal investigation was opened into the events, but it was subsequently decided not to pursue the investigation into the planning and conduct of the rescue operation. The victims' subsequent criminal complaints and civil actions for compensation in respect of non-pecuniary damage were dismissed.[135] Only later it transpired that the gas used by the special unit was a derivative of fentanyl, a toxic chemical gas, but the exact formula has never been disclosed or ascertained.[136]

The applicants before the Court, either hostages or relatives of hostages who died in the course of the rescue operation, complained about violations of the right to life within the meaning of Article 2 ECHR. In its judgment of December 20, 2011, the Court held that the decision to end the negotiations and to storm the building did not violate Article 2 ECHR.[137] As far as the use of the gas was concerned, the Court concluded that, although domestic law allowed the use of weapons and other means against terrorists, it did not indicate the type of

134 No. 18299/03, Judgment of December 20, 2011. See, for a comment of this case in the light of the CWC, V. Vandova, "The European Court of Human Rights's Judgment in the Case of Finogenov and Others v. Russia," in *"Incapacitating Chemical Weapons," Law Enforcement, Human Rights and Policy Perspectives*; Expert Meeting, Montreux, April 24–26, 2012, pp. 46–49, http://www.icrc.org/eng/assets/files/publications/icrc-002-4121.pdf (accessed February 20, 2017).

135 This summary can be found on the homepage of the Court, http://hudoc.echr.coe.int/sites/eng/pages/search.aspx#{"itemid":["002-240"]} (accessed February 20, 2017).

136 Vandova, "The ECtHR's Judgment in Finogenov and Others v. Russia," p. 46.

137 Pargraphs 217–226.

weapons or tools that could be used nor the circumstances in which their use was permitted. It found, however, that the general vagueness of the law did not necessarily result in a breach of Article 2, in particular not in totally unpredictable and exceptional situations such as the present one.[138] Moreover, even though the gas used was dangerous and potentially lethal, it had not been intended to kill, and it could not be said that it was used indiscriminately since it had left the hostages a high chance of survival.[139]

Nevertheless, the ECtHR was of the opinion that the rescue operation had been insufficiently prepared and was implemented in a way that did not satisfy Article 2 ECHR.[140] For instance, the coordination between the various services involved was insufficient: some of the victims of the gas received multiple doses of antidote.[141] Moreover, there were no toxicologists present, and the rescue workers and doctors were not given specific instructions on how to deal with hostages who had been exposed to an unknown gas.[142]

As regards the procedural limb of Article 2, the Court concluded that the investigation into the rescue operation was manifestly incomplete since many facts crucial to the question of possible negligence on the part of the authorities were never established. First and foremost, the composition of the gas was never revealed to the investigators, nor was it ever ascertained when the decision to use the gas was taken or how much time was available to evaluate its possible side-effects. As a result, the investigation into the authorities' alleged negligence was not effective.[143]

To sum up, *Finogenov and Others v. Russia* reiterates and reinforces the principles deriving from the Court's case law in respect of the use of force in law enforcement and, therefore, imposes important restrictions for the future use of gas in this kind of emergency situation. For reasons unknown, the Court did not mention the CWC in its judgment, even though Russia had ratified it on November 5, 1997.

b) Cases involving riot control agents, in particular directed against Turkey

As explained above, "law enforcement including domestic riot control purposes" are considered "purposes not prohibited" under the ECHR.[144] The practice of the ECtHR in numerous cases against Turkey involving the use of tear gas to counter potentially violent demonstrations reflects this explanation. The Court examines

138 Paragraphs 227–236.
139 *Ibid.*
140 Paragraphs 237–266.
141 *Ibid.*
142 *Ibid.*
143 Paragraphs 267–282. As a result of the multiple violations of Article 2 ECHR, the Court awarded, under Article 41 (Just satisfaction), sums between €8 000 and €66 000 to each of the applicants in respect of non-pecuniary damage.
144 Article II.9(d) CWC.

these cases, in particular, from the angle of Article 3 which prohibits inhuman and degrading treatment.[145] For instance, in the case of *Oya Ataman v. Turkey*, it held that:

> [u]nder Article I § 5 of the Convention on the Prohibition of the Development, Production, Stockpiling and Use of Chemical Weapons and on their Destruction of 13 January 1993 ("the CWC"), each State Party undertakes not to use riot control agents as a method of warfare. Tear gas or so-called "pepper spray" are not considered chemical weapons (the CWC contains an annex listing the names of prohibited chemical products). The use of such methods is authorized for the purpose of law enforcement, including domestic riot control (Article II § 9 (d)). Nor does the CWC state which State bodies may be involved in maintaining public order. This remains a matter for the sovereign power of the State concerned. The CWC entered into force with regard to Turkey on 11 June 1997.[146]

From these paragraphs one can deduce that, in these kinds of cases, the appropriate and proportionate use of tear gas qualifies as a justified and proportionate use of force and, as a result, as complying with Article 3 ECHR.[147] Nevertheless, the Court has found violations of this guarantee where legal provisions authorized the use of tear gas or in cases where the law-enforcement forces had made improper or unnecessary use of tear gas (substantive aspect of Article 3).[148] Moreover, even though the threshold of Article 3 is generally not reached by the use of tear gas, the authorities are still under a procedural obligation to conduct an in-depth investigation into alleged human rights violations.[149]

In the recent judgment *İzci v. Turkey*,[150] the Court unanimously, found breaches of the substantive and procedural aspects of Article 3 ECHR due to the disproportionate use of force and the lack of an effective investigation following the use of force and, besides, a violation of Article 11 (Freedom of assembly and association) on account of the failure to respect the applicant's right to freedom of assembly. In this case, the applicant had taken part in a demonstration in Istanbul to celebrate Women's Day which had ended in clashes between the police

145 Article 3 (Prohibition of torture) reads as follows: "No one shall be subjected to torture or to inhuman and degrading treatment or punishment."

146 Application no. 74552/01, Judgment of December 5, 2006.

147 See, for instance, *Çiloğlu and Others v. Turkey*, no. 73333/01, March 6, 2007; or *Oya Ataman v. Turkey*, cited above. On the other hand, the Court has in some instances found a violation of Article 11 (Freedom of assembly and association); see, for instance, *Oya Ataman v. Turkey*, no. 74552/01, December 5, 2006, §§ 28–44.

148 See, for both aspects, for instance, *Abdullah Yaşa and Others v. Turkey*, no. 44827/08, July 16, 2013. See also the case of *Ali Güneş v. Turkey*, no. 9829/07, April 10, 2012.

149 See, for instance, *Mustafa Taştan v. Turkey*, no. 41824/05, June 26, 2012; *Yazıcı and Others v. Turkey (no. 2)*, no. 45046/05, April 23, 2013; or *Abdülsamet Yaman v. Turkey*, no. 32446/96, November 2, 2004.

150 Application no. 42606/05, July 23, 2013.

and protesters. Video footage of the events showed police officers hitting a large number of demonstrators with truncheons and spraying them with tear gas. Women who had taken refuge in shops were dragged out by the police and beaten up. The police officers had not issued any warnings to disperse demonstrators before attacking them, and the demonstrators, for their part, had not responded to the attack, but had only tried to flee.[151]

This case is an example for the repeated violations of the ECHR that occur in demonstrations in Turkey. What is remarkable about the case is the fact that the Court considered these problems as "systematic," recalling that it had already found, in over 40 judgments against Turkey, that the heavy-handed interventions of law-enforcement officials in demonstrations had amounted to violations of Article 3 and/or Article 11 ECHR.[152] The common feature of these cases was the unwillingness of the police forces to show a certain degree of tolerance toward peaceful gatherings and, in some instances, a tendency to precipitate the use of force, including tear gas, by the police.[153] Moreover, in over 20 of the judgments, the Court had already observed the failure of Turkish authorities to carry out effective investigations into allegations of ill-treatment by law-enforcement personnel during demonstrations. It further stressed that 130 applications were pending against Turkey concerning the right to freedom of assembly and the use of force by law-enforcement officials during demonstrations.[154]

As a result, the Court requested the Turkish Government, under Article 46 ECHR, to enact "general measures" in order to prevent similar violations in the future. In particular, it asked the authorities to take steps to ensure that the police act in accordance with Articles 3 and 11 ECHR and that the judicial authorities conduct effective investigations into allegations of ill-treatment in conformity with the obligations under Article 3 in such a way as to secure the accountability of senior police officers. Finally, the Court highlighted, not for the first time, the need for clearer rules regarding the use of violence and of weapons such as tear gas during demonstrations, in particular against non-violent demonstrators.[155]

4. Case involving cluster munitions: *Behrami and Behrami v. France*

One application in which cluster munitions played a role may be mentioned here, namely, that of *Behrami and Behrami v. France*,[156] even though it was ultimately declared inadmissible for lack of jurisdiction.

151 Taken from the legal summary provided by the Court, http://hudoc.echr.coe.int/sites/fra/Pages/search.aspx#{"itemid":["002-7642"]} (accessed February 20, 2017). As far as considerations under Article 46 ECHR are concerned, see paragraphs 94–99 of the judgment.

152 Summary provided by the Court, *op. cit.*

153 Rietiker, "Strange Bedfellows?", p. 155.

154 Summary provided by the Court, *op. cit.*

155 *Ibid.*

156 No. 71412/01, decision of May 2, 2007 [GC].

The two applicants were a Kosovo national (Mr. Behrami) and his son.[157] The application was also filed on behalf of another son who died. At the material time, in March 2000, the applicants lived in the sector of Kosovo for which a multinational brigade led by France was responsible. The brigade was part of the international security force (KFOR) present in Kosovo, mandated by UNSC Resolution 1244 of June 1999. A group of children, including Mr. Behrami's sons, found a number of unexploded cluster bombs which had been dropped during the bombardment of the former Federal Republic of Yugoslavia (FRY) by NATO in 1999. A bomb was thrown into the air by one of the children and exploded, killing one of Mr. Behrami's sons and seriously injuring the other. Police from the UN Interim Administration in Kosovo (UNMIK) – mandated by Resolution 1244 and deployed under the aegis of the United Nations – investigated the incident. They found that the accident amounted to "an unintentional homicide committed by imprudence." It was decided that no criminal prosecution would be brought because the bomb did not explode during the NATO bombardment. Mr. Behrami complained to the Kosovo Claims Office that France had not respected the provisions of Resolution 1244 concerning de-mining. The claim was ultimately rejected on the ground that de-mining had been the responsibility of the United Nations since July 1999.[158]

In one of the most criticized decisions in its history,[159] the ECtHR declared the case of *Behrami and Behrami v. France* inadmissible. In short, the Court was of the opinion that the Convention could not be interpreted in such a way as to place under its control the actions and omissions of contracting parties covered by resolutions of the UNSC and committed prior to or during UN missions aimed at preserving international peace and security.[160] This would amount to interference in the accomplishment of an essential mission of the United Nations in this field or in the effective conduct of such operations. The Court therefore declared itself incompetent *ratione personae* to examine the complaints of the applicants on the merits.[161] According to Alexander Breitegger, since it was the first case ever to involve victims of cluster munitions dealt with by the ECtHR, it has to be considered a lost opportunity to clarify the duties to mark and/or clear unexploded sub-munitions to be respected by those who exercise effective control over a territory.[162]

157 Legal summary of the Court, http://hudoc.echr.coe.int/sites/eng/Pages/search.aspx#{"fulltext":["cluster"],"documentcollectionid2":["GRANDCHAMBER","CHAMBER","DECISIONS"],"itemid":["002-2745"]} (accessed February 20, 2017).

158 *Ibid.*

159 See, for instance, M. Milanović and T. Papić, "As Bad as It Gets: The European Court of Human Rights' *Behrami and Saramati* Decision and General International Law," *ICLQ*, vol. 58, 2009, pp. 267–296.

160 *Ibid.*

161 *Ibid.* For the details of this reasoning, see paragraphs 144–152 of the decision.

162 A. Breitegger, *Cluster Munitions and International Law: Disarmament with a Human Face*, London and New York, 2012, p. 127.

The case having been declared inadmissible by the Court, there was nothing to be executed by the defendant State Party. This tragic episode, originating from human loss caused by cluster munitions, nevertheless confirms the harmful impact those weapons can have on the enjoyment of human rights and, more particularly, the potential relevance of the ECtHR in the implementation of the Oslo Convention.

5. Conclusions

In the absence of traditional implementation and verification mechanisms, the role of the Court and the Committee of Ministers in the execution of judgments involving anti-personnel mines and chemical agents is significant.[163] The added value presented by this procedural opportunity is even more important when considering the nature of the execution of judgments procedure before the Committee of Ministers.[164] The latter is a multilateral forum where all the Foreign Ministers of the 47 Member States – or their deputies – meet several times a year. This being the case, a resolution such as that adopted in the case of *Paşa and Erkan Erol v. Turkey*, mentioned above, can easily influence other States Parties to the ECHR also bound by the Ottawa Convention.[165]

This *erga omnes* effect is another multiplying factor enhancing the positive impact that the system of the ECHR can have on treaties such as the Ottawa Convention, the CWC, or, potentially, the Oslo Convention.[166] The section on the implementation of arms control treaties has revealed allegations of representatives of civil society, in particular HRW and ICBL, of widespread use of cluster munitions and landmines in the ongoing conflict in Ukraine, a State Party to the ECHR. This effect is never the less not limited geographically to Europe since the Committee of Ministers' discussions on topics such as the Ottawa Convention and the CWC, both of which enjoy wide recognition and ratification, are likely to spill over to a universal level.[167]

D. INTERNATIONAL CRIMINAL COURT (ICC)

1. Introductory remarks

At the origin of the creation of the ICC stood the conviction that the most serious crimes concern the international community as a whole and that, therefore, it was

163 Rietiker, "Strange Bedfellows?", p. 154.
164 *Ibid.*
165 In theory, only the respondent State is formally bound by a final judgment; see Article 46 § 1 ECHR: "The High Contracting Parties undertake to abide by the final judgment of the Court in any case to which they are parties."
166 Rietiker, "Strange Bedfellows?", p. 154.
167 *Ibid.*

necessary to put an end to impunity for their perpetrators.[168] The ICC has jurisdiction in respect of genocide, crimes against humanity, war crimes, and the crime of aggression.[169] Article 1 of the Statute adds, however, that the ICC's action shall be "complementary" to that of national criminal courts. In other words, it is only where the national authorities cannot ensure an effective prosecution on their own that the ICC will open proceedings (principle of subsidiarity).[170] It is also relevant to recall that, in accordance with Article 27 of its Statute, the official position of a State agent responsible for a crime does not prevent the ICC from prosecuting that person.

It transpires from the preamble of the Rome Statute that the need to protect individuals, in particular vulnerable groups of victims, has been an important reason for adopting the treaty:

> *The States Parties to this Statute*,
>
> *Conscious* that all peoples are united by common bonds, their cultures pieced together in a shared heritage, and concerned that this delicate mosaic may be shattered at any time,
>
> *Mindful* that during this century millions of children, women and men have been victims of unimaginable atrocities that deeply shock the conscience of humanity,
>
> *Recognizing* that such grave crimes threaten the peace, security and well-being of the world . . .[171]

In addition, the aim of the ICC is not only the prosecution of actual perpetrators, but also the prevention of future crimes.[172] Moreover, certain rights of the victims are also taken into consideration in the Rome Statute, in particular the right to request reparation for the harm caused by criminal acts. Under paragraph 1 of Article 75 of the ICC Statute, the Court can order reparation of its own motion. Pursuant to paragraph 2 of that Article, the ICC can make such an order against the convicted person or order that reparation be made through the Trust Fund provided for in Article 79 of the Statute. Therefore, it can be argued that the ICC, while far from being a human rights instrument, has a positive bearing on the protection of individuals, in particular of the victims of crimes falling under the Court's jurisdiction. This justifies the inclusion of the ICC in the present Chapter.

168 See, in this sense, Articles 1 and 5, as well as paragraphs 4 and 5 of the preamble to the Rome Statute.
169 Article 5 ICC Statute.
170 Article 1 and paragraph 4 of the preamble to the ICC Statute.
171 Paragraphs 1–3 of the preamble (emphasis in the original). See, for a commentary, W. A. Schabas, *The International Criminal Court: A Commentary on the Rome Statute*, Oxford and New York 2010, pp. 31–53.
172 Paragraphs 5 and 9 of the preamble of the Rome Statute.

2. Prosecution for crimes committed by the use of chemical weapons, with particular attention to the potential role of the ICC in the war in Syria

In Resolution 2118(2013), the UNSC stressed that those responsible for any use of chemical weapons in Syria must be held accountable.[173] This almost naturally brings into discussion the possibility that the ICC might eventually deal with this conflict. Syria is not a State Party to the Rome Statute and the only possible way to refer the "situation" to the Prosecutor is through the UNSC acting under Chapter VII of the UN Charter.[174]

If this happens one day, two provisions on war crimes applying to non-international armed conflicts, such as the current conflict in Syria at the time of concluding this study, seem relevant, namely, Article 8.2.e(i), which prohibits "[i]ntentionally directing attacks against the civilian population as such or against individual civilians not taking direct part in hostilities," and Article 8.2.e(xiv) which prohibits "[e]mploying asphyxiating, poisonous or other gases, and all analogous liquids, materials or devices."[175] Whereas use of certain chemical weapons in international armed conflict, considered as prohibited not only by the 1925 Geneva Protocol, but also by customary international law,[176] had already been included in the list of war crimes adopted by the Rome Conference in 1998,[177] Article 8.2.e(xiv) was only introduced by the 2010 Kampala Review Conference on a proposal introduced one year earlier by Belgium and other co-sponsoring States.[178] The adoption, by consensus, of this amendment by the 84 States Parties to the ICC Statute that were present in Kampala is a strong indication that, today, the use of the gases covered by the 1925 Geneva Protocol is prohibited under customary international law also in non-international armed conflict.[179]

173 Paragraph 8 of the preamble and operative paragraph 15 of the Resolution.
174 Article 13(b) of the Rome Statute.
175 See, for a discussion of these issues, D. Akande, "Can the ICC Prosecute for Use of Chemical Weapons in Syria?", *EJIL: Talk!*, August 23, 2013, http://www.ejiltalk.org/can-the-icc-prosecute-for-use-of-chemical-weapons-in-syria/ (accessed February 20, 2017).
176 See this volume, Chapter 3, section A.2.b).
177 Article 8 § 2(b)(xviii) of the Rome Statute.
178 M. Asada, "A Path to a Comprehensive Prohibition of the Use of Chemical Weapons under International Law: From The Hague to Damascus," *Journal of Conflict & Security Law*, 2015, pp. 1–55, 45.
179 *Ibid.*, p. 46. The Resolution (ICC Doc. RC/Res.5, June 10, 2010, preamble, § 8) by which the amendment during the Kampala Review Conference was adopted mentions explicitly in its preamble that "the crimes referred to . . . in Article 8 § 2(e)(xiv) . . . are serious violations of the laws and customs applicable in armed conflict not of an international character, *as reflected in customary international law*" (emphasis added); see in this sense also J. M. Henckaerts and L. Doswald-Beck, *Customary International Humanitarian Law*, vol. I: *Rules*, Cambridge, 2005, pp. 259–263 (Rule 74 of the Study of Customary International Humanitarian Law); and, in contrast, two authors challenging the customary prohibition of use of chemical weapons in non-international armed conflict, J. Blake and A. Mahmud, "A Legal 'Red Line'? Syria and the Use of Chemical Weapons in Civil Conflict," *UCLA L.*

It can be recalled that the UNSC, in its Resolution 2118 adopted on September 27, 2013, "condemned the killing of civilians" resulting from the attacks in Ghouta in August 2013.[180] In addition, the reports from civil society, in particular HRW, indicate several attacks involving chemical weapons launched against the civilian populations between 2013 and 2016, including women and children, causing considerable numbers of deaths and serious injuries. Moreover, in its third report, dated August 24, 2016, the Panel established by the OPCW-UN Joint Investigative Mechanism reiterated its strong conviction that the use of chemicals as weapons, "for any reason and under any circumstances, is totally abhorrent" and that it was absolutely crucial to hold those who use or intend to use chemicals as weapons accountable for their acts.[181] Furthermore, it was convinced that it had enough information to reach a conclusion regarding the authors of the following three cases: regarding Talmenes (April 21, 2014), the Panel concluded that the incident was caused by a Syrian Arab Armed Forces helicopter dropping a device causing damage to the structure of a concrete block building, followed by the release of a toxic substance that affected large numbers of people.[182] A similar conclusion was reached for Sarmin (March 16, 2015), also involving the release by the Government Armed Forces of a toxic substance, matching the characteristics of chlorine, which was fatal to all six occupants. The remnants of the device are reported to be consistent with the construction of a barrel bomb.[183] Regarding Marea (August 21, 2015), the Panel concluded that Islamic State in Iraq and the Levant (ISIL) was the only entity with the ability, capability, motive, and means to use sulfur mustard.[184] Many other cases of use of chemical weapons and/or toxic chemicals have been reported, but their authors could not be clearly identified.[185] In any event, prosecution for "crime against humanity" does not seem excluded, defined as, inter alia, "murder," "when committed as part of a widespread or systematic attack directed against any civilian population, with knowledge of the attack."[186]

For the time being, this discussion is pure speculation. The question of whether the perpetrators of such serious violations of international law committed during the Syrian war will be held accountable one day depends on the UNSC, in particular on its permanent members. On the other hand, a referral to the ICC is not the only possible option to hold responsible the authors of these heinous acts.

Rev. Disc., vol. 61, 2013, pp. 244–260, http://www.uclalawreview.org/pdf/discourse/61-16.pdf (accessed February 20, 2017).

180 Paragraph 8 of the preamble to UNSC Resolution 2188. See also this volume, Chapter 3, section A.2.a).

181 UN Doc. S/2016/738, August 24, 2016, § 82.

182 *Ibid.*, § 54.

183 *Ibid.*, § 56.

184 *Ibid.*, § 58.

185 *Ibid.*, §§ 61–79.

186 Article 7 § 1(a) of the Rome Statute (see, for commentaries, on "murder," Schabas, *The ICC*, pp. 157–158, and on "widespread and systematic," *ibid.*, pp. 147–149).

Another solution could be the creation of an ad-hoc tribunal, following the examples of, inter alia, the ICTY or the ICTR, the Special Court for Sierra Leone (SCSL), the Special Tribunal for Lebanon (STL), and the Extraordinary Chambers in the Courts of Cambodia (ECCC).[187]

3. Potential prosecutions for crimes committed by use of anti-personnel or cluster munitions

The use of anti-personnel mines or cluster munitions was not explicitly included in the list of war crimes of the Rome Statute, due to a lack of consensus among the negotiating States.[188]

As far as anti-personnel mines are concerned, Nigeria was one of the States that had supported the inclusion of the use of mines within the scope of war crimes at the Rome Conference. As there was widespread agreement that a prohibition on the use of anti-personnel mines was not part of customary international law, many States supportive of the Ottawa Convention, including Canada, did not pursue this avenue actively.[189] The debate could not be resolved definitively and was therefore deferred for discussion at a future review conference. In fact, paragraph 2(b)(xx) of Article 8 of the Rome Statute allows the future expansion of the list of prohibited weapons through an amendment procedure.[190] This paragraph reads as follows:

> Employing weapons, projectiles and material and methods of warfare which are of a nature to cause superfluous injury or unnecessary suffering or which are inherently indiscriminate in violation of the international law of armed conflict, provided that such weapons, projectiles and material and methods of warfare are the subject of a comprehensive prohibition and are included in an annex to this Statute, by an amendment in accordance with the relevant provisions set forth in Articles 121 and 123.

187 Underlining the need for a holistic approach, the UN Commission of Inquiry on Syria found that the ICC is the most appropriate judicial mechanism to address the impunity in Syria (Report of the Independent International Commission of Inquiry on the Syrian Arab Republic, Doc. A/HRC/22/59, February 5, 2013, pp. 124–128).

188 See, for a commentary, Schabas, *The ICC*, pp. 243–247.

189 S. Maslen, *Commentaries on Arms Control Treaties*, vol. 1: *The Convention on the Prohibition of the Use, Stockpiling, Production, and Transfer of Anti-Personnel Mines and on Their Destruction*, 2nd edn., Oxford and New York, 2005, p. 259; see also Schabas, *The ICC*, p. 245.

190 See, for a commentary, M. Cottier and D. Krivánek, "Article 8 b) (xx)," in O. Triffterer and K. Ambos (eds.), *Rome Statute of the International Criminal Court, A Commentary*, 3rd edn., Munich, Oxford, and Baden-Baden, 2016, pp. 454–468, 467–468. Maslen, *Commentaries on Arms Control Treaties*, vol. 1, p. 71, is of the opinion that Article 8 § 2 b) (xx), through this formulation, sets a high threshold.

It has been demonstrated above that anti-personnel mines as well as cluster munitions are likely to qualify for being considered "weapons . . . which are of a nature to cause superfluous injury or unnecessary suffering or which are inherently indiscriminate in violation of the international law of armed conflict" within the meaning of this provision.[191]

No amendment was agreed upon at the 2010 Review Conference in Kampala either. In fact, Belgium had initially proposed one which, if accepted, would have made it a war crime to use cluster munitions in international or non-international armed conflicts, as prohibited by the Oslo Convention. This suggestion was later removed in response to concerns regarding the fact that the Oslo Convention had yet to enter into force.[192] This, however, does not mean that the use of cluster munitions could not fall into the category of war crimes under the Rome Statute. If such munitions are used in an international armed conflict as means for an attack intentionally directed against the civil population as such or against individual civilians, the perpetrators could be prosecuted under Article 8 § 2(b)(i) (in an international armed conflict) and § 2(e)(i) (non-international armed conflict) of the Rome Statute.[193] The same reasoning would apply, under Article 8 § 2(b)(v), if such weapons were used in an international armed conflict to attack or bombard towns, villages, dwellings, or buildings which are undefended and which do not constitute military objectives.[194]

In this regard, the case of *Milan Martić* before the ICTY is noteworthy. In early May 1995, ethnic Serb forces had fired cluster munitions by Orkan rocket against Zagreb. Orkan rockets are cluster munitions where each rocket contains 288 sub-munitions which in turn are equipped with 420 small steel balls.[195] These attacks were reported to have killed seven civilians and injured more than 200 others. On June 12, 2007, Milan Martić was convicted by the ICTY of "Violations of the laws or customs of war"[196] *and* crimes against humanity[197] and sentenced to 35 years' imprisonment, inter alia, for having ordered these attacks against civilians in Zagreb. The relevant paragraph of the judgment reads as follows:

> The evidence shows that the M-87 Orkan was fired on 2 and 3 May 1995 from the Vojnić area, near Slavsko Polje, between 47 and 51 kilometres from Zagreb. However, the Trial Chamber notes in this respect that the weapon was fired from the extreme of its range. Moreover, the Trial Chamber notes the characteristics of the weapon, it being a non-guided high dispersion

191 See above, Chapter 3, Section A.2.c).
192 A. Clapham, "Preamble (12th paragraph)," in G. Nystuen and S. Casey-Maslen (eds.), *The Convention on Cluster Munitions: A Commentary*, Oxford and New York, 2010, p. 68, n. 115.
193 See Schabas, *The ICC*, pp. 223–226.
194 For a commentary on this provision, see Schabas, *The ICC*, pp. 231 et seq.
195 Breitegger, *Cluster Munitions and International Law*, p. 69.
196 Article 3 of the Statute of the ICTY.
197 Article 5 of the Statute of the ICTY.

> weapon. The Trial Chamber therefore concludes that the M-87 Orkan, by virtue of its characteristics and the firing range in this specific instance, was incapable of hitting specific targets. For these reasons, the Trial Chamber also finds that the M-87 Orkan is an indiscriminate weapon, the use of which in densely populated civilian areas, such as Zagreb, will result in the infliction of severe casualties . . .[198]

The same events triggered other prosecutions. In its judgment of September 6, 2011, the Trial Chamber of the Tribunal found that Momčilo Perišić, chief of the General Staff of the Yugoslav Army (VJ) from August 1993 to November 24, 1998, exercised effective control over Yugoslav Army officers serving in the Army of Serbian Krajina (SVK). The Chamber established that, although Perišić was immediately notified of both of the SVK's rocket attacks on Zagreb, he had failed to take "necessary and reasonable measures" to punish the perpetrators, whose grave crimes were left unsanctioned. As a result, the Chamber held that Perišić was guilty of having failed to punish his subordinates for their crimes in Zagreb.[199] The Appeals Chamber, however, found that Perišić had not exercised effective control over members of the perpetrators of the crimes committed in Zagreb. On February 28, 2013, it therefore reversed Perišić's convictions for crimes against humanity and violations of the laws or customs of war and entered a verdict of acquittal.[200]

In spite of the final outcome in the latter instance, the two cases decided by the ICTY demonstrate the potential relevance of the ICC for the prosecutions of crimes committed by the use of cluster munitions and anti-personnel mines.

4. Conclusions

In conclusion, it can be asserted that the possibility of involvement of the ICC in the Syrian war, by the prosecution and punishment of the crimes committed by use of chemical weapons, especially against the civilian population, is further evidence for the relevance of the CWC for the protection of human beings. As far as the Ottawa and Oslo Conventions are concerned, even though anti-personnel mines and cluster munitions are not per se included in the ICC's list of prohibited weapons, their use might nevertheless be prosecuted as war crimes or crimes against humanity due to their indiscriminate nature, as indicated by the case law of the ICTY.

198 ICTY, *Prosecutor v. Milan Martić*, Judgment, Case No. IT-95-11-T, June 12, 2007, § 463. An appeal against this judgment was dismissed by the Appeals Chamber (see *Prosecutor v. Milan Martić*, Judgment, Case No. IT-95-11-A, October 8, 2008, in particular §§ 239 et seq.).

199 *Prosecutor v. Momčilo Perišić*, Judgment, Case No. IT-04-81-T, September 6, 2011.

200 *Prosecutor v. Momčilo Perišić*, Judgment, Case No. IT-04-81-A, February 28, 2013.

Part I conclusions

To sum up the Part on arms control treaties dealing with non-nuclear weapons, it has, first, been demonstrated that the borders between the rules applicable in armed conflict and in peacetime, on the one hand, and those applicable in international and non-international armed conflicts, on the other, have become blurred during the last decades. The CWC as well as the Ottawa and Oslo Conventions, which are all applicable in absolute terms, imposing on the States Parties the duty not to use, develop, produce, acquire, stockpile, or retain these weapons "never under any circumstances," fit well into this new legal landscape. The same is true of the new approach to security and development, namely human security and development, which suggests that the concerns for the protection of the human being are intrinsically linked to matters of security and development, replacing the traditional, exclusively State-centered approaches. It is obvious that the humanitarian disaster caused to the civil population by landmines or cluster munitions are tangible examples for this new trend.

As far as the involvement of civil society in the drafting history of the instruments is concerned, the support of the civil society turned out useful for the successful adoption of the CWC, in 1993, and its ratification by many States. It has furthermore been established that the negotiation and adoption of the Ottawa and Oslo Conventions have clearly been driven by humanitarian concerns. It was the civil society that took the lead, outside the traditional arms control machinery and supported by a group of like-minded States, in steering negotiations toward a legally binding instrument prohibiting anti-personnel mines in absolute terms. Thanks to the efforts of certain NGOs, the Ottawa Convention was concluded within a few months. A similar pattern has been successfully followed for the Oslo Convention. As far as the ATT is concerned, its recent adoption has correctly been called the "culmination" of almost two decades of campaigning by civil society. But here also, the ultimate breakthrough has come about thanks to certain States favoring the idea of restrictions in arms trade, in particular the United Kingdom, followed by other EU Member States and numerous African and Latin American countries.

Another element, perhaps the most important one to appreciate the relevance of the treaties examined for the protection of the human being, is the substantive contribution of the specific treaty regimes in this regard. It was noted that the positive impact on the individual generated by the CWC as well as the Ottawa and Oslo Convention is most obviously recognizable in the duty to refrain from using the prohibited weapons, as it transpires from their general clauses (Article I). The impact on the human being is twofold: first of all, from a humanitarian law perspective, since it imposes on the States Parties the duty not to use the weapons as a means of warfare. This aspect is even more important in light of the uncertainty surrounding the question of whether anti-personnel mines as well as cluster munitions comply with core principles of humanitarian law, in particular concerning proportionality, distinction and superfluous injury, and unnecessary suffering. These principles, as well as the Martens Clause, are explicitly referred to in the Ottawa and Oslo Conventions. The CWC is closely linked to the 1925 Geneva Protocol, which attests to its humanitarian logic.

But the instruments are also relevant for human rights law. Insofar as they prohibit the use of the targeted weapons in absolute terms, they protect the human being, in particular the civil population, in war as well as in peacetime. As a matter of fact, weapons such as anti-personnel mines and unexploded cluster munitions represent a significant danger to life and property long after the actual hostilities. The Ottawa and Oslo Conventions go even a step further by taking account of particularly vulnerable groups such as women, children, refugees, and internally displaced persons. Furthermore, these treaties take a victim-based approach by focusing on the dignity and the right to assistance of the injured persons. The CRPD, adopted only a few months before the Oslo Convention, has directly inspired and shaped the latter – another proof of the significant human rights dimension of this treaty.

The ATT constitutes an interesting and the most recent example of a treaty that builds a bridge between human rights, humanitarian law, and arms control law. Its relevance for the protection of the individual has been emphasized. From a theoretical point of view, this instrument hardly fits into the traditional categories and might best be described as being of a *sui generis* nature. The effectiveness and the humanitarian ideals of the ATT have, of course, still to be proven in the harsh realities of international relations and will depend largely on the good faith of the States Parties.

In all the four treaties examined, it has been observed that human rights law in a broad sense has to be taken into account, embracing civil and political rights, as well as economic, social, and cultural rights. A common feature of these treaties is their gender- and age-sensitivity, taking into account particularly vulnerable groups such as women and children.

It has also been shown that the circle of actors involved in the implementation and verification process of the CWC and the Ottawa and Oslo Conventions is surprisingly diverse. Those actors are traditionally advocating the protection of human rights or similar values of general interest. This underlines the relevance of these treaties for the protection of the individual.

It has further been observed that the CWC benefits from the significant support of the organization that administers it, namely the OPCW, which is an arms control institution in the more traditional sense. By contrast, the Ottawa and Oslo

Conventions cannot rely on such an institutional framework, but it was shown that civil society and, perhaps more surprisingly, the ECtHR and the Committee of Ministers of the Council of Europe compensate this gap to a large extent. The particular role of ICBL and the "Landmine and Cluster Munitions Monitor" in the implementation and verification of the Ottawa and Oslo Conventions cannot be overestimated. As far as the ATT is concerned, it is too early to assess the scope and effectiveness of civil society in the implementation and verification, but considering the relevance of this treaty for the human being, the involvement of NGOs in the long preparatory history of this treaty and in the implementation of predecessor mechanisms, civil society is expected to play a significant role on many different levels.

In the last subdivision, finally, it has been shown that the ICC may play a certain role in the implementation of the treaties examined in the present study. The crisis in Syria indicates that that court is likely to be of relevance in future prosecutions of authors of use of chemical weapons. Insofar as the ICC can produce a deterring and preventive effect on future behavior, it contributes to the protection of human rights and of coming generations, as rightly asserted in the preamble of the ICC.

Part II

Humanization of arms control treaties dealing with nuclear weapons

5 Scope of Part II

Apart from the ATT, the most recent but atypical arms control treaty, the first chapter of the present study focused on three very similar treaties aiming at eliminating entire categories of weapons. Instruments dealing with nuclear weapons are less homogenous, prohibiting very different behaviors. The geographical scope of the treaties also varies, ranging from bilateral to regional and universal instruments. Therefore, the selection of the instruments dealt with and the case studies presented in Part II will necessarily be more eclectic than in the first.

Bilateral treaties are largely excluded from this study, which will focus on multilateral and regional agreements.[1] Predominantly, the following treaties will be taken into consideration:

A. TREATY ON THE NON-PROLIFERATION OF NUCLEAR WEAPONS (NPT)

The main pillar of international security in the field of nuclear weapons is the Treaty on the Non-Proliferation of Nuclear Weapons (hereafter "NPT"), signed on July 1, 1968 after more than two decades of Cold War nuclear tension. Initially concluded for 25 years, it was extended indefinitely in 1995. Its adoption was motivated and guided to a large extent by security considerations of those States which had acquired nuclear weapons at the moment of the treaty's conclusion.

1 The most important bilateral treaties in the field of nuclear weapons have been concluded between the Soviet Union (later Russia) and the United States; see, inter alia, the SALT I Agreement of 1972 (including the ABM-Treaty), the SALT II Agreement of 1979, both on strategic arms limitation, the INF Treaty of 1987 on the elimination of intermediate-range and shorter-range missiles, the SORT Treaty of 2002 (sometimes also called the "Moscow Treaty"), aiming at the reduction of the number of operationally deployed strategic nuclear warheads, as well as the START I Treaty of 1991, the START II Treaty of 1993, and, finally, the NEW START Treaty of 2010, all dealing with the reduction and limitation of strategic offensive arms (see, for more details on these treaties, M. I. Shaker, "The Evolving International Regime of Nuclear Non-Proliferation," *Collected Courses of The Hague Academy of International Law*, vol. 321, pp. 9–202, in particular 147–150).

Indeed, the particularity of this instrument is that it draws a sharp distinction between two categories of States Parties and their respective obligations: on the one hand, the nuclear weapon States (NWS), as defined in Article IX(3),[2] which are under an obligation not to transfer nuclear weapons or other nuclear devices or control over such weapons or devices to any State (Article I). The obligations of the non-nuclear weapon States (NNWS), on the other hand, are not to receive the transfer from anyone of nuclear weapons or other nuclear explosive devices, or of the control over such weapons or devices, nor shall they manufacture or otherwise acquire nuclear weapons or other devices, nor seek or receive any assistance in the manufacture of nuclear weapons and other devices (Article II). Article III contains a safeguard provision concerning verification procedures, imposing on the NWS the obligation to conclude agreements with the International Atomic Energy Agency (IAEA) for the purpose of verifying the fulfilment of the obligations assumed under the treaty. These three provisions form the so-called first pillar of the NPT (the non-proliferation obligations). The second pillar preserves all States Parties' rights to use nuclear energy for peaceful purposes (Article IV). The third pillar, finally, is Article VI, the so-called nuclear disarmament obligation – the non-compliance with which is one of the main triggers of the current discussion on the humanitarian approach to nuclear weapons.[3] Finally, it is important to mention that the NPT does not as such prohibit the use of nuclear weapons.

B. TREATIES BANNING NUCLEAR TESTING

At the universal level,[4] two treaties banning nuclear testing were concluded. Having been devised and concluded, inter alia, for public health and environmental reasons,[5] they are relevant for the present study. First, the three powers which were conducting nuclear tests in the 1950s – the United States, the Soviet Union, and Great Britain – began negotiations that ultimately led to the conclusion, in Moscow, on August 5, 1963, of the Treaty Banning Nuclear Weapon Tests in the Atmosphere, in Outer Space and Under Water (also called "Partial Test Ban Treaty" or "Moscow Treaty," hereafter "PTBT").[6]

2 According to this provision, an NWS is one which has manufactured and exploded a nuclear weapon or other nuclear explosive device prior to January 1, 1967 – China, France, Great Britain, Russia, and the United States.

3 See, for more details of the three pillars, D. H. Joyner, *Interpreting the Nuclear Non-Proliferation Treaty*, Oxford and New York, 2011.

4 On the regional level, the treaties establishing nuclear-weapon-free zones, which will be mentioned below, also prohibit nuclear testing (see section C).

5 Regarding the PTBT, see R. Johnson, "Advocates and Activists: Conflicting Approaches on Nonproliferation and the Test Ban Treaty," in A. M. Florini (ed.), *The Third Force, The Rise of Transnational Civil Society*, Tokyo and Washington, 2000, pp. 49–81, 54.

6 *Ibid.* See also G. Venturini, "Test-Bans and the Comprehensive Test Ban Treaty Organization," in J. L. Black-Branch and D. Fleck (eds.), *Nuclear Non-Proliferation in International Law*, The Hague, 2014, pp. 133–158.

Second, during the three decades following the conclusion of the PTBT, efforts were made to expand the scope of the prohibition to test nuclear weapons imposed by that treaty.[7] Only in 1994, after the Soviet Union and the United States had declared national moratoria on nuclear tests,[8] multilateral negotiations with a view to a comprehensive ban took off, leading ultimately to the adoption,[9] on September 10, 1996, of the Comprehensive Test Ban Treaty (CTBT).[10] Despite the broad, almost unanimous support of its adoption[11] and the numerous subsequent signatures (183)[12] and ratifications (166),[13] the treaty has not yet entered into force, in particular due to its unfortunate entry-into-force clause (Article XIV), giving all States with nuclear power and/or research reactors, as listed in Annex 2 to the treaty, a veto power against the CTBT's entry into force.[14] The preparatory history of both the PTBT and the CTBT will be further explained in Chapter 6.

C. TREATIES ON THE DENUCLEARIZATION OF CERTAIN REGIONS (NUCLEAR-WEAPON-FREE ZONES, NWFZ)

The regional approach[15] to strengthen global nuclear non-proliferation and disarmament is of considerable practical relevance, considering in particular the

7 Venturini, "Test-Bans," pp. 142–143.

8 Moreover, the PTBT was supplemented by two consecutive bilateral treaties concluded between the Soviet Union and the United States, namely the Treaty on the Limitation of Underground Nuclear-Weapon Tests (Threshold Test Ban Treaty, TTBT) of July 3, 1974, and the Treaty on Underground Nuclear Explosions for Peaceful Purposes (Peaceful Nuclear Explosions Treaty, PNET) of May 28, 1976 (Shaker, "The Evolving International Regime," p. 151).

9 Venturini, "Test-Bans," p. 143.

10 See also, for an overview of the preparatory work to the CTBT, http://www.ctbto.org/the-treaty/ (accessed February 20, 2017).

11 The CTBT was adopted through UNGA Resolution A/RES/50/245, by 158 votes to three (Bhutan, India, and Libya), with five abstentions (Cuba, Lebanon, Mauritius, Syria, and Tanzania).

12 See https://www.ctbto.org/ (accessed February 20, 2017).

13 *Ibid.*

14 Venturini, "Test-Bans," p. 147. See, for comments on this clause, D. Rietiker, *Le régime juridique des traités de maîtrise des armements: Plaidoyer pour l'unité de l'ordre juridique international*, Berne and Brussels, 2010, pp. 346–349, including the articles referred to. At the moment, nine States mentioned in Annex 2 still have to ratify (China, Congo, DPRK, Egypt, India, Iran, Israel, Pakistan, and the United States).

15 At the universal level, treaties have been concluded to denuclearize certain zones: Antarctic Treaty (adopted on December 1, 1959), Treaty on Principles Governing the Activities of States in the Exploration and Use of Outer Space, including the Moon and other Celestial Bodies (January 27, 1967), Treaty on the Prohibition of the Emplacement of Nuclear Weapons and Other Weapons of Mass Destruction on the Sea-Bed and Ocean Floor and in the Subsoil Thereof (February 11, 1971), and the Agreement Governing the Activities of States on the Moon and Other Celestial Bodies (December 18, 1979).

lack of real progress in universal disarmament.[16] The ultimate goal of NWFZ is to insulate a region totally from the destructive effects of nuclear warfare in general, and from nuclear-weapons deployment and testing in particular.[17]

The legal basis for the group of treaties which have been concluded in the last few decades is Article VII NPT, which states that "[n]othing in this treaty affects the right of any group of States to conclude regional treaties in order to assure the total absence of nuclear weapons in their respective territories."[18] The close relationship that these treaties maintain with the NPT derives also from their procedural limb; in order to verify the respect of the obligations stemming from the regional treaties, the Parties undertake to conclude with the IAEA and bring into force agreements for the application of safeguards in accordance with the NPT.[19]

The pioneering initiative in this development originated in Latin America, which resulted in the adoption of the Tlatelolco Treaty in 1967.[20] According to Cançado Trindade, the establishment of these denuclearized regimes aims at the promotion of peace, at furthering considerations of humanity, and at meeting aspirations of humankind to rid the world of the threat of nuclear weapons forever.[21] Moreover, some of these treaties, contrary to the NPT, prohibit the use of nuclear weapons.[22] The following five treaties have so far been concluded:

- Treaty for the Prohibition of Nuclear Weapons in Latin America and Caribbean (February 14, 1967, hereafter "Treaty of Tlatelolco");
- South Pacific Nuclear Free Zone Treaty (August 6, 1985; hereafter "Rarotonga Treaty");
- Treaty on the South-East Asia Nuclear Weapon Free Zone (December 15, 1995, hereafter "Bangkok Treaty");
- African Nuclear-Weapon-Free Zone Treaty (April 11, 1996, hereafter "Pelindaba Treaty"); and

16 R. Thakur, "Stepping Stones to a Nuclear-Weapon-Free World," in R. Thakur (ed.), *Nuclear Weapons-Free Zones*, London and New York, 1998, pp. 3–32, 8.

17 *Ibid.*

18 As far as the concept of "nuclear-weapon-free zones" is concerned, the UNGA Resolution 3472 B (1975) defines such zones as "any zone recognised as such by the General Assembly of the United Nations, which any group of States, in the free exercises of their sovereignty, has established by virtue of a treaty or convention thereby: a) The statute of total absence of nuclear weapons to which the zone shall be subject, including the procedure for the delimitation of the zone, is defined; b) An international system of verification and control is established to guarantee compliance with the obligations deriving from that statute."

19 See, for instance, Article 8 of the Semipalatinsk Treaty or Article 5 of the Bangkok Treaty. See, for a general discussion of those regional treaties, Shaker, "The Evolving International Regime," in particular pp. 160–178.

20 See M. Serrano, "Latin America – The Treaty of Tlatelolco," in Thakur, *Nuclear Weapons-Free Zones*, pp. 35–58.

21 A. A. Cançado Trindade, *International Law for Humankind: Towards a New Jus Gentium*, 2nd edn., Leiden and Boston, 2013, pp. 405 et seq.

22 Article 1 § 1(a) of the Tlatelolco Treaty and Article 3 § 1(c) of the Bangkok Treaty.

- Treaty on a Nuclear-Weapon-Free Zone in Central Asia (September 8, 2006, hereafter "Semipalatinsk Treaty").

In other words, no less than five regions, and among them entire continents, are today subject to legally binding regimes of denuclearization: Latin America and the Caribbean, the South Pacific, Southeast Asia, Africa, and, most recently, Central Asia. Moreover, Mongolia has declared itself a nuclear-weapon-free State, a status which was internationally recognized by a resolution of the UNGA.[23]

The creation of such a zone in the Middle East has already been seriously discussed for many years.[24] It goes without saying that a legally binding instrument declaring this historically unstable and disputed region nuclear-free forever would constitute an important step for the peace process in the region and give hope for further steps leading to a world free of nuclear weapons. The idea of such a zone has nevertheless encountered a backlash at the NPT Review Conference in 2015, where the disagreement on a conference with a view to establishing such a zone led to the failure of the Conference, as the delegations had been unable to adopt a final document by consensus.[25]

Another aspect plays a significant role in these treaties. The NWS can proceed, by the ratification of protocols to these instruments, to a legally binding recognition of the status of the zones by engaging not to use or threaten to use nuclear weapons against States Parties to the treaties (negative security assurances), nor to contribute to any act that constitutes a violation of the Treaty or of its Protocol by Parties to them. These commitments are not only of a high symbolic character, but also of an appreciable practical importance since they restrict considerably, from a geographical point of view, the margin of maneuver of the NWS in the choice of their nuclear policy.[26] For example, four States recognized as NWS by the NPT (China, France, Russia, and the United Kingdom) ratified the Protocol to the Semipalatinsk Treaty, undertaking a commitment neither to use nuclear

23 UNGA Resolution 55/33S of November 20, 2000.

24 See, for a recent document on this topic, Resolution UNGA 66/25 of December 13, 2011 (Establishment of a nuclear-weapon free zone in the region of the Middle-East).

25 See, for instance, K. Davenport, "UN Acts on Mideast Zone Amid Doubts," *Arms Control Today*, December 2015, https://www.armscontrol.org/ACT/2015_12/News/UN-Acts-on-Mideast-Zone-Amid-Doubts (accessed February 23, 2017).

26 As the ICJ rightly pointed out in the 1996 Advisory Opinion on the *Legality of the Threat and Use of Nuclear Weapons* (para 59 b), not all the protocols have been ratified by all NWS and those that ratified made declarations and reservations. In the case of the Treaty of Rarotonga, for instance, China, when ratifying the 2nd Protocol to this treaty (on October 21, 1988), declared that "the Chinese Government reserves the right to reconsider these obligations if other nuclear weapon States of the contracting parties to the Treaty take action in gross violation of the Treaty and its attached Protocols, thus changing the status of the nuclear free zone and endangering the security interests of China." Such a reservation would have to be scrutinized against the provisions of the regime on reservations under the 1969 VCLT (Articles 19–23) and, moreover, repeats in substance Article 6 of the Protocol that allows withdrawal under certain circumstances.

weapons nor to threaten to do so, against the five States-Parties to this instrument and, as a result, making Central Asia entirely free of nuclear weapons.[27]

After this brief summary of the instruments that will be dealt with in Part II, Chapter 6 will examine the question of to what extent considerations of humanity have played a role in the adoption of certain instruments and to what extent civil society has been involved in their preparation. These considerations are preceded by an introduction on the origins of the antinuclear movement.

27 See, for the text of the Protocol: http://disarmament.un.org/treaties/t/canwfz_protocol/text (accessed March 6, 2017).

6 The preparatory history of the relevant treaties, and in particular the role played by civil society

A. ORIGINS OF THE ANTINUCLEAR MOVEMENT

The event which suddenly changed not only the course of World War II, but also that of human history, was the explosion of the first nuclear weapon in the desert at Alamogordo, New Mexico, on July 16, 1945, followed by the bombings by the United States of Hiroshima, on August 6, 1945, and of Nagasaki, on August 9, 1945.[1] The beginning of this new era, the "Nuclear Age," resulted in the birth of a movement strongly opposing this new weapon. That movement was, on the one hand, largely built up by already existing actors, including civil, education, and pacifist organizations, churches, and women's organizations.[2] On the other hand, and due to the special features of the new type of weapon, in particular its technical complexity, the exact implications of the use of nuclear weapons were virtually out of reach for the political elite, the military leaders, and, above all, ordinary citizens. Therefore, the new era swept an additional group into the peace movement, namely, the relatively small but powerful group of concerned scientists and other professionals.[3] Indeed, who but the persons involved in the development and production of these weapons could have been more qualified subsequently to take the lead against their use?

After having realized that fascist Germany was unable to build nuclear weapons and, in particular, after the defeat of Hitler's armies, the scientists who had been involved in the "Manhattan Project," the American nuclear weapons program, no longer saw a justification for their efforts, even though Japan continued waging war.[4] One of the prestigious members of this new movement of scientists was

1 M. E. Lord, "Nongovernmental Organizations in Arms Control and Disarmament," in R. D. Burns (ed.), *Encyclopedia of Arms Control and Disarmament*, vol. 1/II, New York, Oxford, Singapore, and Sydney, 1993, pp. 405–424, 412.
2 Lord, "Nongovernmental Organizations," p. 412.
3 *Ibid.*
4 R. Maiocchi, *L'ère atomique*, Florence,1993, p. 32. See, for more details on the Manhattan Project, L. S. Wittner, *One World or None: A History of the World Nuclear Disarmament Movement through 1953*, vol. I, Stanford, 1993, pp. 8–11, 31–34.

Albert Einstein, who previously, by a confidential letter addressed to President Franklin D. Roosevelt, had encouraged the development of the nuclear weapon, fearing that Nazi Germany might develop and use it first.[5] Moreover, some scientists involved in the Manhattan Project sought to control its spread and use and, at the end of the war in 1945, founded the Federation of Atomic Scientists, the precursor of the Federation of American Scientists, pointing out that "the value of science to civilization has never been more clear, nor have the dangers of its misuse been greater."[6] The same year, the *Bulletin of the Atomic Scientists* was founded and became one of the principal publications of the US non-governmental arms control community.[7] On July 9, 1955, Albert Einstein and Bertrand Russell issued a manifesto (*Russell-Einstein Manifesto*) among scientists reminding scientists that the already escalating nuclear arms race could only exist thanks to their cooperation and calling on them to confront the danger of nuclear war.[8]

Another prominent nuclear scientist who changed his mind about nuclear weapons was Leonard Szilard, a Hungarian Jew who had fled German persecution. Obsessed by the idea of a Nazi military victory,[9] he was co-author of the above-mentioned letter to President Roosevelt explaining the possibility and advantages of nuclear weapons, and became later directly responsible for the Manhattan Project.[10] Once the scientists of the Manhattan Project had been informed about the plan of launching a nuclear attack against Japan, a group around Szilard and James Franck,[11] another Jewish scientist who left Germany in 1933, drafted a report ("Franck Report"), dated June 11, 1945, recommending not to use the atomic bomb directly against Japan to prompt its surrender, but to use it as a mere means of deterrence in order to intimidate the enemy through an explosion at a remote place in the desert.[12]

5 *Ibid.*, p. 25; Lord, "Nongovernmental Organizations," p. 412.

6 The group included Hans Bethe, George Kistiakowsky, Philip Morrison, and Victor Weisskopf (Lord, "Nongovernmental Organizations," p. 412). The Federation of Atomic Scientists never had more than 3 000 members, but it drew together some 90 percent of the Manhattan Project scientists (Wittner, L. S. and Cooper, S., "Transnational Peace Movements and Arms Control: The Nineteenth and Twentieth Centuries,", in R. D. Burns (ed.), *Encyclopedia of Arms Control and Disarmament*, New York, 1993, p. 498).

7 Lord, "Nongovernmental Organizations," p. 412. It was edited by Eugene Rabinowitch and, for a certain time, by Hyman Goldsmith (Wittner, *One World or None*, vol. I, p. 60). See, for its homepage, http://thebulletin.org/ (accessed February 23, 2017).

8 Lord, "Nongovernmental Organizations," p. 412. Based on the manifesto, a small group of scientists met two years later in Pugwash, Nova Scotia, in order to take up the challenge (see also this volume, Chapter 2, section A).

9 Wittner, *One World or None*, vol. I, p. 9. For more details about Leonard Szilard, see *ibid.*, pp. 5 et seq.

10 Maiocchi, *L'ère atomique*, p. 23.

11 In 1925, James Franck had received the Nobel Prize in Physics.

12 Maiocchi, *L'ère atomique*, pp. 33 et seq. The report contained, for instance, the following warning by the committee: "If the United States were to be the first to release this new weapon of indiscriminate destruction upon mankind, she would sacrifice public support throughout the word, precipitate the race for armaments, and prejudice the possibility of

An overview of the early movement against nuclear weapons would not be complete without mentioning those who suffered the horrors of the first two uses of these weapons, namely, the citizens of Hiroshima and Nagasaki, the so-called "Hibakusha" (atomic bomb-affected persons).[13] As a matter of fact, the two cities in ruins became powerful symbols of world peace, and they have been organizing various activities since 1946, such as popular peace demonstrations, festivals, and poetry readings in memory of the dead.[14] Today, victims still testify to the bombings and to their miraculous survival, as well as to their desperate search in the ruins for their family members.[15] Moreover, August 6 was declared World Peace Day and Hiroshima became a Peace Memorial City. Today, still, the two cities stand for the first victims of nuclear war and their terrible sufferings.[16]

In light of the foregoing, it can be said that the movement against nuclear weapons is as old as the weapons themselves. It grew out of the anticipation of the disastrous and destructive consequences that the use of such a weapon would have. It was made up, on the one hand, of a broad popular peace movement and, on the other hand, of a smaller group but with great authority, namely, the concerned scientists.[17] At first sight, the front of these scientists against nuclear weapons might look surprising, but one must consider the fact that they had been directly involved in the construction of that complex weapon and, therefore, they were the only ones to understand the consequences of its use. Or, as a commentator put it, "seen as the Pandoras guilty of opening the nuclear box, scientists have sought to apply their abilities to ensuring that a cataclysmic nuclear war will not occur."[18]

To reach its goals, the new movement developed very effective means of outreach, in particular relevant publications such as the *Bulletin of the Atomic Scientists*.[19] Finally, the engagement and activities of the victims and survivors of

reaching an international agreement on the future control of such weapons" (Wittner, *One World or None*, vol. I, pp. 25 et seq.).

13 Wittner, *One World or None*, vol. I, p. 46.

14 *Ibid.*

15 See, for some testimonies, Soka Gakkai Hiroshima Peace Committee Hiroshima, *6 August 1945, A Silence Broken*, Tokyo, 2014.

16 Wittner, *One World or None*, vol. I, pp. 48–50.

17 See, for an overview of the World Peace Movement in 1945, Wittner, *One World or None*, vol. I, pp. 40–45. Along with the pacifists and the scientists, he mentions the "World Government Movement," inspired, inter alia, by H. G. Wells's work, *The Shape of Things to Come*, published in 1933 (*ibid.*, p. 44). It grew considerably with the emergence of the nuclear weapon (*ibid.*, pp. 66–71).

18 E. Arnett, "Science, Technology, and Arms Control," in R. D. Burns (ed.), *Encyclopedia of Arms Control and Disarmament*, vol. 1/II, New York, Toronto, Oxford, Singapore, and Sydney, 1993, pp. 477–490, 484. President Ronald Reagan invoked the responsibility of scientists in his 1983 "Star Wars" speech in the following words: "I call upon the scientific community in our country, those who gave us nuclear weapons, to turn their great talents now to the cause of mankind and world peace, to give us the means of rendering these nuclear weapons impotent and obsolete" (*ibid.*, p. 484).

19 Wittner, *One World or None*, vol. I, p. 60.

Hiroshima and Nagasaki have played – and continue to play – a considerable role in the movement.

This summary of the early reactions against nuclear weapons will be followed by a closer look at the preparatory history of certain treaties and, in particular, at the input of civil society in the phases preceding the negotiation of certain treaties restricting these weapons.

B. TREATIES BANNING NUCLEAR WEAPONS TESTS

1. Lobbying in favor of the PTBT (1963)

By 1957, when Great Britain joined the US–Soviet Union arms race by conducting its first hydrogen bomb test, nuclear testing had become "a burning issue," according to Valerian Zorin, the Soviet Ambassador to the United Nations.[20] By 1960, the nuclear powers had tested hundreds of weapons in order to develop more powerful ones.[21] In parallel, new antinuclear groups formed during the late 1950s. Opposing nuclear testing and increasing pressure for a test ban, they were particularly concerned about the health effects of the nuclear tests and the arms race.[22]

Some physicians in Boston, alarmed by the danger of nuclear fallouts, founded the organization "Physicians for Social Responsibility" in 1961.[23] One year later, they published, in the *New England Journal of Medicine*, an article on the medical consequences of nuclear war. This first public attempt to predict casualty levels of thermonuclear weapons in an urban context revealed to the public what the use of nuclear weapons would mean to ordinary citizens.[24] Many joint efforts were undertaken by physicians, dentists, and scientists to demonstrate the dangers of radioactive fallout from nuclear testing.[25] One of them was the "baby teeth campaign" of 1962 to 1963. Dentists collected baby teeth from all over the United States and sent them to the Greater St. Louis Citizens Committee for Nuclear Information, where a team of scientists measured the level of Strontium 90, a radioactive element which could only have come from radioactive fallout deposited in the teeth. The results demonstrated that this element had entered the food chain and posed a serious threat, particularly to children.[26] The alarming

20 Quoted in J. Goldblat and D. Cox, *Nuclear Weapons Tests: Prohibition or Limitation?*, Stockholm and Oxford, 1988, p. 97.

21 Lord, "Nongovernmental Organizations," p. 413.

22 *Ibid.*; and R. Johnson, "Advocates and Activists: Conflicting Approaches on Nonproliferation and the Test Ban Treaty," in A. M. Florini (ed.), *The Third Force, The Rise of Transnational Civil Society*, Tokyo and Washington, 2000, pp. 49–81, p. 54.

23 Lord, "Nongovernmental Organizations," p. 413.

24 *Ibid.*

25 *Ibid.*

26 *Ibid.*

results of the campaign helped to create a popular international movement and to step up pressure on the States conducting nuclear tests.[27]

Moreover, campaigning techniques and increased awareness took new forms. In 1962, Leonard Szilard founded the Council for a Livable World, the first organization devoted exclusively to lobbying for arms control and to supporting candidates for the Senate who favored arms control.[28] A significant contribution to the ultimate conclusion of the PTBT was played by Norman Cousins, a politically engaged journalist who founded, in 1957, the "National Committee for a Sane Nuclear Policy." After having been instrumental in launching a world-wide campaign against nuclear weapons testing and the nuclear arms race by sensitizing public opinion and mobilizing personalities such as Albert Schweitzer and Jawaharlal Nehru, he later became a decisive "behind-the-scenes" player between Washington and Moscow in the negotiations that ultimately led to the conclusion of the PTBT.[29] Indeed, his diplomatic maneuvering, including confidential meetings with President Kennedy and a visit to Khrushchev in April 1963, thus only four months before the conclusion of this treaty in Moscow in August of the same year, is considered to be one of the decisive factors in the preparation of the treaty.[30] According to Lawrence S. Wittner, Cousins's value to Kennedy and Khrushchev lay in the respect which he inspired in each of them as a leader of the world nuclear disarmament movement.[31]

The political event that ultimately turned the scales occurred in October 1962, when the United States detected Soviet nuclear missiles in Cuba and requested their removal. The Cuban missile crisis, which was only one of a series of dangerous episodes in the middle of the Cold War between 1960 and 1962, brought the superpowers to the brink of nuclear war before the Soviet Union agreed to withdraw the missiles.[32] This experience created the political climate in the United States that allowed President Kennedy, followed by President Johnson, to push toward a series of arms control agreements, including the PTBT, which was concluded in Moscow on August 5, 1963.[33] The new treaty was restricted to banning nuclear weapon tests in the atmosphere, outer space, and under water and, therefore, removed the visible mushroom clouds. As a result, and having regard to the fact that civil society's successful campaign had focused on the health

27 *Ibid.*

28 *Ibid.*

29 L. S. Wittner, *Resisting the Bomb, A History of the World Nuclear Disarmament Movement, 1954–1970*, vol. II, Stanford, 1997, p. 425.

30 *Ibid.*

31 *Ibid.* See, for more details on Cousins's role in the negotiations toward the PTBT, *ibid.*, pp. 415–425.

32 Lord, "Nongovernmental Organizations," p. 413. This author mentions the other difficult moments that the newly elected President John F. Kennedy had to face between 1960 and 1962, namely the Bay of Pigs invasion, threatened Communist intervention in Laos, the newly independent Congo, collapse of the summit talks in Vienna with Nikita Khrushchev, and a crisis in Berlin.

33 *Ibid.*, pp. 413 et seq.

risks from nuclear fallout, the antinuclear movement lost its dynamism once the PTBT had been concluded, although a complete test ban remained the ultimate goal for many.[34]

To sum up, it is obvious that the negative impact of nuclear testing on the health of populations and the anticipation of the disastrous consequences of an actual use of such weapons were the main motivations behind the movement's efforts to push the issue on the international agenda. On a political level, the Cuban missile crisis was the trigger for the negotiations between the United States and the Soviet Union toward a binding instrument restricting nuclear tests.

2. The long way toward the CTBT

a) Introductory remarks

After the significant role played by civil society and, especially, scientific circles in the adoption of the PTBT, the next important arms control agreement, the NPT concluded in 1968, is considered more of a product of governments' calculations and security assessments than a response to pressure by civil society.[35] Launched by Ireland in 1958, the NPT was pushed by major military powers from 1965 onward, after they had realized that the value of their own nuclear forces would be at stake if many other States acquired nuclear capability.[36]

In the meantime, civil society, with varying intensity and strength, pursued its efforts for a total ban on nuclear testing because the PTBT was largely viewed as a first step toward a more comprehensive prohibition on nuclear testing.[37] The international antinuclear movement, between the conclusion of the PTBT in 1963 and the beginning of the final negotiations toward the CTBT in the early 1990s, was very diverse insofar as it involved well-established as well as new actors and used new strategies and tactics.[38] For instance, civil society's strategists began to

34 Johnson, "Advocates and Activists," pp. 54 et seq.; and Cooper and Wittner, *op.cit.*, pp. 501 et seq.

35 Johnson, "Advocates and Activists," p. 54. This author adds that this perception did not change in the following years. As a result, the decision on the indefinite extension of the NPT, due in 1995, was ignored by many NGOs. Considering the NPT largely as an instrument of the nuclear status quo, the majority opposed indefinite extension, but was neither organized nor efficient enough to campaign against it (*ibid.*, p. 57).

36 *Ibid.*, p. 54.

37 P. S. Corden, "Historical Context and Steps to Implement the CTBT," in M. Melamud, P. Meerts, and I. W. Zartman (eds.), *Banning the Bang or the Bomb? Negotiating the Nuclear Test Ban Regime*, Cambridge, 2014, pp. 17–31, 19. He indicates that the conclusion of a CTBT in 1963 failed because the United States and the USSR could not agree on on-site inspections and on the issue of placing seismic stations.

38 A new organization, Parliamentarians for Global Action (PGA), a group of legislators from all over the world, was established in Washington, DC in 1978/79 and organized an international campaign against all nuclear testing, joined by the Six Continent Peace Initiative – heads of State of Argentina, India, New Zealand, Kenya, Sweden, and Mexico (Lord, "Nongovernmental Organizations," p. 419).

interact closely with the more active States' delegations in order to seek constructive solutions.[39] For the first time, the movement also resorted to high-profile direct action, in which Greenpeace played a crucial role.[40] Moreover, the movement expanded geographically – the "Nevada-Semipalatinsk" movement revealing itself to be the first genuinely indigenous emergence of antinuclear activism in Soviet civil society.[41] Given that their action turned out to be instrumental for the national moratoria which ultimately made it possible to negotiate the final conclusion of the CTBT, the considerations that follow are dedicated to these two movements: the first engaging in direct, non-violent action, and the second focusing on building public and grassroots movements.[42]

b) Greenpeace (direct, non-violent activism)

One of the best-known NGOs in the environmental and antinuclear fields is Greenpeace, which had been founded by a group of like-minded young people in Vancouver in 1971 to oppose nuclear testing by the United States in Alaska.[43] Soon thereafter, Greenpeace challenged the French nuclear tests in the South Pacific. In the following years, it grew from the "boy's sailing club with a conscience"[44] into "Greenpeace International," an important global organization with several ships. Although it worked on a number of environmental issues, it became famous through its actions against nuclear testing and against the slaughter of whales and seals, provoking its characteristic "David-against-Goliath" confrontations on the sea.[45] It was one of those direct actions that had an unexpected and tragic end.[46] On July 10, 1985, Greenpeace's flagship "Rainbow Warrior" was bombed as it lay at anchor in Auckland Harbor, New Zealand, just as it was about to head off to protest against French nuclear testing in Moruroa, in the South Pacific.[47] The explosion killed a Greenpeace photographer and caused an international incident. After initial confusion, the perpetrators turned out to be French secret service agents trying to prevent the disruption of France's nuclear testing program.[48]

39 These included Australia, Brazil, Canada, the Netherlands, Germany, Japan, Mexico, Indonesia, Iran, and Egypt (Johnson, "Advocates and Activists," p. 55).
40 Johnson calls this period the "wilderness years" ("Advocates and Activists," p. 55).
41 *Ibid.*, p. 56.
42 This distinction is drawn by R. Johnson, "The Role of Civil Society in Negotiating the CTBT," in Melamud et al., *Banning the Bang or the Bomb?*, pp. 96–119, 101.
43 Johnson, "Advocates and Activists," p. 58.
44 *Ibid.* The origin of this description, often used in the 1980s, is not known (*ibid.*, n. 14).
45 *Ibid.*
46 *Ibid.*, p. 59.
47 *Ibid.*; and L. S. Wittner, *Toward Nuclear Abolition: A History of the World Nuclear Disarmament Movement, 1971 to the Present*, vol. III, Stanford, 2003, p. 377.
48 The captured French agents entered into a plea bargain with New Zealand and were sentenced to ten years. Later, the French Government signed an agreement with New Zealand for placing them in French custody, but violated it by releasing the agents (Wittner, *Toward Nuclear Abolition*, vol. III, p. 378).

Despite this incident, Greenpeace continued its high-profile actions against nuclear testing around the globe. Thus, in October 1990, the "MV Greenpeace" was intercepted by the KGB[49] after sending an inflatable dinghy manned by some campaigners and equipped with radiation detectors to the Soviet test site at Novaya Zemlya.[50] The ship and its crew were detained for several days, causing worldwide protests. On October 8, 1990, the Soviet Union carried out the planned test, facing massive criticism.[51] At the time, no one knew that this would be the last test carried out by the Soviet Union; only one year later, on October 5, 1991, President Gorbachev announced a unilateral test moratorium.[52] In parallel, Greenpeace also campaigned successfully in favor of UK, US, and French moratoria.[53] As far as France was concerned, Greenpeace returned to Moruroa with a new "Rainbow Warrior" and smuggled out some samples of lagoon water in order to prove the harm caused to flora and fauna by nuclear testing.[54] Once the results had been published in September 1991, revealing the presence of radioactive plutonium and cesium, and calls for an independent investigation having been ignored by the French Government, Greenpeace hung a large banner from the *Arc de Triomphe* in Paris exclaiming "*Non aux essais.*"[55] In April 1992, France followed the Russian example and announced a unilateral moratorium on testing.[56]

It is certain that the pressure built up by Greenpeace's direct and spectacular actions have played a significant role in the decisions of the Soviet Union and France to stop nuclear testing and, more generally, in the developments leading to negotiations for concluding the CTBT. As far as France is concerned, Rebecca Johnson suggests that it was tactically very wise by Greenpeace to play the science and "soft" health and environmental cards against the last round of tests rather than insisting on the confrontational approach, as Greenpeace had done before.[57]

Whatever the importance of the organization's influence on the memoranda on nuclear testing might have been, the following section will explain to what extent another entity, the Kazakh "Nevada-Semipalatinsk" movement, was even more directly relevant for the Soviet moratorium on nuclear tests.

49 KGB was the Committee of State Security of the Soviet Union (*Комитет государственной безопасности*).

50 Johnson, "Advocates and Activists," p. 60.

51 *Ibid.*

52 *Ibid.*

53 Regarding Greenpeace's actions against UK and US testing, see Johnson, "Advocates and Activists," p. 60.

54 *Ibid.* Moreover, the naturalist Jacques Cousteau revealed deep cracks in the coral atoll where French nuclear tests had been conducted (Johnson, "The Role of Civil Society," p. 107).

55 Johnson, "Advocates and Activists," p. 61.

56 *Ibid.* On June 13, 1995, President Jacques Chirac announced that, even though France would sign the CTBT in the future, it was resuming nuclear testing in the Pacific that September (Wittner, *Toward Nuclear Abolition*, vol. III, p. 462).

57 *Ibid.*

c) The "Nevada-Semipalatinsk" movement (grassroots movement)

One of the most astonishing initiatives against nuclear testing, less known and less spectacular than Greenpeace's actions, arose in Kazakhstan, around the Soviet Union's main test site, called "Polygon," which was located around 150 kilometers from Semipalatinsk, a town of over 300 000 inhabitants.[58] Since 1949, at least 300 nuclear explosions, including numerous atmospheric detonations, had occurred there.[59] Through the conclusion of the PTBT in 1963, atmospheric tests were officially banned, but insufficient safeguards resulted in roughly one out of three of the subsequent underground tests reaching surface level.[60] The impact of the nuclear test program on the surrounding environment and population, in particular on the inhabitants of the city of Semipalatinsk, was disastrous, causing a human tragedy that will be remembered for generations.[61] The suffering endured by local populations exposed to nuclear testing will be described in the chapter on nuclear weapons testing.[62]

In February 1989, after a moratorium which lasted more than one and a half years, the Soviet Union conducted a new series of nuclear tests at Semipalatinsk, two of which released unexpected amounts of radioactive gases into the environment.[63] This pollution was denounced by Olzhas Suleimenov, a renowned Kazakh poet and member of the USSR Supreme Soviet, during a televised awards presentation on February 26, 1989, calling on concerned citizens to meet two weeks later to demonstrate in favor of the closing of the test site of Semipalatinsk.[64] Suleimenov's commitment to civil rights issues was genuine and he was well respected by all ethnic groups throughout Kazakhstan. He possessed the necessary credibility among both Kazakhs and Russians and, as a result, turned out to be the ideal person to embark on what he had triggered by his call.[65] The movement,

58 T. Edmunds, "The Environmental Movement in Kazakstan: Ecology, Democracy and Nationalism," in S. Hussey and P. Thompson (eds.), *The Roots of Environmental Consciousness: Popular Tradition and Personal Experience*, London and New York, 2000, pp. 139–159, 140 et seq.

59 D. J. Peterson, *Troubled Lands: The Legacy of Soviet Environmental Destruction*, Boulder, San Francisco, and Oxford, 1993, p. 202. The first test was conducted on August 29, 1949 (*ibid.*).

60 B. Dave, "Kazakhstan Staggers under Its Nuclear Burden," *Transition*, November 17, 1997, pp. 12–13.

61 Edmunds, "The Environmental Movement in Kazakstan," pp. 140 et seq.

62 This volume, Chapter 7, section C.5.

63 Johnson, "Advocates and Activists," p. 63; and Edmunds, "The Environmental Movement in Kazakstan," p. 146.

64 Johnson, "Advocates and Activists," p. 63; Wittner, *Toward Nuclear Abolition*, vol. III, p. 418; Edmunds, "The Environmental Movement in Kazakstan," p. 146; and Peterson, *Troubled Lands*, p. 204.

65 Edmunds, "The Environmental Movement in Kazakstan," p. 146. He was described to be "a Kazakh who spoke and wrote in Russian and was in many ways more at home in a Russian environment than a Kazakh one" (S. Akiner, *The Formation of Kazakh Identity, From Tribe to Nation-State*, London, 1995, pp. 56 et seq.).

through Suleimenov's membership in the Supreme Soviet, but also thanks to sympathetic parliamentarians, maintained close contact with Moscow.[66] Moreover, it received favorable press coverage, even in the government newspaper *Izvestiya*.[67]

The popular response to Suleimenov's call was overwhelming. Indeed, 5 000 people flocked to the meeting in Almaty, many standing outside, in the winter chill, listening to the loudspeakers transmitting the proceedings. Inside the meeting hall, participants voted for shutting down the Semipalatinsk test site, an end to nuclear weapons production, and a universal ban on nuclear testing.[68] Inspired by reports of demonstrations at the Nevada test site in the United States, they called themselves "Nevada," but the initiative was later referred to as the "Nevada-Semipalatinsk" movement. Symbolically, it later used the logo of a native Kazakh sharing a peace pipe with a Native American.[69] The movement grew quickly and soon organized demonstrations and meetings throughout Kazakhstan, some at the very border of the test site.[70] Within the next few months, the movement launched a petition signed by over a million people, calling for an end to nuclear testing.[71] Thousands of letters and telegrams expressing support for the aims of the movement, as well as charitable donations, were received.[72] On August 6, 1989, 50 000 people attended an antinuclear rally in order to commemorate the Hiroshima bombing, the largest independent event of this kind ever witnessed in the Soviet Union.[73]

In order to push their cause, the movement relied heavily on testimonies of local people and victims of the nuclear tests carried out in Semipalatinsk. A local teacher reported to a journalist in 1990:

> When a test was about to be carried out, we were driven from our houses to the riverside, even at night, and told to push wool into our ears. The light was so bright you could not see a needle on the ground. I saw the yellow and red mushroom clouds and felt the earthquakes. Once my father was sitting near a window and the window smashed and cut his face. During the last blast aboveground, in 1963, the door flew off the oven and fire was thrown into the room, almost blinding my younger brother. On another occasion, the roof fell in and crushed to death a young woman.[74]

66 Peterson, *Troubled Lands*, p. 204.
67 *Ibid.*
68 Wittner, *Toward Nuclear Abolition*, vol. III, p. 418.
69 *Ibid.*
70 Edmunds, "The Environmental Movement in Kazakstan," p. 147; and Peterson, *Troubled Lands*, p. 204.
71 Edmunds, "The Environmental Movement in Kazakstan," p. 146; and Peterson, *Troubled Lands*, p. 204.
72 Edmunds, "The Environmental Movement in Kazakstan," p. 146.
73 Wittner, *Toward Nuclear Abolition*, vol. III, pp. 418 et seq. Following an ancient custom of Kazakhstan of flinging stones into the face of evil, thousands of citizens hurled rocks toward the test site in Semipalatinsk (*ibid.*).
74 *The European*, June 1–3, 1990 (reprinted in Peterson, *Troubled Lands*, p. 202).

The movement spawned various offsprings, such as the Union of Nuclear Test Victims and the Relief Fund for Nuclear Test Victims all over Kazakhstan,[75] and activated a broad range of people, from the intelligentsia to the working class, villagers as well as local professionals and politicians.[76] Moreover, an alliance was forged with the new "Novaya Zemlya-Nevada Committee" to obtain the closing down of the test site in Novaya Zemlya, an archipelago along the eastern edge of the Barents Sea.[77]

The movement also took an international dimension. Suleimenov visited the United States, in December 1989, to consult with the American antinuclear leaders. Ties were established and maintained with Western antinuclear movements, including Greenpeace.[78] In May 1990, the Nevada-Semipalatinsk movement and the International Physicians for the Prevention of Nuclear War (IPPNW) jointly organized the International Citizen's Congress for a Nuclear Test Ban, attracting hundreds of Soviet and other non-governmental participants to Kazakhstan.[79] It included gatherings of bomb survivors and nuclear test victims from the Soviet Union, the United States, Japan, and the South Pacific, who shared stories on cancer, genetic deformations, and leukemia caused by nuclear weapons.[80] Participants agreed that a global coalition would be necessary to end nuclear testing and, as a result, established the Nevada-Semipalatinsk-Moruroa International Movement to Halt Nuclear Weapons Testing.[81]

Another antinuclear meeting organized by the Nevada-Semipalatinsk movement was held in Almaty in late Summer 1993. It called for the creation of a global antinuclear alliance and published data indicating that a zone of ecological danger and radioactive threat to the environment comprised not only the Semipalatinsk region, but also the Almaty area, which was affected by nuclear explosions conducted by China on its Lop Nor test site.[82] In 1993, the movement revealed that, since the mid-1960s, at least 17 underground nuclear explosions had occurred in Western Kazakhstan. Moreover, scientists drew attention to the fact that that region, for the most part situated in the latitude of 45 degrees north,

75 M. Laumulin, "Kazakhstan's Nuclear Policy and the Control of Nuclear Weapons," in G. Quester (ed.), *The Nuclear Challenge in Russia and the New States of Eurasia*, New York and London, 1995, pp. 181–211, 188.

76 Johnson, "Advocates and Activists," p. 64; and Peterson, *Troubled Lands*, p. 204.

77 For Suleimenov, only the closing of the Semipalatinsk site was acceptable, always excluding a "transfer" of nuclear tests to the northern site (Wittner, *Toward Nuclear Abolition*, vol. III, p. 419).

78 In September 1990, a Greenpeace protest ship, sailing from one Soviet port to another, was welcomed by Soviet citizens (Wittner, *Toward Nuclear Abolition*, vol. III, p. 419).

79 Wittner, *Toward Nuclear Abolition*, vol. III, p. 419; and Johnson, "Advocates and Activists," p. 64.

80 Wittner, *Toward Nuclear Abolition*, vol. III, pp. 419 et seq.

81 *Ibid.*, p. 420.

82 Laumulin, "Kazakhstan's Nuclear Policy," p. 206. Lobnor is located some 1 200 kilometers away from Almaty, but the prevailing east wind has borne contaminations to the region (*ibid.*).

had received a maximum fallout of radionuclides caused by tests carried out in Semipalatinsk and other test sites.[83]

As far as its concrete achievements are concerned, it has been suggested that the Nevada-Semipalatinsk movement, through its tireless efforts throughout 1989, succeeded in preventing 11 of the 18 nuclear tests planned for that year. The test carried out at the Semipalatinsk site on October 19, 1989 turned out to be the Soviet Union's last one.[84] Moreover, the movement's activities were certainly instrumental for the Soviet Union's decision on a test moratorium, announced, as indicated above, by President Gorbachev on October 5, 1991.[85] Moscow also declared that the Semipalatinsk test site would be closed by 1993.[86] The closure of the Semipalatinsk testing site has been considered a "stunning victory" for the movement.[87]

d) Assessment

It can be concluded that the considerable efforts made by international NGOs, such as the spectacular direct actions conducted by Greenpeace, as well as the activities of more grassroots-oriented national pressure groups, in particular Nevada-Semipalatinsk, turned out to be instrumental in convincing national decision-makers to decree unilateral moratoria on nuclear testing. The Soviet and French moratoria were followed by that of the United States.[88] This created the conditions for the beginning of the CTBT negotiations in 1994,[89] which were successfully concluded on September 10, 1996.

What are the reasons for this success? It has been asserted that the Nevada-Semipalatinsk movement and its leader, Olzhas Suleimenov, used a very effective strategy of mobilizing local actors and making international appeals, thereby increasing the movement's limited financial resources by cooperating with

83 Laumulin, "Kazakhstan's Nuclear Policy," p. 188. These data have been contested by researchers at the Laboratory for Observation of Radioactive Contamination (*ibid.*).

84 *Ibid.*, p. 147. In November 1989, Soviet Prime Minister Nikolai Ryzhkov announced that further tests at the site would be suspended until the end of that year. The moratorium was extended until end of March 1990, when Deputy Prime Minister Igor Belousov declared that the government had decided to postpone indefinitely all tests at Semipalatinsk (Peterson, *Troubled Lands*, p. 204).

85 Johnson, "The Role of Civil Society," p. 106.

86 Johnson, "Advocates and Activists," p. 64. On August 29, 1991, Kazakh President Nursultan Nazarbaev issued a decree on the closing of the Semipalatinsk test site (Laumulin, "Kazakhstan's Nuclear Policy," p.188; and Edmunds, "The Environmental Movement in Kazakstan," p. 147).

87 K. Watters, "Environmental NGOs and the Development of Civil Society in Central Asia," in M. H. Ruffin and D. C. Waugh (eds.), *Civil Society in Central Asia*, Seattle and London, 1999, pp. 85–108, 86.

88 The Congress mandated the US moratorium in October 1992 (Johnson, "The Role of Civil Society," p. 101).

89 Johnson, "Advocates and Activists," p. 56.

global organizations such as IPPNW and Greenpeace.[90] Nevada-Semipalatinsk understood how to attract public empathy for the unmatched suffering experienced by the inhabitants of the Semipalatinsk region as a result of nuclear testing.[91] Moreover, it perfectly combined nationalist and environmentalist appeals.[92] Indeed, the basis supporting the movement was broad, gathering local working-class people and members of the intelligentsia. Furthermore, Suleimenov, a poet who enjoyed popularity and respect throughout all ethnicities of Kazakhstan and, in addition, maintained close relations with Moscow through his membership in the Supreme Soviet, was the right person for a campaign against nuclear testing. Finally, the timing and political environment surrounding the launch of the Kazakh pressure group was ideal, only a few months before the collapse of the Soviet Union and Kazakhstan's independence.[93]

C. TREATIES ON THE DENUCLEARIZATION OF CERTAIN REGIONS (NWFZ)

1. In general

It is generally acknowledged that the concept and definition of NWFZ – zones of complete absence of nuclear weapons – are relatively simple and unambiguous. It is therefore supposed to be potentially easier for this issue to gain support from civil society.[94] At the time of the establishment of the first NWZF by the 1967 Treaty of Tlatelolco, it was stressed that it came as a response to humanity's concern with its own future, namely the threat of nuclear weapons and, in particular, "for the good of mankind."[95] That initiative was followed by four others of the same kind, in different regions of the globe, but Cançado Trindade argues that basic considerations of humanity have played a role in the establishment of those NWFZ too.[96] The second treaty establishing such a zone, the Rarotonga Treaty regarding a NWFZ in the South Pacific, is generally considered as a direct result of civil society's campaigns and of the support lent by public opinion as a

90 Watters, "Environmental NGOs," p. 86; and Johnson, "The Role of Civil Society," p. 106.
91 Edmunds, "The Environmental Movement in Kazakstan," p. 147.
92 Johnson, "The Role of Civil Society," p. 106.
93 Edmunds, "The Environmental Movement in Kazakstan," p. 147; and Johnson, "The Role of Civil Society," p. 106.
94 M. Hamel-Green, *Regional Initiatives on Nuclear- and WMD-Free Zones: Cooperative Approaches to Arms Control and Non-Proliferation*, UNIDIR, 2005, p. 11.
95 Preamble, § 14, of the Tlatelolco Treaty. See, for a commentary on this treaty, A. García Robles, "Mesures de désarmement dans des zones particulières: le Traité visant l'interdiction des armes nucléaires," *Collected Courses of The Hague Academy of International Law*, vol. 133, 1971, pp. 43–134.
96 A. A. Cançado Trindade, in his dissenting opinion in the case of *Obligations Concerning Negotiations Relating to Cessation of the Nuclear Arms Race and to Nuclear Disarmament (Marshall Islands v. United Kingdom)*, ICJ Reports 2016, § 248.

result of large-scale peace movement actions against nuclear-weapon development and testing in the region.[97] It will be discussed further in the following subdivision.

The third treaty of this kind, the 1995 Bangkok Treaty, was initiated by the Association of Southeast Asian Nations (ASEAN) in order to insulate the region against the policies and rivalries of the NWS.[98] The fourth, the Pelindaba Treaty, adopted in 1996, was prompted, on the one hand, by the African continent's opposition to nuclear tests in the region (prompted by the French tests in the Sahara in 1961) and, on the other, the aspiration of the African people to keep nuclear weapons off their continent.[99] The said treaties having established NWFZ in the southern hemisphere, the fifth of these instruments, the 2006 Semipalatinsk Treaty establishing a NWFZ in Central Asia, follows the same approach and ultimate goal by eradicating nuclear weapons from an important part of the northern hemisphere.

In light of the foregoing, it can be asserted that each of the five treaties reflects the characteristics of each of the five regions, but they all pursue the same cause, namely to free those regions, some of them densely populated, from the fear of nuclear victimization and, more generally, to preserve humankind from the threat of nuclear weapons.[100]

2. The example of the Rarotonga Treaty

The Rarotonga Treaty, establishing a NWFZ in the South Pacific, was the second instrument freeing an entire inhabited region of nuclear weapons. Whereas the first instrument of this kind, the Tlatelolco Treaty, was largely the fruit of efforts of certain interested and engaged governments, in particular Mexico,[101] the

97 M. Hamel-Green, *The South Pacific Nuclear Free Zone Treaty: A Critical Assessment*, Peace Research Centre, Research School of Pacific Studies, Australian National University, Sydney, Australian National University Press, 1990, pp. 56–61, 72–101.

98 A. A. Cançado Trindade, in his dissenting opinion in the case of *Obligations Concerning Negotiations Relating to Cessation of the Nuclear Arms Race and to Nuclear Disarmament (Marshall Islands v. United Kingdom)*, ICJ Reports 2016, § 251.

99 Naciones Unidas, *Las Zonas Libres de Armas Nucleares en el Siglo XXI*, New York and Geneva, UN-OPAL/UNIDIR, 1997, pp. 60–61; and J. O. Ohonvbere, "Africa – The Treaty of Pelindaba," in R. Thakur (ed.), *Nuclear Weapons-Free Zones*, London and New York, 1998, pp. 93–120, 98–99 and 109.

100 A. A. Cançado Trindade, in his dissenting opinion in the case of *Obligations Concerning Negotiations Relating to Cessation of the Nuclear Arms Race and to Nuclear Disarmament (Marshall Islands v. United Kingdom)*, ICJ Reports 2016, § 249; and H. Fujita, "The Changing Role of International Law in the Nuclear Age: From Freedom of the High Seas to Nuclear-Free-Zones," in A. J. M. Delissen and G. J. Tanja (eds.), *Humanitarian Law of Armed Conflict: Challenges Ahead: Essays in Honour of F. Kalshoven*, Dordrecht, 1991, pp. 327–350, 350.

101 Wittner, *Resisting the Bomb*, vol. II, p. 434; and A. A. Cançado Trindade, *International Law for Humankind: Towards a New Jus Gentium*, 2nd edn., Leiden and Boston, 2013, p. 406. Serrano talks of an "imaginative entrepreneurship" between the leading States that enabled the successful conclusion of the treaty and of an example of "modern treaty making"

involvement of civil society became more important in the negotiation of a treaty establishing a NWFZ in the South Pacific. The antinuclear protest movement in the South Pacific is considered to be the most active of its kind and was largely the result of the increasing frustration felt by the populations over the incursions of NWS in the region, such as French nuclear testing at Moruroa and visits made by US nuclear-armed ships, as well as threats of nuclear waste dumping.[102]

Far distant from large centers of population and with no political power to veto the decisions of colonial powers, the Pacific Islands obviously offered ideal locations and conditions for the initial atmospheric nuclear testing programs involving NWS possessing colonial territories in the region.[103] Moreover, the United States, after having ceased nuclear testing in 1963, continued to use the region for other forms of nuclear-weapon-related activities, such as missile testing, and for the deployment of strategic nuclear weapon systems, including permanent bases for nuclear armed forces and regular deployment and transit of mobile nuclear-armed forces.[104] The Soviet Union and China, which did not possess territories in the South Pacific, have nevertheless used the region for missile-testing.[105]

The peak of the French nuclear test program occurred between 1966 and 1974, when 41 tests were conducted in the atmosphere over Moruroa Atoll in French Polynesia. From this site, radioactive clouds drifted across small Pacific Island nations to New Zealand and Australia, depositing their deadly nuclear fallout in the process.[106] Environmental contamination and radiation-related illness among many islanders close to the testing ground, together with hardship and dispossession of land associated with their relocation from test areas, left a legacy of bitterness, distrust, and anger over nuclear testing and related programs in the South Pacific region. Later, their concerns were reinforced by Japanese and American proposals for radioactive waste disposal in the Pacific.[107]

In 1972, activist groups from New Zealand started, as part of a Peace Media project, defying the French Government by sailing small vessels into the test danger zone; only one year later, the movement was already flourishing.[108]

(M. Serrano, "Latin America – The Treaty of Tlatelolco," in Thakur, *Nuclear Weapons-Free Zones*, pp. 35–58, 35).

102 M. Hamel-Green, "The South Pacific – The Treaty of Rarotonga," in Thakur, *Nuclear Weapons-Free Zones*, pp. 59–80, 59 and 62.

103 The United States 1946–1963, Great Britain 1957–1962, and France 1966–1974 used their respective Pacific Island territories for atmospheric test programs, conducting more than 150 atmospheric tests until 1974. Since then, France has continued to test underground at Moruroa Atoll in French Polynesia until 1989 (Hamel-Green, *The South Pacific Nuclear Free Zone Treaty*, p. 83, with further references).

104 *Ibid.*

105 *Ibid.*

106 Wittner, *Toward Nuclear Abolition*, vol. III, p. 12.

107 *Ibid.*, pp. 83 et seq.

108 *Ibid.*, p. 12. Already before, in 1962–1963, peace movements from Australia and New Zealand, as well as the Labour Parties in those countries, then in opposition, were advancing regional denuclearization concepts (Hamel-Green, *The South Pacific Nuclear Free Zone Treaty*, p. 62).

In Australia, the reaction was comparably strong: thousands of people, outraged by the announcement of a new round of French nuclear tests in 1972, held marches in Adelaide, Melbourne, Brisbane, and Sydney. Scientists wrote editorials and issued statements calling for an end to the tests, readers filled whole pages of newspapers with angry letters, and consumers boycotted French products.[109] It turned out that 90 percent of Australians opposed French nuclear testing.[110]

French nuclear testing also spurred resistance in the small island nations of the Pacific, where peace movements and indigenous peoples' groups – supported by certain governments such as those of New Zealand, Fiji, and Papua New Guinea[111] – encouraged the establishment of a regional NWFZ. The People's Charter for a Nuclear-Free and Independent Pacific, drafted and amended at successive conferences of regional peace movements and indigenous groups in 1975, 1978, and 1980, deserves particular attention.[112] It urged governments to establish a NWFZ and called, more generally, for the decolonization of remaining territories and the recognition of the rights of indigenous peoples in the Pacific region.[113]

Moreover, public events were organized throughout the entire region. Thus, in May 1970, 600 people participated in a public meeting on nuclear tests in Suva (Fiji), where it was decided to establish ATOM, an organization against testing on Moruroa.[114] It brought together representatives from the Fiji Council of Churches and the Young Women's Christian Association (YWCA), as well as regional students' organizations, and aimed at raising awareness and resistance to nuclear testing within French Polynesia and at building an antinuclear alliance among churches, unions, and the government.[115] It also linked up with antinuclear groups elsewhere in the Pacific and tried to influence the South Pacific Forum, a regional organization grouping newly independent island States, as well as Australia and New Zealand.[116] In parallel, other antinuclear efforts and movements took off on other Pacific islands, most notably on Tahiti (Polynesia), where the movement even took an international connotation, linking up with antinuclear groups from Australia, France, Japan, New Zealand, and the United States,[117] and on Tinian (Micronesia), where vigorous opposition emerged against the US

109 Wittner, *Toward Nuclear Abolition*, vol. III, p. 12. Australian unions also played a leading role insofar as their members refused to load French ships, service French planes, or carry French mail (*ibid.*).

110 *Ibid.*, with further references.

111 Hamel-Green, *The South Pacific Nuclear Free Zone Treaty*, p. 62.

112 Conference of the Committee on Disarmament (CCD), *Comprehensive Study of the Question of Nuclear-Weapon-Free Zones in All its Aspects*, New York, UNGA Official Records, 30th Session, Supplement No. 27A/, A/10027/Add. 1, 1975, p. 23.

113 Hamel-Green, *The South Pacific Nuclear Free Zone Treaty*, p. 2.

114 Wittner, *Toward Nuclear Abolition*, vol. III, p. 13.

115 *Ibid.*

116 *Ibid.*; and Hamel-Green, *The South Pacific Nuclear Free Zone Treaty*, p. 82.

117 See, for more details, Wittner, *Toward Nuclear Abolition*, vol. III, p. 13.

Government's plan to eject the entire native population in order to enable the establishment of an expanded US Air Force base housing nuclear weapons.[118]

Whereas the efforts of this popular and indigenous peace initiative were instrumental in raising awareness and creating the necessary momentum against nuclear testing in the region during the 1970s, the final breakthrough toward a NWFZ in the South Pacific took place thanks to political changes in New Zealand and Australia.[119] In New Zealand, the Labour Party came to power in 1984 and David Lange, who had always underlined the importance of the antinuclear movement and of a nuclear-free New Zealand, became Prime Minister.[120] Challenged and enormously put under pressure by the United States, which insisted on its nuclear-armed and -powered warships having access to New Zealand's harbors, Lange kept his election promise and, backed by antinuclear demonstrations filling the streets of the capital, barred the visit of the US warship "Buchanan" in early 1985.[121] Bolstered by huge public support for the ban on nuclear warships, he made New Zealand a leading proponent of a NWFZ in the South Pacific and of a comprehensive test ban treaty, declaring proudly before the Labour Party's annual conference that New Zealand had shown that "a small country could speak up for itself and stand up for what is right."[122]

In Australia, too, the climate was propitious for the aspiration to a South Pacific NWFZ. After having made some concessions in the field of uranium mining which provoked strong protests in the Australian nuclear disarmament movement, Australia's newly elected Labour Government, led by Prime Minister Bob Hawke, finally decided to take a firm stance on nuclear issues. Hawke appointed Australia's first minister for disarmament, tripled the size of the disarmament division in the Department of Foreign Affairs, established a peace research center at the Australian National University, and refused to become involved with the Strategic Defense Initiative (SDI), pushed by President Ronald Reagan.[123] In these stormy times, Australia officially proposed negotiations to conclude a legally binding instrument

118 *Ibid.*

119 Thakur, "Stepping Stones to a Nuclear-Weapon-Free World," p. 15, taking the example of NWFZ, argues that timing can be critical with regard to the catalyst that propels countries toward such a zone and determines success or failure of such an approach.

120 Wittner, *Toward Nuclear Abolition*, vol. III, p. 296.

121 *Ibid.*, pp. 296 et seq.

122 In March 1985, Lange, invited to debate the morality of nuclear weapons before the Oxford Union, expressed himself in the following words: "Nuclear weapons make us insecure, and to compensate for our security we build and deploy more nuclear weapons . . . We know that we are seized by irrationality, and yet we persist . . . There is no humanity in the logic which holds that my country must be obliged to play host to nuclear weapons because others in the West are playing host to nuclear weapons . . . That is the logic which refuses to admit that there is any alternative to nuclear weapons when plainly there is. It is a self-defeating logic, just as the weapons themselves are self-defeating" (Wittner, *Toward Nuclear Abolition*, vol. III, p. 297).

123 Wittner, *Toward Nuclear Abolition*, vol. III, p. 298.

providing for the establishment of a NWFZ in the South Pacific region.[124] The proposal was endorsed by the South Pacific Forum in August 1984, negotiated during the following year in a working group of the Forum chaired by Australia, and was soon after signed at the following annual Forum on August 6, 1985.[125] Gathering the necessary eight ratifications, the treaty entered into force on December 11, 1986.[126]

To sum up the observations on the phase preceding actual negotiation of the treaty, it can be concluded that the successful negotiations leading up to the conclusion of the Rarotonga Treaty were rapid and resulted from a large-scale peace movement against nuclear weapon deployment and testing in the South Pacific. The intensive campaigns of indigenous civil societies, frustrated over their powerlessness against incursions of the NWS in their region, were instrumental in engaging the Labour Parties in both Australia and New Zealand and generated the necessary political will to open the negotiations.[127] These two countries' new governments, resolved to challenge US nuclear interests in the region, proved finally decisive for embarking on the formal negotiations that ultimately led to the adoption of the Rarotonga Treaty.

It is noteworthy that the Rarotonga Treaty had the effect of encouraging negotiations for the establishment of a similar zone in the neighboring region of Southwest Asia. These negotiations resulted in the conclusion of the Bangkok Treaty in 1995 and, by the same token, confirmed the continued relevance of regional approaches to the objectives of disarmament and the safeguarding of humankind from the nuclear menace.[128]

D. CONCLUSION

In Part I of the present study, devoted to treaties dealing with non-nuclear weapons, the following factors were, inter alia, identified as essential for the conclusion of the Ottawa and Oslo Conventions: first, a clear and simple goal to be achieved; second, the humanitarian motivations justifying the conclusion of these treaties; third, the involvement of civil society in the process and their successful strategy of building their case around certain triggering events; fourth, the involvement of experts in the process, in particular of medical doctors and

124 Hamel-Green, *The South Pacific Nuclear Free Zone Treaty*, p. 2.

125 *Ibid.*; see also O. Adeniji, *The Treaty of Pelindaba on the African Nuclear-Weapon-Free-Zone*, UNIDIR, New York and Geneva, 2002, p. 20; and Thakur, "Stepping Stones to a Nuclear-Weapon-Free World," p. 9.

126 To date, 13 States have ratified the Rarotonga Treaty: http://disarmament.un.org/treaties/t/rarotonga (accessed February 23, 2017).

127 Hamel-Green, *Regional Initiatives*, pp. 11 et seq.

128 Hamel-Green, *The South Pacific Nuclear Free Zone Treaty*, p. 71. It is also argued that the Rarotonga Treaty served as an important precedent for the Pelindaba Treaty (*ibid.*, pp. 71 et seq.).

surgeons; fifth, the support given to the causes of anti-personnel mines and cluster munitions by certain like-minded States; sixth, the involvement of the victims of these weapons in the negotiation process; and seventh, the treaties have been concluded outside the traditional disarmament fora.[129]

A very similar picture can be drawn for the treaties on nuclear weapons. First, both the ban on nuclear testing and the establishment of a NWFZ are clear and rather simple objectives. Second, the two treaties banning nuclear tests clearly were concluded for the protection of general interests, in particular to enhance the health, safety, and well-being of the local populations. As far as the regional treaties establishing NWFZ are concerned, the opinion of Cançado Trindade according to which basic considerations of humanity played an essential role in the adoption of treaties which free entire inhabited regions from the danger of a nuclear war,[130] is fully shared here.

Third, it has been demonstrated that civil society played a key role in raising awareness and in triggering momentum for opening negotiations for the conclusion of the treaties considered here. Certain events that have shocked public opinion and conscience can be identified as the starting point for the ultimate move toward formal negotiations. It appears that, when civil society became aware of the situation and knew how to benefit from it, the chances for a treaty to be concluded were high. National peace movements, such as the Nevada-Semipalatinsk movement in Kazakhstan and the indigenous movement on the islands of the South Pacific, protesting against nuclear testing and other nuclear-related activities, were crucial elements in these processes. The Pelindaba Treaty establishing a NWFZ in Africa in 1995, which has not been examined here for practical reasons, was due to a similar trend. In February 1960, France conducted its first atmospheric nuclear test in the Sahara Desert, followed by three additional tests in the same year, all of which resulted in significant radioactive fallout in several African countries, with serious consequences for human and animal lives.[131]

Fourth, as outlined above in respect of the Ottawa and Oslo processes, which involved actors with social standing such as medical doctors and surgeons facing new forms of injuries caused by anti-personnel mines and cluster munitions, the antinuclear movement also relied heavily on the expertise of scientists, who were the only ones to understand and predict – at least roughly – the impact of nuclear explosions. The circle included atomic scientists, physicians, and dentists raising public awareness by collecting data and presenting tangible evidence for the devastating force of nuclear weapons.

Fifth, it has been explained that another ingredient for successful campaigns by civil society lies in the support given to the cause by a small circle of interested

129 See this volume, Chapter 2, section D.

130 Cançado Trindade, *International Law for Humankind*, pp. 405 et seq.

131 Adeniji, *The Treaty of Pelindaba*, p. 37. See, for an assessment of this instrument, J. O. Ihonvbere, "Africa – The Treaty of Pelidaba," in Thakur, *Nuclear Weapons-Free Zones*, pp. 93–120.

and engaged States. The role of Australia and New Zealand in pushing the idea of a NWFZ for the South Pacific has been highlighted.

Sixth, the involvement of victims, which was instrumental in the conclusion of the Ottawa and Oslo Conventions, has also played a certain role in the early opposition against nuclear testing in general and, in particular, in the grassroots "Nevada-Semipalatinsk" movement which led to the Soviet Union's moratorium. This was also the case in the popular movement on the islands of the South Pacific, where indigenous people were directly affected by the French nuclear tests. Their effort was one of the driving forces toward a legally binding NWFZ in the South Pacific. Only the last point (seventh) differs insofar as the CTBT has been negotiated within the traditional disarmament machinery. The adoption of this treaty, in 1996, is considered the last success of the CD.

In conclusion, the picture that can be drawn with regard to instruments dealing with nuclear weapons turns out to be very similar to what has been shown concerning treaties on non-nuclear weapons.[132]

132 According to Johnson, even before the breakthroughs of the Ottawa and Oslo processes, civil society penetrated and interacted with negotiations on arms control far more than is generally recognized (Johnson, "The Role of Civil Society," p. 97).

7 Assessing the legality of nuclear weapons in light of humanitarian and human rights law

A. INTRODUCTION

The current debate on the humanitarian impact of nuclear weapons focuses on the disastrous effect that the use of such nuclear weapons might have on combatants and, more so, on the civil population. It raises the question of whether nuclear weapons can be used without violating core principles of humanitarian law. This question will be dealt with in the first section of this chapter (B). The second section (C) will be devoted to the use of nuclear weapons in light of human rights law. From the author's point of view, this assessment has not yet received the attention that it deserves. The third section (D) will be dedicated to other legal duties regarding nuclear weapons, other than the prohibition of the use of these weapons.

Unlike what is the case in the field of non-nuclear weapons, no universal treaty prohibits the use of nuclear weapons. When concluding this study, one of the points in the ongoing debate on the humanitarian impact of nuclear weapons was the filling of this gap. The use of nuclear weapons is nevertheless prohibited by certain treaties establishing regional NWFZ and by the additional protocols thereto, namely, the Tlatelolco[1] and Bangkok[2] Treaties. In addition, as mentioned above, the NWS accepted, by ratifying the protocols to all five treaties establishing NWFZ, the obligation not to use or threaten to use nuclear weapons against the States Parties to the two treaties.[3]

1 Article 1 § 1(a).
2 Article 3 § 1(c). The Semipalatinsk Treaty does not prohibit the use of nuclear weapons, but it obliges the States Parties not to allow their use in their territory (Article 3 § 1(d)(i)).
3 Article 3 of Protocol II to the Tlatelolco Treaty, Article 1 of Protocol I to the Rarotonga Treaty, Article 2 of the Protocol to the Bangkok Treaty, Article 1 of Protocol I to the Pelindaba Treaty, and Article 1 of the Protocol to the Semipalatinsk Treaty.

B. THE PROHIBITION OF USING NUCLEAR WEAPONS IN LIGHT OF HUMANITARIAN LAW

1. The ICJ's Advisory Opinion (1996) and the special features of nuclear weapons

An assessment of the use of nuclear weapons under international humanitarian law has to start from the ICJ's Advisory Opinion on the *Legality of the Threat or Use of Nuclear Weapons.* In that opinion, the Court recognized that nuclear weapons cannot be compared with other arms and underlined their unmatched destructive impact on the human being:

> 35. . . . [The Court] also notes that nuclear weapons are explosive devices whose energy results from the fusion or fission of the atom. By its very nature, that process, in nuclear weapons as they exist today, releases not only immense quantities of heat and energy, but also powerful and prolonged radiation. According to the material before the Court, the first two causes of damage are vastly more powerful than the damage caused by other weapons, while the phenomenon of radiation is said to be peculiar to nuclear weapons. These characteristics render the nuclear weapon potentially catastrophic. The destructive power of nuclear weapons cannot be contained in either space or time. They have the potential to destroy all civilization and the entire ecosystem of the planet.
>
> The radiation released by a nuclear explosion would affect health, agriculture, natural resources and demography over a very wide area. Further, the use of nuclear weapons would be a serious danger to future generations. Ionizing radiation has the potential to damage the future environment, food and marine ecosystem, and to cause genetic defects and illness in future generations.
>
> 36. In consequence, in order correctly to apply to the present case the Charter law on the use of force and the law applicable in armed conflict, in particular humanitarian law, it is imperative for the Court to take account of the unique characteristics of nuclear weapons, and in particular their destructive capacity, their capacity to cause untold human suffering, and their ability to cause damage to generations to come.

Despite its recognition of the special nature of nuclear weapons and their particularly disastrous effect for the human being, the view expressed by the ICJ in its Advisory Opinion was a differentiated one. The starting points of its assessment of nuclear weapons under international law were naturally the Charter of the United Nations and the legality of the use of force in international law (*jus ad bellum*). The Court unanimously reached the conclusion that any use of force which runs counter to the prohibition of the threat or use of force under

Article 2 § 4 of the Charter, a rule of *jus cogens*,[4] and fails to meet the requirements of self-defence within the meaning of Article 51 is unlawful.[5]

Most importantly, in the Court's unanimous view, any use of force proportionate under the law of self-defence must, in order to be legal, also comply with the law governing armed conflict, including the principles and rules of humanitarian law;[6] the latter include, in particular, the distinction between combatants and non-combatants (civilians), and the prohibition of causing unnecessary suffering to combatants.[7] The Court also stressed that these fundamental rules are to be observed by all States whether or not they have ratified the relevant conventions, since they constitute "intransgressible principles of international customary law."[8]

In light of these principles, the ICJ came to the unanimous conclusion that the threat or use of nuclear weapons would "generally" be contrary to the rules of international law applicable in armed conflict, and in particular to those of humanitarian law.[9] But despite the comprehensive body of law protecting the human being in armed conflict, it went on to say the following:

> However, in view of the current state of international law, and of the elements of fact at its disposal, the Court cannot conclude definitively whether the threat or use of nuclear weapons would be lawful or unlawful in an extreme circumstance of self-defence, in which the very survival of a State would be at stake.[10]

This part of the opinion was highly controversial and was adopted by seven votes to seven, with the President's casting vote.[11]

On the one hand, the ICJ's opinion has many positive aspects: The Court recognizes, first of all, that a first strike by nuclear weapons would be illegal under international law; it follows that only in a situation of self-defence, as defined in Article 51 of the Charter and confined by the principles of proportionality and

4 See the case concerning *The Military and Paramilitary Activities in and against Nicaragua (Nicaragua v. United States of America)*, ICJ Reports 1986, § 190.

5 Operative paragraph C.

6 ICJ Reports 1996, § 42, and operative paragraph D.

7 *Ibid.*, § 78.

8 *Ibid.*, § 79. As mentioned above (Chapter 1, section B.1), in its judgment of April 9, 1949 in the *Corfu Channel* case (ICJ Reports 1949, p. 22), the Court already referred to "elementary considerations of humanity."

9 Dispositif, paragraph E, first paragraph.

10 Operative paragraph E, second paragraph. See also M. G. Kohen, "The Notion of 'State Survival' in International Law," in L. Boisson de Chazournes and P. Sands (eds.), *International Law, the International Court of Justice and Nuclear Weapons*, Cambridge, 1999, pp. 293–314.

11 Operative paragraph E.

necessity, such a threat or use could be in conformity with international law. Second, the ICJ points out that such a threat or use would be "scarcely reconcilable" with, and "generally" run against, the basic principles of humanitarian law and, as a result, be contrary to international law. Third, even though the Court did not altogether exclude the lawfulness of a threat or use of nuclear weapons in "extreme circumstances of self-defence, in which the very survival of a State would be at stake," it can nevertheless be argued that the language used by the Court is very strong, setting a high threshold for a lawful use or threat of such weapons.

On the other hand, the opinion has some serious weaknesses. The Court did not declare a threat or use illegal per se, but simply considered itself unable to decide the question (*non liquet*).[12] The same can be argued regarding the "clean" use of smaller, low-yield nuclear weapons whose legality was asserted by the NWS. In other words, the two questions were left open by the Court. From this author's point of view, it is regrettable that the Court failed to take a stronger stance on these central aspects of the issue. The ICJ's conclusion can to a certain extent be explained by the abstract nature of advisory opinions; they are not addressed to States, but aim at "offering legal advice" to the organs of international organizations which request them.[13] In any event, it is suggested that the Court, even back in 1996, had sufficient evidence to declare the use of nuclear weapons categorically and absolutely illegal under international law, even the use of low-yield nuclear weapons, for the reasons that will be examined below.

2. The need to challenge the ICJ's conclusions in light of the humanitarian approach to nuclear weapons

a) Early expressions of a humanitarian approach to nuclear weapons

The idea of putting the humanitarian consequences of the use of nuclear weapons at the center of the debate is not new. On the contrary, as observed above, the movement against nuclear weapons is as old as the weapons themselves.[14] The issue of nuclear disarmament had already been addressed by the UNGA's first resolution, adopted on January 24, 1946 (Resolution 1(I) on the "Establishment of a Commission to Deal with the Problems Raised by the Discovery of Atomic Energy"). Even though it did not use humanitarian language, it nevertheless underlined that the aim of the creation of the new commission was "to deal with

12 See D. Bodansky, "Non Liquet and the Incompleteness of International Law," in Boisson de Chazournes and Sands, *International Law*, pp. 153–170.

13 Advisory opinion, § 15. See also J. Salmon, "Quels sont les destinataires des avis?" in Boisson de Chazournes and Sands, *International Law*, pp. 27–35; and G. Abi-Saab, "On Discretion: Reflections on the Nature of the Consultative Function of the International Court of Justice," in Boisson de Chazournes and Sands, *International Law*, pp. 36–50.

14 This volume, Chapter 6, section A.

the problems raised by the discovery of atomic energy and other related matters"[15] and concluded that the commission was to make proposals "for the elimination from national armaments of atomic weapons and of all other major weapons adaptable to mass destruction."[16] Moreover, in October 1949, the General Advisory Committee to the US Atomic Energy Commission chaired by Robert Oppenheimer – chief scientist of the Manhattan Project – recommended not to produce the hydrogen (H-)bomb, calling it a "weapon of genocide," and stating that it was "beyond military objectives."[17]

During the Cold War, with the perceived success of nuclear deterrence and the aim of non-proliferation as the main objective,[18] humanitarian concerns about nuclear weapons had a difficult stance, but did nevertheless appear from time to time. In 1961, for example, a large majority of States adopted UNGA Resolution 1653 ("Declaration on the prohibition of the use of nuclear and thermo-nuclear weapons"), considering the use of such weapons as not only "contrary to the rules of international law and to the laws of humanity,"[19] but also a "crime against mankind and civilization."[20] Even though this resolution was not accepted by an overwhelming majority,[21] it was subsequently reaffirmed by resolutions adopted by increasingly higher majorities, such as Resolution 46/37D of 1991, which, by 122 votes to 16 (with 22 abstentions), called on the international community, "as a matter of priority," to elaborate a convention prohibiting the use of nuclear weapons on the basis of the draft convention annexed to the resolution.[22] Moreover, the First Special Session of the UNGA devoted to Disarmament, held in 1978, stressed that:

> [m]ankind today is confronted with an unprecedented threat of self-extinction arising from the massive and competitive accumulation of the most destructive weapons ever produced. Existing arsenals of nuclear weapons alone are more than sufficient to destroy all life on earth . . .[23]

The use of nuclear weapons was also condemned by judicial bodies. On December 7, 1963, the District Court of Tokyo delivered the judgment in the case *Shimoda*

15 Preamble to the resolution.
16 Paragraph 5(c) of the resolution.
17 T. Sauer, *Nuclear Inertia: US Nuclear Weapons Policy After the Cold War*, London and New York, 2005, p. 7.
18 T. Sauer and J. Pretorius, "Nuclear Weapons and the Humanitarian Approach," *Global Change, Peace & Security*, vol. 26, no. 3, pp. 233–250, 239.
19 Resolution adopted on November 24, 1961, paragraph 1(b).
20 Paragraph 1(d).
21 55 votes to 20, with 26 abstentions. The negative votes came from Member States of NATO and from allies of the United States (A. A. Cançado Trindade, *International Law for Humankind: Towards a New Jus Gentium*, 2nd edn., Leiden and Boston, 2013, p. 420).
22 Convention on the Prohibition of the Use of Nuclear Weapons, December 6, 1991.
23 Resolution adopted on the Report of the Ad Hoc Committee on the Tenth Special Session, § 11, UNGA, Official Records: Tenth Special Session Supplement No. 4 (A/S-10/4), p. 4.

and Others v. Japan[24] regarding actions brought against Japan by five survivors of the nuclear bombings of Hiroshima and Nagasaki for the damages that they and members of their families had suffered as a result of the atomic bombings by the United States in August 1945. It had been alleged, inter alia, that the dropping of the bombs had been an unlawful act and that Japan's waiver of claims for damages under domestic and international law against the United States gave rise to an obligation of the Japanese Government to pay damages.[25] The action was ultimately dismissed by the Court, basically because of the individuals' lack of international legal personality and, moreover, because Japan had waived all its claims against the United States under the Peace Treaty of 1951. The Court further held that claims by Japanese nationals under domestic law had been waived.[26] What is significant for the present study is the fact that it nevertheless stressed that it was beyond doubt that the bombings of the two cities were contrary to international law:[27]

> . . . [T]he aerial bombardment with an atomic bomb of an undefended city, if not of a defended city, should be regarded as tantamount to a blind aerial bombardment and as such contrary to international law of the time.
>
> (8) . . . Further, it was well known that some 330 000 civilians in Hiroshima and some 270 000 civilians in Nagasaki had their homes there, even though both cities also had what may be called military objectives, such as armed forces, military installations and munitions factories. In these circumstances, it is proper to conclude that the aerial bombardment with an atomic bomb of both Hiroshima and Nagasaki was an illegal act of hostilities under international law as it existed at that time, as an indiscriminate bombardment of undefended cities. This is so since aerial bombardment with an atomic bomb, even if it is confined to military objectives, brings about the same result as a blind aerial bombardment because of the tremendous destructive power of the bomb.
>
> . . .
>
> (11) . . . It is doubtful whether the atomic bomb with its tremendous destructive power was appropriate from the viewpoint of military effect and was really necessary at that time. It is indeed a fact to be regretted that the atomic bombing of the cities of Hiroshima and Nagasaki took away the lives of tens of thousands of citizens, and that among those who have survived are those whose lives are still imperilled owing to its radioactive effects even now after eighteen years. In this sense it is not too much to say that the sufferings

24 *Ryuichi Shimoda et al. v. The State of Japan*, Compensation claim against Japan brought by the residents of Hiroshima and Nagasaki, Tokyo District Court, December 7, 1963.

25 Summary published by the ICRC, http://www.icrc.org/applic/ihl/ihl-nat.nsf/0/AA559087DBCF1AF5C1256A1C0029F14D (accessed February 27, 2017).

26 *Ibid.*, part III of the judgment.

27 Source: *Hanrei Jiho*, vol. 355, p. 17; translated in *The Japanese Annual of International Law*, vol. 8, 1964, p. 231. For the text, see the ICRC website, mentioned above.

> brought about by the atomic bomb are greater than those caused by poisons and poisonous gases; indeed, the fact of dropping this bomb may be regarded as contrary to the fundamental principle of the law of war which prohibits the causing of unnecessary suffering.

In light of these findings, it is highly questionable whether the ICJ did not already have enough evidence at its disposal to declare the use of nuclear weapons unlawful in all circumstances in 1996. The point of view expressed by Cançado Trindade that, even assuming the existence of a legal gap, it would have been possible to fill it,[28] is entirely shared here.

It is particularly surprising that the Court, even though it refers several times to the Martens Clause,[29] mentioned above,[30] neither fully appreciated its legal value nor made adequate use of it. As mentioned above, a contemporary version of this clause can be found in Article 1 § 2 of Additional Protocol I to the Geneva Conventions:

> **General principles and scope of application**
>
> 2. . . . In cases not covered by this Protocol or by other international agreements, civilians and combatants remain under the protection and authority of the principles of international law derived from established custom, from the principles of humanity and from the dictates of public conscience.

From this author's point of view, expressions such as "principles of humanity" and "dictates of public conscience" would hardly fit better anywhere else than into the context of nuclear weapons, the most destructive devices of all. As mentioned in Part I of this study, the ICJ considered this clause an "effective means of addressing the rapid evolution of military technology."[31] A sound application of the clause could have allowed the Court to fill the alleged gap and shift the scale in favor of an absolute prohibition of using nuclear weapons in all circumstances.[32]

These elements having been largely ignored by the ICJ, the opinion expresses, as a result, a backward-oriented, positivist approach in the spirit of the *Lotus* judgment rendered by the Permanent Court of International Justice (PCIJ) in 1929.[33] The main finding in that case, namely, that anything that is not expressly

28 Cançado Trindade, *International Law for Humankind*, p. 419.
29 Paragraphs 78, 84, and 87.
30 See, in particular, this volume, Chapter 3, A.2.c).ee).
31 *The Legality of the Threat or Use of Nuclear Weapons*, ICJ Reports 1996, § 78.
32 See, for this clause, the dissenting Opinion by Judge Weeramantry in the 1996 Advisory Opinion, ICJ Reports 1996, pp. 486 et seq.; and Y. Shigeta, "The Perspective of Japanese International Lawyers," in Boisson de Chazournes and Sands, *International Law*, pp. 435–446, 441.
33 In this sense, see Cançado Trindade, *International Law for Humankind*, pp. 419, 426 et seq. See also, for a broader discussion of the 1996 Opinion, among others, P.-M. Dupuy,

prohibited is permitted (the so-called "Lotus principle")[34] should not have its place in the modern international legal order, in particular where the use of a weapon capable of challenging the survival of humankind is at stake.[35] To follow such a path would mean not only a return from today's intensive cooperation within the international community to a mere situation of coexistence between States, but also a challenge to all the progress accomplished in the field of *jus ad bellum* – toward outlawing wars of aggression altogether – and above all to the development achieved in the domain of humanitarian and human rights law during the second half of the twentieth century,[36] of which certain rules are nowadays recognized by the Court itself to be of a peremptory nature.[37]

In any event, since the ICJ rendered its controversial opinion, more than 20 years have passed. It may well be that the Court would today come to a firmer conclusion on the illegality of nuclear weapons under international law. It is therefore appropriate to add the following observations.

b) Recent developments, in particular the "humanitarian pledge," the ICRC's firm position on nuclear weapons, and the Marshall Islands cases before the ICJ

Even though a renewed interest in the humanitarian idea on nuclear weapons did not arise immediately after the fall of the Iron Curtain, recent developments confirm a growing opposition to nuclear weapons and scepticism concerning the legality of their use under international law. Addressing the 2005 NPT Review Conference, former UNSG Kofi Annan reminded the delegates of the long-lasting suffering that would be caused far beyond the immediate site of "a nuclear catastrophe in one of our big cities":

"Between the Individual and the State: International Law at a Crossroads?" in Boisson de Chazournes and Sands, *International Law*, pp. 449–461.

34 *Lotus* case, PCIJ, Series A no. 10, pp. 20 et seq. See also the following paragraph: "International law governs relations between independent States. The rules of law binding upon States therefore emanate from their own free will as expressed in conventions or by usages generally accepted as expressing principles of law and established in order to regulate the relations between these co-existing independent communities or with a view to the achievement of common aims. Restrictions upon the independence of States cannot therefore be presumed" (p. 18).

35 See, in this sense, the dissenting opinion of Judge Shahabuddeen, *ICJ Reports 1996*, p. 393: "Even if there is no prohibition, is there anything in the sovereignty of a State which would entitle it to embark on a course of action which could effectively wipe out the existence of all States by ending civilization and annihilating mankind? An affirmative answer is not reasonable . . ."

36 See, in this sense, O. Spiermann, "Lotus and the Double Structure of International Legal Argument," in Boisson de Chazournes and Sands, *International Law*, pp. 131–152, in particular 146–148.

37 See this Chapter, section B.1.

> In the chaos and confusion of the immediate aftermath, there might be many questions . . . Imagine, just for a minute, what the consequences would be. Tens, if not hundreds, of thousands of people would perish in an instant, and many more would die from exposure to radiation. The global impact would also be grave . . . Hard-won freedoms and human rights could be compromised. The sharing of nuclear technology for peaceful uses could halt. Resources for development would likely dwindle. And world financial markets, trade and transportation could be hard hit, with major economic consequences. This could drive millions of people in poor countries into deeper deprivation and suffering.[38]

Faced with renewed nuclear proliferation in India, Pakistan, and North Korea, and the truncated nuclear weapons program in Libya and Syria, experienced statesmen such as Henry Kissinger and George Schultz urgently plead for a world without nuclear weapons.[39] The initiative of Schultz, Perry, Kissinger, and Sam Nunn to write an article in the *Wall Street Journal* in 2007 in favor of nuclear disarmament inspired many other (retired) politicians, prime ministers, and ministers of foreign affairs around the globe to do the same.[40] These voices were further reflected in President Obama's famous Prague speech of April 5, 2009, using surprisingly humanitarian language:

> No nuclear war was fought between the United States and the Soviet Union, but generations lived with the knowledge that their world could be erased in a single flash of light. Cities like Prague that existed for centuries, that embodied the beauty and the talent of so much of humanity, would have ceased to exist.[41]

This new spirit in favor of the elimination of nuclear weapons triggered what is now referred to as the "humanitarian initiative," the various aspects of which are addressed here. First of all, new globally acting NGOs have been established, campaigning for the goal of a nuclear-free world. This aspect will be considered in further detail in the section dealing with the contribution of civil society to the implementation of the NPT.[42] In parallel, things started to move on the inter-State level as well. Only one year after the Prague speech, at the 2010 NPT Review Conference, an instrument that does not as such prohibit the use of these weapons,

38 K. Annan, "The Secretary-General Address to the Nuclear Non-Proliferation Treaty Review Conference," May 2, 2005, http://www.un.org/en/conf/npt/2005/statements/npt02sg.pdf (accessed February 27, 2017).

39 Sauer and Pretorius, "Nuclear Weapons," p. 240.

40 G. Schultz, W. Perry, H. Kissinger, and S. Nunn, "Toward a Nuclear Weapon Free World," *The Wall Street Journal*, January 4, 2007.

41 See http://www.acronym.org.uk/old/building-security/reducing-arsenals-incl-start/president-obama-speech-nuclear-disarmament (accessed March 8, 2017).

42 This volume, Chapter 8, section B.2.b).

States Parties expressed, for the first time in such explicit language, their reservations surrounding the possible use of nuclear weapons:

> The Conference expresses its deep concern at the catastrophic humanitarian consequences of any use of nuclear weapons and reaffirms the need for all States at all times to comply with applicable international law, including international humanitarian law.[43]

The inclusion of such language in the final document of 2010 was perhaps not extraordinary or spectacular in itself, but its significance lies in the manner in which it was achieved and in the initiative that it triggered.[44] States such as Switzerland, proud of its humanitarian tradition and host State of the ICRC with headquarters in Geneva, and Norway, despite being a member of a nuclear alliance, were instrumental in inserting such a passage in the NPT's final document and, in this, were backed by the ICRC.[45] At the NPT Preparatory Committee (Prepcom) in May 2012, Switzerland, together with 15 other States, made a Joint Statement on the Humanitarian Dimension of Nuclear Disarmament.[46] Similar statements were made by numerous States at the UNGA's First Committee session in October 2012 and at the NPT Prepcom in April 2013.[47]

Arguing that the humanitarian dimension required increased attention and aware of the fact that an increasing number of countries supported the idea that nuclear weapons are too destructive to be used, the Norwegian Government, in March 2013, organized a conference on the humanitarian impact of nuclear weapons in Oslo.[48] The following year, the Mexican and Austrian Governments organized follow-up meetings in Nayarit and Vienna, respectively. All interested States, as well as UN organizations, representatives of civil society, and other relevant stakeholders, were invited.[49] The fact that this series of humanitarian impact conferences attracted more government delegations than the NPT

43 2010 Review Conference of the Parties to the Treaty on the Non-Proliferation of Nuclear Weapons, Final Document, Doc. NPT/CONF.2010/50 (vol. I), 2010, part I, p. 19.

44 G. Nystuen and K. Egeland, "A 'Legal Gap'? Nuclear Weapons under International Law," *Arms Control Today*, vol. 46, no. 2, March 2016, pp. 8–14, 8.

45 Sauer and Pretorius, "Nuclear Weapons," p. 242.

46 "Joint Statement on the Humanitarian Dimension of Nuclear Disarmament," NPT Preparatory Committee, General Debate, Vienna, May 2, 2012. The 15 States were Austria, Chile, Costa Rica, Denmark, Egypt, Holy See, Indonesia, Ireland, Malaysia, Mexico, New Zealand, Nigeria, Norway, Philippines, and South Africa.

47 "Joint Statement on the Humanitarian Dimension of Nuclear Disarmament," delivered by Benno Laggner, Ambassador of Switzerland, 67th session of the UNGA First Committee, New York, October 22, 2012; and "Joint Statement on the Humanitarian Impact of Nuclear Weapons," Delivered by Ambassador Abdul Samad Minty, Permanent Representative of South Africa to the United Nations, Geneva, April 24, 2013.

48 Nystuen and Egeland, "A 'Legal Gap'?", p. 8; and Sauer and Pretorius, "Nuclear Weapons," p. 242.

49 Sauer and Pretorius, "Nuclear Weapons," p. 242.

Prepcom meetings in 2013 and 2014, one of the main disarmament forums, demonstrated the need to broaden the approach to nuclear weapons and to take into account humanitarian considerations.[50]

The principal aim of these meetings was to demonstrate to a larger public the devastating consequences of the use of nuclear weapons for the human being, as well as to assess the risk of a nuclear war or of the accidental explosion of a nuclear weapon. Sauer and Pretorius consider them to be "a general information campaign, waking up the general public, which has very much forgotten about nuclear weapons since the end of the Cold War."[51] Unfortunately, apart from India and Pakistan, the NWS remained absent in Oslo and Nayarit.[52] In Vienna, in contrast, delegations from India, Pakistan, the United Kingdom, and the United States were attending.[53]

Taking the third conference held in Vienna as an example, expert presentations included various topics such as: "Global Famine after a Regional Nuclear War: Overview of Recent Research,"[54] "The Most Dangerous Machines,"[55] "What is the Risk of Nuclear War,"[56] "Responding to the Humanitarian Consequences of Nuclear Weapons Use in Populated Areas,"[57] "Nuclear Weapons and International Health Law,"[58] "The Use of Nuclear Weapons and International Humanitarian Law,"[59] "The Humanitarian Origins of International Law Regulating Arms,"[60] and "The Fundamental Ethical and Moral Principles on Which International Legal Regulations of Nuclear Weapons are Based."[61]

At the conclusion of the conference, the Austrian hosts submitted a document calling on States and other stakeholders to "fill the legal gap for the prohibition and elimination of nuclear weapons."[62] Some months later, they announced that

50 Nystuen and Egeland, "A 'Legal Gap'?", p. 8.
51 Sauer and Pretorius, "Nuclear Weapons," p. 242.
52 *Ibid.*, pp. 242–243.
53 List of participants: https://www.bmeia.gv.at/fileadmin/user_upload/Zentrale/Aussenpolitik/Abruestung/HINW14/HINW14_participants.pdf (accessed February 27, 2017).
54 M. J. Mills, National Centre for Atmospheric Research. This and all the other presentations can be found on the website of the Vienna Conference: https://www.bmeia.gv.at/en/european-foreign-policy/disarmament/weapons-of-mass-destruction/nuclear-weapons-and-nuclear-terrorism/vienna-conference-on-the-humanitarian-impact-of-nuclear-weapons/ (accessed February 27, 2017).
55 E. Schlosser, author of "Command and Control: Nuclear Weapons, the Damascus Accident, and the Illusion of Safety."
56 S. Baum, Global Catastrophic Risk Institute.
57 R. Muller, Deputy Director of the Office for the Coordination of Humanitarian Affairs (OCHA), Geneva.
58 S. A. Solomon, Acting Legal Counsel at the World Health Organization (WHO), Geneva.
59 H. Durham, International Committee of the Red Cross, Geneva.
60 G. Nystuen, International Law and Policy Institute.
61 N. Hayashi, University of Oslo.
62 Pledge Presented at the Vienna Conference on the Humanitarian Impact of Nuclear Weapons by Austrian Deputy Foreign Minister Michael Linhart, https://www.bmeia.gv.at/fileadmin/

the "Austrian Pledge" would be called the "Humanitarian Pledge," thereby allowing for a broader sponsorship of the document.[63] The most relevant paragraphs of this pledge read as follows:

> In light of the important facts and findings that have been presented at the international conferences in Oslo, Nayarit and Vienna, and after careful consideration of the evidence, We, the States supporting and/or endorsing this pledge, have come to the following inescapable conclusions and make the subsequent pledge to take them forward with interested parties in available fora, including in the context of the NPT and its 2015 Review Conference:
>
> *Mindful of* the unacceptable harm that victims of nuclear weapons explosions and nuclear testing have experienced and recognising that the rights and needs of victims have not yet been adequately addressed,
>
> *Understanding* that the immediate, mid- and long-term consequences of a nuclear weapon explosion are significantly graver than it was understood in the past and will not be constrained by national borders but have regional or even global effects, potentially threatening the survival of humanity,
>
> *Recognizing* the complexity of and interrelationship between these consequences on health, environment, infrastructure, food security, climate, development, social cohesion and the global economy that are systemic and potentially irreversible . . .
>
> *Emphasizing* that the consequences of a nuclear weapon explosion and the risks associated with nuclear weapons concern the security of all humanity and that all states share the responsibility to prevent any use of nuclear weapons . . .
>
> *Mindful* that no national or international response capacity exists that would adequately respond to the human suffering and humanitarian harm that would result from a nuclear weapon explosion in a populated area, and that such capacity most likely will never exist
>
> . . .
>
> We call on all states parties to the NPT to renew their commitment to the urgent and full implementation of existing obligations under Article VI, and to this end, to identify and pursue effective measures to fill the legal gap for the prohibition and elimination of nuclear weapons and we pledge to cooperate with all stakeholders to achieve this goal . . .
>
> We pledge to cooperate with all relevant stakeholders, States, international organizations, the International Red Cross and Red Crescent Movements, parliamentarians and civil society, in efforts to stigmatise, prohibit and eliminate nuclear weapons in light of their unacceptable humanitarian consequences and associated risks.[64]

user_upload/Zentrale/Aussenpolitik/Abruestung/HINW14/HINW14_Austrian_Pledge.pdf (accessed February 27, 2017).

63 Nystuen and Egeland, "A 'Legal Gap'?", p. 8.

64 Emphases in the original.

At the time of writing, 127 States have formally endorsed this pledge.[65]

The 2015 NPT Review Conference was unable to reach agreement on a final document, but by endorsing the Humanitarian Pledge, the majority of the States Parties to the NPT have committed themselves to "pursue effective measures to fill the legal gap for the prohibition and elimination of nuclear weapons."[66] This is generally considered to be a significant achievement and the most important outcome of the 2015 NPT Review Conference.[67]

The position of the ICRC, the most prominent organization assisting the victims of armed conflicts, also attests to a stronger opposition to nuclear weapons more recently. As early as 1945, this organization was at the forefront of the movement against nuclear weapons, issuing a statement on the bombings of Hiroshima and Nagasaki entitled "Mankind is faced with a problem of supreme gravity . . .," expressing the wish that nuclear weapons be abolished.[68] Marcel Junod, ICRC delegate in the Far East at the time, was one of the first foreign doctors to arrive in the city, witnessing first-hand the devastating effects of the bombing and bringing aid to the survivors. His account of the Hiroshima bombing opened with the following words: "The physical impact of the bomb was beyond belief, beyond all apprehension, beyond imagination. Its moral impact was appalling."[69]

During the following decades, the ICRC continued to point at the destructive nature of these weapons, in particular for the civil population, and to urge States to work toward concluding a legally binding agreement on the ban of their use.[70] Following the publication of the ICJ's 1996 Advisory Opinion, the Committee observed at the UNGA that it found it difficult to envisage, in light of the Court's own conclusion that "the destructive power of nuclear weapons cannot be contained in either space or time," how the use of nuclear weapons could be compatible with the rules of international humanitarian law.[71]

65 See http://www.icanw.org/pledge/ (accessed February 27, 2017).

66 See Humanitarian Pledge.

67 See, for instance, B. Fihn, "A New Humanitarian Era: Prohibiting the Unacceptable," *Arms Control Today*, July/August 2015, https://www.armscontrol.org/ACT/2015_0708/Features/A-New-Humanitarian-Era-Prohibiting-the-Unacceptable (accessed February 27, 2017).

68 See, for the statement of September 5, 1945, http://www.icrc.org/eng/resources/documents/statement/69eezs.htm (accessed February 27, 2017).

69 ICRC, "Working Towards the Elimination of Nuclear Weapons," *Background document prepared by the ICRC*, Council of Delegates of the International Red Cross and Red Crescent Movement, November 26, 2011, no. CD/11/4.1, https://www.icrc.org/eng/resources/documents/report/nuclear-background-document-2011-11-26.htm (accessed February 27, 2017).

70 See, for instance, *Draft Rules for the Limitation of Dangers Incurred by the Civil Population in Time of War*, 1958.

71 Statement of the ICRC at the UNGA, 51st session, October 19, 1996, https://www.icrc.org/eng/resources/documents/article/other/57jncx.htm (accessed February 27, 2017).

During the Cold War, the topic of nuclear weapons was politically very sensitive, even for a humanitarian organization such as the ICRC.[72] Its relatively discrete attitude during this period can be explained by its strict policy of neutrality.[73] Recently, the organization's attitude toward nuclear weapons has become more pronounced. In a ground-breaking statement to the "Geneva Diplomatic Corps" on April 20, 2010, just before the 2010 NPT Review Conference, the ICRC's President, Jakob Kellenberger, quoted from the eyewitness account of Junod and made an appeal for banning the use of nuclear weapons, going further than any ICRC president before him.[74] Kellenberger's statement paved the way for further initiatives.[75]

In November 2011, the International Red Cross and Red Crescent Movement, of which the ICRC forms part, adopted a resolution entitled "Working towards the elimination of nuclear weapons," through which the organization updated its position on this matter.[76] The paragraphs that follow illustrate the new humanitarian trend particularly well:

> *The Council of Delegates,*
>
> . . . *concerned* also by the continued retention of tens of thousands of nuclear warheads, the proliferation of such weapons and the constant risk that they could again be used,
>
> *disturbed* by the serious implications of any use of nuclear weapons for humanitarian assistance activities and food production over wide areas of the word . . .
>
> 1. *emphasizes* the incalculable human suffering that can be expected to result from any use of nuclear weapons, the lack of any adequate humanitarian response capacity and the absolute imperative to prevent such use,
> 2. *finds* it difficult to envisage how any use of nuclear weapons could be compatible with the rules of international humanitarian law, in particular the rules of distinction, precaution and proportionality,

72 Sauer and Pretorius, "Nuclear Weapons," p. 239.

73 *Ibid.* See also B. A. Rieffer-Flanagan, "Is Neutral Humanitarism Dead? Red Cross Neutrality Walking the Tightrope of Neutral Humanitarism," *Human Rights Quarterly*, vol. 31, no. 4 (November 2009), pp. 888–915.

74 J. Kellenberger, "Bringing the Era of Nuclear Weapons to an End," *Statement by the President of the ICRC to the "Geneva Diplomatic Corps,"* Geneva, April 20, 2010, https://www.icrc.org/eng/resources/documents/statement/nuclear-weapons-statement-200410.htm (accessed February 27, 2017).

75 R. Johnson, "Linking Humanitarian Law and Nuclear Disarmament Action: The Case for a Nuclear Weapons Convention," *Austrian Review of International and European Law*, vol. 15, 2010, pp. 173–196, 179.

76 Resolution, Working towards the elimination of nuclear weapons, Annex to background document prepared by the ICRC.

3. *appeals* to all States:

> to ensure that nuclear weapons are never again used, regardless of their views on the legality of such weapons . . .
>
> to pursue in good faith and conclude with urgency and determination negotiations to prohibit the use of and completely eliminate nuclear weapons through a legally binding international agreement, based on existing commitments and international obligations . . .[77]

To sum up the ICRC's updated position, it will be noted, first, that the organization, without departing completely from its previous position and the conclusions of the ICJ, seems to take a more global approach, focusing not only on the core principles of humanitarian law, but also working toward the elimination of nuclear weapons by making their future use impossible – in other words, taking a clear disarmament approach. Second, the ICRC insists more heavily on the implications of a possible use of nuclear weapons for its own work and that of other humanitarian assistance organizations, having regard to the experiences made in Hiroshima and Nagasaki.[78] The question is indeed whether the survivors of a nuclear detonation could be efficiently assisted, taking into account the circumstances prevailing in the aftermath of a nuclear blast?[79] Third, the organization emphasizes the long-term effects of nuclear weapons, such as the development of illnesses among the population. The two latter aspects will be examined in more detail in the section below on human rights.[80]

The serious concerns about the catastrophic consequences of the use of nuclear weapons also led to the UNGA's decision to establish, in January 2013, an open-ended working group (OEWG) to develop proposals to activate multilateral nuclear disarmament negotiations.[81] Another OEWG meeting was decided upon in 2015 and took place in Geneva in 2016. As a result of its work, the UNGA adopted, on October 27, 2016, a resolution calling on Member States to launch negotiations in 2017 on a treaty banning nuclear weapons.[82] It noted with satisfaction the OEWG's substantive work,[83] and expressed its deep concern

77 Emphases in the original.

78 Johnson, "Linking Humanitarian Law and Nuclear Disarmament Action," pp. 179–180.

79 See S. Bagshaw, "Responding to the Detonation of Nuclear Weapons: A United Nations Humanitarian Perspective," in J. Borrie and T. Caughley (eds.), *Viewing Nuclear Weapons through a Humanitarian Lens*, New York and Geneva, 2013, pp. 118–130; and L. Maresca, "The Catastrophic Humanitarian Consequences of Nuclear Weapons: The Key Issues and Perspective of the International Committee of the Red Cross," in J. Borrie and T. Caughley (eds.), *Viewing Nuclear Weapons through a Humanitarian Lens*, New York and Geneva, 2013, pp. 131–144, 133–136.

80 See below, in particular this Chapter, sections C.3–4.

81 UNGA Resolution 65/56 (UN Doc. A/RES/67/5), January 4, 2013, "Taking forward multilateral nuclear disarmament negotiations," § 1 of the Preamble.

82 Resolution A/C.1/71/L.41, http://reachingcriticalwill.org/images/documents/Disarmament-fora/1com/1com16/resolutions/L41.pdf (accessed February 27, 2017).

83 Operative, § 1.

"about the catastrophic humanitarian consequences of any use of nuclear weapons."[84] It is no exaggeration to assert that the humanitarian approach to nuclear weapons was one of the driving factors for this resolution. The OEWG and the resolution will be considered further below in the section on the contribution of civil society to the implementation of the NPT.[85]

To sum up, the humanitarian initiative partly resulted from the NNWS' frustration with the NWS' unwillingness and slow pace of disarmament.[86] But it is more than that, namely, a genuine expression of humanity and a reflection of the emergence of a new era in security and disarmament policy in which humanitarian concerns and humanitarian law are growing in importance, and, at the same time, strategic balance and power politics are considered increasingly outdated Cold War concepts.[87] In the same vein, the initiative can also be viewed as an emanation of a more democratic international community in which global problems are discussed and decided by representatives from all States and by civil society, and not exclusively by the permanent members of the UNSC.[88]

In parallel to these developments in political and diplomatic fora, the judicial path was engaged, too, but ultimately was unsuccessful. On April 24, 2014, the Government of the Republic of the Marshall Islands filed an application at the ICJ instituting proceedings against the United Kingdom, Pakistan, and India, in which it claimed that the Respondents have breached their duty to pursue in good faith negotiations leading to nuclear disarmament in all its aspects under strict and effective international control.[89]

It is suggested here that these claims can be regarded as part of the broader humanitarian context. This flows, first of all, from the fact that, in the course of the proceedings, several references were made to the series of Conferences on the Humanitarian Impact of Nuclear Weapons, explained above, and in particular to the statement made by the Marshall Islands during the second of those conferences.[90] Second, during the proceedings, the Applicant drew attention to the devastating effects upon human life of nuclear weapons detonations. Having served as one of the US nuclear testing sites for more than a decade, the Marshall

84 Preamble, § 2.

85 This volume, Chapter 8, section B.2.b).

86 Fihn, "A New Humanitarian Era." See, e.g., Sauer and Pretorius, "Nuclear Weapons," p. 250, arguing that the "recent interest in the humanitarian approach of nuclear disarmament can be explained by a growing frustration with traditional arms control and a lull after initial expectations that the end of the Cold War would result in complete nuclear disarmament."

87 Fihn, "A New Humanitarian Era." Sauer and Pretorius, "Nuclear Weapons," p. 250, suggest that the traditional arms control approach is not only very slow, but also too state-centered.

88 *Ibid.*

89 ICJ, *Obligations Concerning Negotiations Relating to Cessation of the Nuclear Arms Race and to Nuclear Disarmament (Marshall Islands v. United Kingdom)*, October 5, 2016, Preliminary Objections, § 1. See, for the same claims, the cases against India and Pakistan (*ibid.*, § 1).

90 *Obligations Concerning Negotiations Relating to Cessation of the Nuclear Arms Race and to Nuclear Disarmament (Marshall Islands v. United Kingdom)*, Dissenting Opinion of Judge Cançado Trindade, § 259.

Islands can claim to be particular victims of nuclear weapons, although this aspect was not directly at stake in the proceedings before the ICJ. The serious impact of nuclear testing on the peoples and the environment of the Marshall Islands will be addressed in more detail further below.[91]

Ultimately, the high expectations of the disarmament community placed in the proceedings before the ICJ have not been fulfilled, since the cases were dismissed, by nine votes to seven regarding the cases against India and Pakistan and by eight votes to eight, by the President's casting vote, regarding the case against the United Kingdom, on the grounds that no "dispute" existed between the Marshall Islands and the Respondents.[92] In other words, the Court did not have to examine the merits of the case and the question of whether the three States have complied with their duties under Article VI NPT, or corresponding customary law, remains open. This is not the place for an analysis of those judgments, but the various dissenting opinions and the first doctrinal reactions express their surprise about this outcome, the ICJ having for the first time in its history rejected cases on this ground.[93]

c) New evidence for the destructive power of nuclear weapons and for the inability to assist the victims of nuclear explosions

As mentioned above, the main goal of the humanitarian initiative was to collect and present new evidence for the disastrous impact of the use of nuclear weapons for human beings. Two closely linked elements will be addressed in this section. A third element, dealing with the potential global consequences of a limited (regional) nuclear war, will be considered further below in the chapter on human rights.

The first element is the considerable research that has recently been conducted on the effect of nuclear explosions in inhabited regions, in particular in large cities. During the last few years, several studies of this type have been published. In a study presented at the Oslo Conference in March 2013, it has been shown, for instance, that a detonation of a nuclear weapon (of 100 kilotons) over a city of the size of Manchester would create blast and thermal effects killing more than 80 000 people immediately and leaving more than 210 000 people injured, devastating housing and commercial buildings, destroying vital infrastructure, causing massive population displacement, and leaving the local emergency service capacity seriously degraded. Moreover, ongoing radiation would have further health effects and hamper any efforts to respond to the crisis.[94]

91 This Chapter, section C.5.b).

92 Operative paragraphs 1 of the Judgments.

93 See, for instance, C. Tams, "No Dispute About Nuclear Weapons?", *EJIL: Talk!*, October 6, 2016, http://www.ejiltalk.org/no-dispute-about-nuclear-weapons/ (accessed February 27, 2017); and N. Krisch, 'Capitulation in The Hague: The Marshall Islands Cases', *EJIL: Talk!*, October 10, 2016, http://www.ejiltalk.org/capitulation-in-the-hague-the-marshall-islands-cases/ (accessed February 27, 2017).

94 Article 36, "Humanitarian Consequences: Short Case Study of the Direct Humanitarian Impacts from a Single Nuclear Weapon Detonation on Manchester," United Kingdom, 2013,

In another recent study, the immediate humanitarian consequences of a 12-kiloton nuclear explosion in Rotterdam have been examined.[95] In Chapter 1, the study describes in detail the scenario of such an explosion in the port of that city. In Chapter 2, it lays out the effects of a nuclear explosion, such as flash, heat and fire, blast, electro-magnetic pulse (EMP), flooding, radioactivity, fallout, and break-down of traffic, as well as chemical contamination originating from oil refineries and chemical plants in the region.[96] The study demonstrates that, close enough to the explosion, people may die because they are hit by the blast front, by peak dosages of ionising radiation, or by heat and fire. The zone of 100 percent fatalities is the largest regarding heat and fire effects, killing approximatively 7 800 people in the Waalhaven and Heijplaat communities, or in the residential parts of Rotterdam South closest to the explosion.[97] The study estimates that in an area of 300 square kilometers from the detonation, people would be in danger of receiving fatal doses of radiation.[98] As a result of the fact that the center of Rotterdam is directly downwind, 180 000 people would be unable to avoid harmful dosages of radiation. They would be seriously ill and 60 000 of them would die in the hours and days after the detonation.[99] The total amount of people dying as a direct consequence of the nuclear detonation would therefore be between 60 000 and 70 000, not counting the people dying young due to cancer.[100]

The study further estimates that just outside the 100 percent death zone, 7 800 people would be injured and need medical attention, of whom half would have second- and third-degree burns. For the people who would be able to move out of the zone, with fewer than 100 burn beds in the Netherlands, it is hard to imagine how the country would be able to provide the necessary medical care.[101] Moreover, a much larger category of persons would suffer from radiation sickness in various grades; the study assumes that at least an additional 6 000 cancer cases would be announced in the decades after the detonation.[102]

The experts also expect that roughly half the population of the Province of South-Holland would have to be evacuated, as well as the entire population of the Utrecht province – namely, almost 3 000 000 people. If 75 percent were to choose to and be able to leave, this would result in 2 250 000 evacuees, most

p. 14, http://www.article36.org/nuclear-weapons/humanitarian-impacts-from-a-single-nuclear-weapon-detonation-on-manchester/ (accessed February 27, 2017).

95 W. van der Zeijden and S. Snyder, "The Rotterdam Blast," *Pax*, 2014, http://www.paxchristi.net/news-media/resources-pax-christi-member-organisations (accessed February 27, 2017).

96 *Ibid.*, pp. 17–23.

97 *Ibid.*, p. 23.

98 *Ibid.*, p. 24.

99 *Ibid.*

100 *Ibid.*

101 *Ibid.*

102 *Ibid.* The study adds that the number of thyroid cancer cases would partly depend on the ability of the Dutch Government to provide people in affected areas with iodine prophylaxis pills, but concludes that it would almost certainly be impossible to reach all people in time.

of whom would be moving out of their respective areas within the first hours after the detonation.[103] Furthermore, the city of Rotterdam would no longer be the same and its center would be abandoned for a long period of time. Neighborhoods around the center would be affected. By the time Rotterdam city center would be clean enough to be rebuilt, the adjustments and temporary measures may have become permanent and the city, as it once was, would have ceased to exist.[104]

The study concludes that no society can be adequately prepared for any use of nuclear weapons, not even a country as wealthy and well organized as the Netherlands.[105] Similar studies have been conducted and presented for other towns, such as Geneva,[106] Lyon,[107] and Bombay.[108]

Apart from these studies based on concrete scenarios, demonstrating the devastation that would be caused by a nuclear explosion in a city, another factor has gained significance in the recent debate, namely, the recognition that no adequate humanitarian response would be possible in such a situation, in particular in an urban, densely populated area, such as Manchester or Rotterdam. This aspect has already been mentioned above, in connection with the ICRC's approach to nuclear weapons. The following excerpts quoted from a telegram by the first ICRC delegate to reach Hiroshima following the bombing in August 1945 help to concretize this aspect further:

> Visited Hiroshima . . . conditions appalling. City wiped out, eighty percent of all hospitals destroyed or seriously damaged. Inspected two emergency hospitals, conditions beyond description. Effect of bomb mysteriously serious . . . Estimated still over hundred thousands wounded in emergency hospitals . . . sadly lacking bandaging materials, medicines . . . Required: substantial quantities bandages, surgical pads, ointments for burns, sulfamides, also blood plasma and transfusion equipment.[109]

103 *Ibid.* The study stressed that once the extent of the fallout has become clear, many of the evacuees could return home. The experts expect that, all in all, roughly 400 000 people would need long-term relocation. Moreover, of the 1 850 000 people allowed to return home, it is expected that many would be reluctant to go back as a result of the stigmatization and perceived contamination of the areas in which they previously lived.

104 *Ibid.*

105 *Ibid.*, p. 25.

106 J. Borrie and T. Caughley, *An Illusion of Safety: Challenges of Nuclear Weapon Detonations for United Nations Humanitarian Coordination and Response*, UNIDIR, New York and Geneva, 2014, pp. 38 et seq.

107 D. Lalanne, "And If a Nuclear Bomb Exploded in Lyon (France)?" ican and Observatoire des armements, February 2014, http://www.obsarm.org/IMG/pdf/Bombe_sur_Lyon.pdf (accessed February 27, 2017).

108 M. V. Ramana, "Effects of a Nuclear Blast over Bombay," in B. Fihn (ed.), *Unspeakable Suffering: The Humanitarian Impact of Nuclear Weapons*, Geneva, 2013, pp. 94–97.

109 F. Bugnion, "The International Committee of the Red Cross and Nuclear Weapons: From Hiroshima to the Dawn of the 21st Century," *International Review of the Red Cross*, vol. 87, no. 859, 2005, pp. 511–524, 513.

It can also be recalled here that the 2011 Resolution of the Council of Delegates ("Working towards the elimination of nuclear weapons") highlights, in its first operative paragraph, ". . . the lack of adequate humanitarian response capacity and the absolute imperative to prevent such use."[110] Moreover, one of the findings of the Oslo Conference, mentioned above, emphasized that:

> It is unlikely that any State or international body could address the immediate humanitarian emergency caused by a nuclear weapon detonation in an adequate manner and provide sufficient assistance to those affected. Moreover, it might not be possible to establish such capacities, even if it were attempted.[111]

In concrete terms, the severe second- and third-degree burns of the victims would require most intensive medical care and resources, but none would be available.[112] Health professional staff, hospitals, and other health care resources are often concentrated in urban centers and would be disproportionally affected by a nuclear weapons attack. Hospitals would have disappeared or be damaged. If they were still standing, they would likely have no power or water.[113] Laboratories, operating theaters, sterilizers, ventilators, infusion pumps, cardiac monitors, and other equipment would either be smashed, burned, or not working due to electromagnetic pulse and loss of power.[114] In addition, members of emergency services, health care professionals, and others who may be called to assist in response to humanitarian emergencies would face unique dangers and difficulties following any nuclear blast, with widespread and persistent radioactivity severely complicating and hampering access and relief efforts.[115]

The few people who could reach hospitals or clinics would find most of the doctors, nurses, and other health professionals dead or injured.[116] As a matter of fact, in Hiroshima, 270 out of 300 doctors were reported dead, 1 654 out of 1 780 nurses and 112 out of 140 pharmacists were also dead; of 45 hospitals, 42 were no longer functional.[117]

110 See this Chapter, section B.2.b).

111 E. B. Eide, "Chair's Summary: Humanitarian Impact of Nuclear Weapons," March 5, 2013, https://www.regjeringen.no/en/aktuelt/nuclear_summary/id716343/ (accessed February 27, 2017).

112 T.A. Ruff, "The Health Consequences of Nuclear Explosions," in Fihn, *Unspeakable Suffering*, pp. 14–27, 23. See also Borrie and Caughley, *An Illusion of Safety*, p. 76.

113 Ruff, "The Health Consequences of Nuclear Explosions," p. 23.

114 *Ibid.*

115 *Ibid.*, p. 24. See also Borrie and Caughley, *An Illusion of Safety*, p. 76.

116 Ruff, "The Health Consequences of Nuclear Explosions," p. 23.

117 International Committee of Experts in Medical Sciences and Public Health and World Health Organization, Effects of Nuclear War on Health and Health Services, Report of the International Committee of Experts in Medical Sciences and Public Health to Implement Resolution WHA34.38 (1984), Geneva, Albany (NY), WHO Publications Center.

In another recent study, UNIDIR largely confirms these findings, distinguishing nevertheless between nuclear explosions in densely populated environments and detonations in sparsely populated areas in which no people are present. As far as the former situation is concerned, the experts compare the kind of responses needed in the aftermath of a nuclear explosion to those given in the aftermath of a major natural disaster.[118] In this respect, the study concludes that the level of harm and destruction caused would defy any reasonable local preparedness, and assistance would have to come from outside, even more so in cases of multiple nuclear weapon detonations.[119]

d) The particular question of the legality of low-yield and earth-penetrating nuclear weapons

The NWS argued before the ICJ that it was possible to use low-yield (also called "battlefield" or "tactical")[120] nuclear weapons whose limited impact would respect the principles of humanitarian law. The United Kingdom expressed the point of view that, in reality, nuclear weapons could be used in a wide variety of circumstances with very different results in terms of likely civilian casualties. It added that, in certain cases, such as the use of a low-yield nuclear weapon against warships on the High Seas or troops in sparsely populated areas, it might be possible to envisage a use of nuclear weapons which could cause comparatively few civilian casualties.[121]

A similar argument was advanced by the United States. They claimed that, regarding proportionality, the question of whether an attack with nuclear weapons would be disproportionate depended entirely on the circumstances, including the nature of the enemy threat, the importance of destroying the objective, the character, size, and likely effects of the device, and the magnitude of the risk to civilians. In other words, nuclear weapons were not inherently disproportionate.[122]

The Court replied to these arguments in the following terms:

> The Court would observe that none of the States advocating the legality of the use of nuclear weapons under certain circumstances, including the "clean" use of smaller, low yield, tactical nuclear weapons, has indicated what, supposing such limited use were feasible, would be the precise circumstances

118 Borrie and Caughley, *An Illusion of Safety*, p. 76.

119 *Ibid.*

120 There is no definition of a "low-yield" nuclear weapon, but the expression is often used to refer to explosive devices with an explosive output of less than 5 kilotons TNT equivalent. For comparison, the bombs used in Hiroshima and Nagasaki had yields in the range of 12 to 15 kilotons (J. Burroughs, "The Lawfulness of 'Low-Yield,' Earth-Penetrating Nuclear Weapons," Lawyers' Committee on Nuclear Policy, January 20, 2003, http://lcnp.org/wcourt/nwlawfulness.htm (accessed February 27, 2017).

121 Written arguments of the United Kingdom, p. 53 (footnotes omitted).

122 *Ibid.*, p. 23 (footnotes omitted).

> justifying such use; nor whether such limited use would not tend to escalate into the all-out use of high yield nuclear weapons. This being so, the Court does not consider that it has a sufficient basis for a determination on the validity of this view.[123]

In other words, the ICJ left no doubt that it was incumbent on States advocating that a certain type of nuclear weapons could be used in a manner compatible with international law to prove their allegation. It concluded that the NWS had failed to bring sufficient and convincing evidence in support of their claim.

This issue is not only of academic interest, but practically very relevant, considering the fact that in May 2011 Pakistan tested a missile capable of carrying short-range, low-yield nuclear weapons. Experts concluded from this event that Pakistan would consider the use of such weapons in a situation of war with India.[124] The issue had already received attention in expert circles in the aftermath of the 1996 Advisory Opinion, in particular regarding the development of earth-penetrating nuclear weapons that are capable of reaching targets such as underground bunkers, allegedly limiting collateral damage caused to civilians and civil property.[125] The majority of experts seem to be convinced that the use of low-yield, earth-penetrating nuclear weapons cannot meet the criteria of lawfulness identified by the ICJ. As far as the principle of discrimination is concerned, Robert W. Nelson, a physicist with the Princetown's University Program on Science and Global Security and the American Federation of Scientists (AFS), concluded in an article published in 2002, based on analysis of physical constraints, that earth-penetrating warheads cannot penetrate deeply enough to contain the nuclear explosion and would necessarily produce a particularly intense and deadly radioactive fallout.[126] He estimated that a 1-kiloton earth-penetrating

123 Advisory Opinion, ICJ Reports 1996, § 94.

124 See Reuters, "Pakistan Builds Low Yield Nuclear Capability," May 15, 2011, http://www.reuters.com/article/2011/05/15/pakistan-nuclear-idAFL3E7GE02F20110515 (accessed February 27, 2017).

125 Regarding the United States, the most likely weapon to be used for such a purpose is the B61 (or B61-11) air-dropped bomb, a munition that includes a nuclear warhead (D. S. Rudesill, "Regulating Tactical Nuclear Weapons," *The Georgetown Law Journal*, vol. 102, 2013, pp. 99–177, 111). A former Joint Chiefs of Staff's Manual "Doctrine for Joint Theater Nuclear Operations" defined the following categories: very low-yield (less than 1 kiloton), low (1 to 10 kilotons), high (over 50 to 500 kilotons), and very high (over 500 kilotons) (C. J. Moxley Jr., J. Burroughs, and J. Granoff, "Nuclear Weapons and Compliance with International Humanitarian Law and the Nuclear Non-Proliferation Treaty," *Fordham International Law Journal*, vol. 34, no. 4, 2011, pp. 595–696, 642, n. 163).

126 R. W. Nelson, "Low-Yield Earth-Penetrating Nuclear Weapons," *Science and Global Security*, 2002, no. 1, p. 1, http://scienceandglobalsecurity.org/archive/sgs10nelson.pdf (accessed February 23, 2017). See also V. W. Sidel et al., "The Threat of Low-Yield Earth-Penetrating Nuclear Weapons to Civilian Populations: Nuclear "Bunker Busters" and Their Medical Consequences," *IPPNW Special Report*, http://www.ippnw.org/pdf/IPPNWEPWReport.pdf (accessed March 8, 2017).

nuclear weapon used in an urban environment would spread a lethal dose of radioactive fallout over several square kilometers, resulting in tens of thousands of civilian deaths.[127] Similar arguments against the legality of such weapons have been made by other experts.[128] It is estimated, for instance, that a 5-kiloton nuclear weapon, detonating near and upwind from Damascus, Syria, at a depth of 30 feet (9.14 meters) would cause 230 000 fatalities and another 280 000 casualties within two years. The use of a low-yield, earth-penetrating nuclear weapon against the bunker in Baghdad where Saddam Hussein was supposed to live would have caused casualties on a similar scale.[129] Therefore, the principle of distinction would be breached in such a scenario.

In addition, the use of such weapons would also be problematic in light of the principles of necessity and proportionality which command that, if a weapon is available which causes less damage and suffering than a nuclear weapon to carry out the intended mission, the use of nuclear weapons is prohibited.[130] It is argued that the United States possesses a number of conventional weapons capable of destroying hardened targets buried within approximately 50 feet of the surface.[131] In other words, other, less harmful alternatives being available, the use of low-yield, earth-penetrating nuclear weapons is likely to be contrary to the principles of necessity and proportionality.

Even where remote areas are concerned, the use of nuclear weapons would hardly meet the requirements of international humanitarian law because their effects are uncontrollable.[132] To take again a practical example, Professor Brian L. Bengs, Major in the US Air Force, has convincingly demonstrated that a nuclear attack against the Natanz uranium-enrichment facility in the central Iranian desert, located approximately 17 miles from the town of Natanz, would likely be an illegal act.[133] From his point of view, it is difficult to argue that use of a tactical

127 Nelson, "Low-Yield Earth-Penetrating Nuclear Weapons," p. 1.

128 See, for instance, S. Drell, R. Jeanloz, and B. Peurifoy, "Bunkers, Bombs, Radiation," *Los Angeles Times*, 17 March 2002, http://articles.latimes.com/2002/mar/17/opinion/oe-drell17 (accessed February 27, 2017). See also Moxley et al., "Nuclear Weapons and Compliance," in particular pp. 642 et seq.

129 Moxley et al., "Nuclear Weapons and Compliance," p. 643, n. 163.

130 J. Burroughs, "The Vancouver Declaration and the Humanitarian Imperative for Nuclear Disarmament," *Nuclear Abolition Forum*, issue no. 1, October 2011, pp. 1–6, 4, https://www.worldfuturecouncil.org/file/2016/01/NAF_2011_International_humanitarian_Law_and_nuclear_Weapons.pdf (accessed February 23, 2017).

131 R. W. Nelson, "Low-Yield Earth-Penetrating Nuclear Weapons," *FAS Public Interest Report*, January/February 2001, p. 3, https://fas.org/programs/ssp/nukes/newweapons/loyieldearthpenwpnrpt.html (accessed February 27, 2017). See also Moxley et al., "Nuclear Weapons and Compliance," p. 660.

132 Moxley et al., "Nuclear Weapons and Compliance," pp. 642 et seq., 660.

133 In April 2006, the *New Yorker* published an article alleging that the United States was actively planning for a possible attack upon suspected nuclear-weapon-development sites within Iran (S. M. Hersh, "The Iran Plans: Would President Bush Go to War to Stop Tehran from Getting the Bomb?", *New Yorker*, April 17, 2006, http://www.newyorker.com/magazine/2006/04/17/the-iran-plans (accessed February 27, 2017).

nuclear weapon against the Natanz facility would not violate the principles of military necessity and proportionality. The main reason for this allegation is the fact that the only available and appropriate earth-penetrating nuclear weapon (B61-11) has an explosive yield (400 kiloton) that cannot be contained by its limited earth-penetration depth (20 feet).[134] In fact, containment of a nuclear explosion of that size could only be ensured at a depth well in excess of 3 000 feet.[135] As a consequence, the military and civilian personnel in any above- or below-ground structure of the Natanz facility and within approximatively a 1-mile radius would likely be killed immediately as a result of the explosion.[136] Moreover, the resulting radioactive fallout would affect countless civilians unrelated to the Natanz facility and very probably turn the attack into a disproportionate act. The civilian population of the nearby city of Natanz, counting 40 000 inhabitants, would be likely to suffer a high number of injuries and casualties caused by the fallout, unless immediate evacuation takes place. Furthermore, depending on the weather, radioactive fallout could spread to other populated areas in and around Iran, causing additional injuries among civilians.[137]

In his dissenting opinion to the 1996 Advisory Opinion, Judge Schwebel argued that the use of a nuclear depth charge to destroy a submarine that is about to fire nuclear-armed missiles could be lawful:

> . . . At the other extreme is the use of tactical nuclear weapons against discrete military or naval targets so situated that substantial civilian casualties would not ensue. For example, the use of a nuclear depth-charge to destroy a nuclear submarine that is about to fire nuclear missiles, or has fired one or more of a number of its nuclear missiles, might well be lawful. By the circumstance of its use, the nuclear depth-charge would not give rise to immediate civilian casualties. It would easily meet the test of proportionality . . .[138]

According to Moxley, this is a rather unrealistic scenario which, moreover, is likely to provoke a nuclear escalation. This viewpoint is fully shared here.[139] In addition, the proportionality requirement and the prohibition of using means of warfare of a nature to cause superfluous injury and unnecessary suffering contain an implicit requirement of assessing alternatives to the weapon intended for use. In other words, it is suggested that, when looking at the military objective to be achieved, one must assume that there is an obligation to examine whether that objective

134 B. L. Bengs, "Legal Constraints upon the Use of a Tactical Nuclear Weapon against the Natanz Nuclear Facility in Iran," *George Washington International Law Review*, vol. 40, 2008, pp. 323–399, 327 and 371.

135 Nelson, "Low-Yield Earth-Penetrating Nuclear Weapons," p. 9.

136 Bengs, "Legal Constraints," p. 372.

137 *Ibid.*

138 ICJ Reports 1996, pp. 320 et seq.

139 C. J. Moxley Jr., 'The Unlawfulness of the Use or Threat of Use of Nuclear Weapons', *ILSA Journal of International & Comparative Law*, vol. 8, 2002, pp. 447–472, 451 et seq.

could be achieved with a weapon causing less suffering.[140] Having said this, Judge Schwebel expressed doubts that a conventional depth-charge might be enough to successfully destroy the submarine that is about to fire or has already fired nuclear missiles, but did not further elaborate his argument.

Furthermore, the use of nuclear weapons under water might have catastrophic consequences for the maritime environment, protected, inter alia, by Article 35 § 3 of Additional Protocol I to the Geneva Conventions. In its 1996 Advisory Opinion, the ICJ held that States must take environmental considerations into account when applying the necessity and proportionality tests.[141] It is important to mention that the ICRC's Study of customary humanitarian law finds that Rule 45 – prohibiting the use of methods or means of warfare that are intended, or may be expected, to cause widespread, long-term, and severe damage to the natural environment – has become part of universal customary international law, binding on all States whether or not Parties to Additional Protocol I.[142] Even though the criteria for prohibited damage within the meaning of Article 35 § 3 – widespread, long-term, and severe – set a high threshold, as mentioned above, it is suggested that if any means of warfare can meet these criteria, nuclear weapons do, and that many if not all nuclear weapons explosions would contravene this prohibition.[143] In addition, more specific rules protecting the sea might set further limitations to the use of nuclear weapons in this environment.[144] Finally, Judge Schwebel's argument that a nuclear strike could be used to respond to a threat or use of nuclear weapons by the enemy can easily be countered by invoking one of the characteristics of international humanitarian law, namely, that its rules

140 S. O'Connor, "Nuclear Weapons and the Unnecessary Suffering Rule," in G. Nystuen, S. Casey-Maslen, and A. Golden Bersagel (eds.), *Nuclear Weapons under International Law*, Cambridge, 2014, pp. 128–147, p. 143. See also Nystuen and Egeland, "A 'Legal Gap'?", p. 11, arguing that a tactical nuclear strike against a submarine far out at sea may not be a violation of the rule on distinction, but a violation of the prohibition against superfluous suffering.

141 ICJ Reports 1996, § 30; see also, in this respect, E. Brown Weiss, "Opening the Door to the Environment and to Future Generations," in Boisson de Chazournes and Sands, *International Law*, pp. 338–353; and D. Momtaz, 'The Use of Nuclear Weapons and the Protection of the Environment: The Contribution of the International Court of Justice', in Boisson de Chazournes and Sands, *International Law*, pp. 354–374.

142 J.-M. Henckaerts and L. Doswald-Beck, *Customary International Humanitarian Law*, vol. I: *Rules*, Cambridge, 2005, pp. 151–155. France and the United Kingdom have made reservations regarding the application of Protocol I to nuclear weapons. For the text of the UK's reservation, see: https://www.icrc.org/ihl.nsf/NORM/0A9E03F0F2EE757CC1256402003FB6D2?OpenDocument (accessed February 27, 2017). And the French reservation: https://www.icrc.org/applic/ihl/ihl.nsf/Notification.xsp?action=openDocument&documentId=D8041036B40EBC44C1256A34004897B2 (accessed February 27, 2017).

143 J. Burroughs, "International Humanitarian Law," in Fihn, *Unspeakable Suffering*, pp. 68–75, 72.

144 See, for instance, the 1982 UN Convention on the Law of the Sea; its Article 192 reads as follows: "States have the obligation to protect and preserve the marine environment."

must be respected even if the adversary fails to do so. In other words, the principle of reciprocity does not apply when it comes to protecting combatants and civilians affected by armed conflict. This results from common Article 1 of the Geneva Conventions and Article 1 § 1 of Additional Protocol I, which reads: "The High Contracting Parties undertake to respect and to ensure respect for the present Convention *in all circumstances.*"[145]

Moreover, Rule 140 of the compilation of customary international humanitarian law established by the ICRC, mentioned above, recognizes that "[t]he obligation to respect and ensure respect for international humanitarian law does not depend on reciprocity."[146] In other words, even States that have not ratified the Geneva Conventions would be prevented from using nuclear weapons to respond to a threat or use of nuclear weapons.

In light of the foregoing, this author suggests that the NWS have to date not come up with convincing evidence in favor of the possibility of using low-yield nuclear weapons that would respect basic principles of humanitarian law. On the contrary, the weight of evidence shows that there are no "clean" uses and, in particular, that earth-penetrating warheads, whether or not low-yield, would cause significant radioactive fallout and civilian casualties.[147] Purely theoretical scenarios of ideal-condition strikes with allegedly no collateral effects on the civil population are not a realistic basis for a legal analysis of nuclear weapons under international law.[148] In addition, it seems safe to conclude that a situation in which the use of low-yield nuclear weapons is seriously considered would generally not involve a threat to the survival of the State.[149] Accordingly, the ICJ's conclusion of "general" illegality applies to the threat or use of such weapons.[150]

3. A legal update: Toward a presumption of unlawfulness of nuclear weapons under international humanitarian law

In the present subdivision, the author proposes some personal conclusions on the question of the legality of use of nuclear weapons under humanitarian law in light of the recent developments, detailed so far.

Even though the humanitarian approach is not new, as shown above, it has received a new impulse from the numerous voices that have expressed their concern about the potential use of nuclear weapons and, in particular, about the protection of the human being and future generations. To mention only two examples, it can be recalled that the NPT Review Conference, a forum that had

145 Emphasis added.
146 Henckaerts and Doswald-Beck, *Customary International Humanitarian Law*, vol. I, pp. 498–499.
147 Burroughs, "The Vancouver Declaration," p. 5.
148 Moxley et al., "Nuclear Weapons and Compliance," p. 661.
149 *Ibid.*
150 *Ibid.*

traditionally been concerned more with aspects of international security than with humanitarian ideas, voiced in 2010 "its deep concern at the catastrophic humanitarian consequences of any use of nuclear weapons," and that, in 2011, the Council of Delegates of the International Red Cross and Red Crescent Movement found "it difficult to envisage how any use of nuclear weapons could be compatible with the rules of international humanitarian law." Moreover, the outcome of the three conferences in Oslo, Nayarit, and Vienna shows that the humanitarian impact of the use of nuclear weapons has been underestimated. Recent and very concrete studies demonstrate the destructive power of nuclear weapons explosions, in particular in large cities and densely populated regions. A legal assessment cannot remain unaffected by these findings.

Accordingly, the present author suggests that new evidence and information gathered since 1996 confirm that nuclear weapons cannot be used without violating basic rules of international humanitarian law.[151] In light of their particularities, especially the uncontrollability of their impact, these weapons cannot be used without causing considerable collateral damage to civilians and civilian objects. Burroughs argues that the inability to comply with the requirement of discrimination due to the uncontrollability of effects is the most powerful argument in favor of the unlawfulness of the use of nuclear weapons under international humanitarian law.[152] This point of view is shared here without reservations. If cluster munitions directed at the town of Zagreb have been considered to be indiscriminate weapons by the ICTY in the case of *Milan Martić*, as explained in Part I of this volume,[153] it is hard to imagine a situation where the use of nuclear weapons would respect the requirement of distinction in attack. Moreover, the uncontrollability of effects also has a temporal aspect in the same way as anti-personnel mines or ERW. The latter linger and kill and maim civilians, in particular children and women, often years after the cessation of hostilities. The harmful impact of nuclear weapons on future generations will be addressed in more detail in the next section, dealing with human rights.

Essentially the same can be claimed regarding the rule prohibiting unnecessary suffering. The long-term effects of nuclear weapons include a significantly increased risk of cancer mortality throughout the life of the survivors.[154] In light of demonstrable consequences of the use of nuclear weapons, it is not possible, from the present author's point of view, to conceive of circumstances where such

151 See in this sense Johnson, "Linking Humanitarian Law and Nuclear Disarmament Action," p. 194; Burroughs, "International Humanitarian Law," p. 73; and the same author, "Legal Gap or Compliance Gap?", *Arms Control Today*, October 2015, https://www.armscontrol.org/ACT/2015_10/Letter-to-the-Editor/Legal%20Gap%20or%20Compliance%20Gap (accessed February 27, 2017). See, for a more hesitant approach, G. Nystuen, "Conclusions on the Status of Nuclear Weapons under International Law," in Nystuen et al., *Nuclear Weapons under International Law*, pp. 483–486, 486.

152 Burroughs, "International Humanitarian Law," p. 70.

153 This volume, Chapter 4, section D.3.

154 O'Connor, "Nuclear Weapons," p. 147.

injuries and suffering could be deemed necessary or proportionate. As a result, the prohibition not to inflict superfluous injury or unnecessary suffering would be breached by the use of these weapons. It is relevant in this regard to recall that, in the *Ryuichi Shimoda* case, the Tokyo District Court found that the fact of dropping a nuclear bomb "may be regarded as contrary to the fundamental principle of the law of war which prohibits the causing of unnecessary suffering."[155] In addition, as noted above, it is more than doubtful whether any use of nuclear weapons would respect the customary prohibition to deploy means of warfare that cause widespread, long-term, and severe damage to the environment within the meaning of Article 35 § 3 of Additional Protocol I to the Geneva Conventions.[156] In light of what precedes, the principle of proportionality would also be infringed in case of use of nuclear weapons, especially if assessed broadly, as has been suggested for anti-personnel mines and cluster munitions. In other words, the use of nuclear weapons should be justified in light of the larger picture, including its impact on the well-being and health of the people affected, and its consequences for the environment and for future generations.

Apart from these general principles of humanitarian law applicable in armed conflict, on which much legal research has been concentrated in recent years, other rules of international humanitarian law are relevant in connection with nuclear weapons attacks. They have received moderate attention so far, which is surprising considering the precise nature of certain prohibitions. For instance, it is noteworthy to recall the studies of nuclear explosions in Manchester or Rotterdam, detailed above, where it is explained that these towns would no longer be the same, the blast leaving behind devastated housing, commercial buildings, and vital infrastructure. Entire neighborhoods would be abandoned and stigmatized for an indefinite period of time. This brings into play Rule 50 of the Study of customary international humanitarian law indicating that "[t]he destruction or seizure of the property of an adversary is prohibited, unless required by imperative military necessity."[157] In light of the extent of destruction, and in particular due to the long-lasting uselessness of property as a result of radiation, it is difficult to imagine that any nuclear weapon attack against an inhabited town could be legitimized by imperative military necessity.[158] Moreover, in the *Blaškić* case, the ICTY stated that "the notion of 'extensive,' required for the destruction

155 *Ryuichi Shimoda et al. v. The State of Japan*, Tokyo District Court, December 7, 1963, § 11.

156 This Chapter, section B.2.d).

157 Henckaerts and Doswald-Beck, *Customary International Humanitarian Law*, vol. I, pp. 175–177.

158 The violation of this rule through "extensive destruction and appropriation of property, not justified by military necessity and carried out unlawfully and wantonly," constitutes a grave breach under the Geneva Conventions (Article 50 of the First, Article 51 of the Second, and Article 147 of the Fourth Geneva Convention). Under the ICC Statute, "destroying or seizing the enemy's property unless such destruction or seizure be imperatively demanded by the necessities of war" constitutes a war crime in international armed conflict (Article 8(2)(b)(xiii)).

being qualified as a grave breach under the Geneva Conventions and a war crime under the ICTY Statute, has to be evaluated according to the facts of the case" and that "a single act, such as the destruction of a hospital, may suffice to characterize an offence under this count."[159] If the destruction of one single building qualifies as a grave breach, Rule 50 becomes relevant, *a fortiori*, in the event of a nuclear weapon explosion capable of destroying entire cities.

Moreover, the example of an explosion in the port of Rotterdam, causing the destruction of oil refineries and chemical plants in the region and, as a result, provoking further contamination, illustrates the relevance of Rule 42 in the context of a nuclear weapons attack, which imposes on the States Parties a special duty of care in relation to works and installations containing dangerous forces:

> Particular care must be taken if works and installations containing dangerous forces, namely dams, dykes and nuclear electrical generating stations, and other installations located at or in their vicinity are attacked, in order to avoid the release of dangerous forces and consequent severe losses among the civilian population.[160]

Even though the scope of Article 56 of Additional Protocol I is limited to "dams, dykes and nuclear electrical generating stations," it is recognized that, in light of the fact that attacks on such installations may cause severe damage to the civilian population and the natural environment, the same considerations should apply to other installations, such as chemical plants and petroleum refineries.[161]

A nuclear attack against an inhabited city would also destroy historic monuments or sites, museums, theaters, opera houses, concert halls, cinemas, churches, temples, synagogues, mosques and minarets, schools, universities, and many other institutions and buildings dedicated to cultural, educational, scientific, religious, or other similar purposes. Rule 38 of the Study of customary international humanitarian law deals with the "respect" of cultural property during warfare:

> Each party to the conflict must respect cultural property: A) Special care must be taken in military operations to avoid damage to buildings dedicated to religion, art, science, education or charitable purposes and historic monuments unless they are military objectives. B) Property of great importance to the cultural heritage of every people must not be the object of attack unless imperatively required by military necessity.

The freedom of maneuver of many States when attacking cultural property is today further restricted by the 1954 Hague Convention for the Protection of

159 ICTY, *The Prosecutor v. Tihomir Blaškić*, Trial Chamber Judgment, IT-95-14-T, March 3, 2000, § 157.

160 Henckaerts and Doswald-Beck, *Customary International Humanitarian Law*, vol. I, pp. 139–142.

161 *Ibid.*, pp. 141–142.

Cultural Property in the Event of Armed Conflict, ratified by 127 States at the time of writing.[162] The fundamental principles of protecting and preserving cultural property in the Convention are today widely recognized as reflecting customary international law.[163] In the same vein, Rule 40 of the Study of customary international humanitarian law establishes a duty to "protect" cultural property, prohibiting "[a]ll seizure of or destruction or willful damage done to institutions dedicated to religion, charity, education, the arts and sciences, historic monuments and works of art and science."[164]

In addition, it is obvious that the use of a nuclear weapon would also affect the natural environment, crop fields, greenhouses, forests, water courses, lakes, marine ecosystems, wildlife, and domestic animals. As the ICJ in the 1996 Advisory Opinion said, "the radiation released by nuclear explosion would affect health, agriculture, natural resources and demography over a very wide area,"[165] and this most probably for a considerable period of time. Rule 54 of the Study of customary international humanitarian law sets an important limit on the use of nuclear weapons, prohibiting "attacking, destroying, removing or rendering useless objects indispensable to the survival of the civilian population."[166] Additional Protocols I and II provide the following examples of objects indispensable to the survival of the civilian populations in international and non-international armed conflicts: foodstuffs, agricultural areas for the production of foodstuffs, crops, livestock, drinking water installations and supplies, and irrigation works.[167] The list of examples is not exhaustive, as indicated by using the words "such as."[168] Rule 54 is a corollary of the prohibition, valid in international as well as non-international armed conflict, of "the use of starvation of the civilian population as a method of warfare," contained in Rule 53 of the Study of customary international humanitarian law, because attacking objects indispensable to the survival of the civilian population may amount to violations of the prohibition of starvation.[169] The same applies to the denial of access to humanitarian aid intended for civilians in need, including deliberately impeding humanitarian aid, as will be explained further below (Rule 55).

162 See https://www.icrc.org/ihl/INTRO/400 (accessed February 27, 2017).

163 Henckaerts and Doswald-Beck, *Customary International Humanitarian Law*, vol. I, p. 129.

164 *Ibid.*, pp. 132–135. Under the ICC Statute, destruction of buildings dedicated to religion, education, arts, science, or charitable purposes and historic monuments and destruction and seizure that is not imperatively demanded by the necessities of the conflict constitute war crimes in both international and non-international armed conflicts (ICC Statute, Articles 8(2)(b)(ix), 8(2)(b)(xiii), 8(2)(e)(iv) and 8(2)(e)(xii)).

165 ICJ Reports 1996, § 35.

166 Henckaerts and Doswald-Beck, *Customary International Humanitarian Law*, vol. I, pp. 189–193.

167 Article 54 § 2 of Additional Protocol I and Article 14 of Additional Protocol II.

168 Henckaerts and Doswald-Beck, *Customary International Humanitarian Law*, vol. I, p. 193.

169 *Ibid.*, pp. 186 and 188.

Finally, a use of nuclear weapons would also destroy and render unworkable ambulances, hospitals, and clinics, and kill nurses and doctors. Rule 28 of the Study of customary international humanitarian law imposes on States the duty to respect and protect "medical units exclusively assigned to medical purposes . . . in all circumstances." This rule is contained in the First and Fourth Geneva Conventions,[170] and its scope was expanded in Additional Protocol I to cover civilian medical units in addition to military ones.[171] The term "medical units" includes, inter alia, hospitals and similar institutions, blood transfusion centers, preventive medicine centers and institutes, medical depots, and the medical and pharmaceutical stores of such units.[172] Rule 29 imposes an analogous duty to respect and protect medical transports in all circumstances, whether military or civil in nature, and regardless of whether they are conducted by land, such as ambulances, water (hospital ships), and air (medical aircrafts).[173]

In the same logic, it has been indicated above that one of the most significant findings yielded by recent research on the humanitarian impact of nuclear weapons is the awareness of the ICRC and other humanitarian actors of the difficulties to respond adequately to a nuclear disaster. Due to widespread and persistent radioactivity, emergency services and personnel would face unique dangers and problems following nuclear explosions, rendering access to the victims extremely difficult. Therefore, Rule 55 of the Study cited above might come into play in the event of a nuclear attack:

> The parties to the conflict must allow and facilitate rapid and unimpeded passage of humanitarian relief for civilians in need, which is impartial in character and conducted without any adverse distinction, subject to their right of control.[174]

The Additional Protocols implicitly recognize the entitlement of civilian populations to receive humanitarian relief, as they require that relief actions "shall be undertaken" whenever civilians are in need.[175] The ICRC and the United Nations have, on several occasions, highlighted the duty to grant the civilian population adequate access to relief supplies.[176] For example, in a report on

170 Article 19 of the First Geneva Convention and Article 18 of the Fourth Geneva Convention.

171 Article 12 of Additional Protocol I.

172 Henckaerts and Doswald-Beck, *Customary International Humanitarian Law*, vol. I, p. 95.

173 *Ibid.*, pp. 98–102.

174 *Ibid.*, pp. 193–200. The UNSC has repeatedly called for the respect for this rule (see, e.g., as far as situations of children in armed conflicts and the humanitarian assistance to them are concerned, Resolutions 1261 (1999), 1265 (1999), 1296 (2000), and 1314 (2000)).

175 Article 70(1) of Additional Protocol I, and Article 18(2) of Additional Protocol II.

176 For instance, in a statement to the press in 1997 concerning the conflict in Zaire, the ICRC appealed to all parties to "respect the victims' right to assistance and protection" (ICRC, Communication to the Press no. 97/08); other examples are cited in Henckaerts and Doswald-Beck, *Customary International Humanitarian Law*, vol. I, pp. 199–200.

emergency assistance to Sudan in 1996, the UNSG stated that any attempt to diminish the capacity of the international community to respond to conditions of suffering and hardship among the civilian population in that country gave rise to the most serious concerns over the respect of one of the most important recognized humanitarian principles, namely, "the right of civilian populations to receive humanitarian assistance in times of war."[177]

The relevance of such a right in the context of nuclear weapons use is obvious: if adequate access and assistance to victims of a nuclear attack is simply not possible due to the extent of destruction and radiation, such a use will constitute a deliberate violation of this right and, as a result, also of Rule 55 referred to above. For all these reasons, it is relevant to sum up by quoting a report of the World Health Organization (WHO), concluding already in 1987 that, if there is no effective response, the prevention of the use of nuclear weapons is the only realistic possibility to prevent humanitarian disasters of this kind:

> Obviously the health services of the world could in no way cope with such a situation. In sum, in the event of a nuclear war triage would at best be insignificant, rescue work scarcely other than makeshift . . . The great majority of casualties would be left without medical attention of any kind . . . When treatment is ineffective, the only solution available to the health professionals is prevention. Prevention is obviously the only possibility in case of a nuclear war.[178]

To conclude this analysis of the legal situation of nuclear weapons, under international humanitarian law it can be recalled that a prohibition of the latter was already considered "nascent" by the ICJ in 1996.[179] Since the Court's opinion, two decades have passed. On the one hand, the proponents of an absolute prohibition of the use of such weapons have offered a substantial amount of new evidence strengthening their view. On the other hand, the opponents of such a prohibition have not progressed, and have been absent from the negotiation tables during the three humanitarian conferences or, at least, kept silent. From the author's point of view, the burden of proof has now shifted; it is up to them to demonstrate that the use of nuclear weapons could be in compliance with international humanitarian law. Until the NWS have come up with convincing evidence in favor of a possible use of nuclear weapons in full compliance with

177 UNSG, Report on emergency assistance to Sudan, 1996, § 3.

178 WHO, Effects of Nuclear War on Health and Health Services: Report of the WHO Management Group on Follow-up of Resolution WHA36.28: "The Role of Physicians and Other Health Workers in the Preservation and Promotion of Peace" (1987), 2nd edn., WHO, Geneva. In the same line, see Borrie and Caughley, *An Illusion of Safety*, pp. 78 and 81.

179 ICJ Reports 1996, § 73: ". . . The emergence, as *lex lata*, of a customary rule specifically prohibiting the use of nuclear weapons as such is hampered by the continuing tensions between the nascent *opinio juris* on the one hand, and the still strong adherence to the practice of deterrence on the other."

international humanitarian law, a presumption of absolute prohibition under current international law, including for low-yield nuclear weapons, must prevail, in particular if international law is being perceived, as explained in the introductory chapter, as placing the protection of people and the survival of future generations at the center of attention, rather than the survival of States as abstract entities.

C. THE PROHIBITION OF USING NUCLEAR WEAPONS IN LIGHT OF HUMAN RIGHTS LAW

1. Preliminary observations

a) The added value of international human rights law for the use of nuclear weapons

In the preceding Chapter, the limitations on the use of nuclear weapons resulting from international humanitarian law have been examined. In the present chapter, such use will be assessed under another set of rules, namely those of international human rights law. The close relationship between the issue of nuclear weapons and human rights is demonstrated by the fact that many international human rights instruments were adopted as a reaction to the atrocities of World War II, including the bombings of Hiroshima and Nagasaki. Judge Abdul Koroma underlines this link in his dissenting opinion to the 1996 Advisory Opinion:

> It should not be forgotten that the Second World War had witnessed the use of the atomic weapon in Hiroshima and Nagasaki, resulting in the deaths of thousands of human beings. The Second World War therefore came to be regarded as the period epitomizing gross violations of human rights. The possibility that the human rights of citizens, in particular their right to life, would be violated during a nuclear conflagration, is a matter which falls within the purview of the Charter and other relevant international legal instruments.[180]

Even though humanitarian law is generally more specific and has always been considered the primary source of rules governing nuclear weapons as a means of warfare, human rights law adds another significant element to the protection of the human being: First, as will be explained in more detail, human rights instruments apply in all circumstances, except for situations where a State makes use of a derogation clause. As a result, the difficult question of whether the threshold of an armed conflict has been reached in a concrete situation does not have to be addressed, contrary to what is the case in humanitarian law. This advantage is particularly relevant, considering that the effects of a use of nuclear

180 ICJ Reports 1996, p. 557.

weapons can be felt far from the actual place of detonation, including in States that are not necessarily engaged in an armed conflict with the State using nuclear weapons. As a result, more indirect victims could not rely on humanitarian law, but could do so on human rights law. This element will be addressed in greater detail in the subsection dealing with the global impact of a limited (regional) nuclear war on the enjoyment on economic, social, and cultural rights.[181]

Second, while human rights have traditionally been thought to protect the individual against arbitrary interference into his or her rights, the more recent, dynamic jurisprudence of international human rights courts imposes on States Parties the duty to take measures in order to protect the persons under their jurisdiction against harmful acts of other persons or private entities. This type of "positive" obligation of the State to secure rights of individuals against infringements from private actors is today well established in the jurisprudence of human rights bodies and is recognized in various areas, such as domestic violence,[182] violence between prisoners,[183] and environmental pollution by private companies.[184] It will play a significant role in the subsection on "the other legal duties (arms control, non-proliferation, and disarmament obligations)" assessed in light of humanitarian and human rights law.

Third, probably the most significant advantage of human rights law lies in its institutional dimension. In practice, victims of human rights violations, including victims of a potential nuclear weapons use, can rely on treaty bodies and mechanisms providing legal remedies.[185] The reporting procedures within certain UN treaty bodies are also of relevance.[186] This aspect distinguishes human rights law from humanitarian law, which is much less institutionalized, relying largely on the goodwill of the States Parties for implementing its rules and principles.

For instance, what makes the ECtHR so special and effective is that individual applicants have the right – as set out in Article 34 ECHR – to seek redress directly from an independent judicial body that focuses solely on examining allegations of serious human rights violations (the so-called "right of individual application").[187]

181 This Chapter, section C.4.

182 *Opuz v. Turkey*, no. 33401/02, ECHR 2009.

183 *Paul and Audrey Edwards v. United Kingdom*, no. 46477/99, ECHR 2002-II.

184 See, among many others, the cases decided by the ECtHR, *Taşkın and Others v. Turkey*, no. 46117/99, ECHR 2004-X, or *Tătar v. Romania*, no. 67021/01, 27 January 2009, both explained in more detail in section C.4.e).

185 A. Breitegger, *Cluster Munitions and International Law: Disarmament with a Human Face*, London and New York, 2012, p. 92; and L. Doswald-Beck, "Human Rights Law and Nuclear Weapons," in Nystuen et al., *Nuclear Weapons under International Law*, pp. 435–460, 459. See also S. Casey-Maslen, "The Right to a Remedy and Reparation for the Use of Nuclear Weapons," in Nystuen et al., *Nuclear Weapons under International Law*, pp. 461–480.

186 Doswald-Beck, "Human Rights Law and Nuclear Weapons," p. 459.

187 Article 34 ECHR reads as follows: "The Court may receive applications from any person, non-governmental organization or group of individuals claiming to be the victim of a violation by one of the High Contracting Parties of the rights set for in the Convention or

Moreover, the judgments of the Court are binding upon the States Parties to the ECHR and their implementation is supervised by the Committee of Ministers of the Council of Europe, as explained in Part I of this volume.[188] The vast majority of cases are introduced by individuals and there have been only a handful of inter-State claims,[189] which are possible under Article 33 ECHR.[190] In light of the fact that the most recent inter-State applications introduced in Strasbourg had originated from an armed conflict between two States Parties to the ECHR,[191] and given the vast destructions to be expected from a nuclear explosion, such a – coordinated – action would possibly make more sense than thousands of similar applications coming from individual victims of a nuclear attack.

Fourth, the particular nature of certain human rights has to be stressed. It is important to mention that, as is the case with certain principles and rules of humanitarian law, fundamental rules of human rights law have to date attained customary status and, therefore, apply also to States not having ratified the relevant treaties.[192] This is true, for instance, for the right to life or the prohibition of torture or inhuman and degrading treatment, which will be addressed below. Moreover, the normative supremacy of certain human rights has to be emphasized too. In fact, certain rights cannot be derogated from, which is a strong indication for their peremptory nature (*jus cogens*). The ILC, in its Articles on the Responsibility of States for Internationally Wrongful Acts, makes it clear that the circumstances precluding wrongfulness contained in Chapter V of Part One of these Articles do not authorize any derogation from a peremptory rule of general international law.[193] In other words, even a State taking counter-measures may not derogate from such a rule. For example, a genocide cannot justify a counter-genocide.[194] No prior wrong, as evil as it may be, can justify the breach of a rule corresponding to this definition.[195]

In terms of general international law, the VCLT defines a peremptory rule as "a norm accepted and recognized by the international community of States as a

the Protocols thereto. The High Contracting Parties undertake not to hinder in any of the effective exercise of this right."

188 This volume, Chapter 4, section C.1.

189 K. Reid, *A Practitioner's Guide to the European Convention on Human Rights*, 4th edn., London, 2012, p. 56.

190 Article 33 reads as follows: "Any High Contracting Party may refer to the Court any alleged breach of the provisions of the Convention and the Protocols thereto by another High Contracting Party."

191 See, for instance, *Cyprus v. Turkey (IV)*, no. 25781/94, May 10, 2001 and May 12, 2014; *Georgia v. Russia (I)*, no. 13255/07, July 3, 2014; *Georgia v. Russia (II)*, no. 38263/08 (pending); and the pending cases *Ukraine v. Russia (I)*, no. 20958/14, *Ukraine v. Russia (II)*, no. 43800/14, and *Ukraine v. Russia (III)*, no. 42410/15 *(IV)*.

192 Doswald-Beck, "Human Rights Law and Nuclear Weapons," pp. 441 et seq.

193 Article 26 of the ILC Articles.

194 ILC Commentary of Article 26, p. 85, http://legal.un.org/ilc/texts/instruments/english/commentaries/9_6_2001.pdf (accessed February 27, 2017).

195 Doswald-Beck, "Human Rights Law and Nuclear Weapons," p. 442.

whole as a norm from which no derogation is permitted and which can be modified only by a subsequent norm of general international law having the same character."[196] Despite this somewhat circular definition, there is today no doubt about the existence of such higher rules, but what exactly falls under this concept is less clear. International tribunals have generally been hesitant to accept the *jus cogens* nature of rules, but there is widespread agreement that the prohibition of torture[197] and the crime of genocide[198] fall under this definition.

Finally, the obligation to refrain from a breach of such a rule is also one that is of an *erga omnes* nature. In the case of *Barcelona Traction, Light and Power Company, Ltd*, the ICJ defined these obligations as "obligations of a State towards the international community as a whole . . .," adding that "[b]y their very nature the former are the concern of all States . . . and all States can be held to have a legal interest in their protection."[199] The Court gave a number of examples, such as the rules outlawing aggression and genocide, and certain human rights principles such as those prohibiting slavery and racial discrimination.[200] Doswald-Beck is certainly right when she claims that the geographical extent of damage caused by a nuclear weapons explosion is likely to go beyond than just one State, as well as to common areas such as the high seas and the international air space.[201]

The most important consequence of a breach of an *erga omnes* obligation lies in the possibility for any other State than the directly injured State to invoke the responsibility of the State having caused the damage. The condition for such a claim is that the "obligation breached is owed to the international community as a whole."[202] As a result, and accepting that a nuclear attack would entail significant human rights violations, it can be suggested that if State A attacks State B with nuclear weapons, all other States affected would be considered to have a legal interest to act on behalf of State B and could invoke the former's responsibility.

196 Article 53 VCLT (Treaties conflicting with a peremptory norm of general international law). See also Article 64 VCLT (Emergence of a new peremptory norm of general international law).

197 ECtHR, *Al-Adsani v. United Kingdom* [GC], no. 35763/97, § 60, ECHR 2001-XI; ICTY, *Prosecutor v. Furundzija*, case no. IT-95-17/I-T, December 10, 1998, §§ 144 et seq.; and ICJ, *Questions relating to the Obligation to Extradite or Prosecute case*, Judgment, July 20, 2012, ICJ Reports 2012, § 99.

198 *Armed Activities on the Territory of the Congo (Congo v Rwanda)*, Judgment, February 3, 2006, ICJ Reports 2006, § 125.

199 ICJ Reports 1970, § 33.

200 In the Advisory Opinion concerning the *Legal Consequences of the Construction of a Wall in the Occupied Palestinian Territory*, the ICJ recognized the *erga omnes* nature of the right of the Palestinian People to self-determination (ICJ Reports 2004, § 156), referring to the *Eastern Timor* case (ICJ Reports 1995, § 29).

201 Doswald-Beck, "Human Rights Law and Nuclear Weapons," p. 442.

202 Article 48 § 1(b) of the ILC Articles on responsibility of States for internationally wrongful acts.

b) Applicability of human rights law during armed conflict

Generally speaking, humanitarian law applies to the specific situation of an armed conflict, while human rights law is not restricted in the same manner and is in principle applicable at all times, subject to the possibility, offered in certain human rights treaties but hardly invoked in practice, of derogations from certain rights in situations of public emergencies.[203] This does not mean, however, that humanitarian law (*lex specialis*) would, in times of armed conflict, completely displace human rights law (*lex generalis*). Since the aim pursued by the two legal regimes is the same, namely, the protection of the human being, the necessity is one of harmonizing the different categories of rules, and only in the – rare – cases where a real conflict of rules is unavoidable, might human rights law be entirely absorbed by humanitarian law.[204] In most of the cases dealing with use of certain methods of warfare and weapons in armed conflicts, humanitarian law will apply in the first place, and human rights law will come afterwards; and in the interpretation of the latter, the former will be taken into account.[205]

This logic has been followed by international courts. Before the ICJ, it was argued that use of nuclear weapons would necessarily violate the right to life as guaranteed, inter alia, in Article 6 of the ICCPR,[206] whose first paragraph provides that "[e]very human being has the inherent right to life. This right shall be protected by law. No one shall be arbitrarily deprived of his life." The ICJ did indeed acknowledge the continuing applicability of the right to life under the ICCPR in time of warfare. It observed, however, that the test of what is an arbitrary deprivation of life – by the use of a certain type of weapon, for instance – has to be determined by the applicable *lex specialis*, the law governing armed conflict.[207] Even though this straightforward reference to humanitarian law seems simplistic nowadays and has been criticized by some authors for going against the trend to view human rights and humanitarian law as complementary and

203 Breitegger, *Cluster Munitions and International Law*, p. 90; and Doswald-Beck, "Human Rights Law and Nuclear Weapons," p. 438.

204 Breitegger, *Cluster Munitions and International Law*, p. 91. The duty to harmonize different legal norms has recently been reiterated by the ECtHR in the case of *Nada v. Switzerland* [GC], no. 10593/08, ECHR 2012, § 170: "Where a number of apparently contradictory instruments are simultaneously applicable, international case-law and academic opinion endeavour to construe them in such a way as to coordinate their effects and avoid any opposition between them. Two diverging commitments must therefore be harmonized as far as possible so that they produce effects that are fully in accordance with existing law . . .".

205 This corresponds to Article 31 § 3(c) VCLT: "3. There shall be taken into account, together with the context: . . . (c) any relevant rules of international law applicable in the relations between the parties."

206 See, for instance, the statement given by Costa Rica, Verbatim Record, November 14, 1995, p. 31.

207 ICJ Reports 1996, § 25.

permeable,[208] the Court thereby confirmed the relevance of human rights law for the question of nuclear weapons and the continued application of such treaties in time of armed conflict.[209]

The Court confirmed and developed its position on the relationship between humanitarian law and human rights law in its Advisory Opinion on the *Legal Consequences of the Construction of a Wall in the Occupied Palestinian Territory*, delivered on July 9, 2004:

> More generally, the Court considers that the protection offered by human rights conventions does not cease in case of armed conflict, save through the effect of provisions for derogation of the kind to be found in Article 4 ICCPR. As regards the relationship between international humanitarian law and human rights law, there are thus three possible situations: some rights may be exclusively matters of international humanitarian law; others may be exclusively matters of human rights law; yet others may be matters of both these branches of international law. In order to answer the question put to it, the Court will have to take into consideration both these branches of international law, namely human rights law and, as *lex specialis*, in international humanitarian law.[210]

As far as the relationship between humanitarian law and human rights law is concerned, it is significant that this statement was reiterated in the case concerning *Armed Activities on the Territory of the Congo (Democratic Republic of the Congo v. Uganda)* of December 19, 2005, but without the words "as *lex specialis.*"[211]

Marko Milanović has rightly pointed out that it can even be "dangerous" to refer to international humanitarian law as *lex specialis* to human rights law as a whole.[212] As an example, he uses the Bush Administration's denial that persons in Guantanamo were entitled to protection under international human rights law, adding that the US Government invoked two grounds for its approach: first, it argued that the relevant human rights instruments did not apply extraterritorially and, second, it contended that even if they did, they were displaced by international humanitarian law that applied exclusively to the war on terrorism fought by the

208 See, for instance, V. Gowlland-Debbas, "The Right to Life and Genocide: The Court and an International Public Policy," in Boisson de Chazournes and Sands, *International Law*, pp. 315–337, 319 and 325; or T. Wright, "Do Nuclear Weapons Violate the Right to Life under International Law?", *Australian Journal of Peace Studies*, vol. 3, 2008, pp. 99–119, 103 and 106.

209 In the Advisory Opinion on the *Legal Consequences of the Construction of a Wall in the Occupied Palestinian Territory*, the ICJ indicated that there is room for more significant overlap between human rights and humanitarian law (ICJ Reports 2004, §§ 136 et seq.).

210 ICJ Reports 2004, § 106.

211 ICJ Reports 2005, § 216.

212 M. Milanović, *Extraterritorial Application of Human Rights Treaties: Law, Principles and Policy*, Oxford, 2011, p. 234.

United States against Al-Qaeda.[213] Milanović also recalls that since the United States considered the detainees as "unlawful combatants," they enjoyed in reality no protection, not even under international humanitarian law.[214] It is obvious that such an approach should be avoided because it does not guarantee effective protection to the human being.

Moreover, bodies implementing human rights frequently make reference to humanitarian law in order to interpret treaty clauses. For example, in the case of *Democratic Republic of the Congo v. Burundi, Rwanda and Uganda*, the African Commission of Human Rights refers to Geneva Convention IV and its Additional Protocol I in order to reinforce its finding of violations of the right to property, the right to cultural development, and the prohibition of inhuman and degrading treatment under the African Charter on Human and Peoples' Rights (ACHPR).[215] The IACtHR stated that humanitarian law could be used to help interpret human rights rules and stressed, on this basis, the gravity of human rights breaches in the context of an armed conflict.[216] Finally, the ECtHR referred to the Geneva Conventions to reinforce the duty to investigate the whereabouts of missing soldiers under Article 2 ECHR.[217] As a result, it can be observed that when human rights treaty bodies turn to humanitarian law, this is done as a means of interpretation and to reinforce the human rights protection, and not to weaken or restrict its scope.[218]

From a general international law point of view, the ILC, in its 2011 Draft articles on the effects of armed conflicts on treaties, confirmed the principle of continued applicability of human rights in armed conflicts for provisions that cannot be derogated from:

> Although the debate continues whether human rights treaties apply to armed conflict, it is well established that non-derogable provisions of human rights treaties apply during armed conflict. First, the International Court of Justice stated in its *Nuclear Weapons* Advisory Opinion that the protection of the International Covenant of Civil and Political Rights does not cease in times of war, except by operation of article 4 of the Covenant whereby certain provisions may be derogated from in a time of national emergency. The *Nuclear Weapons* opinion is the closest that the Court has come to examining the effects of armed conflict on treaties, including significant

213 *Ibid.*

214 *Ibid.*, p. 235.

215 AComHPR, *Democratic Republic of Congo v. Burundi, Rwanda and Uganda*, Decision, Comm. no. 229/99, May 25, 2006, §§ 79, 84, 87–88.

216 IACtHR, *Bámaca Velásquez v. Guatemala*, Judgment, Series C no. 70, November 25, 2000, § 203; and IACtHR, *Ituango Massacres v. Colombia*, Judgment, Series C no. 148, July 1, 2006, §§ 179–183.

217 *Varnava and Others v. Turkey*, Judgment, nos. 16064/90 et al., September 28, 2009, § 185.

218 Doswald-Beck, "Human Rights Law and Nuclear Weapons," p. 438.

> discussion of the effect of armed conflict on both human rights and environmental treaties . . .[219]

In light of the foregoing, human rights law and humanitarian law have to be perceived as two parallel and complementary, rather than conflicting or excluding, legal regimes, and human rights treaties must be considered applicable to the use of nuclear weapons.

c) Extraterritorial application of human rights treaties in the context of the use of nuclear weapons

In order to be within the scope of a human rights treaty, an act or omission of a State Party, due for instance to the use of nuclear weapons, has to fall into that State's jurisdiction. Most of the modern human rights instruments contain an explicit but very general jurisdictional clause. Article 2 § 1 ICCPR provides that:

> [e]ach State Party to the present Covenant undertakes to respect and to ensure to all individuals within its territory and subject to its jurisdiction the rights recognized in the present Covenant, without distinction of any kind, such as race, colour, sex, language, religion, political or other opinion, national or social origin, property, birth or other status.[220]

Such clauses have been interpreted broadly by the treaty bodies as embracing not only the State's own territory, but also spaces over which it has jurisdiction (or control) outside the national territory.[221] At the universal level, the ICJ, in its Advisory Opinion on the *Legal Consequences of the Construction of a Wall in the Occupied Palestinian Territory*, confirmed the applicability of the ICCPR to Palestinian territories occupied by Israel, relying essentially on the object and purpose of this instrument, as well as on the practice of the Human Rights Committee (HRC).[222]

The question then is: Under which circumstances can an act or omission committed abroad be attributed to a State as falling under its jurisdiction and control? This debate is relevant for the present study. If a nuclear attack occurs within the State's own territory, for example in the context of a non-international

219 Adopted by the ILC at its 63rd session in 2011 and submitted to the GA as part of the Commission's report covering the work of that session (A/66/10), § 49 (references omitted), published in *YBILC*, 2011, vol. II, part 2.

220 See, for another example, Article 1 ECHR (Obligation to respect human rights): "The High Contracting Parties shall secure to everyone within their jurisdiction the rights and freedoms defined in Section I of this Convention."

221 Doswald-Beck, "Human Rights Law and Nuclear Weapons," p. 439.

222 ICJ Reports 2004, § 109; see also §§ 110–111. See also the case concerning *Armed Activities on the Territory of the Congo (Democratic Republic of the Congo* v. *Uganda)*, Judgment, ICJ Reports 2005, § 220.

armed conflict or of the fight against terrorist groups, the question of jurisdiction would not be controversial. More delicate is the question of whether a State can be held responsible, under human rights instruments, for an attack that is aimed at another State and, in other terms, whether the victims of such a violation could complain about the foreign State's conduct?

This raises the issue of the extraterritorial application of human rights treaties in the case of armed attacks, where the State cannot claim to have physical control over people, for instance over detainees. Several cases are relevant in this regard. The Inter-American Commission on Human Rights (IAComHR) applied the American Declaration on the Rights and Duties of Man (ADRDM) to an attack of a civilian plane over international waters conducted by Cuban military planes. In spite of the fact that the ADRDM has no jurisdictional clause, the Commission held that this action fell within Cuba's jurisdiction, since the effect of firing on the planes "placed the civilian pilots . . . under their authority."[223] The Commission took the same approach when it had to apply the jurisdictional clause of the ACHR.[224] In an inter-State petition, Ecuador complained about human rights breaches by Colombian military personal perpetrated, inter alia, by the air bombing of alleged positions of the Revolutionary Armed Forces of Colombia (FARC) on the territory of Ecuador. It held that in order to establish jurisdiction, it was "necessary to determine whether there [was] a causal nexus between the extraterritorial conduct of the State and the alleged violation of the rights and freedoms of an individual."[225]

On the other hand, the Commission also found that it was not necessary to show a territorial presence and the ability to respect the whole range of human rights duties in the context concerned, but rather that:

> the obligation does arise in the period of time that agents of a State interfere in the lives of persons who are on the territory of the other State, for those agents to respect their rights, in particular, their right to life and human treatment.[226]

The ECtHR's approach to extraterritorial application of the ECHR, in particular in situations where actual control over a territory is not easy to establish, is more ambiguous. In the controversial decision on admissibility in *Banković and Others v. 17 NATO Member States*, the Grand Chamber of the Court rejected the proposition that control over the airspace above, rather than the territory in which victims of NATO airstrikes during Operation Allied Force resided, would suffice to bring these victims under the jurisdiction of respondent States. In other words,

223 IAComHR, *Alejandre and Others v. Cuba*, case no. 11.589, report no. 86/99, September 29, 1999, § 25.
224 Article 1 § 1 ACHR.
225 IAComHR, *Ecuador v. Colombia*, report, admissibility (2010), no. 112/10, § 99.
226 *Ibid.*, § 100.

it rejected the argument of the applicants that the air superiority of the attackers amounted to "effective control" and would, therefore, fall under the jurisdiction of the defending States.[227] As a result, the Court did not accept a simple "cause-and-effect" notion of jurisdiction within the meaning of Article 1 ECHR.[228]

In the subsequent cases, the Court has not strictly followed this approach. In *Issa and Others v. Turkey*, a chamber of the ECtHR accepted, in principle, that the victims could come under Turkish jurisdiction, thereby accepting that a temporary but effective overall control over a portion of territory during ad hoc military operations was sufficient in respect of alleged arrests, torture, and killings during military operations on the ground by Turkish armed forces against Kurds in Northern Iraq in 1995.[229] The following paragraph is noteworthy:

> Moreover, a State may also be held accountable for violation of the Convention rights and freedoms of persons who are in the territory of another State but who are found to be under the former State's authority and control through its agents operating – whether lawfully or unlawfully – in the latter State . . . Accountability in such situations stems from the fact that Article 1 of the Convention cannot be interpreted so as to allow a State party to perpetrate violations of the Convention on the territory of another State, which it could not perpetrate on its own territory . . .[230]

The reason for the adoption of this more flexible approach compared with the solution of the Grand Chamber in *Banković* cannot be easily deduced from the Chamber judgment, but the latter was confirmed in other cases. In *Pad and Others v. Turkey*, the victims, Iranian nationals living close to the Turkish border, were allegedly attacked by a Turkish helicopter. Even though it was undisputed that they were killed by Turkish forces, it was debated whether the killing took place on the Turkish or the Iranian side of the border. Relying explicitly on *Issa*, the Chamber did not find it necessary to determine the exact location of the event, given that the Turkish Government had already admitted that the fire discharged from the helicopters had caused the killing of the applicants' relatives, who had been suspected of being terrorists.[231]

In other words, the Court has accepted that since the applicants were killed by Turkish agents, they fell within the jurisdiction of Turkey, regardless of whether the killing took place in Turkey or in Iran.[232] This approach has been confirmed

227 ECtHR, *Banković and Others v. 17 NATO Member States*, decision [GC], no. 52207/99, December 12, 2001, § 75.

228 *Ibid.*

229 ECtHR, *Issa and Others v. Turkey*, no. 31821/96, judgment, November 16, 2004, §§ 74–75.

230 *Ibid.*, § 71.

231 *Pad and Others v. Turkey* (dec.), no. 60167/00, June 28, 2007, § 54.

232 Milanović, *Extraterritorial Application*, p. 185.

by subsequent cases, in which extraterritorial jurisdiction was not always admitted in the concrete circumstances, but which explicitly referred and applied the *Issa* criteria.[233]

To sum up, without having officially abandoned the *Banković* approach, the ECtHR seems to accept a "cause-and-effect" notion of jurisdiction in situations of bombing or shooting of persons, even outside the border of the State and without necessarily establishing effective control over a certain territory. In other words, "jurisdiction" within the meaning of Article 1 ECHR may arise from State control over an individual, the potential victim of a human rights violation, rather than over territory.[234]

This author advocates, based on the human rights treaty bodies' general acceptance of an extraterritorial application of these instruments, that it is very likely that a nuclear attack would fall under the jurisdiction of a State within the meaning of the clauses contained in these treaties. He finds confirmation of this conclusion in a modern approach to treaty interpretation. In fact, it is one of the characteristics of human rights treaties that they have to be interpreted in a teleological manner, giving full effect to their object and purpose within the meaning of Article 31 § 1 VCLT.[235] In the language of the ECtHR, for instance, this means that the Convention has to be interpreted in a manner that renders the rights guaranteed "practical and effective," and not "theoretical or illusory."[236] Reiterating the ICJ's approach in the case of the *Legal Consequences of the Construction of a Wall in the Occupied Palestinian Territory*,[237] referred to above, this author is of the opinion that there is nothing that would prevent the application of this principle to Article 1 ECHR, even though this principle has been applied by the Court when interpreting the scope of individual rights protected by the Convention. Given the devastating consequences on the enjoyment of human rights by the affected population, including non-derogable rights such as the right to life or the prohibition of torture, and the huge number of potential victims, an appropriate, effective, and fair interpretation of the notion of "jurisdiction" would necessarily lead to the conclusion that the use of nuclear weapons by a State

233 *Solomou and Others v. Turkey*, Judgment, no. 36832/97, June 24, 2008, §§ 44–45, 51; *Andreou v. Turkey*, decision, no. 45653/99, June 3, 2008; and *Ben El Mahi and Others v. Denmark*, decision, no. 5853/06, December 11, 2006.

234 Milanović, *Extraterritorial Application*, p. 186.

235 Article 31 § 1 VCLT reads as follows: "A treaty shall be interpreted in good faith in accordance with the ordinary meaning to be given to the terms of the treaty in their context and in the light of its object and purpose."

236 See, among many others, ECtHR, *Artico v. Italy*, May 13, 1980, § 33, Series A no. 37; and *Airey v. Ireland*, October 9, 1979, § 24, Series A no. 32, where the Court held: "The Convention is intended to guarantee not rights that are theoretical or illusory but rights that are practical and effective." See also D. Rietiker, "The Principle of 'Effectiveness' in the Recent Jurisprudence of the European Court of Human Rights: Its Different Dimensions and Its Consistency with Public International Law – No Need for the Concept of Treaty *Sui Generis*," *Nordic Journal of International Law*, vol. 79, no. 2, 2010, pp. 245–277.

237 ICJ Reports 2004, § 109.

against another would fall under its jurisdiction within the meaning of the clauses contained in the relevant treaties. In other words, human rights treaty bodies, many of which have been created as a reaction to the atrocities committed in World War II, are unlikely to refuse to hear potential cases from victims of an attack involving the most inhuman weapon.

After these preliminary observations, the following subsection will focus on the different human rights that might be affected by the use of nuclear weapons. Three different scenarios are proposed: First, the relevance of the civil and political rights of victims directly affected by a nuclear weapons attack; second, the difficulties associated with complying with human rights law after a nuclear attack; third, the case of a limited (regional) nuclear war and its global impact on the enjoyment of economic, social, and cultural rights of people, including victims living far away from the actual place of nuclear weapons detonations. Finally, the rights of particularly vulnerable groups, such as indigenous peoples, women, and children, will be assessed in light of the harm caused to them by nuclear testing and accidents occurring in nuclear power plants, in particular in Chernobyl and Fukushima. Those examples convey an idea of the human suffering and destruction in case of actual use of nuclear weapons.

2. The most important civil and political rights likely to be affected by nuclear attacks

a) Right to life

The right to life, its special status in international law, and its role in the 1996 Advisory Opinion have already been addressed in the introductory chapter to Part II. The present subsection will expand this aspect without, however, going into the details of the abundant case law of the different courts.

The right to life is guaranteed by various international instruments, in particular by Article 6 ICCPR, Article 3 UDHR, and,[238] on a regional level, Article 2 ECHR and Articles 4 ACHR and ACHPR. As far as the ICCPR is concerned, the non-derogable nature of the right to life is stated in absolute terms in its Article 4,[239] and the qualification "inherent" in Article 6 ICCPR is meant to denote its significance as well as, as some have argued, its parallel existence in customary international law.[240] It is even considered a rule of *jus cogens* by certain commentators.[241]

238 Article 3: "Everyone has the right to life, liberty and security of persons."

239 See, *a contrario*, Article 15 § 2 ECHR, which excludes from the non-derogability of Article 2 "deaths resulting from lawful acts of war."

240 See, for instance, Y. Dinstein, "The Right to Life, Physical Integrity, and Liberty," in L. Henkin (ed.), *The International Bill of Rights: The Covenant on Civil and Political Rights*, New York, 1981, pp. 114–137, 115.

241 See, for an overview and further references, M. Nowak, *UN Covenant on Civil and Political Rights, CCPR Commentary*, Kehl, Strasbourg, and Arlington, 2nd edn., 2005, p. 122; and B. G. Ramcharan, "The Concept and Dimensions of the Right to Life," in B. G. Ramcharan

It is relevant to briefly mention here the principles established by the ECtHR and the IACtHR regarding attacks conducted in armed conflicts in order to draw some conclusions on the lawfulness of a potential use of nuclear weapons. As far as the practice of the ECtHR is concerned, the most relevant cases arose out of the internal conflicts in Chechnya (Russia) and Turkey. Article 2 ECHR provides the following:

1. Everyone's right to life shall be protected by law. No one shall be deprived of his life intentionally save in the execution of a sentence of a court following his conviction of a crime for which this penalty is provided by law.
2. Deprivation of life shall not be regarded as inflicted in contravention of this Article when it results from the use of force which is no more than absolutely necessary:

   (a) in defence of any person from unlawful violence;
   (b) in order to effect a lawful arrest or to prevent the escape of a person lawfully detained;
   (c) in action lawfully taken for the purpose of quelling a riot or insurrection.

It derives from this article that, unlike Article 6 ICCPR, the ECHR does not spell out that the right to life will be breached if a person is "arbitrarily deprived of life," the relevant criterion for a violation being the use of force that is not "absolutely necessary" for the purpose of the three exceptions found in Article 2 § 2 ECHR.

The relevant cases have generally been brought by relatives of civilians who died during combat operations against rebel groups. In order to ensure that the use of force was no more than "absolutely necessary," the Court examined whether the planning of the operation was such as to "avoid" or at least "minimise deaths." In one of the leading cases, the ECtHR examined whether these criteria were complied with by Turkey:

> . . . In the light of the above considerations, the Court agrees with the Commission that the responsibility of the State is not confined to circumstances where there is significant evidence that misdirected fire from agents of the State has killed a civilian. It may also be engaged where they fail to take all feasible precautions in the choice of means and methods of a security operation mounted against an opposing group with a view to avoiding and, in any event, to minimising, incidental loss of civilian life . . .[242]

It is evident that the language used much resembles the vocabulary of international humanitarian law, described above, even though the Court did not refer

(ed.), *The Right to Life in International Law*, Dordrecht, Boston, and Lancaster, 1985, pp. 1–32, 14 et seq.

242 *Ergi v. Turkey*, July 28, 1998, § 79, *Reports of Judgments and Decisions* 1998-IV.

expressly to Common Article 3 of the Geneva Conventions or Additional Protocol II.[243] The same approach was used in subsequent cases, in particular in cases against Russia which conducted air operations against rebels during the Second Chechen War:

> 190. . . . According to the servicemen's statements, bombs and other non-guided heavy combat weapons were used against targets both in the centre and on the edges of the village . . .
>
> 191. The Court considers that using this kind of weapon in a populated area, outside wartime and without prior evacuation of the civilians, is impossible to reconcile with the degree of caution expected from a law-enforcement body in a democratic society. No martial law and no state of emergency has been declared in Chechnya, and no derogation has been made under Article 15 of the Convention . . . The operation in question therefore has to be judged against a normal legal background. Even when faced with a situation where, as the Government submit, the population of the village had been held hostage by a large group of well-equipped and well-trained fighters, the primary aim of the operation should be to protect lives from unlawful violence. The massive use of indiscriminate weapons stands in flagrant contrast with this aim and cannot be considered compatible with the standard of care prerequisite to an operation of this kind involving the use of lethal force by State agents.[244]

In a subsequent case, the ECtHR accepted that Russia had had no other choice than to carry out aerial strikes in order to regain a town that was defended by well-equipped rebels. The Court nevertheless concluded that there had been a violation of the right to life, in particular for having exceeded what was necessary in the concrete situation:

> Against this background and in the light of the principles stated in paragraph 178 above, the Court may be prepared to accept that the Russian authorities had no choice other than to carry out aerial strikes in order to be able to take over Urus-Martan, and that their actions were in pursuit of the aim set out in paragraph 2(a) of Article 2 of the Convention, as alleged by the Government. It is, however, not convinced, having regard to the materials at its disposal, that the necessary degree of care was exercised in preparing the operation of 19 October 1999 in such a way as to avoid or minimise, to the greatest extent possible, the risk of a loss of life, both for the persons at whom the measures were directed and for civilians . . .[245]

243 These norms apply in non-international armed conflict.

244 *Isayeva v. Russia*, no. 57950/00, February 24, 2005; see also *Isayeva and Others v. Russia*, nos. 57947/00, 57948/00, and 57949/00, February 24, 2005, § 199.

245 ECtHR, *Khamzayev and Others v. Russia*, no. 1503/02, § 180, May 3, 2011.

In this case, the Russian operation resulted in six deaths, 16 injuries, and 13 houses destroyed, caused by the use of high-explosive fragmentation bombs of caliber 250–270kg. These weapons were considered "indiscriminate weapons" by the Court,[246] which concluded that the use of such bombs in inhabited areas was "manifestly disproportionate" to the aim of dislodging the extremists.[247]

The IACtHR, too, had to decide cases involving attacks by armed forces. Article 4 ACHR of 1969 was inspired by the ICCPR that had been concluded three years earlier. Therefore, it refers to the criterion of "arbitrary deprivation" of life. In the case of *Zambrano Vélez et al. v. Ecuador*, the Court held that lethal force must be absolutely necessary in relation to the force or threat to be countered. When excessive force is used, any resulting deprivation of life is arbitrary.[248]

Another leading case, *Santo Domingo Massacre v. Colombia*, involved the dropping of cluster munitions against guerrillas. The Court held that that there had been a violation of the right to life due to a lack of precautions to avoid or minimize deaths among the civilian population.[249] The weighty arguments in favor of a violation were the facts that the pilot had not been able to see exactly where the bomblets would fall, air support for the army on the ground was not really necessary, the use of cluster bombs should have been avoided in a populated area, and the defendant State could not present any evidence that sufficient regard was given to the presence of civilians in the vicinity.[250]

In light of the foregoing, it appears that both regional human rights courts avoided referring directly to international humanitarian law; Doswald-Beck rightly observes that much effort was focused on the question of whether all reasonable efforts were made to avoid casualties (sufficient precaution in attack), rather than on the issue of whether civilian deaths and injuries were "excessive" in relation to the military objective pursued. From her point of view, this is not surprising for human rights institutions, less familiar with considerations of military advantage and the proportionality rule within the meaning of international humanitarian law.[251]

In any event, the large number of deaths likely to be caused by a nuclear explosion is unlikely to meet the high standards ("absolutely necessary" and "strictly proportionate") within the meaning of the ECtHR's and the IACtHR's case law.[252] In other words, a State having decided to use nuclear weapons would have to prove that sufficient precautions had been taken to "avoid or minimize"

246 *Ibid.*, § 185.
247 *Ibid.*, § 189.
248 IACtHR, *Zambrano Vélez et al. v. Ecuador*, Judgment, Series C no. 166, July 4, 2007, § 84, with other references.
249 IACtHR, *Santo Domingo Massacre v. Colombia*, Judgment, Series C no. 259, November 30, 2012, §§ 216–230.
250 *Ibid.*
251 Doswald-Beck, "Human Rights Law and Nuclear Weapons," pp. 448–449.
252 *Ibid.*, p. 450.

incidental loss of life, among civilians as well as among those at whom the measures were directed.[253] Such proof seems impossible to administer in light of the uncontrollable effects of a nuclear detonation. It is also important to recall that the right to life can be relevant, and violated, even if no individual has actually died; it is sufficient that the person has been exposed to life-threatening treatment.[254] In other words, a person who has been exposed to a lethal dose of radiation yet survives could invoke a breach of Article 2 ECHR. Finally, the presence of radiation after an attack would also hamper the ability to search for, rescue, and care for the wounded, which could amount to further violations of the right to life.[255] This aspect will be considered below.[256]

Considering the above case law, it seems that the use of nuclear weapons would, under normal circumstances and on account of its indiscriminate and disproportionate effect, constitute an "arbitrary"[257] deprivation of life in the sense of Article 6 § 1 ICCPR. In light of these observations and of the fundamental nature of the right to life, considered by the ECtHR as "one of the most fundamental provisions in the [ECHR],"[258] Professor Gowlland-Debbas is certainly right when she argues that the choice should

> be clear in balancing the survival of one State against the potential destruction of mankind, of civilisation, of the unborn, of the earth and its ecosystem, of the future environment and . . . of the right to life of all other living beings.[259]

This point of view was confirmed by the HRC, the body in charge of the implementation of the ICCPR, which devoted two General Comments on the right to

253 *Khamzayev and Others v. Russia*, no. 1503/02, § 180, May 3, 2011.

254 *Makaratzis v. Greece* [GC], no. 50385/99, ECHR 2004-XI, § 49: "In the present case, the force used against the applicant was not in the event lethal. This, however, does not exclude in principle an examination of the applicant's complaints under Article 2, the text of which, read as a whole, demonstrates that it covers not only intentional killing but also situations where it is permitted to use force which may result, as an unintended outcome, in the deprivation of life (see *İlhan v. Turkey* [GC], no. 22277/93, § 75, ECHR 2000-VII). In fact, the Court has already examined complaints under this provision where the alleged victim had not died as a result of the impugned conduct."

255 Doswald-Beck, "Human Rights Law and Nuclear Weapons," p. 451.

256 See this Chapter, section C.3.

257 The expression "arbitrary" is not easy to define and has been criticized since the drafting of Article 6 ICCPR as being ambiguous (Dinstein, "The Right to Life," p. 116).

258 See, for instance, *Makaratzis v. Greece* [GC], no. 50385/99, December 20, 2004, § 56: "Article 2, which safeguards the right to life and sets out the circumstances when deprivation of life may be justified, ranks as one of the most fundamental provisions in the Convention, from which no derogation is permitted (see *Velikova v. Bulgaria*, no. 41488/98, § 68, ECHR 2000-VI). Together with Article 3, it also enshrines one of the basic values of the democratic societies making up the Council of Europe. The circumstances in which deprivation of life may be justified must therefore be strictly construed . . .".

259 Gowlland-Debbas, "The Right to Life and Genocide," p. 337.

life. In its General Comment of 1982 (General Comment No. 6), which does not specifically deal with nuclear weapons, the HRC held, inter alia, that:

> 1. . . . [The right to life] is the supreme right from which no derogation is permitted in time of public emergency which threatens the life of the nation (article 4) . . . It is a right which should not be interpreted narrowly.
>
> 2. . . . Every effort [the States] make to avert the danger of war, especially thermonuclear war, and to strengthen international peace and security, would constitute the most important condition and guarantee for the safeguard of the right to life . . .[260]

The HRC's General Comment No. 14, adopted in 1984, went even further by dealing specifically with the prevention of war, weapons of mass destruction, and, in particular, nuclear weapons:

> 2. In its previous general comment, the Committee also observed that it is the supreme duty of States to prevent wars. War and other acts of mass violence continue to be a scourge of humanity and take the lives of thousands of innocent human beings every year.
>
> 3. . . . [R]epresentatives from all geographical regions have expressed their growing concern at the development and proliferation of increasingly awesome weapons of mass destruction, which not only threaten human life but also absorb resources that could otherwise be used for vital economic and social purposes, particularly for the benefit of developing countries, and thereby for promoting and securing the enjoyment of human rights for all.
>
> 4. The Committee associates itself with this concern. It is evident that the designing, testing, manufacture, possession and deployment of nuclear weapons are among the greatest threats to the right to life which confront mankind today. This threat is compounded by the danger that the actual use of such weapons may be brought about, not only in the event of war, but even through human or mechanical error or failure . . .
>
> 6. The production, testing, possession, deployment and use of nuclear weapons should be prohibited and recognized as crimes against humanity.
>
> 7. The Committee accordingly, in the interest of mankind, calls upon all States, whether Parties to the Covenant or not, to take urgent steps, unilaterally and by agreement, to rid the world of this menace.[261]

260 HRC, General Comment No. 6, Sixteenth Session, 1982, Compilation of General Comments and General Recommendations Adopted by Human Rights Treaty Bodies, UN Doc. HRI/GEN/1/Rev.1 at 6 (1994).

261 HRC, General Comment No. 14 (Article 6), Twenty-third session, 1984, Compilation of General Comments and General Recommendations Adopted by Human Rights Treaty Bodies, UN Doc. HRI/GEN/1/Rev.1 at 18 (1984).

This comment deserves our attention for several reasons: First, the mere fact that the HRC, a human rights body, deals with issues of prevention of war and nuclear weapons constitutes evidence for the growing interconnection between these fields of international law. Second, the HRC goes even further by calling on States to take urgent measures to remove the threat of nuclear weapons, a call that one would normally expect from a disarmament body. Third, the HCR not only condemns the use of nuclear weapons, but also their production, testing, possession, and deployment. This aspect will be addressed in more detail below.[262] Fourth, the Committee urges States to recognize these acts as crimes against humanity. Fifth, it recalls that the risk generated by nuclear weapons not only resides in their intended use as a means of warfare, but also in the possibility of accidental explosions caused by human or technical error. All in all, and despite the fact that the HRC was criticized by some States, in particular France, as well as by some commentators for having overstepped its mandate,[263] General Comment No. 14 can be considered as containing a clear statement to the effect that nuclear weapons "are among the greatest threats to the right to life which confront mankind today."[264]

The HRC also dealt with individual communications involving nuclear weapons, made under the First Optional Protocol to the ICCPR. In the case of *Aalbersberg et al. v. The Netherlands*,[265] the applicants challenged the Dutch Supreme Court's refusal to declare that the use of nuclear weapons would, under all circumstances, be contrary to the Netherlands' obligations under international law. Unsurprisingly, the Committee concluded that the applicants were not "actually affected" by any alleged violation because, fortunately, no nuclear explosion had occurred.[266] Even though this communication was declared inadmissible for formal reasons, it is another example of the relevance of human rights law in the field of nuclear arms control.

b) Prohibition of genocide

The prohibition of genocide is another guarantee that might prove relevant in the field of nuclear weapons and that can be considered a human rights rule in the broader sense, applying both in time of peace and during actual hostilities.[267]

262 Below, section D.

263 See D. McGoldrick, *The Human Rights Committee: Its Role in the Development of the International Covenant on Civil and Political Rights*, Oxford and New York, 1991, pp. 335 et seq.; and Gowlland-Debbas, "The Right to Life and Genocide," p. 328.

264 General Comment No. 14, § 4.

265 *Aalbersberg et al. v. The Netherlands*, UN Human Rights Committee, Communication no. 1440/2005, UN Doc. CCPR/C/87/D/1440/2005, August 2, 2005. Before the HRC, the Dutch Government argued, inter alia, that it would never use nuclear weapons against its own citizens within its territory (§ 4.4).

266 *Ibid.*, § 6.3.

267 Article I of the Convention on the Prevention and Punishment of the Crime of Genocide (December 9, 1948). The applicability of the Convention in all circumstances was explicitly

In the proceedings leading to the 1996 Advisory Opinion certain States maintained before the Court that the number of deaths occasioned by the use of nuclear weapons would be enormous and that the victims could, in certain cases, include persons of particular national, ethnic, racial, or religious grounds. They also argued that the intention to destroy such groups could be inferred from the fact that the State using such weapons had omitted to take account of their well-known disastrous effects.[268] Strictly following the wording of Article I of the Genocide Convention,[269] the ICJ pointed out that:

> the prohibition of genocide would be pertinent in this case if the recourse to nuclear weapons did indeed entail the element of intent, towards a group as such, required by the provision quoted above [Article II]. In the view of the Court, it would only be possible to arrive at such a conclusion after having taken due account of the circumstances specific to each case.[270]

In other words, the Hague Court confirmed the relevance of the prohibition of genocide – as a rule of *jus cogens*[271] – in respect of nuclear weapons, provided that the perpetrators of a nuclear attack aimed at the destruction of one of the groups enumerated in Article II of the Genocide Convention.[272]

c) The prohibition of torture, and degrading and inhuman treatment

Only the right to life and the prohibition of genocide have been invoked explicitly before the ICJ in the 1996 advisory proceedings. It is suggested here that other human rights guarantees are relevant in the context of nuclear weapons.

In light of the gravity of the injuries caused by a nuclear explosion, depriving the victims of their dignity, survivals of a potential nuclear weapons explosion could possibly invoke the prohibition of torture and inhuman and degrading treatment, proscribed at the universal level by Article 7 ICCPR.[273] The immediate

recalled by the ICJ in the case on the *Application of the Convention on the Prevention and Punishment of the Crime of Genocide (Bosnia and Herzegovina v. Yugoslavia (Serbia and Montenegro)*, Preliminary Objections, ICJ Reports 1996, § 31.

268 ICJ Reports 1996, § 26.

269 Article II of the Convention defines "genocide" as "any of the following acts committed with intent to destroy, in whole or in part, a national, ethnical, racial or religious group, as such (a) Killing members of the group; (b) Causing serious bodily or mental harm to members of the group . . .".

270 ICJ Reports 1996, § 26.

271 Case of *Armed Activities on the Territory of the Congo (New Application: 2002) (Democratic Republic of the Congo v. Rwanda)*, Jurisdiction and Admissibility, Judgment, ICJ Reports 2006, § 64.

272 See the dissenting opinion of Judge Weeramantry (ICJ Reports 1996, p. 517) and of Judge Koroma (*ibid.*, pp. 576 et seq.).

273 Article 7 ICCPR: "No one shall be subjected to torture or to cruel, inhuman or degrading treatment or punishment. In particular, no one shall be subjected without his free consent to medical or scientific experimentation."

casualties reported from Hiroshima, spreading over 13 square kilometers, included severe burns, flash blindness, ruptured organs, compound fractures, fractured skulls, and penetrating and other blunt force wounds.[274] Those not killed suffered severe burns and/or painful effects of radiation poisoning, as well as other serious long-term health effects, such as damage to the thyroid gland and the development of cancers. Moreover, due to the radiation that affects the immune system, the injured would not recover in the way they could have from conventional weapons lacking such radiation.[275] In this context, it is relevant to quote the following paragraph of Judge Weeramantry's dissenting opinion, underlying the notion of dignity:

> . . . when a weapon has the potential to kill between one million and one billion people, as WHO has told the Court, human life becomes reduced to a level of worthlessness that totally belies human dignity as understood in any culture. Such a deliberate action by an State is, in any circumstances whatsoever, incompatible with a recognition by it of that respect for basic human dignity on which world peace depends, and respect for which is assumed on the part of all Member States of the United Nations . . . No weapon ever invented in the long history of man's inhumanity to man has so negatived the dignity and worth of the human person as has the nuclear bomb.[276]

In Europe, the prohibition of torture and inhuman and degrading treatment is, in particular, protected by Article 3 ECHR, whose wording is short and clear: "No one shall be subjected to torture or to inhuman or degrading treatment or punishment." The case law of the ECtHR in the field of torture and inhuman and degrading treatment is particularly rich and detailed. Therefore, the following observations will be limited to some thoughts on this provision.

The value and the extraordinary status of the prohibition of torture and inhuman and degrading treatment in a democratic society, as well as the absolute nature of this right, have been summarized by the ECtHR in the case of *El-Masri v. The Former Yugoslav Republic of Macedonia*. This case originated from the extraordinary rendition, illegal detention, and torture of the applicant, arrested by the Macedonian authorities acting in collaboration with the Central Intelligence Agency (CIA). The Court said the following:

> 195. The Court reiterates that Article 3 of the Convention enshrines one of the most fundamental values of democratic societies. Unlike most of the substantive clauses of the Convention, Article 3 makes no provision for

274 Maresca, "The Catastrophic Humanitarian Consequences of Nuclear Weapons," p. 132, n. 274.
275 Doswald-Beck, "Human Rights Law and Nuclear Weapons," p. 452.
276 Dissenting opinion of Judge Weeramantry, section III.10(g), ICJ Reports 1996, p. 507.

> exceptions and no derogation from it is permissible under Article 15 § 2 even in the event of a public emergency threatening the life of the nation . . . The Court has confirmed that even in the most difficult circumstances, such as the fight against terrorism and organized crime, the Convention prohibits in absolute terms torture and inhuman or degrading treatment or punishment, irrespective of the conduct of the person concerned . . .[277]

In light of the last sentence cited, even a nuclear attack would not authorize a State to use nuclear weapons as a means of retaliation if it is accepted that such a use would involve violations of the prohibition of torture and inhuman and degrading treatment.

In order to be within the ambit of Article 3 ECHR, ill-treatment must attain a minimum level of severity (so-called "threshold theory").[278] Once this level is reached, the Court usually determines which of the three categories of treatments is involved (torture, inhuman treatment, or degrading treatment), but the assessment is a relative one:

> 196. In order for ill-treatment to fall within the scope of Article 3 it must attain a minimum level of severity. The assessment of this minimum depends on all the circumstances of the case, such as the duration of the treatment, its physical or mental effects and, in some cases, the sex, age and state of health of the victim . . . Further factors include the purpose for which the treatment was inflicted together with the intention or motivation behind it . . .[279]

As far as nuclear weapons are concerned, it seems clear that their use would at least amount to "degrading" treatment, since it deprives the victims of their basic dignity.[280] The human suffering involved would easily reach this threshold since it is treatment "such as to arouse in the victims feelings of fear, anguish and inferiority capable of humiliating and debasing them."[281] By comparison, the ECtHR has held in several cases involving relatively minor ill-treatments, for instance handcuffing imposed on detainees and prisoners, that there were violations of Article 3 ECHR.[282]

277 *El-Masri v. the former Yugoslav Republic of Macedonia* [GC], December 13, 2012.

278 See, for more details, D. Harris, M. O'Boyle, and C. Warbrick, *Law of the European Convention on Human Rights*, 3rd edn., Oxford, 2014, pp. 236 et seq.

279 *Ibid.*

280 See, in this sense, dissention opinion of Judge Koroma in the 1996 Advisory Opinion on the *Legality of the Threat or Use of Nuclear Weapons*, p. 577: "It should be recalled that both human rights law and international humanitarian law have as their raison d'être the protection of the individual as well as the worth and dignity of the human person, both during peacetime or in an armed conflict."

281 See, for instance, *Kudla v. Poland* [GC], no. 30210/96, October 26, 2000, § 92.

282 See, for instance, *Henaf v. France*, no. 65436/01, ECHR 2003-XI; *Mouisel v. France*, no. 67263/01, ECHR 2002-IX; or *Kashavelov v. Bulgaria*, no. 891/05, January 20, 2011.

It may also be argued that the use of nuclear weapons could amount to "inhuman" treatment, given the fact that, as observed above, numerous victims could suffer injuries that would inflict enormous suffering and pain and, within a few weeks, lead to their demise. The release of ionizing radiation and radioactive fallout can result in radiation sickness, with most people not being aware that they have been exposed to a potentially lethal radiation dose until days or weeks after the explosion.[283] The period preceding death could certainly be qualified as "acute mental and physical suffering" that would "expose [the victims] to a real risk of dying under most distressing circumstances." The ECtHR held, in a different situation, that such circumstances, involving "compelling humanitarian considerations," were likely to amount to "inhuman" treatment in breach of Article 3.[284]

It is also noteworthy that, in the case of *Selçuk and Asker v. Turkey*, the ECtHR held that there was inhuman treatment when, as a part of a security operation, the security forces destroyed the elderly applicants' home and property in a contemptuous manner and in their presence, without regard to their safety or welfare, depriving them of their livelihood and shelter and causing them great distress.[285] It is obvious that the destruction of one's home by a nuclear blast, as described above, is very likely to have a similar effect and could amount, on its own, to a breach of Article 3 ECHR.

Finally, the following paragraph of the *El-Masri* judgment shows that a particular stigma attaches to "torture," defined as a deliberate inhuman treatment that intentionally inflicts severe pain or suffering with the aim, inter alia, of obtaining information, inflicting punishment, or intimidating:

> 197. . . . In addition to the severity of the treatment, there is a purposive element, as recognised in the United Nations Convention against Torture and Other Cruel, Inhuman or Degrading Treatment or Punishment, which came into force on 26 June 1987, which defines torture in terms of the

283 Maresca, "The Catastrophic Humanitarian Consequences of Nuclear Weapons," pp. 132 et seq.

284 *D. v. United Kingdom*, no. 30240/96, May 2, 1997, § 54. In this case, the applicant, suffering from AIDS, was ordered to be returned to his national State of St. Kitts after he had completed his prison sentence for drug smuggling. Pending his removal and the outcome of the proceedings in Strasbourg, he had been placed in a hospice and was in the terminal stage of his sickness when the ECtHR ruled that his return would be contrary to Article 3 ECHR.

285 *Selçuk and Asker v. Turkey*, April 24, 1998, § 77, *Reports of Judgments and Decisions* 1998-II: ". . . [The Court] recalls that Mrs Selçuk and Mr Asker were aged respectively 54 and 60 at the time and had lived in the village of İslamköy all their lives . . . Their homes and most of their property were destroyed by the security forces, depriving the applicants of their livelihoods and forcing them to leave their village. It would appear that the exercise was premeditated and carried out contemptuously and without respect for the feelings of the applicants. They were taken unprepared; they had to stand by and watch the burning of their homes; inadequate precautions were taken to secure the safety of Mr and Mrs Asker; Mrs Selçuk's protests were ignored, and no assistance was provided to them afterwards."

> intentional infliction of severe pain or suffering with the aim, *inter alia*, of obtaining information, inflicting punishment or intimidating (Article 1 of the United Nations Convention) . . .

On account of this definition, it seems safe to argue, first, that the use of nuclear weapons, in particular in an inhabited area, is a deliberate act capable of "causing very serious and cruel suffering" among the civilian population. Second, it is likely that, in the logic of a policy of deterrence, the use of nuclear weapons would have the aim of intimidating the targeted victims and government. Third, the assessment that the Court has to make under Article 3 ECHR "depends on all the circumstances of the case, such as the duration of the treatment, its physical or mental effects and, in some cases, the sex, age and state of health of the victim."[286] In other words, the special needs of particularly vulnerable persons, such as children, women, or elderly persons, can be taken into consideration. It has been observed in Part I, in respect of cluster munitions and anti-personnel mines, that, in time of war and its aftermath, these categories of persons are most affected by the horrors of warfare.[287] This is *a fortiori* in the case of nuclear explosions, as will be shown in the Chapter dealing with nuclear weapons testing. Fourth, in the case of *Selmouni v. France*, decided in 1999, the ECtHR took the view that the increasingly high standard required in the area of the protection of human rights inevitably requires greater firmness in assessing breaches of the fundamental values of democratic societies.[288] In light of this statement, it found a violation of the prohibition of torture in the very specific circumstances of the case not entailing physical suffering to an extent that had been necessary to amount to torture in earlier cases.[289] The Court held that the ill-treatment had to be considered "as a whole."[290] In light of the foregoing, it is from this author's point of view, not excluded that the use of nuclear weapons would amount to torture within the meaning, inter alia, of Article 3 ECHR.

These examples show that, apart from the physical harm to which the survivors of a nuclear explosion are exposed, mental suffering can be decisive to find a violation of Article 3 ECHR. A similar phenomenon will be considered below in the subsection dealing with the difficulties with regard to respecting human rights after a nuclear explosion, for instance in the case of the Fukushima accident.[291]

286 *El-Masri v. the former Yugoslav Republic of Macedonia* [GC], December 13, 2012, § 196.
287 This volume, Chapter 3, section A.3.b)cc).
288 *Selmouni v. France* [GC], no. 25803/94, § 101, ECHR 1999-V.
289 The applicant was, inter alia, dragged along by his hair, made to run along a corridor with police officers positioned on either side to trip him up, he was made to kneel down in front of some police officers, of whom one showed him his penis and urinated on him. Later he was threatened with a blowlamp, then with a syringe (§ 103).
290 *Ibid.*, § 105.
291 This Chapter, section C.3.

d) Right to respect for private life and home, and right to property

In addition to the above-mentioned rights, other provisions of international human rights law might be relevant in situations of nuclear explosions and could be invoked, at least subsidiarily, before an international judicial body. For instance, protection against the disastrous consequences for health, as described in the rubric of Article 3 ECHR, is also covered by the right to respect for private life, one of the aspects of Article 8 ECHR, which extends to both physical and mental integrity.[292]

The right to respect of one's home, another guarantee stemming from Article 8 ECHR, might also come into play. An interference with this right can be justified by showing the existence of a legal basis, of a legitimate aim, and of a necessity of the measure in a democratic society. Typical interferences with the exercise of this right are the denial of access and occupation,[293] and expulsion or eviction.[294] The denial of access to one's home can in addition constitute an interference with the right to property, guaranteed, among others, by Article 1 of Protocol no. 1 to the ECHR.[295] All three regional human rights bodies have found serious violations of the right to home as well as the right to property in extreme cases of a deliberate burning of houses.[296] In a case against Russia, it has been found that both Article 8 and Article 1 of Protocol no. 1 have been breached due to the destruction of the applicants' property following an aerial attack during the second Chechen war. The ECtHR held that the "Suppression of Terrorism Act" vested wide powers in State agents within the zone of a counter-terrorism operation and did not define with sufficient clarity the scope of those powers and the manner of their exercise so as to afford individuals adequate protection against arbitrariness.[297] Therefore, the Court concluded that the interference with the applicants' rights under Article 1 of Protocol no. 1 as well as Article 8 ECHR was not "lawful" within the meaning of the Convention and that, as a result, there had been violations of these guarantees.[298]

292 See, for instance, *Nada v. Switzerland* [GC], no. 10593/08, September 12, 2012, § 15, with further references.

293 *Wiggins v. United Kingdom*, no. 7456/76, February 8, 1978, DR 13, pp. 40 et seq. (inadmissible).

294 See, for instance, *Larkos v. Cyprus* [GC], no. 29515/95, ECHR 1999-I; and *Iatridis v. Greece* [GC], no. 31107/96, ECHR 1999-II.

295 See, for instance, *Loizidou v. Turkey* [GC], no. 15318/89, December 18, 1996, §§ 63 et seq.

296 ECtHR, *Akdivar and Others v. Turkey*, September 16, 1996, § 88; *Reports of Judgments and Decisions* 1996-IV; *Bilgin v. Turkey*, no. 23819/94, § 108, November 16, 2000; IACtHR, *Moiwana Village v. Suriname*, Judgment, Series C no. 145, June 15, 2005, § 134; and *Ituango Massacres v. Colombia*, Judgment, Series C no. 148, July 1, 2006, §§ 182, 194, and 197; ACommHPR, *Sudan Human Rights Organisation and the Centre on Housing Rights and Evictions v. The Sudan*, Decision, Comm. nos. 279/03 and 296/05, May 27, 2009, § 216.

297 *Khamzayev and Others v. Russia*, no. 1503/02, § 217, May 3, 2011. See also *Khamidov v. Russia*, no. 72118/01, § 143, ECHR 2007-XII (extracts); and *Selçuk and Asker v. Turkey*, April 24, 1998, § 86, *Reports of Judgments and Decisions* 1998 II.

298 *Khamzayev and Others v. Russia*, no. 1503/02, § 219, May 3, 2011.

Moreover, the ECtHR held in several cases that breaches of the respect for individuals' homes are not confined to concrete or physical breaches, but might also include noise, emissions, smells, or other forms of nuisances.[299] It is suggested here that, even when a building resists a nuclear blast, an area within the radius of the explosion might not be habitable for a long time or forever due to the radioactive fallout. This might amount to a de facto expulsion or eviction, and even assuming that the interference with the right has a legal basis in national or international law and pursues a legitimate aim within the terms of paragraph 2 of Article 8 ECHR, such as the protection of the interest of national security, a nuclear attack against a populated area would be disproportionate and, as a result, breach Article 8 ECHR. Doswald-Beck rightly argues that the enormous destructive impact of a nuclear explosion, and the long-term radioactive poisoning, are likely to result in breaches of Article 8 and/or Article 1 of Protocol no. 1.[300]

It is true that both Article 8 ECHR and Article 1 of Protocol no. 1 can be derogated from "in time of war or other public emergency threatening the life of the nation."[301] Such a derogation has to be strictly construed and does not give a *carte blanche* to the State invoking it, the derogation being limited "to the extent strictly required by the exigencies of the situation, provided that such measures *are not inconsistent with its other obligations under international law*."[302] In other words, the protection of international humanitarian law, in particular its fundamental principles, would remain relevant.[303]

e) Non-exhaustive list of potential human rights violations: Use of nuclear weapons as a total denial of all basic human rights

It has been shown in this subsection that the use of nuclear weapons, in particular in inhabited areas, is likely to have disastrous consequences for the enjoyment of the right to life and the prohibition of inhuman and degrading treatment of civilians. It has also shown that such a use might amount to torture and, provided that the specific intent to destroy a protected group is established, to a breach of the prohibition of genocide – both of which are *jus cogens* rules. Finally, the right

299 See, for instance, *Hatton v. United Kingdom* [GC], no. 36022/97, July 8, 2003 § 96; and *Giacomelli v. Italy* [GC], 59909/00, November 2, 2006, § 76.

300 Ibid., p. 459.

301 Article 15 (Derogation in time of emergency): "1. In time of war or other public emergency threatening the life of the nation any High Contracting Party may take measures derogating from its obligations under this Convention to the extent strictly required by the exigencies of the situation, provided that such measures are not inconsistent with its other obligations under international law. 2. No derogation from Article 2, except in respect of deaths resulting from lawful acts of war, or from Articles 3, 4 (paragraph 1) and 7 shall be made under this provision . . .".

302 Emphasis added.

303 Regarding the derogation clause, see Doswald-Beck, "Human Rights Law and Nuclear Weapons," pp. 451–452.

to respect for private life and home, as well as the right to property, are other human rights that might be heavily infringed upon by nuclear explosions.

These are only some of the rights, probably the most obvious ones, that are likely to be denied in situations of nuclear attack. The list is not meant to be exhaustive insofar as only a few, if any, rights would remain unaffected by a nuclear explosion. Indeed, a detonation in a town would destroy churches, mosques, temples, and cemeteries, depriving the different religious groups of their places of worship and prayer, protected by the most relevant human rights treaties.[304] Moreover, a nuclear explosion is likely to destroy the buildings and infrastructures of media organs, such as buildings of the written press as well as television and radio stations. As a result, even the most basic enjoyment of the freedom of expression would be jeopardized, too.[305] Similarly, a nuclear explosion would destroy the premises of private associations and trade unions and, therefore, deprive them of the possibility to gather peacefully, in flagrant violation of the right of freedom of assembly and association.[306] Furthermore, a nuclear blast could cause the destruction of court buildings and law firms and lead to the death of judges, lawyers, and other judicial staff. The paralyzation of the judiciary authorities would lead to the deprivation, at least temporarily, of the right to a fair trial.[307] Finally, a nuclear explosion would bring about the destruction of schools, universities, and libraries, and the death of their staff, depriving the people of their right to education.[308]

For practical reasons, the impact of nuclear weapons on these freedoms and rights has not been examined in detail here; thus the examples given here are not exhaustive. It is sufficient, for the purpose of the present study, to conclude that the use of such weapons would amount to a total denial of all basic human rights.

3. Duty to respect human rights after a nuclear explosion

a) Positive obligation of States to protect life and dignity after a nuclear accident or catastrophe

It has already been shown that one of the aspects that make nuclear weapons so fatal is the fact that no adequate rescue and medical response is possible due to

304 Regarding Europe, see Article 9 ECHR; for instance, *Cyprus v. Turkey* [GC], no. 25781/94, May 10, 2001, §§ 241 et seq. This right is also protected by Article 18 ICCPR, Article 12 ACHR, and Article 8 ACHPR.

305 See, for Europe, Article 10 ECHR; for instance, *Bankovićand Others v. Belgium and Others* [GC], no. 52207/99, December 12, 2001 (inadmissible), in which the applicants complained, inter alia, about the bombing of the building of *Radio Televizije Srbije* (RTS). In one of its most criticized decisions, the Court declared the case inadmissible for lack of jurisdiction. See also Article 19 ICCPR, Article 13 ACHR, and Article 9 ACHPR.

306 See, for instance, *Cyprus v. Turkey* [GC], no. 25781/94, May 10, 2001, §§ 255 et seq. (Article 11 ECHR). See also Article 21 ICCPR, Article 15 ACHR, and Article 11 ACHPR.

307 Article 14 ICCPR, Article 6 ECHR, Article 8 ACHR, and Article 7 ACHPR.

308 See, for instance, Article 2 of Protocol no. 1 to the ECHR, Article 5(e)(v) ICESCR, Article 26 ACHR (at least implicit), and Article 17 § 1 ACHPR.

the complete destruction of infrastructures, the death of medical personnel, and the long-lasting radioactivity rendering access to the area very difficult. The presence of radiation after a nuclear attack would seriously hamper the ability to search for, rescue, and care for the wounded. This author fully agrees with Doswald-Beck, who claims that this could amount to a violation of the right to life by the attacking State.[309]

It has also been explained above that the right to life forbids the use of force that is not "absolutely necessary" and, therefore, encompasses the duty to "avoid or minimalize" loss of life, civil as well as among the enemy combatants. But the duties inherent in the right to life do not stop there, since a State might be under the obligation to provide adequate medical care in response to a harmful event.[310]

The question has to be raised, first, who would owe the duty to avoid or minimalize deaths in the aftermath of a nuclear explosion. In the event of a nuclear attack by a State against a group of individuals within its own territory, that State would have to remedy the consequences of a use of nuclear weapons, since the situation falls under its jurisdiction. The question is more difficult to answer in the case of a State attacking another one. First of all, it is suggested that the State targeted by the attack remains *a priori* responsible since the explosion, and its effects, are felt on its own territory. In this regard, it is relevant to recall that, according to the case law of the ECtHR, even if the territorial State has no effective control over a part of its territory, this territory falls, in terms of international law, within its jurisdiction.[311] This does not mean, however, that this State would be necessarily responsible for all potential human rights violations, the ECtHR admitting but a limited responsibility for human rights violations on territories over which the State does not have full authority.[312] The precise extent of that responsibility could only be determined by an assessment of the concrete actions and omissions of the territorial State. A minimum duty to be expected from the territorial State might be that of asking for and allowing international assistance, including from relevant organizations such as the ICRC. It is noteworthy to mention that, in 2016, the ILC adopted the Draft articles on the protection of persons in the event of disasters, Article 13 of which imposes on

309 Doswald-Beck, "Human Rights Law and Nuclear Weapons," p. 451.

310 *Ibid.*, p. 450.

311 *Ilaşcu and Others v. Moldova and Russia* [GC], no. 48787/99, § 331, ECHR 2004-VII; *Catan and Others v. the Republic of Moldova and Russia* [GC], nos. 43370/04, 8252/05, and 18454/06, § 109, ECHR 2012 (extracts); and *Sargsyan v. Azerbaijan* [GC], no. 40167/06, § 151, ECHR 2015.

312 See, for instance, the case of *Catan and Others v. the Republic of Moldova and Russia* [GC], nos. 43370/04, 8252/05, and 18454/06, § 109, ECHR 2012 (extracts), concerning the territory of Transdniestria, where the ECtHR held what follows: "Moldova's obligation under Article 1 of the Convention . . . was, however, limited in the circumstances to a positive obligation to take the diplomatic, economic, judicial or other measures that were both in its power to take and in accordance with international law."

the States affected by a disaster the duty to seek external assistance when the disaster exceeds its national response. Article 14 adds that the provision of external assistance requires the consent of the affected States, but that consent shall not be withheld or withdrawn arbitrarily.[313] As far as the attacking State is concerned, the question of whether it would be responsible for omitting positive measures with a view to limiting deaths and destruction would depend, from the author's point of view, on its presence on the territory and whether or not it has effective control over it.

Several cases may illustrate the positive duties after a life-threatening incident in the aftermath of a nuclear explosion. In the case of *Neira Alegria et al. v. Peru* concerning the use of force to suppress a prison riot, for example, over 100 inmates died and 34 were injured, many of them crushed to death. One of the violations of the right to life found by the IACtHR in this case was the fact that no effort had been made to find and rescue persons who might still have been alive.[314] The significance of subsequent medical care to prevent loss of life as well as the duty to investigate the whereabouts of missing persons – soldiers or civilians – have been examined in other cases, in particular by the ECtHR. A concrete example is the case of *Varnava and Others v. Turkey*, where the Court held that in a zone of international conflict, States are under an obligation to protect the lives of those not, or no longer, engaged in hostilities, and that this duty also extends to the provision of medical assistance to the wounded. The Court further found that where combatants have died, or succumbed to wounds, the need for accountability would necessitate the proper disposal of remains and require the authorities to collect and provide information about the identity and fate of the persons concerned, or authorize institutions such as the ICRC to do its work in this field.[315] It concluded that "Article 2 therefore imposes a continuing obligation on the respondent Government to account for the whereabouts and fate of the missing men in the present case . . ."[316]

The right to life is not the only guarantee that might come into play in the aftermath of a nuclear explosion. The prohibition of inhuman or degrading

313 Eighth report on the protection of persons in the event of a disaster, Special Rapporteur E. Valencia-Ospina, UN Doc. A/CN.4/697, March 17, 2016, p. 103. It is important to mention that the draft articles take a broad definition of "disaster," including natural and man-made ones: "'Disaster' means a calamitous event or series of events resulting in widespread loss of life, great human suffering and distress, displacement, or large-scale material, economic or environmental damage, thereby seriously disrupting the functioning of society."

314 IACtHR, *Neira Alegria et al. v. Peru*, Judgment, Series C no. 20, January 19, 1995, §§ 74–76.

315 *Varnava and Others v. Turkey*, ECtHR, Judgment, nos. 16064/90 et al., September 18, 2009, § 185; see also the case of *Ahmet Özkan and Others v. Turkey*, Judgment, no. 21689/93, April 6, 2004, §§ 307 et seq.

316 *Varnava and Others*, § 186.

treatment is another potentially relevant rule in such a scenario. The occurrence of forced disappearances illustrates the mental distress of people worrying about the whereabouts of their family members after a nuclear attack. The ECtHR has held that the burden on the relatives of missing people who are kept in ignorance of the fate of their loved ones and have suffered the anguish of uncertainty can fall within the ambit of Article 3 ECHR and amount to degrading and inhuman treatment.[317] In such cases, the essence of the human rights violation lies in the authorities' reactions and attitudes to the situation once it has been brought to their attention.[318] The ECtHR held, in such cases, that the finding of a violation is not limited to cases where the respondent State has been held responsible for the disappearance, but can also arise out of the failure of the State to react to the relatives' quest for information.[319] In such a situation, the Grand Chamber of the Court held that, in the context of the disappearances occurring in 1974 during the conflict between Cyprus and Turkey:

> . . . the military operation resulted in a considerable loss of life, large-scale arrests and detentions and enforced separation of families. The overall context must still be vivid in the minds of the relatives of persons whose fate has never been accounted for by the authorities. They endure the agony of not knowing whether family members were killed in the conflict or are still in detention or, if detained, have since died. The fact that a very substantial number of Greek Cypriots had to seek refuge in the south coupled with the continuing division of Cyprus must be considered to constitute very serious obstacles to their quest for information. The provision of such information is the responsibility of the authorities of the respondent State. This responsibility has not been discharged. For the Court, the silence of the authorities of the respondent State in the face of the real concerns of the relatives of the missing persons attains a level of severity which can only be categorised as inhuman treatment within the meaning of Article 3.[320]

Finally, humanitarian organizations are confronted with the question of how, in a situation of emergency, the survival and safety of unaccompanied or orphaned children, women, elderly persons, or persons with disabilities could be ensured, including the administration of basic needs such as access to uncontaminated food and potable water and to adequate sanitation facilities in order to prevent the outbreak of diseases.[321] Such a protection would have to include measures against sexual and gender-based violence, which often occurs in humanitarian emergencies,

317 *Ibid.*, § 200.
318 *Ibid.*; see also *Orhan v. Turkey*, no. 25656/94, § 358, June 18, 2002.
319 *Varnava and Others*, § 200.
320 *Cyprus v. Turkey* [GC], no. 25781/94, § 157, ECHR 2001-IV. See also *Dodov v. Bulgaria*, no. 59548/00, January 17, 2008; and *Medova v. Russia*, no. 25385/04, January 15, 2009.
321 Bagshaw, "Responding to the Detonation of Nuclear Weapons," p. 122.

particularly in camp settings.[322] It is suggested here that, in a situation short of special measures of protection, the effects of nuclear explosions, combined with the poor health and living conditions in its aftermath, could amount to degrading or inhuman treatment, or even torture, within the meaning of Article 3 ECHR and the case law of the ECtHR, especially when the victims are members of particularly vulnerable groups.[323]

b) Right to health in the aftermath of the Fukushima accident (2011)

Sadly enough, the Fukushima accident offers a "real-life" example for the difficulties with regard to reacting adequately to a nuclear weapons explosion as a means of warfare.

On March 11, 2011, Japan was hit by an earthquake and tsunami that caused an accident in the Fukushima Daiichi nuclear power plant. The earthquake, of a magnitude of 9.0, occurred off the east coast of Japan in the Pacific Ocean. It gave rise to a tsunami with waves of up to 40 meters high.[324] As a result of the earthquake and tsunami, almost 16 000 people died and more than 6 000 were injured.[325] Designed to resist waves of a maximum height of 5.7 meters, the walls of the power plant failed to contain the impact of the tsunami, causing a total power blackout in units 1 to 5 of the plant, as well as the breakdown of the communication system within and outside the plant. The complete power outage in units 1 to 3 led to the failure of the reactor cooling system, causing damage to the fuel contained in the reactors. Ultimately, as a result of the meltdown, a series of explosions occurred.[326]

To reduce the impact of the Fukushima tragedy on people to mere cancer statistics would be too narrow and not responsive to the human suffering endured by the affected population.[327] It is relevant for the present study to highlight that the Special Rapporteur on the right of everyone to the enjoyment of the highest

322 *Ibid.*

323 See also the above-mentioned Draft articles on the protection of persons in the event of disasters, which determine that, in responding to disasters, States "shall respect and protect the inherent dignity of the human person" (Article 5) and that "[p]ersons affected by disasters are entitled to the respect, protection and fulfillment of their human rights" (Article 6). In the response to disasters, the "needs of the most vulnerable" shall be taken into account (Article 7).

324 Report of the Special Rapporteur on the right of everyone to the enjoyment of the highest attainable standard of physical and mental health, Anand Grover, UN Doc. A/HRC/23/41/Add. 3, July 2013, § 6.

325 *Ibid.*

326 *Ibid.*, § 7.

327 International Physicians for the Prevention of Nuclear War (IPPNW), Critical Analysis of the UNSCEAR Report "Levels and effects of radiation exposure due to the nuclear accident after the 2011 Great East-Japan Earthquake and tsunami," June 5, 2014, p. 18, http://www.fukushima-disaster.de/fileadmin/user_upload/pdf/english/Akzente_Unscear2014.pdf (accessed February 27, 2017).

attainable standard of physical and mental health, Anand Grover, visited Japan in November 2012, in order to ascertain the country's efforts to implement the right to health in the aftermath of the nuclear accident of March 11, 2011. In his report, he stated that the nuclear accident in Fukushima has affected the right to health of evacuees and residents alike, and has had an impact on physical as well as mental health, particularly of pregnant women, older persons, and children.[328] He added that the evacuation had caused the breakdown of families and communities, and had given rise to mental health concerns.[329] Certain of his findings deserve to be briefly exposed here.

In the aftermath of a nuclear accident, the right to health commands rigorous and continued monitoring of individual health because the effects of radiation exposure are not always immediately known or treatable.[330] The early capture and registration of information are crucial to the effective monitoring of the human health impact of radiation exposure.[331] The Special Rapporteur criticized the fact that a basic survey was sent out only three months after the nuclear accident had occurred and relied solely on the memory of respondents of their activities around the time of the accident.[332] In health monitoring, special attention has to be paid to children, as they are most at risk of thyroid cancer caused by radioactive iodine intake.[333] Anand Grover observed that the thyroid screening of children was insufficient and delayed, which prevented parents from taking efficient mitigating action against potential thyroid cancer and was in breach of their right to health.[334] This problem was coupled with the difficulty faced by parents in obtaining access to the results of their children's thyroid check-ups as a result of the bureaucracy and the cumbersome applicable legislation in the field of freedom of information.[335]

The Special Rapporteur also recalled that the right to health imposes on States the duty to mitigate the effect of nuclear accidents on the mental health of the victims by alleviating stress and anxiety caused by radiation exposure and separation of families.[336] The effect of nuclear disasters on mental health was documented by

328 Report Grover, § 11.
329 *Ibid.*
330 *Ibid.*, § 22.
331 IAEA, "Generic Procedures for Medical Response during a Nuclear or Radiological Emergency, Emergency Preparedness and Response," Vienna, April 2005, pp. 137 et seq., http://www-pub.iaea.org/MTCD/Publications/PDF/EPR-MEDICAL-2005_web.pdf (accessed February 27, 2017).
332 Report Grover, § 27.
333 *Ibid.*, § 28.
334 *Ibid.*, § 31.
335 *Ibid.*, § 32.
336 *Ibid.*, § 36. See also, in this regard, T. Morris-Suzuki, "Introduction," in Greenpeace, "Lessons from Fukushima," 2012, pp. 11–13, http://www.greenpeace.org/slovenia/Global/slovenia/Dokumenti/Lessons-from-Fukushima.pdf (accessed February 27, 2017).

the incidents in Three-Mile Island, as well as in Chernobyl.[337] In fact, following the Chernobyl accident, women with young children were found to be most vulnerable to the effects on mental health of this nuclear tragedy, and the latter's negative consequences were still visible more than six years after the accident.[338] Anand Grover also noted that the anxiety and stress of evacuees, residents, and their families were attributable to the effects of radiation leakage on their health – in particular of children, the cost of evacuation, and the loss of livelihoods, as well as the uncertainty surrounding the future.[339]

To sum up, Anand Grover explored relevant aspects of the right to health in situations of a large-scale nuclear accident. His conclusions and criticism of the conduct of the responsible Japanese authorities are relevant for the present analysis dealing with the human rights implications of nuclear activities, in particular when he focuses on the rights of vulnerable groups such as women, children, and older people, or on especially exposed persons, in particular power plant workers. His broad analysis rightly goes beyond mere illness and death statistics by taking into consideration the social and economic aspects of the victims' right to health.

4. The scenario of a limited (regional) nuclear war and its impact on the global enjoyment of economic, social, and cultural rights

a) Impact of a regional nuclear war on global development, health, and environment

The observations that have so far been made in this chapter concern mostly the immediate impact of a nuclear explosion on the local population through thermal radiation (heat) and blast waves causing serious casualties in large areas.[340] An element that has gained ground in recent years is the recognition that the use of nuclear weapons, in particular if it triggers subsequent nuclear explosions in retaliation, would affect the whole planet, or at least entire regions. Recent studies have tried to assess the impact of a nuclear war more globally, taking into account factors such as displacement of people, climate change, environment, and development. The UNIDIR study (mentioned above[341]) analyzed the consequences of a regional nuclear war in South Asia, a densely populated area. Based on previous studies, it modelled the consequences of a nuclear conflict between India

337 See, for instance, E. J. Bromet et al., "Mental Health of Residents near the Three Mile Island Reactor: A Comparative Study of Selected Group," *Journal of Preventive Psychiatry*, vol. 1(3), 1982, 225–276.

338 J. Havenaar et al., "Long-Term Mental Health Effects of the Chernobyl Disaster: An Epidemiologic Survey in Two Former Soviet Regions," *American Journal of Psychiatry*, vol. 154(11), 1997, pp. 1605–1607, 1606.

339 Report Grover, § 38.

340 Maresca, "The Catastrophic Humanitarian Consequences of Nuclear Weapons," p. 132.

341 Borrie and Caughley, *An Illusion of Safety*, and this Chapter, section B.2.c).

and Pakistan in which each side used 50 15kt weapons, predominantly against the others' urban areas. Such a conflict could produce about 21 million short-term fatalities.[342]

UNIDIR comes to the conclusion that the scale of human displacement in such a regional nuclear conflict, the loss of people forced to flee areas affected by the detonations and those compelled to move because of fallout, and fear of radiation or further nuclear strikes, would be massive. It suggests that, conservatively estimated, the number of displaced people could be comparable to the short-term fatalities, thus 21 million.[343] In the aftermath, people would most likely flee from cities into the surrounding countryside, but, unless adequate humanitarian assistance such as emergency shelter, medical care, food, sanitation, clean water, and security could be provided quickly, they would be compelled to move on as local resources became depleted.[344]

As far as nuclear war and climate change are concerned, it was already recognized during the Cold War that a large-scale nuclear war between the former USSR and the United States of America could lead to globally lower temperatures, often referred to as "nuclear winter."[345] It was nevertheless only recently acknowledged that the use of only 0.03 percent of the global nuclear arsenal could cause such an effect. Taking again an India–Pakistan nuclear conflict as a scenario, it is suggested that 100 15kt airbursts in an urban environment would produce so much soot from burning cities that it would have significant effects on the climate.[346] Recent research has demonstrated that temperatures could globally fall below those of the Little Ice Age of the fourteenth to nineteenth centuries due to the light blocked from reaching the planet's surface.[347] Such a fall in temperature would shorten the growing seasons throughout the world for at least a decade after this kind of conflict.[348] Recent studies suggest that agricultural production in parts of the United States and China would decline by about 20 percent for four years, and by 10 percent for a decade.[349] In addition, major ozone depletion in

342 O. B. Toon et al., "Consequences of Regional-Scale Nuclear Conflicts," *Science*, vol. 315, 2007, pp. 1224–1225, http://climate.envsci.rutgers.edu/pdf/SciencePolicyForumNW.pdf (accessed February 27, 2017).

343 Borrie and Caughley, *An Illusion of Safety*, p. 43. In 2013, there were estimated to be 33.3 million internally displaced persons globally and 10.4 million refugees of concern to UNHCR.

344 *Ibid.*, p. 44.

345 *Ibid.*

346 A. Robock and O. B. Toon, "Self-Assured Destruction: The Climate Impacts of Nuclear War," *Bulletin of the Atomic Scientists*, vol. 68, no. 5, 2012, pp. 66–74.

347 Borrie and Caughley, *An Illusion of Safety*, p. 44.

348 *Ibid.*

349 L. Xia and A. Robock, "Impacts of a Nuclear War in South Asia on Rice Production in Mainland China," *Climatic Change*, vol. 116, 2013, pp. 357–372; and M. Özdoğan, A. Robock, and C. J. Kucharik, "Impacts of a Nuclear War in South Asia on Soybean and Maize Production in the Midwest United States," *Climatic Change*, vol. 116, 2013, pp. 373–387.

the atmosphere is expected in such a scenario, allowing more ultraviolet radiation to reach the surface, affecting human health as well as the environment.[350]

Past famines indicate that the consequences of food shortages are likely to be disproportionally felt by the poorest and most vulnerable, since food becomes scarcer and prices rise. These individuals would suffer most by such a scenario both in the immediate aftermath of the incident and in the long term.[351] In other words, while a nuclear explosion would not discriminate between rich and poor in its immediate impact, its long-term consequences would.[352] IPPNW thus argued that, based on recent academic research, the number of people threatened by famine caused by a nuclear war would amount to 2 billion.[353] Such a situation would cause immense pressure on States and international relief organizations. By comparison, the World Food Programme (WFP) currently provides food assistance to 80 million people per year.[354]

A last noteworthy aspect is environmental sustainability. Disasters have in general devastating effects on the environment, depending on their type, severity, and location. They affect key natural resources such as fields, soil, forests, and biodiversity, and restoring them is often impossible in the short term.[355] Obviously, a nuclear explosion would have a particularly harmful effect on the environment, from water to soil.[356] Such a scenario would disproportionately affect the rural, often poorer, population. The effects of radiation on the human being are exacerbated by a nearly irreversible environmental contamination, leading to the loss of livelihood and lands; the decontamination and storage of radioactive materials after the use of nuclear weapons would be a complex, expensive, lengthy, and hazardous process, with no guarantee of success.[357] According to UNDP and the UN International Children's Emergency Fund (UNICEF), the radioactive fallout from the Chernobyl disaster contaminated large areas of Ukraine, Belarus, and Russia, "affecting life in rural communities for decades to come."[358] They note

350 M. J. Mills et al., "Massive Global Ozone Loss Predicted Following Regional Nuclear Conflict," *Proceedings of the National Academy of Sciences*, vol. 105, no. 14, 2008, pp. 5307–5312.

351 R. Acheson, "Wider Consequences – Impact on Development," in Fihn, *Unspeakable Suffering*, pp. 59–65, 65.

352 "Disaster Proofing the Millennium Development Goals (MDGs): Enhancing Resilience and Accelerating Achievement of MDGs and HFA Implementation in Asia and the Pacific Region by 2015," Asian Disaster Preparedness Center, p. 3, http://www.preventionweb.net/publications/view/16098 (accessed February 27, 2017).

353 I. Helfand, "Nuclear Famine: Two Billion People at Risk? Global Impacts of Limited Nuclear War on Agriculture, Food Supplies, and Human Nutrition," IPPNW and Physicians for Social Responsibility, 2nd edn., 2013, http://www.psr.org/assets/pdfs/two-billion-at-risk.pdf (accessed February 27, 2017).

354 WFP, http://www.wfp.org/logistics (accessed February 28, 2017).

355 "Disaster Proofing the Millennium Development Goals," p. 10.

356 Acheson, "Wider Consequences," p. 63.

357 *Ibid.*

358 "The Human Consequences of the Chernobyl Nuclear Accident: A Strategy for Recovery," A Report Commissioned by UNDP and UNICEF with the support of UN-OCHA and

furthermore that "[a]griculture and forestry are forbidden in wide areas. Poverty forces many people to eat contaminated berries, mushrooms, game and fish, to feed contaminated hay to their cattle and to burn radioactively contaminated firewood in their stoves."[359]

Recent research also identifies the impact of a regional nuclear war on the global economy and development.[360] Such a conflict would lead to tens of millions of people being killed or injured, and millions more losing members of their families, their homes, jobs, and most of their material possessions. As a result, it is likely to cause other effects, such as economic disruption, loss of wealth with macroeconomic impact, increased market volatility, loss of investor confidence, and potential for political turmoil, as well as the diversion of resources from global development and poverty reduction to meet emergency needs, with negative effects in particular for the most vulnerable people.[361]

b) Introductory remarks on economic, social, and cultural rights

The aim of this subsection is to demonstrate that the rights of numerous people living far away from the actual war theater would be infringed by an exchange of nuclear weapons. The following rights will be considered: the right to development, the right to the highest standard of health, the right to a healthy environment, and the right to an adequate standard of living, including the right to food and water. These rights belong to the category of economic, social, and cultural rights; they are inter-related and sometimes overlapping.

Like civil and political rights, examined above,[362] economic, social, and cultural rights are generally considered applicable extraterritorially.[363] The rights that will be examined in this Chapter all have an environmental connotation. In this context, it is suggested by Birnie, Boyle, and Redgwell that there is no reason, if States can be held responsible for their failure to control their soldiers abroad, why States should not be liable for their failure to control transboundary pollution and environmental harm emanating from industrial activities within their territories.[364]

WHO, 2012, http://www.unicef.org/newsline/02chernobylstudy.htm (accessed February 28, 2017).

359 *Ibid.*, p. 5.

360 See for more details L. J. Dumas and T. D. Nelson, "Estimating the Economic Consequences of a Nuclear Weapons Explosion: Critical Factors," in Fihn, *Unspeakable Suffering*, pp. 50–57.

361 Borrie and Caughley, *An Illusion of Safety*, p. 45.

362 This Chapter, section C.2.

363 See, for instance, Committee on Economic, Social and Cultural rights (CESCR), General Comment No. 8, The Relationship between Economic Sanctions and Respect for Economic, Social and Cultural Rights, UN Doc. E/C.12/1997/8, December 12, 1997, § 13; and AComHPR, *Association pour la sauvegarde de la paix au Burundi v. Tanzania, Kenya, Uganda, Rwanda, Zaire and Zambia*, Decision, Comm. no. 157/96, May 23, 2003, § 75.

364 P. Birnie, A. Boyle, and C. Redgwell, *International Law and the Environment*, 3rd edn., Oxford and New York, 2009, p. 299.

This opinion is shared here since these activities take place within States' jurisdiction and control, and only the effects are of an extraterritorial nature.[365] The authors mentioned add that denial of transboundary protection to claimants guaranteed by human rights treaties would be hard to reconcile with the principles of equality of access to justice and non-discrimination.[366] As a result, a State using nuclear weapons could be held accountable for the human rights violations that occur on the territories of other States. This is only natural and fair, considering the transboundary impact of a nuclear weapons detonation.

The present Chapter examines the global consequences of a regional nuclear war on the global environment, health, and development. Since many of the States on whose territories the effects of such a war are felt, in particular through fallout and radiation, are not engaged in the regional conflict in which the nuclear explosions took place, it is less relevant whether the treaties containing the rights assessed in this Chapter are applicable in an armed conflict. Moreover, it is suggested that as the relevant treaties do not contain any derogation clauses, there is no reason why economic, social, and cultural rights should not apply during armed conflicts.[367] On the contrary, the CESCR has suggested, in the context of the civil war in Colombia, that economic, social, and cultural rights are even more important in times of crises and war:

> The Committee reminds the State party that it is precisely in situations of crisis, that the Covenant requires the protection and promotion of all economic, social and cultural rights, in particular of the most marginalized and disadvantaged groups of the society, to the best of its ability under the prevailing adverse conditions.[368]

Human rights, and in particular economic, social, and cultural rights, are often defined in terms of three types of duties:[369] the first of which "respects" these rights, namely, the negative duty not to interfere with rights and freedoms of individuals by State action.[370] It has been suggested that, in the context of an armed attack, the obligation to "respect" entails "the obligation not to destroy

365 *Ibid.*

366 *Ibid.*, p. 300.

367 Doswald-Beck, "Human Rights Law and Nuclear Weapons," p. 457. This was explicitly acknowledged for the right to health by the Special Rapporteur on the situation of human rights in Kuwait under Iraqi occupation, Walter Kälin, Special Rapporteur of the Commission on Human Rights in accordance with Commission resolution 1991/67, UN Doc. E/CN.4/1992/26, January 16, 1992, § 208.

368 CESCR, Concluding Observations: Colombia, UN Doc. E/C.12/COL/CO/5, May 21, 2010, § 7.

369 CESCR, General Comment no. 9 (Substantive Issues Arising in the Implementation of the International Covenant on Economic, Social and Cultural Rights), UN Doc. E/C.12/1998/24, 1998.

370 M. Gondek, *The Reach of Human Rights in a Globalising World: Extraterritorial Application of Human Rights Treaties*, Antwerp, 2009, p. 60.

minimal essential levels of economic, social and cultural achievements."[371] The second type of duty is to "protect" rights, namely, to adopt measures to prevent other individuals or groups from violating the integrity, freedom of action, or other human rights of the individual, including the prevention of infringements of his or her material resources.[372] The third type is the duty to "fulfil" (or to "facilitate" or to "provide"), requiring the State to take the measures necessary to ensure for each individual within its jurisdiction opportunities to obtain satisfaction of the needs, recognized in the human rights instruments, which cannot be secured by personal efforts.[373]

The explosion of nuclear weapons, and *a fortiori* a regional nuclear war, could most likely amount to a breach of the duty to "respect" the mentioned rights.[374] This aspect will be examined in more detail in the present section. The duty to "protect" could become relevant when a non-State actor, for instance a terrorist organization, uses a nuclear weapon. In such a scenario, the victims could complain about the violation of their human rights against the State if they can prove that the State did not prevent the violations, for instance, as far as NWS are concerned, by neglecting the security concerning their own stockpiles of nuclear arms or other nuclear devices, thus allowing the illegal appropriation of such material by terrorists. Such duties are comparable with what the ECtHR calls "positive obligations," mentioned above.[375]

c) The right to development and the right not to be discriminated against

Today, the right to development is considered a human right that can be invoked by individuals and peoples.[376] On the universal level, this right stems, inter alia, from the UN Declaration on the Right to Development, adopted in 1986. On a regional level, Article 22 ACHPR provides for the right of all peoples to their economic, social, and cultural development.[377] This provision is significant since it entails one of the few "hard law" provisions guaranteeing the right to development in contemporary international human rights law.[378]

371 W. Kälin and L. Gabriel, *Human Rights in Times of Occupation: The Case of Kuwait*, Bern, 1994, p. 24.

372 A. Eide, "Realization of Social and Economic Rights and the Minimum Threshold Approach," *Human Rights Law Journal*, vol. 10(1–2), 1989, pp. 35–51, 37.

373 *Ibid.* See also Gondek, *The Reach of Human Rights in a Globalising World*, pp. 62–63.

374 Doswald-Beck, "Human Rights Law and Nuclear Weapons," p. 455.

375 See this Chapter, section C.3.a).

376 Cançado Trindade, *International Law for Humankind*, p. 358.

377 Article 22: "1. All peoples shall have the right to their economic, social and cultural development with due regard to their freedom and identity and in the equal enjoyment of the common heritage of mankind. 2. States shall have the duty, individually or collectively, to ensure the exercise of the right to development."

378 O. C. Okafor, "A Regional Perspective: Article 22 of the African Charter on Human Rights and Peoples' Rights," in *Realizing the Right to Development, Essays in Commemoration of*

The preamble of the 1986 Declaration underlines that the human being shall be placed at the center of the development debate.[379] This has also been explained above in the introductory chapter on "human development."[380] The essence of the right to development is summarized in the general clause enshrined in its Article 1 § 1, according to which the right to development is an "inalienable human right" by virtue of which "every human person and all peoples" are entitled to participate in, contribute to, and enjoy economic, social, cultural, and political development, in which all human rights and fundamental freedoms can be fully realized. In other words, it is understood that economic development is not an end in itself, but rather a tool to achieve wider objectives, in particular social justice.[381]

More recently, the trend to view poverty through the human rights lens has gained much support, building upon the assumption that poverty is a grave denial of human rights.[382] For instance, a lack of access to food prevents the poor from living free from hunger, while discrimination experienced in social and political life deprives them of their dignity. Such circumstances are today considered violations of rights because they affect the ability of people to live a dignified life.[383] Poverty is, moreover, closely linked to discrimination because it disproportionately affects members of socially disadvantaged groups, including certain ethnic or religious minorities, indigenous peoples, women, children, persons with disabilities, and elderly people, as these groups are subject to increased vulnerability due to various forms of discrimination.[384] Discrimination causes poverty, but poverty also causes discrimination.[385] It has been mentioned above that the effects of a regional nuclear war would be disastrous for global economy and

25 years of the United Nations Declaration on the Right to Development, United Nations, Office of the High Commissioner, New York and Geneva, 2013, pp. 374–384. The ACommHPR had the opportunity to apply the right guaranteed under Article 22 in the case of *Centre for Minority Rights Development (Kenya) and Minority Rights Group International (on behalf of Endorois Welfare Council) v. Kenya*, ACommHPR, 276/2003, February 4, 2010. See, for a comment on the case, K. De Feyter, "Indigenous Peoples," in *Realizing the Right to Development, Essays in Commemoration of 25 years of the United Nations Declaration on the Right to Development*, United Nations, Office of the High Commissioner, New York and Geneva, 2013, pp. 159–168, 164–167.

379 Paragraph 13 of the preamble reads as follows: "Recognizing that the human person is the central subject of the development process and that development policy should therefore make the human being the main participant and beneficiary of development . . .".

380 This volume, Chapter 1, section B.3.

381 Cançado Trindade, *International Law for Humankind*, p. 359.

382 S. R. Osmani, "Human Rights and Poverty: Building on the Capability Approach," *Journal of Human Development*, vol. 6(2), 2006, pp. 205–219, 206.

383 A. Sen, "Human Rights and Development," in B. A. Andreassen and S. P. Marks (eds.), *Development as a Human Right: Legal, Political and Economic Dimensions*, 2nd edn., Intersentia, 2010, p. 3.

384 Report of the independent expert on the question of human rights and extreme poverty, Magdalena Sepúlveda Carmon, UN Doc. A/63/274, August 13, 2008, § 20.

385 *Ibid.*, § 29.

development. Climate change could lead to a famine threatening billions of people. And the poorest populations, particularly vulnerable when disasters strike, would suffer the most from the consequences of such a scenario. The link between a nuclear explosion and development is clearly established.

The two main means to implement the right to development, in the sense of the 1986 Declaration, are the duty of States to cooperate with each other, on the one hand, and positive obligations to promote development and progress, on the other. As far as the first is concerned, Article 3 § 3 of the 1986 Declaration imposes on States the duty to cooperate with each other in ensuring development and eliminating obstacles to development.[386] The CESCR emphasized that it was incumbent on States Parties, and other actors in a position to assist, to provide international assistance and cooperation, in particular of an economic and technical nature, to enable developing countries to meet their core obligations.[387] The duty to cooperate and to assist other States, in particular less developed ones, would be crucial in the aftermath of a regional nuclear war, leaving behind radioactivity whose appropriate decontamination and storage require sophisticated, expensive tools and infrastructure.

The notion of "sustainable" development has evolved as a response to the possible conflict between economic development and environmental protection and conservation.[388] It can be traced back to the Rio Declaration on Environment and Development, adopted in 1992, after the proclamation of the 1986 Declaration of the right to development.[389] Principle 1 of the Rio Declaration states that "human beings are at the centre of concerns for sustainable development" and that they are "entitled to a healthy and productive life in harmony with nature." In the context of nuclear weapons, assessed in light of the right to development, it is also relevant to refer to Principle 25 of the Rio Declaration: "Peace, development and environmental protection are interdependent and indivisible." The scenario of a regional nuclear war illustrates the link between peace, development, and environment. The use of nuclear weapons would poison key natural resources, from water to soil, and therefore disproportionately affect the rural population dependent on agricultural products. Such a scenario demonstrates that nuclear explosions are simply not compatible with sustainable development. Therefore, the duty to respect the right to development would be grossly violated by waging such a war.

386 See also Articles 4 § 2 and 6 § 1.

387 Article 2 § 1 ICESCR. See also CESCR, General Comment No. 3, The Nature of State Parties Obligations (Article 2 § 1), fifth session, December 14, 1990, §§ 13–14.

388 B. Boer, "Environmental Law and Human Rights in the Asia-Pacific," in B. Boer (ed.), *Environmental Law Dimensions of Human Rights*, Oxford, 2015, pp. 135–179, 139; and S. Atapattu, "Sustainable Development and the Right to Health," in M.-C. Cordonier Segger and C. G. Weeramantry (eds.), *Sustainable Justice: Reconciling Economic, Social and Environmental Law*, Leiden, 2005, pp. 355–363, 357.

389 UN Doc. A/CONF.151/5/Rev.1 (1992), adopted on June 13, 1992.

The concept of sustainable development is in constant evolution. Between June 20 and 22, 2012, Brazil hosted the UN Conference on Sustainable Development in Rio de Janeiro. The outcome of this Conference is summarized in Resolution 66/288 adopted by the UNGA on July 27, 2012, entitled "The Future We Want." The Resolution reiterates the importance of peace and security for development and builds a bridge to most relevant human rights in the development context:

> We also reaffirm the importance of freedom, peace and security, respect for all human rights, including the right to development and the right to an adequate standard of living, including the right to food, the rule of law, gender equality, women's empowerment and the overall commitment to just and democratic societies for development.

It follows from this paragraph that the right to development can be regarded as an "umbrella right,"[390] aiming at the realization of other human rights, including that of not being discriminated against. As observed above in the subsection on civil and political rights, the use of nuclear weapons would constitute a denial of many of these rights. Considering the close relationship of development, environment, and peace with economic, social, and cultural rights, the impact of a nuclear detonation is capable of challenging the very essence of the latter rights, too. Some of these rights will be dealt with in the present chapter.

d) The rights to the highest standard of health and to a healthy environment

The human right to the highest standard of health is recognized in numerous international instruments, such as the UDHR,[391] the 1965 International Convention on the Elimination of All Forms of Racial Discrimination (ICEAFRD),[392] the CEDAW,[393] and the UNCRC.[394] In addition, several regional human rights instruments also recognize the right to health, such as the European Social Charter of 1961 as revised in 1996,[395] the ACHPR,[396] and the 1988 Additional Protocol to the American Convention on Human Rights in the Area of Economic, Social and Cultural Rights.[397]

390 Sen, "Human Rights and Development," p. 11.

391 Article 25 § 1 reads as follows: "Everyone has the right to a standard of living adequate for the health of himself and of his family, including food, clothing, housing and medical care and necessary social services."

392 Article 5(e)(iv).

393 Articles 11 § 1(f) and 12.

394 Article 24.

395 Article 11.

396 Article 16.

397 Article 10. Similarly, the right to health has been proclaimed by the Commission on Human Rights, as well as in the Vienna Declaration and Programme of Action of 1993 and other international instruments.

The ICECSR contains nevertheless the most comprehensive provision on the right to health in international human rights law. In accordance with Article 12 § 1 of the Covenant, States Parties recognize "the right of everyone to the enjoyment of the highest attainable standard of physical and mental health," while paragraph 2 enumerates, by way of illustration, a number of "steps to be taken by the States parties . . . to achieve the full realization of this right." With a view to implementing this provision, the CESCR adopted, on August 11, 2000, General Comment No. 14 on the "Right to the highest attainable standard of health."[398] Interestingly for the present study, it observes, in the subdivision dealing with the duty to "respect" the right to the highest standard of health, that:

> States should . . . refrain from unlawfully polluting air, water and soil, e.g. . . . from using or testing nuclear . . . weapons, if such testing results in the release of substances harmful to human health.[399]

As to the right to a healthy environment – a relatively recent concept – no global human rights treaty explicitly mentions it. In its General Comment No. 14 on the right to the highest attainable standard of health (Article 12 ICESCR), the CESCR affirms that this right includes the right to a healthy environment. On the regional level, the African Charter on Human and Peoples' Rights was the first international instrument to include an explicit guarantee of environmental quality: "All peoples shall have the right to a general satisfactory environment favourable to their development." Subsequently, the 1988 Protocol on Economic, Social and Cultural Rights (Protocol of San Salvador) to the American Convention on Human Rights enshrined the "right to a healthy environment." In Europe, the ECtHR has developed a particularly dynamic interpretation of the right to life and the right to respect of private life in the sense of a right to an adequate environment, as will be seen further below regarding, in particular, the right to water.[400]

The author shares the point of view that *any* use of nuclear weapons would have extremely harmful effects on human health.[401] The following findings of the Special Rapporteur on the situation of human rights in Kuwait under Iraqi occupation, even though not related to the use of such weapons, are very relevant and give a concrete idea about the potential impact of nuclear weapons on the right to the highest standard of health:

> . . . not only in peacetime but also in times of armed conflict, the deliberate causing of large-scale environmental damage which severely affects the health

398 CESCR, General Comment No. 14, The Right to the Highest Attainable Standard of Health (Article 12 of the ICESCR), UN Doc. E/C.12/2000/4, August 11, 2000.

399 *Ibid.*, § 34.

400 Below, subsection e).

401 Doswald-Beck, "Human Rights Law and Nuclear Weapons," p. 456.

> of a considerable proportion of the population concerned, or creates risks for the health of future generations, amounts to a serious violation of the right to the enjoyment of the highest attainable standard of health as embodied in article 12 of the [ICESCR].[402]

The effects of nuclear weapons on health are expected to be incomparably higher than that of conventional weapons, even for people living far away from the actual explosions. Another aggravating factor for the enjoyment of the right to health is the disruption of health services caused by nuclear explosions, as observed above.[403]

How could, in concrete terms, nuclear explosions occurring, for instance, in a regional nuclear war, affect the right to health and the right to a healthy environment, including of people living far away from the actual explosion? The answer lies in the causal link between radioactivity, fallout, and cancer. It is scientifically proven that radiation exposure can damage living cells, killing some and modifying others. The destruction of a sufficient number of cells will inflict noticeable harm on organs which may result in death.[404] If altered cells are not repaired, the resulting modification will be passed on to further cells and may eventually led to cancer. Modified cells that transmit hereditary information to the offspring of an exposed individual might cause hereditary disorder.[405] Radiation exposure has been associated with most forms of leukemia, as well as cancer of the thyroid, lung, and breast, although the exact number of deaths that might be attributed to radiation exposure, for instance, from nuclear testing, is difficult to assess.[406]

As far as the nuclear bombings in Japan are concerned, studies have revealed the following for survivors: the risk of developing leukemia is five-and-a-half times greater than in the general public;[407] children appear to be twice as sensitive as adults to leukemia-causing effects of radiation – unborn children exposed to radiation in the uterus are even more sensitive; the risk for developing any type of cancer for those highly exposed to an atomic blast is about 50 percent higher; the female breast cancer risk is more than twice as high as normal and women who are exposed when under the age of 20 are found to be at an even higher risk; the

402 Report prepared by Walter Kälin, UN Doc. E/CN.4/1992/26, § 208.

403 This Chapter, section C.3.

404 Report of the UN Scientific Committee on the Effects of Atomic Radiation (UNSCEAR) to the UNGA, vol. 1, 2000, § 8, http://www.unscear.org/docs/reports/gareport.pdf (accessed February 28, 2017).

405 *Ibid.*

406 See the website of CTBTO Preparatory Commission: http://www.ctbto.org/nuclear-testing/the-effects-of-nuclear-testing/general-overview-of-theeffects-of-nuclear-testing/ (accessed February 28, 2017).

407 American Cancer Society, "Radiation Exposure and Cancer," https://archive.org/stream/RadiationExposureAndCancer/Radiation%20Exposure%20And%20Cancer_djvu.txt (accessed March 8, 2017).

risk of developing lung cancer is 50 percent higher; and, finally, the risk for multiple myeloma is more than twice as high as in the general population.[408]

The accident at the Chernobyl nuclear power plant in 1986 was the most serious incident involving radiation exposure. It caused the death, within a few days or weeks, of 30 workers and radiation injuries to over 100 others. It also brought about the immediate evacuation of around 116 000 persons from areas surrounding the reactor and the permanent relocation, after 1986, of about 220 000 people from Belarus, the Russian Federation, and Ukraine.[409] Moreover, it caused serious social and psychological disruptions in the lives of those affected and vast economic losses for the entire region. Large areas of the three countries were contaminated and deposits of released radionuclides were measurable in all countries of the northern hemisphere.[410] The number of thyroid cancers in individuals exposed in childhood, in particular in the severely contaminated areas, turned out to be considerably higher than expected based on previous knowledge and the high incidence and short induction period are considered unusual.[411] In a recent report,[412] the German affiliate of IPPNW and the *Gesellschaft für Strahlenschutz*[413] summarized the tragic consequences of the Chernobyl accident on the Ukrainian population as follows:

> Even though the lack of large-scale independent long-term studies does not permit a complete picture to be made of the current situation, a number of trends can be shown: a high mortality rate and an almost 100% morbidity rate can be observed among people, such as liquidators, who were exposed to high radiation levels. 25 years after the reactor catastrophe cancer and other diseases have emerged on a scale that, owing to the long latency period, might have appeared inconceivable immediately following the catastrophe . . . The number of non-cancerous diseases is far more dramatic than had ever before been imagined. "New" symptoms, such as the premature aging of liquidators, raise questions that research is still unable to answer. . . . By 2050 thousands more cases of illnesses will be diagnosed that will have been caused by the Chernobyl nuclear catastrophe. The delay between cause and noticeable physical reaction is insidious. Chernobyl is far from over.[414]

408 *Ibid.*
409 UNSCEAR Report to the UNGA, vol. 1, 2000, § 18.
410 *Ibid.*, and §§ 99 et seq.
411 *Ibid.*, § 102.
412 S. Pflugbeil, H. Paulitz, A. Claussen, and I. Schmitz-Feuerhake, "Health Effects of Chernobyl, 25 Years after the Reactor Catastrophe," Berlin, April 8, 2011, p. 8, http://www.ratical.org/radiation/Chernobyl/HEofC25yrsAC.html (accessed February 28, 2017).
413 Society for Radiation Protection (Engl.)
414 See, for a recent report on the accident in Fukushima of March 11, 2011, published by the German Affiliate of IPPNW: H. Paulitz, W. Eisenberg, and R. Thiel, "Health Consequences Resulting from Fukushima," Berlin, March 6, 2013, http://www.ippnw.de/commonFiles/

In light of these pessimistic previsions, it is safe to claim that the use of nuclear weapons in the context of a regional nuclear war, for instance, would amount to a breach, by these States, of the duty to respect the rights to health and to a healthy environment.[415] The exact impact on these rights is hard to predict, since the effect of nuclear weapons cannot be limited either in space or in time, but the effect of the radioactive fallout would be felt and cause damage in populations far away from the actual explosion, and leave its deadly traces for many future generations.

e) The right to an adequate standard of living, in particular the rights to food and to water

The right to an adequate standard of living is recognized in several international instruments. The Universal Declaration of Human Rights covers it in its Article 25, including the right to adequate food and the right to health. Article 11 § 1 of the 1966 ICESCR deals more comprehensively than any other instrument with this right:

> The States Parties to the present Convention recognize the right of everybody to an adequate standard of living for himself and his family, including adequate food, clothing and housing, and to the continuous improvement of living conditions.

It is noteworthy that Article 28 § 1 CRPD largely reflects the wording of Article 11 § 1.

One of the key elements of the right to an adequate standard of living is the right to food. Under Article 11 § 2, the States Parties to the ICESCR recognize that more immediate and urgent steps may be necessary to ensure the "fundamental right of everyone to be free from hunger." The CESCR devoted its General Comment No. 12 of 1999 to the right to adequate food, in which it recognizes that this right is of "crucial importance for the enjoyment of all rights."[416] It recalls that millions of people are chronically hungry and suffer from famine as a result of natural disasters and of the increasing incidence of civil strife and wars.[417] It states that the obligation to "respect" existing access to adequate food requires States Parties to the ICESCR not to take any measures that would prevent such access.[418]

pdfs/Atomenergie/Fukushima/Health_consequences_Fukushima_en.pdf (accessed February 28, 2017).

415 Doswald-Beck, "Human Rights Law and Nuclear Weapons," p. 455.

416 CESCR, General Comment No. 12, Right to Adequate Food (Twentieth Session, 1999), UN Doc. E/C.12/1999/5 (1999), § 1.

417 *Ibid.*, § 5.

418 *Ibid.*, § 15.

UNGA Resolution 66/28 of 2012, mentioned above, also reiterates the right to adequate food and the fundamental rights of everyone to live free from hunger.[419] The resolution stresses that food security and nutrition has become a pressing global challenge for present and future generations.[420] It also emphasizes that a significant part of the world's poor live in rural areas and highlights the need to strengthen agricultural and rural development, notably in developing countries, in an economically, socially, and environmentally sustainable manner.[421] It further reaffirms the necessity to promote, enhance, and support more sustainable agriculture, while conserving natural resources and biodiversity and enhancing resilience to climate change and natural disasters.[422]

Why is all this relevant in the context of nuclear weapons? In other words, how could the right to adequate food be affected by a regional nuclear war, including the right of people living far away? One of the key issues of the right to adequate food is the access to food, in quantity and quality.[423] Regarding quantity, it has been observed above that nuclear explosions, for instance in a regional nuclear war, would have significant effects on agriculture and on food security and nutrition. Global temperatures would fall sharply due to the blockage of sunlight causing shorter growing seasons. As a result, there would be a decline in production ("nuclear winter"). In other words, waging a nuclear war would be likely to cause a global "nuclear famine" and, as a result, constitute a serious violation of the obligation to respect the right to food of millions of people. So far as the quality of food is concerned, the CESCR observes, in its General Comment No. 12 on the right to adequate food, that food has to be "free from adverse substances." As explained above, vegetation can be contaminated through nuclear fallout on the external surfaces of plants or by absorption through the roots. Exposure is also possible through the consumption of milk and meat from animals grazing on contaminated vegetation. The Chernobyl experience has nevertheless shown that, often, poorer people have no choice and are obliged to consume contaminated products offered by nature, such as mushrooms, berries, and fish, which affects their right to the highest attainable standard of health.

The right to water has been recognized in a wide range of international documents and gained importance in recent years. It is embedded in a number of other rights, in particular the right to an adequate standard of living, the right to food, the right to health, the right to development, or the right to life, but it is today also generally considered an independent human right.[424]

419 UNGA Resolution 66/288, § 108.

420 *Ibid.* The conference reiterated the "Five Rome Principles for Sustainable Global Food Security," adopted on November 16, 2009 (Food and Agricultural Organization of the United Nations (FAO), document WSFS 2009/2).

421 *Ibid.*, § 109.

422 *Ibid.*, § 111.

423 General Comment No. 12, § 8.

424 E. Brown Weiss, *International Law for a Water-Scarce World*, The Hague Academy of International Law Monographs, vol. 7, Boston and Leiden, 2013, pp. 214–224; and

The CESCR has described this human right in its General Comment No. 15 of 2002 ("Right to water"), where it interprets the word "including" contained in the above-mentioned Article 11 § 1 as denoting not to draw up an exhaustive catalogue of rights and considers that the right to water clearly falls within the category of guarantees essential for securing an adequate standard of living, in particular because water constitutes one of the most fundamental elements of human survival.[425] Article 14 § 2(h), of the CEDAW stipulates that States shall ensure to all women the right to "enjoy adequate living conditions, particularly in relation to . . . water supply," and Article 24 § 2(c), of the UNCRC requires States Parties to combat disease and malnutrition through, inter alia, "the provision of adequate nutritious foods and clean drinking-water, taking into consideration the dangers and risks of environmental pollution." The 2012 UN Conference on Sustainable Development recognized that water was at the "core of sustainable development,"[426] recalled the importance of the "human right to safe drinking water and sanitation," and reaffirmed the commitment to the International Decade for Action, "Water for Life", 2005–2015,[427] stressing the need to adopt measures to significantly reduce water pollution.[428] Moreover, in 2013, the European Parliament recognized the right to water as a basic human right.[429]

The right to water has also been recognized and shaped by international human rights bodies. In the case of *Centre for Minority Rights Development (Kenya and Minority Rights Group/Kenya)*, the African Commission of Human and Peoples' Rights (AComHPR) linked the right of access to sources of water, inter alia, to the right to development.[430] In another case, the African Commission explicitly referred to the CESCR's General Comment No. 14 on the right to the highest attainable standard of health, underlining that "the failure to enact or enforce laws to prevent the pollution of water . . . violates the right to health."[431]

J. Murillo Chávarro, *The Human Right to Water: A Legal Comparative Perspective at the International, Regional and Domestic Level*, Cambridge, 2015, pp. 353–354.

425 General Comment No. 15, The Right to Water (Articles 11 and 12 of the Covenant), January 20, 2003, UN Doc. E/C.12/2002/11, § 3.

426 Resolution 66/288, § 119.

427 *Ibid.*, § 121.

428 *Ibid.*, § 124.

429 European Parliament, Resolution on the Commission Communication on Water Management in Developing Countries and Priorities for EU Development Cooperation, P5_TA(2003)0377 (September 5, 2003).

430 *Centre for Minority Rights Development (Kenya) and Minority Rights Group International (on behalf of Endorois Welfare Council) v. Kenya*, ACommHPR, 276/2003, February 4, 2010, § 286: ". . . The Endorois were relegated to semi-arid land, which proved unsustainable for pastoralism, especially in view of the strict prohibition on access to the Lake area's medicinal salt licks or traditional water sources . . .".

431 *Sudan Human Rights Organization and the Centre on Housing Rights and Evictions v. The Sudan*, Decision, nos. 279/03 and 296/05, May 27, 2009, § 210 (original in French).

General Comment No. 15 of the CESCR, mentioned above, offers an authoritative comment on the right to water, stressing the importance of adequate water supply for the respect of human rights, dignity, and the fight against poverty:

> Water is a limited natural resource and a public good fundamental for life and health. The human right to water is indispensable for leading a life in human dignity. It is a prerequisite for the realization of other human rights. The continuing contamination, depletion and unequal distribution of water is exacerbating existing poverty.[432]

The right to water entitles every human being to sufficient, safe, acceptable, physically accessible, and affordable water for their personal and domestic use.[433] Water is above all an essential element of life and a minimum intake is necessary to prevent death by dehydration.[434] General Comment No. 15 further emphasizes that water should be treated as a "social and cultural good," and not primarily as an economic one.[435] General Comment No. 15 also stresses that the realization of the right to water must be ensured for present and future generations.[436] It suggests that States should ensure that natural water resources are protected, inter alia, from contamination by harmful substances.[437] The water quality required for personal or domestic use must be safe, i.e. free from micro-organisms, chemical substances, and radiological hazards threatening a person's health.[438] Toxic contamination is particularly serious, and while the contaminants can be removed from surface waters, flushing them from lakes can take between decades and more than a century.[439] The contamination of the ground water, whether from pesticides or other toxics, presents a special challenge since 29.9 percent of the total supply of freshwater is found in groundwater and only 0.26 percent in lakes, rivers, and reservoirs.[440] Moreover, polluted water resources can adversely affect the environment by damaging ecosystems, and contamination kills plants, fish, and other fauna.[441]

432 General Comment No. 15, § 1.
433 *Ibid.*, § 2; L. Boisson de Chazournes suggests that three elements characterize the right to water, namely: availability, quality, and accessibility (*Fresh Water in International Law*, Oxford, 2013, p. 155).
434 Murillo Chávarro, *The Human Right to Water*, p. 7.
435 General Comment No. 15, § 11.
436 *Ibid.* See also Brown Weiss, *International Law for a Water-Scarce World*, p. 195.
437 *Ibid.*, § 8.
438 *Ibid.*, § 12(b).
439 National Research Council of the United States and Royal Society of Canada, *The Great Lakes Water Quality Agreement: An Evolving Instrument for Ecosystem Management*, Washington, DC, National Academy Press, 1985, pp. 47–74.
440 Murillo Chávarro, *The Human Right to Water*, p. 1.
441 Brown Weiss, *International Law for a Water-Scarce World*, p. 206.

The ECtHR has also significantly contributed to the emergence of a right to water, namely under the label of the right to respect for private and family life and home, in particular as regards the contamination of groundwater, an aspect that is very relevant for the duty to respect the right to water. In the case of *Dubetska and Others v. Ukraine*, decided in 2011,[442] the ECtHR concluded that there had been a violation of Article 8 ECHR, since the State had failed to protect the applicants' home and private and family life from excessive pollution generated by two-State-owned industrial facilities, a coal-mining enterprise and a coal-processing factory. It was established that the operations of the two facilities had adverse environmental effects, due for instance to the penetration of heavy metals into the soil and groundwater. In the case of *Taşkın and Others v. Turkey*,[443] the ECtHR held that the defendant State had failed to comply with its positive obligation to protect the individuals against contamination of groundwater by toxic waste, including cyanide, stressing that the water was being used by the inhabitants of the region. In the case of *Tătar v. Romania*,[444] the applicants alleged that the technology used by a gold and silver mining company, using cyanide, was dangerous to their lives and that, on January 30, 2000, a large quantity of polluted water containing sodium cyanide and other substances was leaked into various rivers and traveled 800 kilometers in 14 days, crossing several borders and polluting drinking water sources. The ECtHR decided that Romania had failed to assess adequately the potential risk of the mining activities and to take measures to guarantee the applicants' right to respect of their private and family life under Article 8 ECHR.[445]

As far as water contamination by the use of nuclear weapons is concerned, General Comment No. 15 states explicitly that the obligation to "respect" the right to water includes the prohibition of diminishing or polluting water, for example through the "use and testing of weapons,"[446] without referring specifically to nuclear weapons. The nuclear weapons tests on the Marshall Islands, whose catastrophic impact on the local population will be examined in the next Chapter, have demonstrated that a nuclear explosion can affect people's right to water in different ways. In a nuclear explosion, radioactivity penetrates the atmosphere, soil, and water.[447] At Bikini Atoll, for example, the soil and the water contained radioactive isotopes of cesium, cobalt, strontium, americium, and plutonium after the most powerful test.[448] The radioactivity in the lagoon and sea

442 *Dubetska and Others v. Ukraine*, no. 30499/03, February 10, 2011.
443 *Taşkın and Others v. Turkey*, no. 46117/99, ECHR 2004-X.
444 *Tătar v. Romania*, no. 67021/01, January 27, 2009.
445 See, in particular, §§ 121–125 (in French).
446 General Comment No. 15, § 21.
447 R. Levy Guyer, "Radioactivity and Rights – Clashes at Bikini Atoll," *Am J Public Health*, vol. 91(9), 2001, pp. 1371–1376, 1373, http://www.ncbi.nlm.nih.gov/pmc/articles/PMC1446783/pdf/0911371.pdf (accessed February 28, 2017). See also M. Kunz and J. E. Viñuales, "Environmental Approaches to Nuclear Weapons," in Nystuen et al., *Nuclear Weapons under International Law*, pp. 269–291, 284.
448 Levy Guyer, "Radioactivity and Rights," p. 1373.

eventually diluted slowly and steadily into the ocean, whereas the radioactivity on the islands remained.[449] Through oceanic and atmospheric circulation, the contaminants were carried from Bikini around the entire globe.[450] In the desert of Nevada, where clean water is already scarce, US underground nuclear testing conducted between 1951 and 1992 is estimated to have contaminated more than 6 trillion liters of groundwater.[451] In Semipalatinsk, the former Soviet Union's favorite nuclear test site, local water bodies were reported to show concentrations of radioactive uranium isotopes well above the normal values.[452] These examples taken from the field of nuclear weapons testing convey an idea of the potential impact on the right to water of an actual use of such weapons.

In the context of the right to water, the transboundary nature of such pollution and the need to apply the relevant human rights treaties accordingly have to be emphasized. A regional nuclear war is likely to pollute international watercourses. The harmful act would take place in one or two countries, but harm would also be caused in other States. In other words, the pollution of an international watercourse caused by an upstream State has a direct impact on the right to water of the people living in downstream areas.[453] This aspect is significant, considering that a large number of rivers, lakes, and aquifers are internationally shared.[454] Murillo Chávarro advocates extraterritorial application of the right to respect, for example, the duty not to pollute water, based on State practice and the close relation maintained by the right to water with international water law.[455]

Finally, the situation and needs of indigenous populations deserve particular attention in relation to the right to water. The IACtHR and the IACommHR, in particular, have contributed to a better protection of the rights of indigenous peoples, especially the right to enjoy their traditional lands. This aspect will be examined more closely in the next subsection dealing with the impact of nuclear tests on the enjoyment of human rights; but the following passage of the decision

449 *Ibid.*

450 *Ibid.* The same phenomenon could be observed as a result of the Fukushima nuclear power plant accident in 2011. Only a few months after this accident, namely by August 2011, elevated levels of cesium-134 in bluefin tuna (a fish that spawns in the western Pacific, near Japan) caught off the Californian coast have been detected. A. Hutchinson, "Is Radioactive Water Worth Worrying About?", *The New Yorker*, April 30, 2015, http://www.newyorker.com/tech/elements/is-radioactive-water-from-fukushima-worth-worrying-about (accessed February 28, 2017).

451 S. Kellman, 'Nuclear Fallout: Nevada Takes Hard Look at Contaminated Groundwater From Historic Testing Grounds', *Water News*, 15 November 2009, http://www.circleofblue.org/2009/world/news-nuclear-fallout-nevada-takes-hard-look-at-contaminated-groundwater-from-historic-testing-grounds/ (accessed February 28, 2017).

452 R. Prăvălie, "Nuclear Weapons Tests and Environmental Consequences: A Global Perspective," *Ambio*, October 2014, http://www.ncbi.nlm.nih.gov/pmc/articles/PMC4165831/ (accessed February 28, 2017).

453 Murillo Chávarro, *The Human Right to Water*, p. 350.

454 *Ibid.*, p. 354.

455 *Ibid.*, pp. 350–352.

in *Xákmok Kásek Indigenous Community v. Paraguay*, in which the IACtHR referred to the right to access to water as part of a right to a decent existence, is particularly relevant for the right to water:

> The culture of the members of the indigenous communities corresponds to a specific way of life, of being, seeing and acting in the world, constituted on the basis of their close relationship with their traditional lands and natural resources, not only because these are their main means of subsistence, but also because they are an integral element of their cosmology, their spirituality and, consequently, their cultural identity.[456]

Regarding the access to water of acceptable quality, the Court considers "that the measures taken by the State . . . have not been sufficient to provide the members of the Community with water in sufficient quantity and of adequate quality, and this has exposed them to risks and disease."[457] In light of the particular relation between indigenous peoples and their traditionally possessed lands, it is not hard to imagine the challenges that these peoples would be facing in case of nuclear explosions and the contamination of their natural resources, including water, resulting from them. The huge impact that nuclear weapons testing has had on indigenous peoples and other particularly vulnerable categories of people will be addressed in the following section.

5. Human rights of particularly vulnerable groups, assessed in light of the harm caused by nuclear testing and nuclear power plant accidents

a) Introduction

In addition to their actual use during hostilities, it is important to recognize that the testing of nuclear weapons also has negative effects on human rights. Moreover, the reliance on the use of nuclear weapons as means of warfare might presuppose prior testing. Therefore, this subsection is closely linked to the last one, having dealt with, inter alia, the relevance of human rights law for the prohibition of the use of nuclear weapons. Lessons can also be drawn from nuclear accidents, such as those having occurred in Chernobyl and, more recently, in Fukushima. The "real-life" examples that will be given are capable of conveying only a slight idea of what human life and environment would look like in the aftermath of one or several detonations of nuclear weapons during an armed conflict.

The aim of this subsection is to analyze the impact of nuclear weapons testing and nuclear power plant accidents on the enjoyment of the rights of particularly

456 Paragraph 174 (footnote omitted).

457 IACtHR, *Xákmok Kásek Indigenous Community v. Paraguay*, Judgment of August 24, 2010, Series C no. 214, § 196.

vulnerable groups of people. It begins with a brief outline of the tragic circumstances that have accompanied the nuclear tests, as well as their effects on the local population and environment. The example chosen concerns the nuclear testing by the United States on the Marshall Islands.

b) Indigenous peoples' rights, assessed in particular in light of their special relationship with their land

Probably the best proof that nuclear testing is closely linked to nuclear disarmament and that such testing causes serious human suffering is established by the fact that the applicant State, the Marshall Islands, in the course of the proceedings before the ICJ in the cases of *Obligations Concerning Negotiations Relating to Cessation of the Nuclear Arms Race and to Nuclear Disarmament*, mentioned above, repeatedly drew attention to the devastating effects upon human life of nuclear weapons detonations. For instance, in the case opposing them to the United Kingdom, the applicant State stressed, in its oral arguments presented on March 11, 2016, the "tragic losses for the Marshallese," and the "dire health consequences suffered by the Marshallese following nuclear contamination, including extreme birth defects and cancers."[458]

Between 1946 and 1958, 67 nuclear weapon tests were carried out by the United States in the Marshall Islands, most of them at Bikini (23 tests) and Enewetak Atolls (43 tests). The total explosive yield of the tests was approximately 100 megatons (equivalent to 100 million tons of Trinitrotoluene, TNT), which is equivalent to more than 7 000 Hiroshima bombs.[459] On March 1, 1954, the "Castle Bravo" test on Bikini Atoll resulted in a blast that had 1 000 times the explosive power of the Hiroshima bombing, and that turned out to be the most powerful detonation ever carried out by the United States. Radioactive fallout was unexpectedly deposited on Rongelap, Utrik, and other inhabited atolls to the east and southeast of Bikini Atoll.[460] The Marshallese people were

458 ICJ, Doc. CR 2016/5, of March 11, 2016, p. 9, § 10.

459 Division of Cancer Epidemiology and Genetics, National Cancer Institute, National Institutes of Health, and Department of Health and Human Service, "Estimation of the Baseline Number of Cancers among Marshallese and the Number of Cancers Attributable to Exposure to Fallout from Nuclear Weapons Testing Conducted in the Marshall Islands," September 2004, p. 1, http://marshall.csu.edu.au/Marshalls/html/Radiation/NCI-report.pdf. See also D. Pevec, "The Marshall Islands Nuclear Claims Tribunal: The Claims of the Enewetak People," *Denv. J. Int'l L. & Pol'y*, vol. 35, no. 1, 2006, pp. 221–239, 221. The tests conducted on the territory of the Marshall Islands made up 32 percent of the atmospheric tests conducted by the United States (Report of the Special Rapporteur on the implications for human rights of the environmentally sound management and disposal of hazardous substances and wastes, Calin Georgescu, A/HRC/21/48/Add.1, § 15).

460 Report, Georgescu, A/HRC/21/48/Add.1, § 13. The fallout caused contamination over an area of more than 11 000 km^2, spreading traces of radioactive material as far as Australia, India, Japan, the United States, and parts of Europe (homepage of CTBT preparatory commission: http://www.ctbto.org/nuclear-testing/the-effects-of-nuclear-testing/the-united-states-nuclear-testing-programme/ (accessed February 28, 2017)).

told that the tests were necessary for the eventual well-being of all people in the world.[461]

In September 2004, a report compiled by the Division of Cancer Epidemiology and Genetics of the US National Cancer Institute, National Institutes of Health, and the Department of Health and Human Service, concluded that the nuclear testing program in the Marshall Islands will cause about 500 additional cancer cases among Marshallese exposed during the years 1946 to 1958, about a 9 percent increase over the number of cancers expected in the absence of exposure to regional fallout.[462]

A review report issued in 2010 reduced the excess number of cancer cases to 170.[463] According to Calin Georgescu, the UN Special Rapporteur on the implication for human rights of the environmentally sound management and disposal of hazardous substances and wastes, who was charged by the Human Rights Council to undertake a mission to the Marshall Islands, it is important, however, not to limit too narrowly the assessment to cancer statistics, but also to take into account social, economic, cultural, and psychological aspects.[464] As far as the latter are concerned, survivors of the tests provided compelling testimony about their psychological trauma from witnessing the explosions, and their effect on their stress and anxiety are to be recognized as a legitimate and serious health issue. As a result, the fear of some inhabitants of the Marshall Islands of the radiation that they believe still contaminates their lands and affects their health should not be underestimated.[465]

In order to protect them from the effects of nuclear testing, the inhabitants, in particular, from Bikini, Enewetak, Rongelap, and Utrok Atolls, have been displaced several times. The various forced relocalizations turned them into "nomads."[466] As a result of their forced displacement due to nuclear testing in the region, the peoples of the Marshall Islands were disconnected from their lands and their cultural and indigenous way of living.[467] Laurence Carucci, an American professor of anthropology, testifying before the Nuclear Claims Tribunal, explained the Enewetak people's relationship with the land in the following words:

461 Petition from the Marshallese people concerning the Pacific Islands (T/PET.10/29), March 9, 1956, enclosure IV.

462 National Cancer Institute et al., "Estimation of the Baseline Number of Cancers"; see also National Cancer Institute, "Dose Estimation and Predicted Cancer Risk for Residents of the Marshall Islands Exposed to Radioactive Fallout from the U.S. Nuclear Weapons Testing at Bikini and Eniwetok," https://dceg.cancer.gov/research/how-we-study/exposure-assessment/nci-dose-estimation-predicted-cancer-risk-residents-marshall-islands#purpose (accessed February 28, 2017).

463 Report, Georgescu, A/HRC/21/48/Add.1, § 23.

464 *Ibid.*, § 28.

465 *Ibid.*, § 26. See also IAEA, "Radiation, People and the Environment," Vienna, February 2004, p. 46, https://www.iaea.org/sites/default/files/radiation0204.pdf (accessed March 1, 2017).

466 Report, Georgescu, A/HRC/21/48/Add.1, § 33.

467 *Ibid.*

> For Marshall Islanders in general, and Enewetak people in particular, land is a part of one's person and one's entire identity. It is an integral part of a person's sense of who they are in the world and how their life makes sense as part of certain culture. One's sense of self, both personal and cultural, is deeply embedded in a particular parcel of land on a particular atoll . . .
>
> When Enewetak people were moved to Ujelang in 1947, this sense of communal origin, of land as the visible representation of centuries of human labor, was lost . . . Enewetak people were distraught, heartbroken, and in general state of mental and emotional trauma when they were forced to leave their homeland. Their very embeddedness in a place in the word, the very processes through which the community had scratched their being into the physical contours of the earth, and the historied place that gave them a sense of meaningful connection with their communal past, were gone.[468]

Through their displacement, the Marshallese were deprived of the possibility of using their lands according to their traditions and customs. For example, as a result of the contamination of certain islands and atolls by nuclear fallout, they are today unable to perform their traditional migratory practices and harvest their cultural goods, such as fish, fruits, medicines, or materials for housing, as they have done before.[469]

Another, closely related aspect concerns the access to safe food and potable water. The Marshallese eat primarily seafood, supplemented by pandanus fruit, coconut, and other fruits. The fallout contaminated local food supplies and led to illnesses and, ultimately, to the stigmatization of these foods.[470] In spite of the fact that the United States informed the people about the danger of the consumption of local food and provided imported canned food, many Marshallese people continued to eat local food, due to lack of understanding of the health risk, and succumbed to illnesses. This situation was moreover aggravated by the fact that the Marshallese take much of their fresh water supply from coconuts, leading to highly limited access to drinking water during the period of nuclear testing.[471]

The Enewetak people finally returned to its atoll in 1980, but their suffering did not end there; indeed, the severe damage caused to the land by the nuclear weapons testing, the residual radiation contamination over large parts of the Enewetak Atoll, the inability to grow adequate food crops for local consumption and to use the land for productive economic purposes, as well as the required

468 *In the Matter of the People of Enewetak, et al.*, NCT No. 23-0902, cited by Pevec, "The Marshall Islands Nuclear Claims Tribunal," p. 223.

469 Report, Georgescu, A/HRC/21/48/Add.1, § 33.

470 *Ibid.*, § 28.

471 *Ibid.* Coconuts on Bikini Atoll are still radioactive because coconut palm trees absorb caesium-137 and other radioactive elements from the soil. These elements are then concentrated in the fruit. See http://www.ctbto.org/nuclear-testing/the-effects-of-nuclear-testing/the-united-states-nuclear-testing-programme/ (accessed February 28, 2017).

reliance on imported food continue to prolong the hardship to the Enewetak people. Professor Carucci, quoted above, expressed this misery as follows:

> Since their return in 1980, Enewetak people have struggled with life on the New Enewetak, a place reminiscent of their homeland yet, in so many ways, a radically different location than the atoll on which people lived in the 1940s . . . They cannot be at home in the very land that is their home since the contours of the land are no longer the same, its productive capacity is lacking, and, without those products, the wide array of day-to-day activities that allowed people to make local products into canoes, and sleeping mats, and foods, have lost their meaning . . .[472]

The Marshallese are only one example of indigenous peoples who were deprived of their lands, had to sacrifice their traditions, and were pushed into a lifestyle they could never get used to. Other indigenous peoples affected from nuclear testing all over the world experienced a similar destiny. Their suffering equally deserves to be reflected here, but this is not possible for practical reasons.

A legal assessment of the situations of the Marshallese peoples and other indigenous peoples has to start from the UN Declaration on the Rights of Indigenous Peoples (DRIP), which was adopted by the UNGA on September 13, 2007, after many years of preparatory work.[473] Certain authors are of the opinion that many of its provisions reflect customary international law.[474] In any event, this declaration cannot be ignored by a State acting in good faith and constitutes, therefore, the basis for the present discussion. In addition, the International Labour Organization's (ILO) Convention No. 169 ("Indigenous and Tribal Peoples Convention"), adopted in 1989, is also noteworthy.[475] Even though this treaty has to date only been ratified by 22 States, it reflects, according to some authors, customary international law.[476]

472 *In the Matter of the People of Enewetak, et al.*, NCT No. 23-0902.

473 UNGA Resolution 61/295, adopted by 143 against four States (Australia, Canada, New Zealand, and the United States), 11 States abstaining, and 34 States not participating in the vote.

474 M. Barelli, "The Role of Soft Law in the International Legal System: The Case of the United Nations Declaration on the Rights of Indigenous Peoples," *ICLQ*, vol. 58, 2009, pp. 957–983, 966 et seq.; and C. Charters, "The Road to the Adoption of the Declaration on the Rights of Indigenous Peoples," *New Zealand Yearbook of International Law*, vol. 4, 2007, pp. 121–133, 123.

475 This convention entered into force on September 5, 1991. See C. Metcalf, "Indigenous Rights and the Environment: Evolving International Law," *Ottawa L. Rev.*, vol. 35, 2003–2004, pp. 101–140; and R. K. Hitchcock, "International Human Rights, the Environment, and Indigenous Peoples," *Colo. J. Int'l Envtl. L. & Pol'y*, vol. 5, 1994, pp. 1–22.

476 K. Göcke, "Indigenous Peoples in the Nuclear Age: Uranium Mining on Indigenous' Lands," in J. L. Black-Branch and D. Fleck (eds.), *Nuclear Non-Proliferation in International Law*, vol. I, The Hague 2014, pp. 199–223, 212 et seq.

The concept of property of indigenous peoples is fundamentally different from the Western one, in particular insofar as it exceeds the idea of possession and appropriation of an object. In fact, property is defined in cultural and spiritual terms.[477] All indigenous peoples have a particular relationship with their land. Article 26 DRIP contains and underlines the importance of the right of these communities to their own land. In addition, its Article 25 recognizes the special, spiritual relationship that indigenous peoples maintain with their traditionally owned lands in the following terms:

> Indigenous peoples have the right to maintain and strengthen their distinctive spiritual relationship with their traditionally owned or otherwise occupied and used lands, territories, waters and coastal seas and other resources and to uphold their responsibilities to future generations in this regard.[478]

Indigenous peoples' rights to culture and cultural heritage, in particular in connection to their land, have also increasingly gained judicial recognition in recent years. The jurisprudence of the IACtHR is particularly interesting in this field. In the *Moiwana* case, the Court determined that indigenous peoples, by the fact of their sole existence, are entitled to live freely in their own territory and that their close ties with the land must be recognized and understood as the fundamental basis of their cultures, their spiritual life, their integrity, and their economic survival.[479] In the case of *Yakye Axa v. Paraguay*, the Court explicitly recognizes the need to respect the indigenous peoples' cultural diversity and, therefore, the importance of their communal property rights:

> The culture of the members of the indigenous communities directly relates to a specific way of being, seeing, and acting in the world, developed on the basis of their close relationship with their traditional territories and the resources therein, not only because they are their main means of subsistence, but also because they are part of their worldview, their religiosity, and therefore, of their cultural identity.[480]

In the case of *Tingni Mayagna (Sumo) Indigenous Community v. Nicaragua*, the Court added that the particular link that unites indigenous peoples with their

477 D. Shelton, "The Inter-American Human Rights Law of Indigenous Peoples," *U. Haw. L. Rev.*, vol. 35, 2013, pp. 937–982, 968; and S. J. Rombouts, *Having a Say, Indigenous Peoples, International Law and Free, Prior and Informed Consent*, Oisterwijk, 2014, p. 67.

478 The ILO Convention No. 169 contains a similar guarantee (Article 23 § 1).

479 *Moiwana Cmty v. Suriname*, Preliminary Objections, Merits, Reparations, and Costs, Judgments, IACtHR, Series C no. 124, § 131 (June 15, 2005).

480 *Yakye Axa v. Paraguay*, Merits, Reparations and Costs, Judgment, IACtHR, Series C no. 125, § 135 (June 17, 2005); see also *Mayagna (Sumo) Awas Tingni Cmty. v. Nicaragua*, Merits, Reparations, and Costs, Judgment, IACtHR, Series C no. 79, § 149 (August 31, 2001). See also Shelton, "The Inter-American Human Rights Law of Indigenous Peoples."

lands has to be appreciated and exercised in view of the preservation of their cultural heritage in favor of future generations:

> [f]or indigenous communities, relations to the land are not merely a matter of possession and production but a material and spiritual element which they must fully enjoy, even to preserve their cultural legacy and transmit it to future generations.[481]

It is obvious that the forced removal of the indigenous peoples from their territory, even if it was in order to protect them against the direct impact of the nuclear weapons tests, are hardly reconcilable with this provision. The same would be true, *a fortiori*, for a removal as a result of a nuclear attack. It is noteworthy that Article 16 of ILO Convention No. 169 contains a special provision prohibiting removal of indigenous peoples from their lands. If relocation is considered necessary, the authorities are obligated to receive free and informed consent from the affected peoples or, at least, proceed according to the applicable law. In any event, the people shall be entitled to return as soon as possible to their lands or, at least, to territories that are equal and suitable. If this is not possible, they shall at least be entitled to compensation. In fact, as far as the Marshall Islands are concerned, a Nuclear Claims Tribunal was created in 1988 that has the power to allocate compensation for the consequences of the US nuclear tests.[482]

In addition, Article 30 of the declaration forbids "military activities" in the lands or territories of indigenous peoples, unless justified by a relevant public interest or otherwise freely agreed with or requested by the indigenous peoples. This provision reinforces the argument against nuclear testing or nuclear warfare on indigenous lands.

It has also been mentioned above that the territory which the Marshallese, in particular the Enewetak peoples, found after their return, contaminated by radioactive fallout, had nothing much in common with the land they had to leave many years ago. In this regard, the relevance of Article 29 § 1 DRIP is also worth mentioning:

> 1. Indigenous peoples have the right to the conservation and protection of the environment and the productive capacity of their lands or territories and resources . . .

In the same logic, it has also been underlined above that, in particular, the Marshallese peoples are, as a result of the environmental contamination, largely

481 *Mayagna (Sumo) Awas Tingni Cmty.*, § 149.

482 See Pevec, "The Marshall Islands Nuclear Claims Tribunal." The tribunal was established on the basis of the "Agreement between the Government of the United States and the Government of the Marshall Islands for the Implementation of Section 177 of the Compact of Free Association pmbl."

deprived of the enjoyment of their traditional practices and customs with regards cultural goods, including food supplies, potable water, and medicines. The DRIP also addresses these aspects, inter alia, in the following provisions:

> Indigenous peoples have the right to maintain and develop their political, economic and social systems or institutions, to be secure in the enjoyment of their own means of subsistence and development, and to engage freely in all their traditional and other economic activities[483] . . . Indigenous peoples have the right to their traditional medicines and to maintain their health practices, including the conservation of their vital medicinal plants, animals and minerals . . .[484]

In light of the foregoing, it is asserted here that the rights of indigenous peoples impose important limitations on the freedom of States to conduct nuclear tests and, *a fortiori*, launch nuclear attacks. Finally, it is worth recalling that it derives from the IACtHR's case law mentioned above that one of the reasons to protect the rights of indigenous peoples is to preserve their cultural legacy in order to be transmitted to future generations. This constitutes another example of the relevance of nuclear activities – weapons testing as well as potential use – for the rights of future generations.

c) Women's rights, in particular their reproductive rights

The Special Rapporteur, Calin Georgescu, in his report mentioned above, is of the opinion that the specific effects of radiation on the health of women caused by the testing program on the Marshall Islands have not yet been fully addressed.[485] Recent research on the health impact of exposure to radiation in the Semipalatinsk region shows a considerable gender difference in cancer rates, in particular esophagus cancer and higher rates of breast cancer.[486] Moreover, studies have concluded that pregnant women are particularly susceptible to thyroid cancer, a fact that affects not only them, but also their infants.[487] It has also been mentioned above that, as a result of the nuclear attacks against Hiroshima and Nagasaki, female breast cancer risk is more than twice as high as normal and women who are exposed when under the age of 20 are found to be at an even higher risk.[488]

Regarding the legal assessment of this situation, it has to be reiterated that no universal, legally binding instrument exists that protects the rights of women in a

483 Article 20 § 1.
484 Article 24 § 1.
485 Report, Georgescu, A/HRC/21/48/Add.1, § 27.
486 S. Bauer et al., "Radiation Exposure due to Local Fallout from Soviet Atmospheric Nuclear Weapons Testing in Kazakhstan: Solid Cancer Mortality in the Semipalatinsk Historical Cohort," 1960–1999, *Radiation Research*, vol. 164, 2005, pp. 409–419, 416 et seq.
487 Report, Georgescu, A/HRC/21/48/Add.1, § 27.
488 This Chapter, section C.4.d).

global manner, contrary, for example, to the rights of children or of persons with disabilities. Discriminatory treatment and practices against women are prohibited by the CEDAW, concluded in 1979. The Protocol to the African Charter on Human Rights and Peoples' Rights on the Rights of Women in Africa, adopted in 1993, also warrants mention in this regard.[489] Its Article 3 § 1 guarantees the "right to dignity inherent in a human being" and, according to Article 15, States Parties "shall ensure that women have the right to nutritious and adequate food," including access to clean drinking water and means of producing nutritious food.[490] It is obvious that these provisions, considering the problems revealed by the Special Rapporteur, are very relevant in the context of nuclear weapons tests.

Moreover, the Rapporteur reiterated the relevance and importance of the Guiding Principles on Internal Displacements, which list the guarantees of persons against forced displacement and their protection and assistance during displacement, as well as during return or resettlement and reintegration.[491] As far as the situation of the Marshallese women is concerned, Principle 4 § 2 is noteworthy, stating that certain persons, such as expectant mothers, mothers with young children, or female heads of household shall be entitled to protection and assistance required by their condition and to treatment which takes into account their special needs. According to Principle 8, a displacement should not be carried out in a manner that breaches the "rights to life, dignity, liberty and security of those affected."[492]

Nuclear testing also affects women with regard to their reproductive rights. The Special Rapporteur took note of compelling testimony by women returning from Rongelap Atoll (Marshall Islands) and drew attention to the alarmingly high rates of stillbirths, miscarriages, congenital birth defects, and reproductive problems, such as changes in menstrual cycles and the subsequent inability to conceive, even concerning women who previously had no such health issues. Those women who gave birth frequently experienced fetal disorders leading to the death of the baby, resulting in shame and trauma from which they still suffer today.[493] Women expressed their fears of reproduction and motherhood as a result of their exposure to nuclear tests or in the event of a nuclear weapon explosion.[494]

The CESCR's General Comment No. 14 concerning the Right to the Highest Attainable Standard of Health (Article 12 ICESCR) defines "reproductive health" in the following terms:

489 It was adopted by the 2nd Ordinary Session of the Assembly of the African Union, Maputo, July 11, 2003, and entered into force on November 25, 2005.

490 Article 15(a).

491 Report, Georgescu, A/HRC/21/48/Add.1, § 32. These principles were published in the "Report of the Representative of the Secretary-General, Francis M. Deng, submitted to the United Nations Commission on Human Rights, pursuant to Commission Resolution 1997/39, Addendum," UN Doc. E/CN.4/1998/53/Add.2.

492 Report, Georgescu, A/HRC/21/48/Add.1, § 32.

493 *Ibid.*, § 30.

494 *Ibid.*

> Reproductive health means that women and men have the freedom to decide if and when to reproduce and the right to be informed and to have access to safe, effective, affordable and acceptable methods of family planning of their choice as well as the right of access to appropriate health-care services that will, for example, enable women to go safely through pregnancy and childbirth.[495]

In other words, women have the right to decide "freely and responsibly" about the number and spacing of their children.[496] This is an aspect of the broader concept of autonomy, a principle that is well known in health law and one of the most basic fundamental rights.[497] Decisions on reproduction require that individuals have access to information about reproductive matters and have the power and resources required to carry out their decisions.[498] This includes that States should not allow coercion, such as non-consensual sterilization or mandatory testing for sexually transmitted diseases.[499] In its Resolution 66/288 ("The future we want"), the UNGA explicitly reiterated its commitment to address and promote women's sexual and reproductive health, as well as to ensure universal access to safe, effective, affordable, and acceptable modern methods of family planning.[500]

According to Article 14 (Health and reproductive rights) of the Protocol to the African Charter on Human Rights and Peoples' Rights on the Rights of Women in Africa, the States "shall ensure that the right to health of women, including sexual and reproductive rights, is respected and promoted." This duty includes, inter alia, the right to control their fertility, the right to decide whether to have children and the number of children, as well as the right to be informed on their health status in accordance with internationally recognized standards and best practices.[501] Again, the jurisprudence of the ECtHR is relevant in the field of

495 UN Doc. E/C.12/2000/4, August 11, 2000, note 12. See also R. J. Cook and V. Undurraga, "Article 12," in M. A. Freeman, C. Chinkin, and B. Rudolf (eds.), *The UN Convention on the Elimination of All Forms of Discrimination against Women*, Oxford 2012, pp. 311–333, 320–323.

496 C. Makhlouf Obermeyer, "A Cross-Cultural Perspective on Reproductive Rights," *Human Rights Quarterly (HRQ)*, vol. 17, 1995, pp. 366–381, 369.

497 J. Rothmar Herrmann, "Reproductive Health," in B. Toebes, M. Hartlev, A. Hendriks, and J. Rothmar Herrmann (eds.), *Health and Human Rights in Europe*, Cambridge, Antwerp, and Portland, 2012, pp. 145–176, p. 147.

498 Makhlouf Obermeyer, "A Cross-Cultural Perspective," p. 369.

499 CEDAW General Recommendation No. 24 (General Comments), February 5, 1999, § 22.

500 A/RES/66/288, September 11, 2012, § 241.

501 Article 14 § 1(a), (b), and (e). See also Article 16 § 1(e) of CEDAW: "1. States Parties shall take all appropriate measures to eliminate discrimination against women in all matters relating to marriage and family relations and in particular shall ensure, on a basis of equality of men and women: . . . (e) The same rights to decide freely and responsibly on the number and spacing of their children and to have access to the information, education and means to enable them to exercise these rights."

reproductive rights and health. In the case of *Evans v. United Kingdom*,[502] the Court was confronted with a "frozen embryo disposition dispute." Most importantly, the Grand Chamber of the ECtHR admitted that the decision to become a parent falls into the ambit of the right to respect of private life (Article 8 ECHR), which also incorporates the right to personal autonomy and development:[503] "The Grand Chamber considers that . . . the right to respect for the decision to become a parent in the genetic sense . . . falls within the scope of Article 8."[504]

The conclusion that Article 8 ECHR is applicable to decisions to become genetic parents was confirmed in the same year in the case of *Dickson v. United Kingdom*.[505] This case concerned access to artificial insemination by two prisoners who met through an inmates' pen pal network. The UK courts refused such technique to the applicants due, inter alia, to the lack of an adequate support network for the potential child.[506] As far as applicability of Article 8 ECHR is concerned, the Court considered that the situation of the applicants concerned both their private and family lives.[507] What is important for the present study is the conclusion of the Court in both cases that the decision to have (or not to have) children is covered by Article 8 ECHR and constitutes undoubtedly, therefore, a human right. This finding was later confirmed by the ECtHR in other instances.[508] On the universal level, the right of two partners to have children is guaranteed by Article 23 § 2 ICCPR (Right to found a family).[509] As a consequence, States Parties are under the primary duty to refrain from restricting natural reproduction.[510]

A particularly serious interference with the right to procreation constitutes compulsory sterilization. ***V.C. v. Slovakia*** is a landmark case in the field of forced sterilization of a Roma woman in Slovakia. This case demonstrates that this kind of situation can involve the prohibition of inhuman and degrading treatment (Article 3 ECHR). The ECtHR held what follows:

> The Court notes that the sterilisation procedure grossly interfered with the applicant's physical integrity as she was thereby deprived of her reproductive

502 *Evans v. United Kingdom* [GC], no. 6339/05, ECHR 2007-I.
503 *Ibid.*, § 71.
504 *Ibid.*, § 72.
505 *Dickson v. United Kingdom* [GC], no. 44362/04, ECHR 2007-V.
506 *Ibid.*, § 13.
507 *Ibid.*, § 66.
508 See, for instance, the case of *S.H. and Others v. Austria* [GC], no. 57813/00, ECHR 2011, in which the applicants challenged Austria's restrictive laws on assisted reproduction. The Grand Chamber of the ECtHR held: "The Court considers that the right of a couple to conceive a child and to make use of medically assisted procreation for that purpose is also protected by Article 8, as such a choice is an expression of private and family life. Article 8 of the Convention therefore applies to the present case" (§ 82). On the merits, the Court rejected the claims of both couples, considering that the Austrian legislation was a careful and cautious attempt to reconcile social realities with its approach of principle in this field (§ 114).
509 Nowak, *UN Covenant on Civil and Political Rights*, p. 533.
510 *Ibid.*

> capability. At the time of her sterilisation the applicant was twenty years old and therefore at an early stage in her reproductive life[511] . . . Thus, the sterilisation procedure, including the manner in which the applicant was requested to agree to it, was liable to arouse in her feelings of fear, anguish and inferiority and to entail lasting suffering. As to the last-mentioned point in particular, the applicant experienced difficulties in her relationship with her partner and, later, husband as a result of her infertility. She cited her infertility as one of the reasons for her divorce in 2009. The applicant suffered serious medical and psychological after-effects from the sterilisation procedure, which included the symptoms of a false pregnancy and required treatment by a psychiatrist. Owing to her inability to have more children the applicant has been ostracised by the Roma community.[512]

The Court concluded that, although there was no indication that the medical staff had acted with the intention of ill-treating the applicant, they had nevertheless displayed gross disregard for her right to autonomy and choice as a patient and, as a result, the sterilization of the applicant amounted to a breach of Article 3 ECHR.[513] Without neglecting the factual differences between the two situations, certain parallels can be drawn with the situation of Marshallese women as described by the Special Rapporteur: victimization of female members of minority/ indigenous groups; absence of intention of the authorities to inflict physical and moral harm, but gross negligence in protecting the women; massive interference in physical integrity of the victims, thereby depriving them of their reproductive capability; important psychological harm caused by infertility, reinforced through the cultural context; and, lastly, decrease of prospect for marriage because of social stigmatization and risk of marginalization and exclusion from the group.

To sum up, it is suggested here that the choice of women to have children is significantly reduced as a result of negative impact of nuclear testing on their reproductive health, as described above. As a result, they have to bear interference in their rights to respect private and family lives in the sense, inter alia, of Article 8 ECHR, or of the right to found a family within the meaning of Article 23 § 2 of the ICCPR.

d) Children's rights

Closely linked to the reproductive rights of women are the rights of children, in particular the right to life and to the highest attainable standard of health. A confirmation of this link can be found in Article 24 § 2(d) UNCRC, which directs States Parties to ensure access to essential health services for the child and his or her family, including pre-and post-natal care for mothers. It is well recognized that the key determinants of children's health, nutrition, and development depend

511 *V.C. v. Slovakia*, no. 18968/07, November 8, 2011, § 116.
512 *Ibid.*, § 118.
513 *Ibid.*, § 119.

on the mother's health and the role of the parents.[514] A significant number of deaths of infants occur during the neonatal period, related to the poor health of the mother prior to, and during, the pregnancy and the immediate post-partum period, and to suboptimal breastfeeding practices.[515] In other words, the health and health-related behaviors of parents have a major impact on children's health.[516]

The impact of nuclear testing has affected children and young adults in a disproportionate way. Among the population in the vicinity of Semipalatinsk, high rates of cancer – including leukemia, infant mortality, and stillborn children were reported.[517] An important part of the local population is considered to have reproductive cells negatively affected by nuclear testing, leading to genetic problems among their offspring. Moreover, chromosomal abnormalities in the third generation following exposure are expected to be even more serious. Other children are born with considerable bone deformations, some without arms and legs.[518] Regarding the Marshall Islands, the Special Rapporteur, Calin Georgescu, observed that an unusually high incidence of stunted growth as well as a high number of instances of thyroid cancer is established among Marshallese children. Similar effects have been reported in children in other irradiated environments, with a higher incidence of thyroid cancer as a result of the intake of iodine-131, especially through drinking milk contaminated with this element, which accumulates in the thyroid. This inhibits growth and the child's abilities and is also likely to lead to mental disability.[519]

In a report on the health consequences of the nuclear accident in Fukushima, the authors conclude that a decline in the birth rate was documented nine months after the nuclear catastrophe.[520] Japan also experienced a rise in infant mortality, with 75 more children dying in their first year of life than expected statistically.[521] Moreover, in the Fukushima Prefecture alone, almost 55 600 children were diagnosed with thyroid gland nodules or cysts. In contrast to cysts and nodules found in adults, these findings in children must be classified as pre-cancerous.

514 Committee on the Rights of the Child, General Comment No. 15 (2013) on the right of the child to the enjoyment of the highest attainable standard of health (Article 24), CRC/C/GC/15, April 17, 2013, § 18.

515 *Ibid.*

516 *Ibid.*

517 D. J. Peterson, *Troubled Lands: The Legacy of Soviet Environmental Destruction*, Boulder, San Francisco, and Oxford, 1993, p. 203. See also M. Laumulin, "Kazakhstan's Nuclear Policy and the Control of Nuclear Weapons," in G. Quester (ed.), *The Nuclear Challenge in Russia and the New States of Eurasia*, New York and London, 1995, pp. 181–211, p. 187. These conditions have often been referred to as "Semipalatinsk AIDS" (*ibid.*; and T. Edmunds, "The Environmental Movement in Kazakstan: Ecology, Democracy and Nationalism," in S. Hussey and P. Thompson (eds.), *The Roots of Environmental Consciousness: Popular Tradition and Personal Experience*, London and New York, 2000, pp. 139–159, p. 141).

518 R. Elegant, "Fallout," *The National Review*, September 2, 2002, pp. 30–32, 32.

519 Report, Georgescu, A/HRC/21/48/Add.1, § 31.

520 Paulitz et al., "Health Consequences resulting from Fukushima," p. 2.

521 *Ibid.*

There were also the first documented cases of thyroid cancer in children.[522] The special vulnerability of children confronted with nuclear activities has also been recognized by the Special Rapporteur for the right to health in the aftermath of the Fukushima accident, Anand Grover, observing that children are most at risk of thyroid cancer caused by radioactive iodine intake.[523] It has also been mentioned above that the follow-up of thyroid screening of children was inadequate, which prevented parents from taking efficient mitigating action against potential thyroid cancer in breach of their children's right to health.[524]

Furthermore, the recent report, mentioned above, on the consequences of the Chernobyl accident on the Ukrainian population highlights the particularly serious consequences for children:

> Particularly tragic is the fate of the thousands of children who were born dead or died in infancy, who were born with malformations and hereditary diseases, or who are forced to live with diseases they would not have developed under normal circumstances . . . The genetic defects caused by Chernobyl will continue to trouble the world for a long time to come – most of the effects will not become apparent until the second or third generation.[525]

In this report, it was observed, inter alia, that the number of fatalities among infants as a result of Chernobyl was about 5 000.[526] According to the UN Scientific Committee on the Effects of Atomic Radiation (UNSCEAR), between 12 000 and 83 000 children were born with congenital deformations in the region of Chernobyl, and around 30 000 to 207 000 genetically damaged children worldwide.[527] It also referred to another study showing that after 1986, in the aftermath of Chernobyl, around 800 000 fewer children were born in Europe than expected.[528] Moreover, infant mortality in Sweden, Finland, and Norway increased by a significant 15.8 percent compared to the trend for the period 1976 to 2006.[529] In Germany, scientists observed a significant increase in trisomy 21 in newly born children in the nine months following Chernobyl.[530] Another study reported 179 brain tumors diagnosed among children under the age of 3 in Ukraine in the aftermath of Chernobyl (1986–2002), compared to only nine cases between 1981 and 1985.[531]

522 *Ibid.*
523 This Chapter, section C.3.b).
524 *Ibid.*
525 Pflugbeil et al., "Health Effects of Chernobyl," p. 8.
526 *Ibid.*, summary of findings, p. 6, § 8.
527 *Ibid.*, p. 6, § 10.
528 *Ibid.*, p. 6, § 11.
529 *Ibid.*, p. 7, § 14.
530 *Ibid.*, § 15.
531 *Ibid.*, § 16, referring to Y. A. Orlov and A. V. Shaversky, "Indices of Neuro-Oncological Morbidity Dynamics among Younger Children in Ukraine," *Int. J. Rad. Med.*, 2004 6(1–4), pp. 72–77.

In light of these dramatic pictures, it is obvious that nuclear testing runs diametrically counter to the right of the child to the enjoyment of the highest attainable standard of health. The relevant paragraphs of Article 24 UNCRC (Health and health services) read as follows:

> 1. States Parties recognize the right of the child to the enjoyment of the highest attainable standard of health and to facilities for the treatment of illness and rehabilitation of health . . .
> 2. States Parties shall pursue full implementation of this right and, in particular, shall take appropriate measures:
>
> (a) To diminish infant and child mortality;[532] . . .
> (c) To combat disease and malnutrition, including within the framework of primary health care, through, *inter alia*, the application of readily available technology and through the provision of adequate nutritious foods and clean drinking-water, taking into consideration the dangers and risks of environmental pollution;
> (d) To ensure appropriate pre-natal and post-natal health care for mothers . . .

As far as infant and child mortality is concerned, one of the major problems linked to nuclear activities, Article 12 § 2(a) of the ICESCR provides, moreover, that States must take those steps necessary for "the provision for the reduction of the still-birth rate and of infant mortality and for the healthy development of the child." The African Charter on the Rights and Welfare of the Child, adopted on July 11, 1990, imposes on States the duty to take measures "to reduce infant and child mortality rates."[533] In spite of the vagueness in the formulation of the duties of States in the implementation of these duties, the CRC stated unambiguously that "States have an obligation to reduce child mortality."[534] With the adoption of Millennium Development Goal (MDG) No. 4, aiming at reducing the under-5 infant mortality by two-thirds by 2015, infant mortality has become a concern of the entire international community.[535] Despite the considerable decline in preventable child deaths since 1990, the current trends are not sufficient to meet MDG No. 4.[536]

532 While the infant mortality rate is the probability of dying between birth and one year (per 1 000 live births), the child mortality rate is often referred as the probability of dying between birth and five years (G. Van Bueren, *The International Law on the Rights of the Child*, Dordrecht, Boston, and London, 1995, p. 303).

533 Article 14 § 2(a).

534 General Comment No. 15 (2013), § 33. Van Bueren, *The International Law on the Rights of the Child*, pp. 302–303, is also in favor of an interpretation of Article 24 § 2 CRC in the sense of a legally binding duty to reduce infant and child mortality.

535 J. Tobin, *The Right to Health in International Law*, Oxford, 2012, p. 256.

536 See United Nations, "The Millennium Development Goals Report," 2015, pp. 32–37, http://www.un.org/millenniumgoals/2015_MDG_Report/pdf/MDG%202015%20 rev%20(July%201).pdf (accessed February 28, 2017).

The legal obligation to reduce infant and child mortality rates is moreover confirmed by Article 6 UNCRC (Right to life, survival and development) providing for the following guarantees:

1. States Parties recognize that every child has the inherent right to life.
2. States Parties shall ensure to the maximum extent possible the survival and development of the child.

While the first paragraph of Article 6 contains a provision guaranteeing the right to life of children, paragraph 2 addresses the "survival and development" of the child. This aspect is noteworthy in the context of nuclear testing and other harmful nuclear activities insofar as it derives from the preparatory work of this provision that States Parties are under the (positive) duty to promote measures and conditions for the protection of life and the survival and development of the child.[537] The Committee of the Rights of the Child (CRC) expects States to interpret "development" in its broadest sense as a "holistic concept, embracing the child's physical, mental, spiritual, moral, psychological and social development."[538] Its implementation measures should be aimed at achieving the optimal development for all children.[539] Nuclear testing producing harmful nuclear contamination is hardly compatible with the duty to create an environment in which children can develop and grow up healthily and happily.

Moreover, it has been observed above that nuclear testing on the Marshall Islands has deprived the local peoples of their natural environment and products, including food and drinking water. Such activities would have to be assessed under Article 24 § 2(c) UNCRC, which imposes on States Parties the duty to adopt measures with a view to ensuring access to nutritionally adequate, culturally appropriate, and safe food, taking into account the specific context.[540] Moreover, the CRC recognized that safe and clean drinking water is essential for the full enjoyment of life and other rights of the child.[541] Finally, the Committee also noted that "States should take measures to address the dangers and risks that local environmental pollution poses to children's health in all settings."[542]

The right of children to health has also been addressed by the ECtHR, even though the ECHR does not expressly address the right to health or to health care. To name just one case, in *Oyal v. Turkey*, the State failed to take preventive

537 Considerations of the 1988 Working Group, E/CN.4/1988/28, pp. 5–7, in S. Detrick, *The United Nations Convention on the Rights of the Child, A Guide to the "Travaux Préparatoires,"* Dordrecht, Boston, and London, 1992, pp. 120 et seq.

538 Committee on the Rights of the Child, General Comment No. 5 (General measures of implementation of the CRC), UN Doc. CRC/GC/2003/5, November 27, 2003, § 12.

539 *Ibid.*; see also J. Zermatten, *La Convention des droits de l'enfant vingt ans plus tard*, Essai d'un bilan, Sion, 2010, pp. 41–44.

540 General Comment No. 15 (2013), § 43.

541 *Ibid.*, § 48.

542 *Ibid.*, § 49.

measures against the spread of HIV through blood transfusion. As a consequence, a newborn baby was infected with HIV at a state hospital. The ECtHR considered the redress offered by the national authorities as clearly insufficient and therefore found a violation of the positive obligation under the right to life (Article 2 ECHR):

> 72. . . . the Court . . . considers that the most appropriate remedy in the circumstances would have been to have ordered the defendants, in addition to the payment of non-pecuniary damages, to pay for the treatment and medication expenses of the first applicant ***during his lifetime.***[543] The Court concludes therefore that the redress offered to the applicants was far from satisfactory for the purposes of the positive obligation under Article 2 of the Convention.[544]

Following this approach, a State bound by a human rights treaty such as the ECHR would have to compensate the costs for the health problems caused by nuclear testing or by an accident occurring in a nuclear power plant, and this even during the entire life of the victim.

In light of the foregoing, it is obvious that States that take children's rights seriously have to refrain from nuclear testing, in particular atmospheric testing or underground and other testing that releases harmful radiation to the environment, as well as from other harmful nuclear activities.

6. Conclusions of the present chapter, in particular in light of the rights of future generations

It has been demonstrated in the first subsection of this Chapter that human rights law is applicable in armed conflict and therefore imposes important limits on the use of nuclear weapons, which had already been indicated by the ICJ in its Advisory Opinion of 1996. There are several parallels with the conclusions of Part I that can be identified here, in particular with those relating to anti-personnel mines and cluster munitions.

Regarding jurisdiction, a dynamic and effective interpretation of human rights law and practice leads to the conclusion that a nuclear attack of one State on the territory of another, even without full control over the territory, would fall into the jurisdiction of the attacking State, which could therefore be held responsible for human rights violations resulting from such an attack. Jurisdiction of the State victim of an attack on his territory is not completely excluded, even though it concerns only a limited responsibility.

543 Emphasis added.
544 *Oyal v. Turkey*, no. 4864/05, March 23, 2010.

In the second subsection, it has been asserted that the most relevant civil and political rights concerned in the case of a nuclear attack are the right to life, the prohibition of genocide if the specific intent to destroy a group of people is established, the prohibition of degrading and inhuman treatment, including torture, and the right to respect for private life and home, as well as the right to property. This is not very different from what has been observed, in Part I of the present study, for anti-personnel mines and cluster munitions. As far as the immediate victims of a nuclear attack are concerned, in particular when directed against an inhabited area, it is likely that many of these rights would be breached. It has also been shown that the list of potential human rights violations committed by a nuclear attack, proposed in the present study, is not exhaustive since the use of nuclear weapons, in particular in an attack against the civil population, would amount to a total destruction of human rights.

Furthermore, the difficulties in respecting human rights in the aftermath of a nuclear attack have been demonstrated in the third subsection, especially those due to the fact that no appropriate rescue and medical response is possible. This is another important argument in favor of the illegality of nuclear weapons. It is hard to imagine how the duty to avoid and minimalize deaths in a life-threatening situation imposed by the relevant human rights instruments, in particular the right to life, could be respected. The observations of the Special Rapporteur on the right of everyone to the enjoyment of the highest attainable standard of physical and mental health, made after having visited Fukushima, reveal the problems encountered by victims – and particularly by vulnerable persons – of a nuclear accident in respect of their right to health.

In the fourth subsection, the importance of economic, social, and cultural rights in the context of a regional nuclear war has been stressed. These rights also turned out to be relevant in the context of the use of anti-personnel mines and cluster munitions, examined in Part I of this study. They would be even more so in a situation where nuclear weapons have been used. In light of the transboundary impact on health and environment of such a situation, due to fallout and radioactivity, the importance of extraterritoriality of these rights has also been emphasized. It has also been shown that it is likely that the rights examined would be breached in such a scenario, namely the right to development, the right to the highest standard of health, and the right to a healthy environment, as well as the right to an adequate standard of living, including the right to food and water. The duty to "respect" the latter right is particularly relevant in the context of a regional nuclear war due to the likely contamination of lakes, watercourses, and groundwater.

Another important conclusion that can be drawn from the assessment of the potential effect of nuclear weapons on economic, social, and cultural rights, given the experience of the Chernobyl accident, is the fact that the consequences of a regional nuclear war would affect the poor people in a disproportionate manner. In other words, whereas it has been shown in the subsection dealing with humanitarian law that the use of a nuclear weapon, in particular where directed against an inhabited area, affects civil population and armed forces alike, it would further discriminate against those who have already endured hardship in their daily lives. Again, similar conclusions have been drawn in Part I concerning anti-personnel mines and cluster munitions, weapons that are often used today in conflicts fought in developing countries.

In the fifth subsection, an assessment has been made, following the example of the Ottawa and Oslo Conventions in the first Part, in light of particularly vulnerable groups. It has been stressed that testing of nuclear weapons has always been conducted far from the capitals of the nuclear weapon States, mainly on the territory of indigenous peoples. The Marshallese peoples will never fully recover from their multiple forced displacements and the same applies to many other indigenous peoples who are victims of past nuclear testing. Following the work of the Special Rapporteur, Calin Georgescu, it has also been asserted in the same subsection that women are particularly vulnerable to nuclear tests, especially regarding their reproductive rights. Those rights go hand in hand with the rights of the children and it has been explained that children are often more affected by nuclear testing than adults. The same has been shown for victims of accidents having occurred in nuclear power plants, such as those in Chernobyl and Fukushima.

The victimization of women and children raises the topic of rights of future generations, in particular taking into account the fact that after Chernobyl many children were born with congenital deformations and that the latency period for many types of cancer is 25 to 30 years.[545] Moreover, the contamination of land by anti-personnel mines and ERW, addressed in Part I, attests to the hardship and the human rights violations caused by certain conventional weapons long after the actual fighting has ceased. This is even more true in the context of nuclear weapons. The use of nuclear weapons, assessed in the context of economic, social, and cultural rights, involves the rights and interests of future generations, given their deep impact on human health, environment, and development. Concepts such as "sustainable development" spawn principles of equity and intra- and inter-generational rights. They seek to ensure that both present and future generations will benefit from an equitable share of natural resources for their development and in relation to environmental protection.[546] In other words, each generation must use the natural and cultural heritage in a manner which allows that heritage to be passed on to future generations in the condition in which it was received.[547] Certain treaties explicitly oblige States not to perform activities which would likely

545 Pflugbeil et al., "Health Effects of Chernobyl," p. 5.

546 *Ibid.*

547 E. Weiss, "Implementing Intergenerational Equity," in M. Fitzmaurice, D. Ong, and P. Merkouris (eds.), *Research Handbook on International Environmental Law*, Cheltenham, 2010, pp. 100–116, 110–112.

breach intergenerational rights,[548] such as the 1996 Protocol (as amended in 2006) to the 1972 London Dumping Convention.[549]

As has been admitted by the ICJ in its 1996 Advisory Opinion nuclear weapons have the "potential to destroy all civilization and the entire ecosystem of the planet" and their use "would be a serious danger to future generations." The Court adds that "[i]onizing radiation has the potential to damage the future environment, food and marine ecosystem, and to cause genetic defects and illness in future generations."[550] The relevance of these principles in the field of nuclear weapons had already been expressed by Judge Weeramantry in his dissenting opinion in the *Nuclear Test* case, decided in 1995. While the ICJ's judgment declined to take jurisdiction because underground rather than atmospheric tests had been involved in 1974, Judge Weeramantry argued that the Court had a duty to protect the rights of future generations:

> This Court must regard itself as a trustee of those [future generations'] rights in the sense that a domestic court is a trustee of the interests of an infant unable to speak for itself . . . The rights of the people of New Zealand include the rights of unborn posterity. Those are rights which a nation is entitled, and indeed obliged, to protect.[551]

The fact that, by 2050, many cases of illnesses may be diagnosed that will have been caused by the Chernobyl nuclear catastrophe of 1986 confirms the threat of long-term harm caused by radioactivity and, therefore, the impact of a potential nuclear war on present and future generations.[552]

To sum up this Chapter, human rights law, in addition to humanitarian law, imposes significant limitations on the use of nuclear weapons, as has already been found to be the case in Part I of this study in respect of chemical weapons, anti-personnel mines, and cluster munitions. The application of human rights treaties in such situations would depend, in practice, on the ratification of these treaties by the responsible States or on the existence of a corresponding

548 A. Anastassov, "The Sovereign Right to Peaceful Use of Nuclear Energy and International Environmental Law," in J. L. Black-Branch and D. Fleck (eds.), *Nuclear Non-Proliferation in International Law*, The Hague, 2014, pp. 159–197, 172.

549 Convention on the Prevention of Marine Pollution by Dumping of Waste and Other Matter (November 13, 1972) and Protocol Thereto (November 7, 1996), amended in 2006. Paragraph 8 of its preamble reads as follows: "*The Contracting Parties to this Protocol* . . . *Being Convinced* that further international action to prevent, reduce and where practicable eliminate pollution of the sea caused by dumping can and must be taken without delay to protect and preserve the marine environment and to manage human activities in such a manner that the marine ecosystem will continue to sustain the legitimate uses of the sea and will continue to meet the needs of *present and future generations*" (emphasis added).

550 ICJ Reports 1996, § 35.

551 *Nuclear Test Case (New Zealand v. France)*, ICJ Reports, 1995, p. 288 (Dissenting Opinion of Judge Weeramantry, p. 341).

552 Pflugbeil et al., "Health Effects of Chernobyl," p. 8.

customary international law rule. A particularly convincing argument in favor of the absolute unlawfulness of nuclear weapons can be derived from the continued applicability of human rights that cannot be derogated from in situations of emergency, such as the right to life or the prohibition of inhuman and degrading treatment, including torture, or the rights that are of a *jus cogens* nature, such as the right to life or the prohibition of torture or of genocide, which can be invoked by all States thanks to their *erga omnes* nature.

D. THE OTHER LEGAL DUTIES (ARMS CONTROL, NON-PROLIFERATION, AND DISARMAMENT OBLIGATIONS) ASSESSED IN LIGHT OF HUMANITARIAN AND HUMAN RIGHTS LAW

1. Introduction

In Part I on treaties dealing with non-nuclear weapons (CWC and Ottawa and Oslo Conventions), it has been asserted that the prohibition of using the relevant weapons is the core duty under those instruments and that the so-called arms control, non-proliferation, and disarmament duties aim at rendering impossible their actual use.[553] The same applies, *a fortiori*, to nuclear weapons, the most destructive weapons invented to date. These obligations contribute directly to the respect of humanitarian law and the protection of human rights.

Another question is whether humanitarian and human rights law render activities other than the use of nuclear weapons, in particular development, manufacture and production, possession, or threat of use, per se illegal or impose at least some restrictions on the freedom of States. Such activities are prohibited, in particular, by the NPT and the regional treaties establishing NWFZ. These questions will be addressed in the current subsection.

2. The limitations to the development, manufacture, production, acquisition, possession, and threat of use of nuclear weapons imposed by humanitarian law

The relevance of the Martens Clause for the use of nuclear weapons has already been mentioned above.[554] It is noteworthy to reiterate that the ICJ has considered this clause, in its 1996 Advisory Opinion, an “effective means of addressing the rapid evolution of military technology.”[555] In other words, this clause is capable of limiting the States’ engagement in weapons that might turn out to be inhuman and, therefore, it is particularly relevant for the development, manufacture, production, acquisition, possession, and threat of use of nuclear weapons.

553 This volume, Chapter 3, section B.
554 This Chapter, section B.2.a).
555 *Legality of the Threat or Use of Nuclear Weapons*, ICJ Reports 1996, § 78.

Another, somehow similar, provision is foreseen in common Article 1 of the Geneva Conventions and Article 1 § 1 of Additional Protocol I, referred to above, imposing the duty to "respect" and "ensure" respect for international humanitarian law by armed forces in all circumstances. This general clause not only applies in actual combat, but also in peacetime. It is suggested that common Article 1 imposes on States Parties the obligation to undertake everything they can to ensure that the rules of international humanitarian law are respected by their own organs, as well as by entities under their jurisdiction.[556]

Moreover, it has also been observed that Article 36 of Additional Protocol I to the Geneva Conventions imposes on States Parties, in the study, development, acquisition, or adoption of a new weapon or means or method of warfare, the duty to determine whether its use would, in some or all circumstances, be prohibited by this Protocol or by any other rule of international law.

It is advocated here that, in light of the assessment made above of the use of nuclear weapons under humanitarian and human rights law, States, acting in good faith, should reasonably come to the conclusion, based on common Article 1 of the Geneva Convention and Article 1 § 1 of Additional Protocol I, combined with Article 36 of Additional Protocol I, that they have to refrain from developing, manufacturing, producing, acquiring, and possessing nuclear weapons.

In addition, deployment and readiness to use nuclear weapons run counter to the UN Charter's clear injunction that the threat of force is the exception, not the rule.[557] According to the ICJ, if the envisaged use of force is itself unlawful, the readiness to use it would be a threat prohibited under Article 2 § 4 of the UN Charter.[558] Moreover, a direct threat to use an already deployed nuclear weapon might also be contrary to international humanitarian law.[559] The ICJ stated that "[i]f an envisaged use of weapons would not meet the requirements of humanitarian law, a threat to engage in such use would also be contrary to that law."[560] Furthermore, under Article 51 § 2 of Additional Protocol I to the Geneva Conventions, "[a]cts *or threats* of violence the primary purpose of which is to

556 L. Boisson de Chazournes and L. Condorelli, "Common Article 1 of the Geneva Conventions Revisited: Protecting Collective Interests," *International Review of the Red Cross (IRRC)*, no. 837, vol. 82, 2000, pp. 67–87. Common Article 1 also implies an "external" element, imposing on States Parties the duty to ensure that third States comply with international humanitarian law (see K. Dörmann and J. Serralvo, "Common Article 1 to the Geneva Conventions and the Obligation to Prevent International Humanitarian Law," *International Review of the Red Cross (IRRC)*, no. 895/896, vol. 96, 2014, pp. 706–736).

557 Article 2 § 4 of the UN Charter: "All Members shall refrain in their international relations from the *threat* or use of force against the territorial integrity or political independence of any state, or in any other manner inconsistent with the Purposes of the United Nations" (emphasis added).

558 *Legality of the Threat or Use of Nuclear Weapons*, ICJ Reports 1996, § 47.

559 G. Nystuen, "Threats of Use of Nuclear Weapons and International Humanitarian Law," in Nystuen et al., *Nuclear Weapons under International Law*, pp. 148–170, 162.

560 *Legality of the Threat or Use of Nuclear Weapons*, ICJ Reports 1996, § 78.

spread terror among the civilian population are prohibited."[561] Such acts or threats are today also prohibited by customary international humanitarian law in international and non-international armed conflicts.[562] From this author's point of view, it is likely that, if the criterion of "primary purpose" is fulfilled, a concrete threat to use nuclear weapons would run counter to Article 51 § 2 of Additional Protocol I.[563]

3. The limitations imposed by human rights law

a) Development, manufacture, production, acquisition, and possession in light of the right to development

As indicated in the Chapter dealing with the use of nuclear weapons assessed in light of human rights law, the HRC, in its General Comment No. 14 on the right to life adopted in 1984, condemned not only the use of nuclear weapons, but also other activities in the following terms: "It is evident that the *designing, testing, manufacture, possession and development* of nuclear weapons are among the greatest threats to the right to life which confront mankind today."[564] In other words, it is justified to raise the question of whether activities prior to the actual use of nuclear weapons, such as development, manufacture, production, and possession, can amount to actual violations of human rights. The following assessment is limited to the right to development. According to the "Nuclear Weapons Cost Study" published by "Global Zero" in 2011, global annual expenditure on nuclear weapons amounts to US $105 billion.[565] NWS are expected to spend at least US $1 trillion over the next ten years.[566] Moreover, the costs of such weapons are not limited to their production and storage, but consist also in the delivery and targeting systems and in the maintenance of their command-and-control systems.[567] Another study concluded that nuclear weapons competition

561 Emphasis added.

562 See Henckaerts and Doswald-Beck, *Customary International Humanitarian Law*, vol. I, Rule 2, pp. 8–11.

563 See, for a more cautious view, Nystuen, "Threats of Use of Nuclear Weapons," p. 168.

564 General Comment No. 14, § 4 (emphasis added).

565 International Peace Bureau, Parliamentarians for Nuclear Nonproliferation and Disarmament, and World Future Council, "Move the Nuclear Weapons Money: A Handbook for Civil Society and Legislators," 2016, p. 6, https://www.worldfuturecouncil.org/time-move-nuclear-weapons-money-new-resource-launched-parliamentary-event-geneva/ (accessed February 28, 2017), p. 6.

566 *Ibid.*

567 S. Schwartz (ed.), *Atomic Audit: The Costs and Consequences of U.S. Nuclear Weapons Since 1940*, Washington, DC, 1998. The United States is said to spend US $30 million just to maintain the stockpiles (M. Gillis, *Le désarmement: Un guide de référence*, 3rd edn., New York, 2013, p. 27).

causes high socio-economic costs and diverts resources away from poverty alleviation.[568]

The link between development and disarmament was already recognized by the drafters of the UN Charter. According to its Article 26, the UNSC is supposed to propose plans to be submitted to the Member States of the organization for the establishment of a system for the regulation of armaments "in order to promote the establishment and maintenance of international peace and security with the least diversion for armaments of the world's human and economic resources." It is furthermore noteworthy to mention that the UNGA's Declaration of the United Nations on the Right to Development, adopted on December 4, 1986,[569] explicitly refers to disarmament:

> *The General Assembly,*
>
> *Reaffirming* that there is a close relationship between disarmament and development and that progress in the field of disarmament would considerably promote progress in the field of development and that resources released through disarmament measures should be devoted to the economic and social development and well-being of all peoples and, in particular, those of the developing countries . . .[570]
>
> All States should promote the establishment, maintenance and strengthening of international peace and security and, to that end, should do their utmost to achieve general and complete disarmament under effective international control, as well as to ensure that the resources released by effective disarmament measures are used for comprehensive development, in particular that of the developing countries.[571]

Moreover, the UNGA has regularly reiterated the relationship between disarmament and development in its annual resolutions. In such a resolution adopted in 2015, the UNGA clearly takes a human-centered approach and language, insofar as it refers to "poverty eradication and the elimination of diseases that afflict humanity," bringing other rights, such as the right to the highest standard of health, into play.[572]

In light of the foregoing, it can be concluded that the development, manufacture, and production, as well as the possession due to associated maintenance costs, of nuclear weapons have a negative impact on the right to development.

568 S. Willett, *The Costs of Disarmament: The South Asian Arms Dynamic*, Geneva, 2004, quoted in P. Lewis, B. Unal, and S. Aghlani, "Nuclear Disarmament: The Missing Link in Multilateralism," Chatham House, October 2016, p. 10, https://www.chathamhouse.org/publication/nuclear-disarmament-missing-link-multilateralism (accessed February 28, 2017).

569 UN Doc. A/RES/41/128.

570 Preambular, § 12 (emphasis in the original).

571 Article 7.

572 Resolution A/C.1/70/L.10, October 15, 2015, preamble, § 6.

b) Possession and threat of nuclear weapons as potential human rights violations

Deployment of nuclear weapons, coupled with declared policies that the weapons may be used when vital interests are at stake, casts a shadow over the right to life.[573] In his argument to the International Court of Justice in the 1996 Advisory Opinion proceedings, Australian Foreign Minister Gareth Evans observed:

> The threat of global annihilation engendered by the existence of such weapons, and the fear that this has engendered amongst the entire post-war generation, is itself an evil, as much as nuclear war itself. If not always at the forefront of our everyday thinking, the shadow of the mushroom cloud remains in all our minds. It has pervaded our thoughts about the future, about our children, about human nature. And it has pervaded the thoughts of our children themselves, who are deeply anxious about their future in a world where nuclear weapons remain.[574]

This raises the question of whether a human rights violation has to be materialized in order to constitute an arguable claim before a human rights body, or whether it is sufficient that an individual is threatened to be restricted in the exercise of his or her rights? In other words, could the possession of nuclear weapons as such constitute a breach of human rights, other than the right to development?

In certain specific situations, the ECtHR has accepted that an applicant may be only a "potential" victim of a human rights violation, but can nevertheless present a valid claim of breach of his or her rights; for example, where he or she was unable to establish that the legislation complained of had actually been applied to him or her on account of the secret nature of the measures,[575] or where an alien's removal had been ordered, but not enforced, and where enforcement would have exposed him or her in the receiving country to treatment contrary to Article 3 of the Convention or to an infringement of his or her rights under Article 8 of the Convention.[576] Moreover, it is open to a person to contend that a law violates his or her rights, in the absence of an individual measure of implementation, if he or she is required either to modify his or her conduct or risks being prosecuted or if he or she is a member of a class of people who are at risk of being directly affected

573 See D. Rietiker and J. Burroughs, "The Incompatibility of WMDs with the Right to Life (Article 6 ICCPR) – a Submission to the HRC," *Swiss Lawyers for Nuclear Disarmament (SLND) and International Association of Lawyers Against Nuclear Arms (IALANA)*, September 7, 2016, https://safna.org/2016/09/08/the-incompatibility-of-wmd-to-the-right-to-life-article-6-iccpr-a-submission-to-the-un-human-rights-committee/ (accessed February 28, 2017).

574 Verbatim Record, Public Sitting, *Legality of the Use by a State of Nuclear Weapons in Armed Conflict* and *Legality of the Threat or Use of Nuclear Weapons*, October 30, 1995, p. 42.

575 *Klass and Others v. Germany*, September 6, 1978, § 36, Series A no. 28,

576 *Soering v. United Kingdom*, July 7, 1989, Series A no. 161.

by the legislation, such as homosexuals threatened by a legislation that prohibits, under sanction, certain same-sex practices.[577]

Such scenarios are very specific and do not match with the situation of possession of nuclear weapons. In other words, if it is not excluded that possession, or at least concrete threat of use of nuclear weapons, would infringe on human rights, it might be difficult in practice to demonstrate before a tribunal that one is a victim of a potential violation. This has been confirmed, inter alia, by the case of *Aalbersberg et al. v. The Netherlands*,[578] mentioned above,[579] where the applicants challenged the Dutch Supreme Court's refusal to declare that the use of nuclear weapons would, under all circumstances, be contrary to the Netherlands' duties under international law. The HRC concluded that the applicants were not "actually affected" by any alleged violation because no nuclear explosion had been taken place.[580]

This might be different in a situation of concrete threat to use nuclear weapons, particularly in light of the prohibition of torture and inhuman or degrading treatment. In this regard, it is worth mentioning the case of *Gäfgen v. Germany*, decided by the ECtHR in 2010.[581] In this case, the applicant suffocated an 11-year-old boy to death and hid his corpse near a pond. Meanwhile, he sought a ransom from the boy's parents and was arrested shortly after having collected the money. He was taken to a police station where he was questioned about the victim's whereabouts. The next day, the deputy chief police officer ordered one of his subordinate officers to threaten the applicant with physical pain and, if necessary, to subject him to such pain in order to make him reveal the boy's location. Following these orders, the police officer threatened the applicant that he would be subjected to considerable pain by a person specially trained for such purposes. Some ten minutes later, for fear of being exposed to such treatment, the applicant disclosed where he had hid the victim's body.[582] The Court replied in the following terms to the question of whether threat of torture or inhuman and degrading treatment can amount to a violation of Article 3 ECHR:

> 103. The Court ... considers that the real and immediate threats of deliberate and imminent ill-treatment to which the applicant was subjected

577 *Burden v. United Kingdom* [GC], no. 13378/05, § 34, ECHR 2008; *Michaud v. France*, no. 12323/11, §§ 51–52, ECHR 2012; and *Sejdić and Finci v. Bosnia and Herzegovina* [GC], nos. 27996/06 and 34836/06, § 28, ECHR 2009.

578 *Aalbersberg et al. v. The Netherlands*, UN HRC, Communication no. 1440/2005, UN Doc. CCPR/C/87/D/1440/2005, August 2, 2005. Before the HRC, the Dutch Government argued, inter alia, that it would never use nuclear weapons against its own citizens within its territory (§ 4.4).

579 This Chapter, section C.2.a).

580 *Ibid.*, § 6.3.

581 *Gäfgen v. Germany* [GC], no. 22978/05, ECHR 2010.

582 Legal summary provided by the ECtHR: http://hudoc.echr.coe.int/eng#{"itemid": ["002-906"]} (accessed February 28, 2017).

> during his interrogation must be regarded as having caused him considerable fear, anguish and mental suffering . . .
>
> 104. The Court further observes that the threat was not a spontaneous act but was premeditated and calculated in a deliberate and intentional manner.
>
> 105. As regards the purpose of the threats, the Court is satisfied that the applicant was intentionally subjected to such treatment in order to extract information on J.'s whereabouts.
>
> 106. The Court further notes that the threats of deliberate and imminent ill-treatment were made in the context of the applicant being in the custody of law-enforcement officials, apparently handcuffed, and thus in a state of vulnerability . . .
>
> 108. . . . It reiterates that according to its own case-law . . . which also refers to the definition of torture in Article 1 of the United Nations Convention against Torture . . . a threat of torture can amount to torture, as the nature of torture covers both physical pain and mental suffering. In particular, the fear of physical torture may itself constitute mental torture.

In light of the foregoing paragraphs, the Court came to the conclusion that the method of interrogation to which the applicant was subjected was sufficiently serious to amount to inhuman treatment prohibited by Article 3 ECHR.[583] Given the reasoning of the Court in the *Gäfgen* case, this author is of the opinion that a real and imminent threat of using nuclear weapons might, contrary to mere possession of such weapons, amount to inhuman treatment of the population targeted insofar as it is capable of causing considerable fear, anguish, and mental suffering, in particular when its primary purpose is to spread terror among the population, as indicated above in the assessment of threat of use of nuclear weapons made in light of humanitarian law.[584] It is also undeniable that the threat of use of nuclear weapons would generally be a premeditated and calculated act and that victims of a nuclear attack would be extremely vulnerable, in particular when such an attack is directed against the undefended civilian population.

c) Positive obligation of States to prevent accidental nuclear explosions and those caused by terrorists

A further question is whether a State possessing nuclear weapons could be held responsible for an accidental explosion if it turns out that such explosion could have been avoided. This question is even more relevant given that it is well established how close humanity has come to nuclear weapons use owing to accidents or miscalculations during the Cold War.[585]

583 *Gäfgen v. Germany*, § 108.
584 This Chapter, section D.2.
585 Lewis et al., "Nuclear Disarmament," p. 6, with further references in footnote 6.

In this regard, it is worth reiterating the ECtHR's far-reaching, particularly dynamic jurisprudence in the field of environmental protection, transforming the right to live in an adequate environment into an individual human right. The cases regarding the right to water, explained above, are appropriate examples for this dynamic interpretation.[586] Especially under Articles 2 (Right to life) and 8 ECHR (Right to respect for private life and home), States are nowadays obliged to prevent environmental disasters, to inform the affected populations about possible risks, and, in the event of materialization of such a risk, to investigate the accident, pay compensation to the victims, and, under certain circumstances, prosecute and punish the responsible officials in an adequate manner.[587]

Regarding dangerous activities, which includes possessing and maintaining nuclear arsenals, the case of *Öneryildiz v. Turkey* is noteworthy.[588] In this first environmental case involving loss of life (Article 2 ECHR) decided by the Court, the two applicants alleged that the national authorities were responsible for the deaths of their close relatives and for the destruction of their property due to a methane explosion at the municipal waste dump in an area of Istanbul. In April 1993, such an explosion occurred, followed by a landslide that destroyed ten dwellings and killed 39 people.[589] In its judgment of November 30, 2004, the Grand Chamber of the ECtHR reiterated that the right to life contains not only a negative obligation to refrain from the use of force by State agents, but also imposes a positive obligation on the States Parties to take appropriate steps to safeguard the lives of those within their jurisdiction. This obligation applies to any activity, whether public or not, "in which the right to life may be at stake, and *a fortiori* in the case of industrial activities, which by their very nature are dangerous, such as the operation of a waste-collection site."[590] The ECtHR included the public's right to information among the preventive measures that the State must take to protect the right to life and found that the defendant State had breached its obligations in this regard.[591]

In light of this judgment, it is not hard to imagine that a State possessing nuclear weapons but not applying the necessary precaution in respect of such weapons and causing an accidental explosion could be held responsible *vis-à-vis* the victims. Even though the majority of nuclear weapons and related devices are said to be kept adequately, some of those weapons and materials pose

586 This Chapter, section C.4.e).

587 For an overview, see D. Shelton, "Human Rights and the Environment: What Specific Environmental Rights Have been Recognized?," *Denv. J. Int'l L. & Pol'y*, vol. 35, 2006, pp. 129–171.

588 *Öneryildiz v. Turkey* [GC], no. 48939/99, November 30, 2004.

589 *Ibid.*, see the legal summary provided by the Court, http://hudoc.echr.coe.int/eng#{%22itemid%22:[%22002-4094%22]} (accessed November 11, 2016).

590 *Ibid.*, § 71. The Court held that the primary duty on the State is to put into place a legislative and administrative framework designed to provide effective deterrence against threats to the right to life (§§ 91 et seq.).

591 See in particular §§ 90 and 108 et seq.

considerable risks.[592] Such a risk is moreover amplified by the fact that many nuclear weapons are on a high state of alert and ready to be used within a few minutes.[593]

Yet another question is whether a State could be held responsible for an explosion caused by a terrorist group if it turns out that the group was able to steal or otherwise acquire a bomb from that State. Non-state actors, in particular terrorists, have in the past shown clear interest in obtaining and threatening the use of nuclear weapons.[594] Former US President Obama warned in Prague in April 2009: "One terrorist with one nuclear weapon could unleash massive destruction."[595] These concerns have also been at the heart of the Nuclear Security Summits (NSS) held annually since 2010.[596] In addition, an amendment to the Convention on the Physical Protection of Nuclear Material (CPPNM) came into force on May 8, 2016, requiring States Parties to protect nuclear facilities and apply that protection to nuclear material in domestic use, storage, and transport.[597]

In light of the foregoing, it does not seem unlikely that a terrorist group, in addition to the desire to produce a nuclear device on their own, could seek to acquire a nuclear warhead through theft or through an insider assisting in the illegal acquisition.[598] It is suggested here that a State might be held responsible under human rights law for the use of nuclear weapons by non-State actors if it could reasonably have prevented the acquisition of the weapons by these groups. This can be deduced from the relevant case law of human rights courts regarding the positive duty to prevent harm from materializing, including when being caused by private actors. In the European human rights system, such protection is granted by an extensive and dynamic interpretation of the right to life (Article 2 ECHR). In a case against Turkey, the ECtHR had to deal with an allegation of the applicant, relying on the right to life (Article 2 ECHR), that his brother was killed by or with the connivance of State agents in a context of Kurdish separatism.[599] The relevant paragraphs of the judgment read as follows:

> 62. The Court recalls that the first sentence of Article 2 § 1 enjoins the State not only to refrain from the intentional and unlawful taking of life, but also to take appropriate steps to safeguard the lives of those within its jurisdiction . . . It also extends in appropriate circumstances to a positive obligation on the authorities to take preventive operational measures to protect an individual or individuals whose life is at risk from the criminal acts of another individual . . .

592 Gillis, *Le desarmement*, p. 27.
593 *Ibid.*
594 Lewis et al., "Nuclear Disarmament," p. 17.
595 Remarks by President Barack Obama, April 5, 2009, http://www.acronym.org.uk/old/building-security/reducing-arsenals-incl-start/president-obama-speech-nuclear-disarmament (accessed March 8, 2017).
596 Lewis et al., "Nuclear Disarmament," p. 17.
597 *Ibid.*, p. 18.
598 *Ibid.*, p. 17, with further reference in n. 73.
599 *Kılıç v. Turkey*, no. 22492/93, ECHR 2000-III.

In light of the right to life protected by Article 2 ECHR, it can be argued that States possessing nuclear weapons are under the duty to take appropriate measures to protect their population against nuclear attacks by terrorist groups, including by illegal acquisition of nuclear devices from their own arsenals. Such a duty is confirmed by the recent, above-mentioned ILC's "Draft articles on the protection of persons in the event of disasters," whose Article 11 imposes on States the duty to "reduce the risk of disasters by taking the necessary and appropriate measures . . . to prevent the creation of new risk and reduce existing risk . . ."[600] One can raise the question, given the growing threat of terrorism, whether an effective protection of stored nuclear weapons can be guaranteed at all. In any event, from the author's point of view, it is obvious that the most appropriate way to fulfill the duty to protect the right to life is simply to get rid of these highly controversial and extremely dangerous weapons by fulfilling their disarmament duties under Article VI NPT and, thereby, excluding the possibility of illegal appropriation of such devices by those groups.

d) The right to receive information about the risks inherent in the possession of nuclear weapons

A question that would deserve deeper reflection is whether, under the right to life or the right to respect for private and family life and home, the population of a State possessing nuclear weapons has at least the right to be informed about the storage and maintenance of nuclear weapons. This is not the place for a detailed analysis of this question, but it can be reiterated that, in the case of *Guerra v. Italy*,[601] the ECtHR found a violation of the right to respect for private and family life (Article 8 ECHR), stating that the applicants had waited throughout the operation of fertilizer production at the company for essential information that would have enabled them to assess the risks they and their family might run if they continued to live at Manfredonia, a town particularly exposed to danger in the event of an accident at the factory.[602] Another relevant case concerned the risks attached to a potential eruption of the volcano Vesuvius and the measures taken by the authorities to combat those risks.[603] The applicants, who lived near the volcano, alleged, inter alia, that the lack of adequate information on the risks they faced was in breach of their right to respect for their private and family life. The case was ultimately declared inadmissible for failure to exhaust domestic remedies, but it constitutes nevertheless an example for the importance of the duty to inform

600 UN Doc. A/CN.4/697, p. 103.

601 *Guerra and Others v. Italy* [GC], no. 14967/89, February 19, 1998.

602 *Ibid.*, § 60. Referring to the fact that workers from the factory had died of cancer, the applicants also argued that the failure to provide the information in issue had infringed their right to life as guaranteed by Article 2 of the Convention. The Court did not separately examine this complaint (*ibid.*, §§ 61 et seq.).

603 ECtHR, *Viviani and Others v. Italy* (dec.), no. 9713/13, March 24, 2015.

the local population about risks to life inherent in dangerous or hazardous activities.[604]

Access to information can also be inferred from the freedom of opinion and expression. Such a right is granted by Article 19 ICCPR, paragraph 2 of which declares that everyone shall have the right to freedom of expression, which includes "freedom to seek, receive and impart information and ideas of all kinds." In its General Comment No. 34 on Article 19 ICCPR, dated September 12, 2011, the HRC holds the following:

> 18. Article 19, paragraph 2 embraces a right of access to information held by public bodies. Such information includes records held by a public body, regardless of the form in which the information is stored, its source and the date of production . . . As has already been noted, taken together with article 25 of the Covenant, the right of access to information includes a right whereby the media has access to information on public affairs and the right of the general public to receive media output.[605]

This right has moreover been confirmed by the HRC in individual communications.[606] It is noteworthy to mention that, in a recent, ground-breaking judgment against Hungary, the Grand Chamber of the ECtHR also explicitly recognized such a right despite the fact that the text of Article 10 § 1 ECHR does not refer to it. The Court was of the opinion that whether and to what extent the denial of access to information constituted an interference with an applicant's freedom of expression had to be assessed in each individual case and in light of the particular circumstances, including: (i) the purpose of the information request; (ii) the nature of the information sought; (iii) the role of the applicant; and (iv) whether the information was ready and available.[607]

Regarding access to information concerning nuclear weapons and their potential risk to the population of the State holding them, as such without doubt a question of considerable public interest (ii), it would be interesting to find out whether a journalist, a representative of civil society, or a researcher (iii) seeking in vain before national authorities access to information with a view to inform the broader public (i), and provided that the information sought does not necessitate the collection of any data by the State,[608] could successfully file an application to an international human rights court. Such an application could in principle be

604 *Ibid.*

605 UN doc. CCPR/C/GC/34, September 12, 2011.

606 See, in particular, *Gauthier v. Canada* (Communication no. 633/1995, May 5, 1999); *Toktakunov v. Kyrgyzstan* (Communication no. 1470/2006, March 28, 2011); and *Rafael Rodríguez Castañeda v. Mexico* (Communication no. 2202/2012, August 29, 2013).

607 *Maygar Helsinki Bizottság v. Hungary* [GC], no. 18030/11, §§ 158–170, November 8, 2016.

608 *Ibid.*, § 169.

rejected if the refusal to grant access by the national authorities is considered necessary in a democratic society, in particular on grounds of national security. In the case of *Hadjianastassiou v. Greece*,[609] the ECtHR held that the conviction of the applicant, a captain in the air force, for disclosure of a project for the manufacture of a guided missile undertaken by the air force, classified as "military secret," was necessary in a democratic society:

> Like the Government, the Court takes the view that the disclosure of the State's interest in a given weapon and that of the corresponding technical knowledge, which may give some indication of the state of progress in its manufacture, are capable of causing considerable damage to national security.[610]

The latter case, involving an army member being criminally charged for divulgation of a "state secret," however, differs considerably from the situation of a journalist, an NGO, or a researcher seeking information in order to inform the broader public of the danger inherent in the possession of nuclear weapons.

609 *Hadjianastassiou v. Greece*, December 16, 1992, Series A no. 252.
610 *Ibid.*, § 45.

8 Implementation and verification of the relevant treaties by human rights actors and institutions

A. INTRODUCTORY REMARKS

In the first Part of the present study, dealing with treaties restricting or prohibiting non-nuclear weapons, it has been shown that the assistance of human rights actors in the implementation and verification of the respect of treaty obligations is remarkable. This conclusion can be interpreted as attesting to the relevance of this type of arms control treaties for the protection of the human being. It has also been observed that where strong implementation and verification mechanisms are lacking, in particular within the Ottawa and Oslo Conventions, civil society as well as the ECtHR together with the Committee of Ministers of the Council of Europe fill at least part of the gap.

The following subsection is devoted to the question of whether the same applies to treaties dealing with nuclear weapons. The actors potentially involved in the implementation and verification of the treaties are identical to those in the Chapter 4 of Part I, namely civil society (section B, below), international and regional human rights bodies (section C, below), as well as the ICC (section D, below). For practical reasons, the role of international and regional human rights bodies has been studied already in the different subsections of Part II and does not need to be re-examined here.

B. CIVIL SOCIETY: THE EXAMPLE OF THE NPT

1. General observations

It has been observed above that the antinuclear movement was instrumental in the pre-negotiation phase of certain treaties, in particular the PTBT and the CTBT, as well as treaties establishing regional NWFZ.[1] The present subsection will consider the extent to which civil society is also involved in the implementation and verification of these treaties. From the outset, treaties dealing with nuclear weapons benefit from stronger implementation and verification structures than treaties such as the Ottawa or Oslo Conventions. The IAEA plays a central role

1 This volume, Chapter 6, sections B and C.

in the implementation of international safeguards in conformity with Article III NPT.[2] Certain regional organizations have also been attributed functions of verification, in particular the Nuclear Energy Agency (NEA), Euratom, and the Agency for the Prohibition of Nuclear Weapons in Latin America (OPANAL).[3] Due to these strong institutional structures of specialized agencies, the role of civil society is likely to be more limited here. Moreover, civil society might have only restricted access, or no access at all, to information on nuclear weapons due to secrecy, in spite of freedom of information legislation in many countries.[4] Does this mean that civil society is completely irrelevant in the implementation process? Far from that, as will be shown in the present subsection. As far as verification of compliance in the proper sense is concerned, VERTIC (UK), a highly specialized entity, can be mentioned here. This NGO has already been referred to above, in connection with verification in the CWC.[5] Its Nuclear Verification and Monitoring Programme focuses on the use of nuclear material and is active in three sectors: non-proliferation, disarmament, and nuclear testing.[6] As far as non-proliferation is concerned, it provides training on the Comprehensive Safeguard Agreements and the Additional Protocol concluded between States and the IAEA. Its aim is to support international organizations in achieving the broad application of such safeguards and to ensure that the States have appropriate and individually tailored safeguard coverage.[7]

Moreover, civil society has been extremely active and helpful in the implementation of Article VI NPT, as the following subsection will show. Even though all three pillars of the NPT – non-proliferation (Articles I–III), peaceful use of nuclear energy (Article IV), and disarmament (Article VI) – are of concern to civil society, it is safe to claim that the disarmament pillar lies at the center of these organizations' aims. It should not be forgotten that the organizations engaging in the arms control process are all firmly rooted in the peace movement.[8] In the same vein, civil society engages in the consolidation of existing and establishment of new NWFZ, which equally, but maybe more realistically, aspires to a world without nuclear weapons.[9]

2 See, for a commentary on the role of the IAEA, M. I. Shaker, "The Evolving International Regime of Nuclear Non-Proliferation," *Collected Courses of The Hague Academy of International Law*, vol. 321, pp. 9–202, 43–47.

3 *Ibid.*, pp. 53–59.

4 H. Born, B. Gill, and H. Hänggi, "Introduction," in H. Born, B. Gill, and H. Hänggi (eds.), *Governing the Bomb: Civilian Control and Democratic Accountability of Nuclear Weapons*, Oxford and SIPRI, 2010, pp. 1–24, 22 et seq.

5 This volume, Chapter 4, section B.1.

6 See the website of VERTIC: http://www.vertic.org/pages/homepage/programmes/verification-and-monitoring/nuclear-materials.php (accessed February 28, 2017).

7 *Ibid.*

8 C. Kissling, *Civil Society and Nuclear Non-Proliferation: How do States Respond?*, Aldershot, 2008, pp. 53 and 78.

9 *Ibid.*, p. 76.

The present subsection concentrates on the contribution of civil society to the NPT review process, the main international forum for discussing on a regular basis the problems of implementation of the duties imposed by that treaty. It will be shown that the participation of NGOs in this task has been modest, but has currently been growing. Moreover, a recent forum – the Open-Ended Working Group (OEWG) on disarmament, which met in 2013 and 2016 – has proven more accessible for civil society and has played a considerable role in pushing the disarmament debate more prominently on the international agenda. It will also be examined in the following observations.

2. The contribution of civil society in implementing Article VI NPT

a) The growing importance of Article VI NPT

In accordance with Article VIII § 3 NPT, periodic Review Conferences take place every five years with a view to assuring that the purposes of the treaty are being realized. This provision, adopted in 1968, does not explicitly mention the participation of civil society's representatives.

As far as the aim of disarmament in the sense of Article VI NPT is concerned, it has received increased attention in recent NPT review cycles. During the 1995 and 2000 Review Conferences, the goal of general and complete disarmament was recalled and even strengthened. The 1995 Review Conference not only prolonged the NPT for indefinite duration, but also adopted, by consensus, a decision on Principles and Objectives for Nuclear Non-Proliferation and Disarmament, which set forth a "program of action" for the implementation of Article VI.[10] Five years later, on the basis of the 1995 Principles and Objectives, the 2000 Review Conference elaborated, again by consensus, "Thirteen Practical Steps towards Nuclear Disarmament under Article VI."[11] One of those steps confirmed the "unequivocal undertaking of the nuclear-weapon States to accomplish the total elimination of their nuclear arsenals" (step 6), while another repeated the ultimate goal of "general and complete disarmament" (step 11).

It may be added that, even though these concrete proposals have not so far been followed by practical measures of implementation, many NNWS have reiterated the call for further action to implement Article VI NPT at the 2005 and 2010 Review Conferences. One of the recommendations made at the end of the 2010 Conference is unambiguous: "States parties agree to commence

10 See Decision 2 in the annex of the Final Document of the 1995 NPT Review Conference (Doc. NPT/CONF.1995/32), http://www.un.org/Depts/ddar/nptconf/2142.htm (accessed February 28, 2017).

11 2000 Review Conference of the Parties to the Treaty on the Non-Proliferation of Nuclear Weapons (NPT), New York, USA, April 24–May 19, 2000, Final Document, Part II, at 14, para 15 (UN Doc. NPT/CONF.2000/28).

multilateral negotiations leading to the conclusion of a nuclear weapons Convention . . .".[12] As far as the 2015 Review Conference is concerned, it has already been observed that no agreement on a final document could be reached, but that the endorsement of the Humanitarian Pledge, by which a majority of States Parties to the NPT have committed themselves to "pursue effective measures to fill the legal gap for the prohibition and elimination of nuclear weapons," was considered the most significant result of the Conference.[13]

b) The structure of the civil society involved in the NPT review process and the OEWG, including the survivors and victims of Hiroshima and Nagasaki ("Hibakusha")

The structure of the civil society recently represented at the NPT Review Conferences and PrepComs is similar to that which was instrumental in the negotiations leading to most of the treaties on nuclear weapons described above.[14] It ranges from strong activist associations and popular grass-roots movements to associations of professionals and politicians, especially parliamentarians[15] and mayors.[16] Among the associations of professionals, IPPNW still play an important role. Organizations established by other professionals, lawyers for instance, such as the International Association of Lawyers against Nuclear Arms (IALANA),[17] joined the movement more recently. Moreover, think tanks – sometimes called academic-policy-analysis institutes – often benefit from broad knowledge and specialized expertise in their ranks and are therefore influential, too.[18] The Arms Control Association (ACA), with headquarters in Washington, DC, is one of the most prominent of those entities.[19]

12 Final Document, vol. II, p. 705 (UN Doc. NPT/Conf.2010/50).
13 This volume, Chapter 7, section B.2.b).
14 This volume, Chapter 6.
15 See, for the statement delivered by Jeremy Corbyn, Co-Chair of Parliamentarians for Nuclear Non-Proliferation and Disarmament UK Section, at the 2014 PrepCom, http://www.reachingcriticalwill.org/images/documents/Disarmament-fora/npt/prepcom14/statements/29April_HoC.pdf (accessed February 28, 2017).
16 L. S. Wittner, "Where Is the Nuclear Abolition Movement Today?", in K. Vignard and J. Linekar (eds.), *Civil Society and Nuclear Disarmament*, disarmament forum, UNIDIR, 4/2010, pp. 3–13, 3 et seq.
17 The IALANA was founded in 1988 in Stockholm. Today, it has its headquarters in Germany and runs offices in the Pacific region, Japan, the United States, and Switzerland. See, for more information, http://en.ialana.de (accessed February 28, 2017). See, for their statement at the 2014 PrepCom, http://www.reachingcriticalwill.org/images/documents/Disarmament-fora/npt/prepcom14/statements/29April_IALANA.pdf (accessed February 28, 2017).
18 Kissling, *Civil Society and Nuclear Non-Proliferation*, p. 52.
19 See, for more information, http://www.armscontrol.org/ (accessed February 28, 2017). See, as far as the statement of Daryl Kimball, Executive Director, at the 2014 PrepCom is concerned: http://www.reachingcriticalwill.org/images/documents/Disarmament-fora/npt/prepcom14/statements/29April_Kimball-Walker.pdf (accessed February 28, 2017).

In addition, the antinuclear organizations try to maximize their efforts by building up large networks or campaigns. One of the well-established campaigns against nuclear weapons is Abolition 2000, an entity created in 1995 as a reaction by NGOs against the States Parties' failure to put the disarmament obligations under Article VI on the NPT agenda. During the 1995 NPT Review Conference, a number of NGOs got together to sign their Abolition Statement.[20] The International Campaign to Abolish Nuclear Weapons (ICAN) was initiated by IPPNW in 2006, largely due to dismay among the civil society about the failure of the 1995 NPT Review Conference. It is inspired and shaped by the success of the International Campaign to Ban Landmines and is today backed by a large number of national and international organizations.[21]

Particularly interesting for the present study, dealing with the interaction between the protection of the human being and arms control, is the fact that survivors and victims of the nuclear bombs dropped on Hiroshima and Nagasaki are given a certain place in the NPT Review process. In this regard, Mayors for Peace, whose aim it is to abolish nuclear weapons as of 2020, play a particular role. This organization is growing very fast and now counts almost 7 200 member cities.[22] During the PrepComs of 2013 and 2014, for instance, the Mayors of Hiroshima and Nagasaki, who are also the President and Vice President of Mayors for Peace, took the floor in order to remind the delegations present of the horrors and human suffering caused by the bombings of their towns in August 1945 and to express their wish for a world free of nuclear weapons.[23] Moreover, actual survivors and victims ("Hibakusha") of the nuclear catastrophes of Hiroshima and Nagasaki have been given a voice in the NPT review process. At the PrepCom of 2013, Toshiki Fujimori, the assistant Secretary-General of Nihon Hidankyo, the Japan Confederation of A- and H-Bomb Sufferers Organizations, addressed the delegations, recalling the human disaster that he – then a young child – and his family had been facing since August 1945 and urging the international community to abolish nuclear weapons:

20 Wittner, "Where Is the Nuclear Abolition Movement Today?", p. 5.

21 *Ibid.*; see, for more information, http://www.icanw.org/ (accessed February 28, 2017). Also noteworthy is the Middle Powers Initiative, founded in 1998, which is a collaboration among several international NGOs and "middle power" governments; see, for more information, http://middlepowers.org (accessed February 28, 2017). Finally, Global Zero was established by a group of high-ranking political and military leaders in December 2008; see, for more details, http://www.globalzero.org/ (accessed February 28, 2017).

22 On December 1, 2016, it had 7 196 member cities; see, for more details, http://www.mayorsforpeace.org/english/index.html (accessed February 28, 2017).

23 See, for the statements of Matsui Kazumi, Mayor of Hiroshima (2013), and those of Tomihisa Taue, Mayor of Nagasaki (2014), http://www.reachingcriticalwill.org/images/documents/Disarmament-fora/npt/prepcom13/statements/24April_M.Kazumi.pdf (accessed February 28, 2017) and http://www.reachingcriticalwill.org/images/documents/Disarmament-fora/npt/prepcom13/statements/24April_T.Taue.pdf (accessed February 28, 2017).

> My family consisted of 12 members: Grandfather, father, mother and 9 brothers and sisters. Excluding 4 children who had been evacuated away from Hiroshima, the other 8 members of my family were all affected by the A-bomb. My 4th sister, who was in the first year of a girls high school, had been mobilized together with her schoolmates, to work in the building evacuation work near the ground zero area. After the bombing, my parents and other sisters looked for her many days in the area, but her remains were nowhere to be found. Among the students who were mobilized from different places to work inside Hiroshima City on that morning, more than 6 000 students were killed . . . By the end of that year, a total of 210 000 people were killed in Hiroshima and Nagasaki . . . I sincerely ask all of you to accept our heartfelt appeal. We urge you to set a clear path leading to the abolition of nuclear weapons in the 2015 NPT Review Conference. This is the desire of the Hibakusha.

This kind of intervention aims at increasing the awareness of States' delegations of the human impact of nuclear weapons by going beyond a discourse dominated by security considerations.[24]

c) From the limited but growing role of the civil society in the NPT review process to the democratic, participatory OEWG

Traditionally, the NPT review process was only open to States Parties.[25] The participation of civil society in the Review Conferences and PrepComs has nevertheless been gradually admitted in recent years. Canada's statement addressed to the 2002 NPT PrepCom, supported by interventions by other delegations, emphasized the crucial role of "partnerships with civil society" in pursuing non-proliferation, arms control, and disarmament objectives. Canada, in particular, urged States to consider measures "to enhance the participation of civil society in the preparatory process and at Review Conferences."[26] More recently, the participation of civil society in the NPT review process reached high levels. For instance, at the 2005 Review Conference, nearly 1 800 representatives of civil society registered, ten times more than at the 1994 PrepCom; to those, one may add the hundreds of unregistered people who travelled to New York in order to make their

24 R. Tyson of Reaching Critical Will (RCW) put it correctly in the following way: "A critical function of NGOs is to re-humanize the effects of nuclear weapons for delegations in order to move the deliberations from a dry, rationalist debate to one of conscious commitment to progress towards genuine disarmament" (RCW, *News in Review*, no. 4, May 1, 2003, p. 1).

25 *Ibid.*, p. 37. This author adds that States that have signed the treaty but not ratified it were allowed to participate without taking part in the votes. Non-parties could attend as observers, but could only submit their views in writing.

26 Remarks by The Hon. Christopher Westdal, Ambassador for Disarmament, to the Preparatory Committee for the Conference of the Parties of the Treaty on the Non-Proliferation of Nuclear Weapons, New York, April 9, 2002.

voices heard on the occasion of the numerous other events taking place in tandem.[27]

The role of civil society in the formal negotiations within the NPT review mechanism is, however, still limited. NGOs have struggled hard for some kind of recognized standing. The Second PrepCom session (January 1994), preparing for the 1995 Review Conference, agreed for the first time to the presence of representatives of civil society, starting with the Third PrepCom, which took place in September 1994.[28] Since then, such representatives can be accredited to the review process, which entitles them to register for the meetings of the PrepComs and the Review Conferences, to receive a badge, to enter the UN Headquarters in New York, Geneva or Vienna; and to attend the public meetings of the sessions.[29] In this regard, it has to be noted that the public, open meetings are still largely outweighed by the closed ones.[30] Moreover, civil society representatives may officially address the delegations within the limited time frame allocated to them.[31] This procedure was tested for the first time at the 1997 PrepCom and was formalized in the 2000 Final Document with regard to the Seventh review process. In the 2005 Review Conference, for instance, civil society was given three hours to present topics. The same time slot was also reserved during the 2010 and 2015 Review Conferences.[32]

Apart from interventions during the official meetings of the Review Conferences and the PrepComs, more spontaneous gatherings, meetings, consultations, briefings, roundtables, and panels take place, where members of the civil society can exchange their points of view and engage in discussions with the governmental representatives on their issues and concerns. Moreover, the NGOs also organize their own events, inside and outside the premises of the United Nations. For instance, on May 1, 2005, shortly before the Review Conference started, civil society managed to organize a mass demonstration in which approximately 45 000 people marched through Manhattan toward Central Park.[33] A very impressive series of side events were organized in 2010 and 2015.[34] A particularly original idea came from Parliamentarians for Nuclear Non-Proliferation and Disarmament (PNND), which initiated and coordinated "Global Wave" in 2015, an action event organized by people around the world before or at the opening of the NPT

27 Kissling, *Civil Society and Nuclear Non-Proliferation*, p. 51. The author adds that 1 000 people came from Japan, among which only 200 were formally registered for the actual Conference.

28 *Ibid.*, p. 55.

29 *Ibid.*

30 *Ibid.*, p. 58.

31 *Ibid.*, p. 55.

32 See, for the 2015 NPT Review Conference, http://www.reachingcriticalwill.org/disarmament-fora/npt/2015/ngos (accessed February 28, 2017).

33 *Ibid.*, p. 52.

34 See, for the 2015 NPT Calendar of events, http://www.reachingcriticalwill.org/disarmament-fora/npt/2015/calendar (accessed February 28, 2017).

Review Conference in order to "wave goodbye to nuclear weapons" and aiming at engaging civil society, policy makers, and media in supporting a successful NPT Review Conference.[35]

Finally, a rather recent phenomenon in relation to the NPT review process is noteworthy. It is a fact that a certain influence can be exercised on the negotiations through the incorporation of representatives into the delegations of States, such as representatives of NGOs, scientific or political researchers, as well as national parliamentarians.[36] This practice is in full conformity with a recommendation contained in the UN Study on Disarmament and Non-Proliferation Education of 2002, which encourages Member States to include non-governmental advisors and/or parliamentarians in delegations to meetings on arms control or disarmament.[37]

To sum up, even though much progress has been achieved in respect of civil society participation in the NPT review mechanism, its role remains limited, especially when compared to other international fora, for instance those concerned with human rights issues. This can be explained by the intergovernmental nature of the NPT review process, the confidential features of arms control negotiations and the special consideration of security that are inherent in this domain.[38] But, as mentioned in the introduction to this subsection, a new forum has allowed civil society to participate more broadly and efficiently in the nuclear disarmament debate, namely, the United Nations' OEWG, convened pursuant to UNGA Resolution 70/33 ("Taking forward multilateral nuclear disarmament negotiations"), adopted on December 7, 2015, and mandated, inter alia, to "substantively address concrete effective legal measures, legal provisions and norms that would need to be concluded to attain and maintain a world without nuclear weapons."[39] The OEWG was clearly set up against a background of growing concern about the "catastrophic humanitarian consequences of any use of nuclear weapon," on the one hand, and the growing frustration among NNWS about the NWS' failure to fulfill their disarmament commitments under Article VI NPT, on the other.[40]

35 See, for more information, http://mailing.pnnd.org/2015-04-21-en-web.html (accessed February 28, 2017).

36 In the 2005 NPT Review Conference, for instance, the Czech Republic, Germany, Japan, Kyrgyzstan, the Netherlands, New Zealand, the Republic of Korea, and the United Kingdom included one or several political researchers, and Germany added a scientific researcher to its delegation. Other delegations, such as Bangladesh, Canada, the Holy See, Ireland, and New Zealand, had one or two civil society representatives, and Germany, Indonesia, Ireland, the Netherlands, and Sweden integrated one or several parliamentarians into their delegations (Kissling, *Civil Society and Nuclear Non-Proliferation*, p. 60).

37 UNGA Resolution A/57/124, August 30, 2002, p. 17, recommendation no. 8.

38 Kissling, *Civil Society and Nuclear Non-Proliferation*, pp. 55 and 69.

39 Operative § 2 of UNGA Resolution 70/33.

40 Preamble, § 2 of UNGA Resolution 70/33. See also M. Brehm, "Whose Security Is It Anyway? Towards a Treaty Prohibition of Nuclear Weapons," *EJIL:Talk!*, May 31, 2016, http://www.ejiltalk.org/whose-security-is-it-anyway-towards-a-treaty-prohibition-of-nuclear-weapons/ (accessed February 28, 2017).

The OEWG held in 2016 gathered in three sessions during a total of 15 days at the UN premises in Geneva. Its sessions were attended by 100 States – all the NWS chose to stay absent – by representatives of international organizations, as well as by a large number of NGOs.[41] The structure of the OEWG was comparable to that of the three conferences on the humanitarian impact of nuclear weapons (Oslo, Nayarit, and Vienna) mentioned above.[42] Presentations by experts from academia and civil society were followed by a general debate, questions were addressed to the panelists, and there was a real exchange of views between States and civil society. Panels included interventions on various topics with regard to advancing in the field of nuclear disarmament, such as the question of the possible pathways to take forward multilateral nuclear disarmament negotiations,[43] the identification of legal provisions to be adopted to attain and maintain a world without nuclear weapons,[44] and additional measures to increase awareness of the complexity of the interrelationship between the wide range of humanitarian consequences of any nuclear detonation.[45] The last-mentioned topic indicates that, in substance too, there was considerable overlap between the OEWG and the three conferences on the humanitarian impact of nuclear weapons.

Paragraph 1 of UNGA Resolution 70/33 indicates that multilateral disarmament negotiations have to be conducted in a "comprehensive, inclusive, interactive and constructive manner." These principles have, from this author's point of view, been fully respected during the OEWG. According to its final report, deliberations were conducted without prejudice to their eventual outcome and to national positions: this allowed "for frank, constructive and participatory discussion."[46] As mentioned above, the circle of participants at the OEWG was very large and access for civil society almost unlimited. As a matter of fact, pursuant to paragraph 5 of Resolution 70/33, the OEWG had to convene in Geneva "with the participation and contribution of international organizations and civil society representatives, in accordance with established practice . . .". In reality, all relevant NGOs which were granted access to the UN premises, namely entities having consultative status with the UN Economic and Social Council (ECOSOC) or being accredited to the Department of Public Information (DPI), could register and attend the meetings of the OEWG.[47] Even other interested organizations, relevant for and competent in the areas of arms control and disarmament, could register and

41 *Ibid.*

42 This volume, Chapter 7, section B.2.b).

43 Panelist N. Ritchie, Lecturer, University of York (Final report of the OEWG, "Taking forward multilateral nuclear disarmament negotiations," UN Doc. A/71/371, September 1, 2016, § 17).

44 Panelist S. Casey-Maslen, Professor of International Law, University of Pretoria (*ibid.*).

45 Panelists I. Helfand (IPPNW) and S. Sekkenes, UN Development Programme (UNDP) (*ibid.*).

46 Final report of the OEWG, § 12.

47 See http://www.reachingcriticalwill.org/disarmament-fora/oewg/2016/may (accessed February 28, 2017).

participate, subject to the agreement of Member States (on a no-objection basis).[48] During the actual exchange of views, civil society's representatives were largely on an equal footing with the delegations of States thanks, in particular, to the generous and sensible attitude to civil society's concerns demonstrated by the chairperson of the OEWG, Ambassador Thani Thongphakdi from Thailand.[49] Only very few sessions were held in private, excluding NGOs from participating. Moreover, during the three sessions, civil society organized many side events, as was the case during the recent NPT Review Conferences and PrepComs.[50]

A last remark concerns the high quality of civil society participating in the OEWG. Apart from the numerous valuable interventions made by important antinuclear "activists," some in-depth, more "neutral" and academic statements by well-respected think tanks[51] and professional groups[52] engaged in the field of arms control were tabled, thereby greatly clarifying the discussions.

In light of the foregoing, it seems safe to argue that the OEWG, much more than the NPT Review Conferences where the standing of civil society is still reduced, reflects a contemporary multilateral and truly democratic and participatory disarmament forum.[53]

48 *Ibid.*

49 This author followed certain sessions of the 2016 OEWG and experienced the generous and respectful manner in which Ambassador Thani chaired the group.

50 *Ibid.*

51 See, among others, Acronym Institute for Disarmament Diplomacy, "Security and Humanitarian Implications of Relying on Nuclear Weapons for Deterrence, and Effective Legal Alternatives," A/AC.286/NGO/22, May 9, 2016, http://www.reachingcriticalwill.org/images/documents/Disarmament-fora/OEWG/2016/Documents/NGO22.pdf (accessed March 1, 2017); Arms Control Association, "Options for Moving Forward on Disarmament," A/AC.286/NGO/23, May 9, 2016, http://www.reachingcriticalwill.org/images/documents/Disarmament-fora/OEWG/2016/Documents/NGO23.pdf (accessed March 1, 2017); or Global Security Institute, "Respond to the Critical Moment," A/AC.286/NGO/11, Rev. 1, May 3, 2016, http://www.reachingcriticalwill.org/images/documents/Disarmament-fora/OEWG/2016/Documents/NGO11.pdf (accessed March 1, 2017).

52 See, among others, IALANA, "A Legal Instrument for the Prohibition and Elimination of Nuclear Weapons," A/AC.286/NGO/12, May 2, 2016, http://www.reachingcriticalwill.org/images/documents/Disarmament-fora/OEWG/2016/Documents/NGO12.pdf (accessed February 28, 2017); International Council of Nurses, the International Physicians for the Prevention of Nuclear War, the World Federation of Public Health Associations, and the World Medical Association, "The Health and Humanitarian Case for Banning and Eliminating Nuclear Weapons," A/AC.286/NGO/18, May 4, 2016, https://ippnweupdate.files.wordpress.com/2016/04/health-and-humanitarian-case-for-banning-and-eliminating-nuclear-weapons_oewg-may-2016.pdf (accessed February 28, 2017); or James Martin Center for Non-proliferation Studies at the Monterey Institute of International Studies, "Disarmament and Non-Proliferation Education," A/AC.286, Misc.1/Rev.1, April 17, 2016, http://www.reachingcriticalwill.org/images/documents/Disarmament-fora/OEWG/2016/Documents/MISC1Rev1.pdf (accessed February 28, 2017).

53 As such, the OEWG follows what R. Rydell calls "democratic revolution" within the United Nations ("The United Nations and a Humanitarian Approach to Nuclear Disarmament,"

d) Specific proposals submitted by civil society on the implementation of Article VI NPT

In recent years, specific proposals, introduced or at least backed by civil society, on the implementation of Article VI have played a growing role. One of the first proposals was that of a comprehensive nuclear weapons convention. Already in 1997, Costa Rica had requested the UNSG to circulate to all UN Member States a "Model Nuclear Weapons Convention."[54] It is largely a product of civil society, namely, of a consortium of international experts convened by IALANA, the International Network of Engineers and Scientists against Proliferation (INESAP), and IPPNW.[55]

The Model Convention is inspired by the CWC, which has pursued quite successfully the elimination of an entire category of weapons, and is designed to prohibit the production of fissile material for nuclear-weapon use as well as the development, testing, stockpiling, transfer, use, and threat of use of nuclear weapons.[56] Such an instrument would include a phased program for the complete elimination of these weapons within a specific time frame.[57] The NGOs involved, by drafting the Model Convention, have invested a substantial amount of energy to encourage governments seriously to consider the idea of a treaty that provides a roadmap to a world without nuclear weapons.[58] In 2008, at the request of Costa Rica and Malaysia, former UNSG Ban Ki-moon circulated an updated version of this text, which he later considered to be "a good point of departure" for the negotiation of a treaty on the prohibition on nuclear weapons.[59] The idea of a comprehensive convention was reiterated by certain representatives of civil society and of States during the 2016 OEWG,[60] but it was also felt that the wide gap between the NWS and the NNWS regarding nuclear disarmament renders this approach too ambitious and that it was inappropriate and technically very difficult

International Humanitarian Law and Nuclear Weapons, Nuclear Abolition Forum, issue no. 1, 2011, pp. 25–35, 30).

54 Letter of October 31, 1997 from the Chargé d'affaires a.i. of the Permanent Mission of Costa Rica to the UNSG (UN Doc. A/C.1/52/7, November 17, 1997). At the 2010 Review Conference, Costa Rica submitted a working paper on the Model Nuclear Weapons Convention (NPT/Conf.2010/PC.I/WP.17). For the consideration by the Conference of the Model Convention, see 2010 Review Conference of the Parties to the Treaty on the Non-Proliferation of Nuclear Weapons, Final Document, Volume II (NPT/Conf.2010/50, vol. II), pp. 702–705.

55 D. Hawkins, "Now We Can: Civil Society and Governments Moving towards a Ban on Nuclear Weapons," in K. Vignard and J. Linekar (eds.), *Civil Society and Nuclear Disarmament*, disarmament forum, UNIDIR, 4/2010, pp. 39–47, 40.

56 *Ibid.*

57 Final report of the OEWG, § 37.

58 Hawkins, "Now We Can," p. 41.

59 Press Release, UNSG Ban Ki-moon, "The United Nations and Security in a Nuclear-Weapon-Free World," UN Doc. SG/SM/11881, October 24, 2008.

60 Final report of the OEWG, § 37; see also the document introduced by Costa Rica and Malaysia, "Model nuclear weapons convention," A/AC.286/WP.11, February 24, 2016.

to negotiate detailed provisions for the verified elimination of nuclear weapons without the involvement of States possessing such weapons.[61] Moreover, it is suggested here that the Model Convention needs updating, for instance concerning its entry-into-force clause which resembles the clause of the CTBT and due to which that treaty has been awaiting its introduction into force for more than 20 years.[62]

Not all the NGOs dealing with nuclear disarmament rallied behind the idea of a comprehensive convention. The idea of a "ban treaty" has been advanced for a certain period of time, in particular by ICAN.[63] This is the favorite approach of the majority of States having participated in the 2016 OEWG. Following this idea, inspired by the positive experiences of the Ottawa and Oslo Conventions, prohibition would precede elimination.[64] In other terms, such an instrument would only be an interim or partial step toward nuclear disarmament, since it does not include a duty to eliminate nuclear weapons.[65] According to the advocates of such a treaty, a prohibition can and should be pursued independently of the process of elimination and, therefore, would not necessarily presuppose the participation of the NWS. They argue that a ban treaty would not only prevent States Parties from assisting in nuclear-weapon-related activities, but also greatly change the normative landscape by delegitimizing and stigmatizing nuclear weapons and codifying the prohibition of nuclear weapons under international law.[66]

Moreover, the idea of a framework agreement providing for the taking of a range of legal measures according to a negotiated sequence has also been promoted more recently.[67] Such an instrument could, for instance, adopt features of the CCW, insofar as a framework agreement could provide for a preamble and

61 Final report of the OEWG, § 37.

62 See Article XV of the Model Convention and Article XIV of the CTBT.

63 M. Fraser, "The Illegality of Nuclear Weapons," *Nuclear Abolition Forum*, issue no. 1, 2011, pp. 36–39, 37; and N. Ritchie, "The Story So Far: The Humanitarian Initiative on the Impacts of Nuclear Weapons," *ILPI-UNIDIR Vienna Conference Series*, no. 1, p. 5, http://www.unidir.org/files/publications/pdfs/the-story-so-far-en-616.pdf (accessed February 28, 2017).

64 Brehm, "Whose Security Is It Anyway?". See for the possible elements of such an instrument, Final report of the OEWG, § 35.

65 Final report of the OEWG, § 36.

66 *Ibid.*; and Brehm, "Whose Security Is It Anyway?". See, for a document explaining this approach in detail, "Article 36" and the Women's International League for Peace and Freedom, "A Treaty Banning Nuclear Weapons," A/AC.286/NGO/3, February 24, 2016, http://www.reachingcriticalwill.org/images/documents/Disarmament-fora/OEWG/2016/Documents/NGO3.pdf (accessed February 28, 2017).

67 Brehm, "Whose Security Is It Anyway?"; and Final report of the OEWG, § 30. See also the document introduced during the OEWG, Middle Powers Initiative, "Options for a Framework Agreement," A/AC.286/NGO/20, May 4, 2016, http://www.reachingcriticalwill.org/images/documents/Disarmament-fora/OEWG/2016/Documents/NGO20.pdf (accessed February 28, 2017).

definitions, as well as for some technical rules[68] and final clauses.[69] Subsequent protocols, which the States Parties to the agreement would be free to ratify, could provide for the prohibition of different activities, such as possession, transfer, testing, and use, as well as a duty to eliminate stockpiles.[70] The advantage of such an approach is its flexibility, which leaves room for confidence-building measures and allows for a smooth transition toward nuclear disarmament by taking into account the concerns and interests of all States, NWS as well as NNWS.[71]

During the OEWG, certain States expressed their preference for a step-by-step (or "progressive") approach.[72] Supporters of this approach conceive a prohibition intervening only once the "minimization point" of the nuclear weapons elimination process has been reached – the final "building block."[73] This moment would be reached when nuclear weapons are reduced to very low numbers and once a reliable verification regime has been established.[74] In other words, the elimination of stockpiles would precede prohibition.[75] In parallel, NWS as well as NNWS should participate in any effective legal and non-legal measure of unilateral, bilateral, plurilateral (regional), or multilateral nature, such as the entry into force of the CTBT, the negotiation of a fissile-material treaty, the conclusion of a post-NEW START Treaty, or the strengthening of existing and the creation of new NWFZ.[76] Considering the numerous unfulfilled disarmament promises made by the NWS in the past, such a minimum approach does not go far enough and is acceptable neither for the majority of States nor for the representatives of civil society which have participated in the OEWG.

On October 27, 2016, the UNGA adopted, by 123 votes against 38, and 16 abstentions, a resolution to launch negotiations in 2017 on a treaty banning nuclear weapons. This historic resolution might mark the end of two decades of paralysis in multilateral nuclear disarmament efforts.[77] It is clearly inspired by the humanitarian initiative insofar as the UNGA declares itself "[d]eeply concerned about the catastrophic humanitarian consequences of any use of nuclear

68 Scope of application, relations with other international agreements, dispute settlement, indications concerning potential verification and review mechanisms, general rules of implementation, etc.

69 These could include clauses on, inter alia, signature, ratification, acceptance, approval, accession, entry into force, review and amendments, provisional application, denunciation, reservations, depositary, and authentic texts.

70 Contrary to such an agreement, the protocols to the 1980 Convention prohibit not different activities, but different types of conventional weapons.

71 Final report of the OEWG, § 38.

72 Brehm, "Whose Security Is It Anyway?".

73 *Ibid.*

74 Final report of the OEWG, § 40.

75 Brehm, "Whose Security Is It Anyway?".

76 Final report of the OEWG, §§ 40 and 41.

77 Resolution A/C.1/71/L.41; for the text, see: http://reachingcriticalwill.org/images/documents/Disarmament-fora/1com/1com16/resolutions/L41.pdf (accessed February 28, 2017).

weapons."[78] It also notes with satisfaction that the OEWG "engaged in structured and substantive discussion in a comprehensive, inclusive, interactive and constructive manner"[79] and explicitly recognizes the value of the participation and contribution of civil society in the work of the OEWG.[80] The UNGA also encourages all Member States to participate in the conference, which will be open to international organizations and civil society.[81] Given the current international climate necessitating increased political attention to disarmament and non-proliferation issues, the UNGA

> [c]alls upon States participating in the conference to make their best endeavour to conclude *as soon as possible* a legally binding instrument to prohibit nuclear weapons, leading towards their total elimination.[82]

3. Conclusion

The involvement of civil society in the implementation of nuclear arms control treaties demonstrates that this field is relevant for individuals. It is also recognized that the disarmament pillar (Article VI NPT) has gained importance in the most recent review cycles. Even though the role of civil society has traditionally been limited within the NPT, a tendency toward a more participatory cooperation has been observed in recent years. The fact that actual survivors and victims of the nuclear attacks against Hiroshima and Nagasaki have been given a voice is of more than only symbolic value and proves that the NPT review cycles have not remained immune to growing "humanization." In other words, mere considerations of State security are increasingly challenged by humanitarian and human rights concerns. Similar conclusions have already been drawn in Part I of this volume, especially with regard to the Ottawa and Oslo Conventions.

Even more effective and human-centered than the NPT review cycle was the 2016 OEWG, as it allowed for genuinely democratic and participatory discussions between States and civil society. It is probable that, after the failure of the 2015 NPT Review Conference, the OEWG will be the starting point for the elaboration of a new legally binding instrument permanently prohibiting nuclear weapons. At the time of writing, several options are on the table and, considering the adoption of the above-mentioned UNGA resolution calling to start negotiations, in 2017, with a view to concluding as soon as possible a legally binding instrument prohibiting nuclear weapons, the near future will show which one will be favored and retained. In any event, the most promising options, namely that of a

78 Preamble, § 2.
79 Operative § 1.
80 Operative § 3.
81 Operative §§ 9 and 10.
82 Preamble, § 13, and operative § 12 (emphasis added).

comprehensive nuclear weapons convention and a ban treaty, as well as the option of a framework convention, have been introduced and largely endorsed by civil society; they have been preceded by instruments that were clearly inspired by humanitarian concerns, such as the CWC, the Oslo and Ottawa Conventions, and the CCW, respectively. In other words, whatever solution is ultimately adopted, the humanitarian and human rights discourse will play a prominent role therein.

C. POTENTIAL PROSECUTION OF USE OF NUCLEAR WEAPONS BY THE ICC

1. Introduction

Even though the actual use of nuclear weapons is not the only activity related to nuclear weapons which has harmful effects on humans and which might trigger individual criminal responsibility, the following subsection will concentrate on this aspect. Moreover, the present study aiming at examining the relation between the human being and weapons, the observations that follow will focus on the use of nuclear weapons as possible war crimes, crimes against humanity, or acts of genocide, but exclude consideration of the crime of aggression that concerns primarily violations of *jus ad bellum*, within the meaning of the UN Charter and UNGA Resolution 3314 (XXIX) of December 14, 1974, rather than breaches of international law protecting the individual during armed conflict and other situations of violence.[83]

As a result of a substantial overlap between international humanitarian law and the ICC Statute, the following observations reflect to some extent the findings of the Chapter dealing with the lawfulness of nuclear weapons under international humanitarian law.[84]

83 See new Article 8bis of the Rome Statute, which defines "crime of aggression" as "planning, preparation, initiation or execution, by a person in a position effectively to exercise control over or to direct the political or military action of a State, of an act of aggression which, by its character, gravity and scale, constitutes a manifest violation of the Charter of the United Nations" (§ 1). Moreover, its paragraph 2 defines "acts of aggression" and enumerates the different acts that might qualify as such; for instance, invasion or attack of the territory of another State, military occupation, bombardment, blockade of ports, or the sending by or on behalf of a State of armed bands, groups, irregulars or mercenaries, which carry out acts of armed forces amounting to acts of aggression.

84 See this volume, Chapter 7, section B. For this relationship, see also A. Golden Bersagel, "Use of Nuclear Weapons as an International Crime and the Rome Statute of the International Criminal Court," in G. Nystuen, S. Casey-Maslen, and A. Golden Bersagel (eds.), *Nuclear Weapons under International Law*, pp. 221–243, 230–239.

2. The use of nuclear weapons as a potential war crime

a) The different war crime provisions relevant to the use of nuclear weapons

In the Chapter on treaties dealing with non-nuclear weapons, it has been shown that the drafters of the Rome Statute on the ICC included in the list of war crimes certain weapons whose use is prohibited by specific treaties or rules of customary international law, such as asphyxiating, poisonous, and other gases, prohibited as early as in 1925 by the relevant Geneva Protocol.[85] In contrast, nuclear weapons, such as anti-personnel mines and cluster munitions, have not been included in this list, even though a proposal to do so was put forward at the Rome Conference.[86] The strong resistance by some States, in particular the NWS, prevailed in the end and no reference to nuclear weapons was made.[87] In 1996, only two years before the Rome Statute was adopted, the ICJ had delivered its Advisory Opinion on the *Legality of the Threat or Use of Nuclear Weapons*, in which it concluded that, under current international law, no weapon-specific prohibition, including one of a customary nature, of the use of nuclear weapons existed per se.[88] This finding, although very controversial, gave the adversaries to the inclusion of nuclear weapons in the ICC's list of crimes a powerful and convenient argument. Later, during the Review Conference of the Rome Statute in Kampala (2010), the Mexican delegation proposed to include the use or threat of nuclear weapons as a separate war crime in Article 8 § 2(b).[89] This proposal was rejected, as it was considered too controversial and might have endangered other achievements of the Conference.[90]

The fact that the use of nuclear weapons is not recognized, per se, as a separate war crime does not mean that the authors of such a use would be immune against prosecution within the ICC. On the contrary, as observed above,[91] the highly indiscriminate nature of nuclear weapons is incompatible with the principle of distinction, one of the key principles of the law of arms conflict. As a result, and on account of their destructive power, nuclear weapons could easily cause harm amounting to "grave breaches" within the meaning of Article 147 of the Fourth

85 Article 8.2.e(xiv); see this volume, Chapter 4, section D.2.

86 A. Cassese, P. Gaeta, and J. Jones (eds.), *The Rome Statute of the International Criminal Court: A Commentary*, vol. I, Oxford, 2002, pp. 79 and 396. In particular, the Non-Aligned Movement (NAM) favored the inclusion of nuclear weapons, but the testing of nuclear weapons in May 1998 by Pakistan and India undermined its ability to pressure the other nuclear powers to concede (*ibid.*, p. 132, with reference).

87 *Ibid.*, p. 369.

88 ICJ Reports1996, §§ 51 et seq.

89 See an amendment proposal by Mexico, UN Doc. C.N.725.2009.TREATIES-6 (October 29, 2009).

90 F. Leggeri and F. Gouttefarde, "La Conférence de révision," in J. Fernandez and X. Pacreau (eds.), *Statut de Rome de la Cour pénale internationale, Commentaire article par article*, vol. II, Paris, 2012, pp. 251–268, 255.

91 This volume, Chapter 7, section B.3.

Geneva Convention relative to the Protection of Civilian Persons in Time of War,[92] especially when used against inhabited areas. The individuals responsible for such breaches could be charged, at least, for wishful killing (Article 8 § 2(a)(i))[93] and for wishfully causing great suffering or serious injury to body or health (*ibid.*, (iii)),[94] as well as for extensive destructions of property not justified by military necessity and carried out unlawfully and wantonly (*ibid.*, (iv)).[95]

If the nuclear attack was intentionally directed against the civilian population as such or against individuals not participating directly in the hostilities, perpetrators could be prosecuted under Article 8 § 2 (b)(i)[96] or, in non-international armed conflicts, on the basis of Article 8 § 2(e)(i).[97] Moreover, if the attack was intentionally directed against civilian objects – that is, objects which are not military objectives – Article 8 § 2(b)(ii) might apply.[98] In addition, a prosecution could be based on Article 8 § 2(b)(v), if a nuclear attack is launched against towns, villages, dwellings, or buildings which are undefended and which are not military objectives.[99]

92 Article 8 § 2(a) incorporates the list of grave breaches contained in the four Geneva Conventions of 1949.

93 See, for instance, regarding the ICTY, *Prosecutor v. Delalic et al.*, Case No. IT-96-21-T, Judgment, Trial Chamber, November 16, 1998, § 424; and *Prosecutor v. Blaskic,* Case No. IT-95-14-T, Judgment, Trial Chamber, March 3, 2000, § 153.

94 The ICTY recognized that this crime covers both physical as well as mental pain or suffering (*Prosecutor v. Naletilic and Martinovic*, Case No. IT-98-34-T, Judgment, Trial Chamber, March 13, 2003, § 339; and *Prosecutor v. Delalic et al.*, § 442). Moreover, the acts don't have to be carried out for a specific purpose (*Prosecutor v. Naletilic and Martinovic*, §§ 340 et seq.; and *Prosecutor v. Delalic et al.*, § 442).

95 These acts are grave breaches under the First (Article 50), Second (Article 51), and Fourth (Article 147) 1949 Geneva Conventions. The protected property includes civilian hospitals (see, in particular, Articles 18 and 19 of the Fourth Geneva Convention). Regarding the *mens rea* requirement for "destruction" of property, the perpetrator must have acted with the intent to destroy it or in reckless disregard of the likelihood of its destruction (*Prosecutor v. Brdjanin*, Case No. IT-99-36-T, Judgment, Trial Chamber, September 1, 2004, §§ 589 et seq.).

96 The conventional basis of this provision is the Additional Protocol I to the Geneva Conventions, in particular its Articles 51 § 2 and 85 § 3. In the *Galic* case, the ICTY Trial Chamber accepted that both intention and recklessness could enter into play. It required that the Prosecutor shows that the perpetrator was aware or should have been aware of the civilian status of the persons attacked (*Prosecutor v. Galic*, Case No. IT-98-29-T, Judgment, Trial Chamber, December 5, 2003, §§ 54 et seq.).

97 See also, regarding non-international armed conflicts, Article 8 § 2(c)(i), incriminating violence to life and person – in particular, murder of all kinds, mutilation, cruel treatment, and torture – committed against persons taking no active part in the hostilities.

98 This crime is based largely on Article 52 of Additional Protocol I, which reflects customary international law (J.-M. Henckaerts and L. Doswald-Beck, *Customary International Humanitarian Law*, vol. I: *Rules*, Cambridge, 2005, pp. 25 et seq.).

99 The conventional roots of these provisions are, in particular, Article 25 of the Regulations annexed to Hague Convention IV of 1907 and Article 59 of Additional Protocol I (see W. A. Schabas, *The International Criminal Court: A Commentary on the Rome Statute*, Oxford and New York, 2010, pp. 231–232). See, for the definition of "undefended," R. Arnold and S. Wehrenberg, "Article 8 § 2(b)(v)," in O. Triffterer and K. Ambos (eds.), *Rome Statute*

According to Article 8 § 2(b)(iv), it is also a war crime to launch an attack in the knowledge that if it will cause incidental loss of life or injury to civilians or damage to civilian objects or widespread, long-term, and severe damage to the natural environment which would be clearly excessive in relation to the concrete and direct overall military advantage anticipated. This provision addresses the problem of collateral damages and fits well into the context of nuclear weapons, characterized by their uncontrollable effects. The disastrous consequences for the environment of the actual use of nuclear weapons can easily be imagined in light of the above observations concerning nuclear weapons testing.[100] Moreover, as regards the elements of distinction, military necessity, and proportionality, inherent in Article 8 § 2(b)(iv),[101] it has been explained that even the use of a low-yield or earth-penetrating nuclear weapon, assuming it to be technically feasible, would fail to meet these requirements.[102]

The prosecution of yet other war crimes enumerated in the long list of Article 8 of the Rome Statute is not excluded when the use of nuclear weapons is considered. For instance, as indicated above, indiscriminate attacks by nuclear weapons on inhabited towns would not spare places of worship, churches, temples, mosques, or cemeteries, nor schools, universities, and hospitals.[103] Moreover, they would destroy museums, theaters, and other cultural institutions and treasures. As a result, Article 8 § 2(b)(ix) and, in non-international armed conflict, Article 8 § 2(e)(iv), might come into play, incriminating intentionally directing attacks against buildings dedicated to religion, education, art, science, or charitable purposes, historic monuments, hospitals, and places where the sick and wounded are collected, provided they are not military objectives.[104]

Finally, it was again the ICJ that observed, in its 1996 Advisory Opinion, that the radiation released by a nuclear explosion would affect agriculture and natural

of the International Criminal Court: A Commentary, 3rd edn., Munich, Portland, and Oxford, 2016, pp. 380–382.

100 This volume, Chapter 7, section C.5. Regarding the damage to environment, the wording of Article 8 § 2(b)(iv) resembles much of Article 55 § 1 of Additional Protocol I. See also the 1976 Convention on the Prohibition of Military or Any Other Hostile Use of Environmental Modification Techniques.

101 See, for a commentary, Schabas, *The International Criminal Court*, pp. 229–231.

102 This volume, Chapter 7, section B.2.d).

103 This volume, Chapter 7, section C.2.e).

104 See for a commentary on these provisions, Schabas, *The International Criminal Court*, pp. 235–237. Regarding more specifically the protection of cultural property, see also the Hague Convention for the Protection of Cultural Property in the Event of Armed Conflict of 1954, including its two Protocols. See, for two important cases involving those conventions, *Prosecutor v. Kordic and Cerkez*, Case No. IT-95-14/2-T, Judgment, Trial Chamber, February 26, 2001; and *Prosecutor v. Strugar*, Case No. IT-01-42-T, Judgment, Trial Chamber, January 31, 2005. See finally also Article 8 § 2(b)(xiii), and, regarding non-international armed conflicts, Article 8 § 2(e)(xii), prohibiting the destruction or seizing the enemy's property unless such destruction or seizure be imperatively demanded by the necessities of war.

resources over a wide area.[105] The negative impact of the use of nuclear weapons on the right to food and water has been mentioned already.[106] As a result, Article 8 § 2(b)(xxv), which prohibits "intentionally using starvation of civilians as a method of warfare by depriving them of objects indispensable to their survival, including willfully impeding relief supplies as provided for under the Geneva Conventions," should be remembered. It suggests that "starvation" covers above all suffering from lack of food and clean water;[107] it is not, however, restricted to deprivation of food or water, but may apply also to clothing necessary for the civilian population, medical supplies, or objects indispensable to produce, harvest, and process foodstuffs.[108] Considering the destructive power and indiscriminate nature of nuclear weapons, it is likely that such goods would be destroyed within a large perimeter around the point of impact. Furthermore, many victims of a nuclear attack who are not killed immediately in the blast are likely to die slowly from hunger, cold, and diseases, a scenario that is covered by the common definition of "starvation."[109] Finally, the wording of Article 8 § 2(b)(xxv) suggests that this crime extends to the interruption of relief supplies. In this respect, it can be recalled that one of the most important challenges identified by the ICRC is how survivors of a nuclear detonation could be efficiently assisted.[110]

To sum up this subsection, it can be claimed that different provisions on war crimes might come into play in situations of actual use of nuclear weapons. In this regard, a declaration made by France upon ratification of the Rome Statute will be analyzed briefly below.

b) The invalidity of the "interpretative declaration" of France of June 9, 2000

When France ratified the Rome Statute on June 9, 2000, it made several "interpretative declarations," among which the following concerns the use of nuclear weapons:

105 ICJ Reports 1996, § 35; quoted above, this volume, Chapter 7, section B.1, B.3 and C.6 (for B.1, see p. 142).

106 This volume, Chapter 7, section C.4.e).

107 See, for a commentary, M. Cottier and E. Richard, "Article 8 § 2(b)(xxv)," in Triffterer and Ambos, *Rome Statute of the International Criminal Court*, pp. 508–519.

108 *Ibid.*, p. 461. See in this sense Article 54 of Additional Protocol I (Protection of objects indispensable to the survival of the civilian population), which constitutes the treaty basis for this war crime.

109 See, in this sense, the definition of "starvation" provided by *New Shorter Oxford English Dictionary*, vol. 2, 1993: "die, especially slowly from hunger, cold, grief, disease etc."

110 This volume, Chapter 7, section B.2.c). Regarding the *actus reus* of this war crime, the starvation has to be used "as a method of warfare," with the purpose of gaining military advantage. On the other hand, the prohibition of starvation as a method of warfare does not prohibit siege warfare, the imposition of a naval blockade, or an embargo of a city, as long as the purpose is to achieve a military objective and not to starve a civilian population (Henckaerts and Doswald-Beck, *Customary International Humanitarian Law*, vol. I: *Rules*, pp. 188 et seq.).

> 2. The provision of Article 8 of the Statute, in particular paragraph 2(b) thereof, relate solely to conventional weapons and can neither regulate nor prohibit the possible use of nuclear weapons nor impair the other rules of international law applicable to other weapons necessary to the exercise by France of its inherent right of self-defense, unless nuclear weapons or the other weapons referred to herein become subject in the future to a comprehensive ban and are specified in an annex to the Statute by means of an amendment adopted in accordance with the provisions of Articles 121 and 123.

Under Article 120 of the Rome Statute, "[n]o reservations may be made to this Statute." According to Article 2 § 1(d) VCLT, a "reservation" means a

> unilateral statement, however phrased or named, made by a State, when signing, ratifying, accepting, approving or acceding to a treaty, whereby it purports to exclude or to modify the legal effects of certain provisions of the treaty in their application to that State.[111]

In one of the leading cases in the field of reservations to multilateral treaties, *Belilos v. Switzerland*,[112] the ECtHR held that, "in order to establish the legal character of such a declaration, one must look behind the title given to it and seek to determine the substantive content."[113] In light of that quotation, the ECtHR characterized the "interpretative declaration" made by Switzerland as a "reservation" and, subsequently, examined its validity under the applicable provision dealing with reservations.[114] As a result, it is suggested here that France intended to exclude, from the scope of the Rome Statute, a whole category of weapons, and by far the most devastating, harmful, and indiscriminate one. In other words, even though France named its statement "interpretative declaration," it is ultimately a reservation within the meaning of Article 2 § 1(d) VCLT. In other terms, France's declaration is contrary to Article 120 of the Rome Statute, which does not authorize reservations.

111 France has not ratified the VCLT, but the definition deriving from Article 2 § 1(d) is uncontested and of a customary nature (see M. Villiger, *Commentary on the 1969 Convention on the Law of Treaties*, Leiden and Boston, 2009, pp. 87 and seq.; and P. Gautier, 'Article 2', in O. Corten and P. Klein (eds.), *The Vienna Convention on the Law of Treaties: A Commentary*, Oxford and New York, 2011, pp. 23–56, pp. 48 et seq.). It has also been quoted in several international decisions (case concerning the *Delimitation of the Continental Shelf between the United Kingdom of Great Britain and Northern Ireland, and the French Republic*, Reports of International Arbitral Awards *(RIAA)*, vol. XVIII, § 55, pp. 169 et seq.).

112 No. 10328/83, April 29, 1988; see also ECtHR, *Weber v. Switzerland*, no. 11034/84, May 22, 1990.

113 *Belilos v. Switzerland*, § 49.

114 Article 64 ECHR (*Belilos v. Switzerland*, §§ 51–59). The same approach was adopted by other international bodies, for instance by the HRC in its General Comment No. 24, Doc. CCPR/C/21/rev.1/Add.6, November 11, 1994, § 3. In order to be precise, it has to be said that following numerous modifications of the ECtHR, the provision dealing with reservations is now Article 57 ECHR.

In light of what precedes, it is not even necessary to determine whether the French "declaration" is compatible with the object and purpose of the Rome Statute.[115] In any event, this author shares New Zealand's view expressed in the declaration joined to its instrument of ratification of September 7, 2000, that is, three months after the deposit of the French declaration, but without explicitly referring to the latter. According to this declaration, the core principles of humanitarian law apply independently from a certain type of weapon and, therefore, it would be inconsistent with these principles to limit the scope of Article 8 of the Rome Statute to acts involving conventional weapons.[116] To support its argument, New Zealand referred to the 1996 Advisory Opinion where the ICJ stated that the conclusion that humanitarian law did not apply to nuclear weapons

> would be incompatible with the intrinsically humanitarian character of the legal principles in question which permeates the entire law of armed conflict and applies to all forms of warfare and to all kinds of weapons, those of the past, those of the present and those of the future.[117]

The Government of New Zealand, most likely in response to another French declaration,[118] further recalled that international humanitarian law applies equally to aggressor and defender States and that its application does not depend on a determination of whether or not a State is acting in self-defense.[119]

To sum up, the French interpretative declaration, excluding the use of nuclear weapons from the scope of war crimes, has to be considered a reservation within the meaning of Article 2 § 1(d) VCLT and is therefore incompatible with Article 120 of the Rome Statute. It has no legal effect.

115 The "object and purpose" test according to Article 19(c) of the VCLT is not applicable here because Article 120 of the Rome Statute prohibits any reservation.

116 See, in particular, the first paragraph of New Zealand's declaration: "1. The Government of New Zealand notes that the majority of the war crimes specified in article 8 of the Rome Statute, in particular those in article 8(2)(b)(i)–(v) and 8(2)(e)(i)–(iv) (which relate to various kinds of attacks on civilian targets), make no reference to the type of the weapons employed to commit the particular crime . . . Accordingly, it is the view of the Government of New Zealand that it would be inconsistent with principles of international humanitarian law to purport to limit the scope of article 8, in particular article 8(2)(b), to events that involve conventional weapons only."

117 ICJ Reports 1996, § 86.

118 The first French declaration reads as follows: "The provisions of the Statute of the International Criminal Court don't preclude France from exercising its inherent right of self-defence in conformity with Article 51 of the Charter."

119 Paragraph 3 of the declaration, referring to the 1996 Advisory Opinion, §§ 40–42. See also, concerning the validity of the French reservation, F. Coulée, "Article 120," in Fernandez and Pacreau, *Statut de Rome de la Cour pénale internationale*, pp. 2103–2116, 2115 et seq.

3. The use of nuclear weapons as a crime against humanity

Whereas the ICJ, in its Advisory Opinion of 1996, did not address the question of whether the use of nuclear weapons would constitute a crime against humanity, the UNGA stated, as early as in 1961 and by a large majority, that "the use of nuclear weapons . . . would be a crime against humanity."[120] This statement has regularly been reaffirmed by the UNGA, most recently in 2015.[121]

Under the Rome Statute, a crime against humanity means one of the acts listed in Article 7 when consciously committed as part of a widespread or systematic attack against any civilian population.[122] The term "widespread" refers to the large-scale nature of the attack and the number of targeted persons.[123] In the *Tadić* case, the Trial Chamber of the ICTY asserted that a "widespread attack" may be the "cumulative effect of a series of inhumane acts or the singular effect of an inhuman act of extraordinary magnitude."[124] The second part of the sentence is of obvious relevance to the use of a nuclear weapon against a town or other inhabited area.[125] In the context of nuclear weapons, "murder" (Article 7 § 1(a)) might be the act that would qualify as a crime.[126] In the case of *Akayesu*, the ICTR Trial Chamber stated that the crime of murder, in the context of crimes against humanity under Article 3 of its Statute, was the "unlawful, intentional killing of a human being" when, "at the time of the killing the accused or a subordinate had the intention to kill or inflict bodily harm on the deceased having known that such bodily harm is likely to cause the victim's death, and is reckless whether death ensues or not."[127] This means that *dolus eventualis* or recklessness is sufficient to

120 UNGA Resolution 46/37D (preamble, § 8), adopted on December 6, 1991 by 122 votes to 16, with 22 abstentions.

121 UNGA Resolution 70/62, December 11, 2015 (preamble, § 6), "Convention on the Prohibition of the Use of Nuclear Weapons," adopted by 130 votes in favor against 48 against, with 8 abstentions.

122 Under Article 7 § 2(a), "attack directed against any civilian population" means "a course of conduct involving the multiple commission of acts referred to in paragraph 1 against any civilian population, pursuant to or in furtherance of a State or organizational policy to commit such attack."

123 *Prosecutor v. Kordic*, Case No. IT-95/14/2-A, Judgment, Appeals Chamber, December 17, 2004, § 94.

124 ICTY, *Prosecutor v. Dusko Tadić*, Judgment (Trial Chamber), Case No. IT-94-1, May 7, 1997, § 648.

125 S. Casey-Maslen, "Use of Nuclear Weapons as Genocide, a Crime against Humanity or a War Crime," in Nystuen et al., *Nuclear Weapons under International Law*, pp. 193–220, 204.

126 Article 7 § 1(a) does not require premeditation of the murder; in this respect, the French version is more precise ("*meutre*," and not "*assassinat*"); see, for more details, Y. Jurovics, "Article 7," in Fernandez and Pacreau, *Statut de Rome de la Cour pénale internationale*, pp. 417–478, 419 et seq. See also Schabas, *The International Criminal Court*, p. 158. For the mental element of the crime, see Article 30 of the Rome Statute.

127 *Prosecutor v. Akayesu*, Case No. ICTR-96-4-T, Judgment, Trial Chamber, September 2, 1998, § 589.

constitute *mens rea*. In light of this precedent and essentially for the reasons exposed in the subsection on war crimes, an attack on an inhabited area by means of nuclear weapons, capable of causing the death of and injuries to thousands of people, would be likely to meet the criteria of crimes against humanity within the meaning of Article 7 of the ICC Statute.

Moreover, in the context of nuclear weapons and considering what has been said on the crime of starvation, one cannot exclude the relevance of the crime of "extermination" within the meaning of Article 7 § 2(b) that "includes the intentional infliction of conditions of life, *inter alia* the deprivation of access to food and medicine, calculated to bring about the destruction of part of a population."[128]

4. The use of nuclear weapons as genocide

A significant overlap can occur between crimes against humanity and genocide.[129] As far as the latter is concerned – according to the ICTY Appeals Chamber, "one of the worst crimes known to humankind"[130] and not by chance enumerated first in the Rome Statute – it has been recalled above that the ICJ, in its 1996 Advisory Opinion, clearly affirmed the relevance of this rule in the context of nuclear weapons, the condition being that the perpetrators of a nuclear attack intended to destroy one of the groups enumerated in Article II of the Genocide Convention.[131] This condition was maintained in the Rome Statute, adopted two years after the Advisory Opinion, which defines genocide as any of the acts listed in Article 6 "committed with intent to destroy, in whole or in part, a national, ethnical, racial or religious groups, as such."[132]

As far as the *actus reus* of genocide is concerned, the obvious consequences of the use of nuclear weapons would be swift and widespread death and injury.[133] The destructive power of nuclear weapons is likely to cause the death of thousands of people and to provoke significant injuries to others. As a result, Article 6 (a) and (b) might be applicable, punishing the act of "killing members of the group"[134]

128 See, in this sense, Casey-Maslen, "Use of Nuclear Weapons as Genocide," p. 204.

129 See Schabas, *The International Criminal Court*, p. 135.

130 *Prosecutor v. Krstić*, Case No. IT-98-33-A, Judgment, Appeals Chamber, April 19, 2004, § 134.

131 ICJ Reports 1996, § 26.

132 The ICTY Trial Chamber observed that Article 4 § 2 of its Statute requires the "intent to destroy, in whole or in part, a national, ethnical, racial or religious group, as such" (*Prosecutor v. Sikirica et al.*, Case No. IT-95-8-T, Judgment, Trial Chamber, September 3, 2001, §§ 57 et seq.). The ICTR Appeals Chamber confirmed that genocide is a crime of "specific intent" (*Prosecutor v. Ntakirutimana et al.*, Case No. ICTR-96-10-A and ICTR-96-17-A, Judgment, Appeals Chamber, December 13, 2004, § 364; and *Prosecutor v. Niyitegeka*, Case No. ICTR-96-14-A, Judgment, Appeals Chamber, 9 July 2004, § 54).

133 Casey-Maslen, "Use of Nuclear Weapons as Genocide," p. 196.

134 In the case of *Kayishema & Ruzindana*, Case No. ICTR-95-1-T, Judgment, Trial Chamber, May 21, 1999, the ICTR Trial Chamber found that there was "virtually no difference

and "causing serious bodily or mental harm to members of the group."[135] But even the third category (c) listed in Article 6 might be relevant in the circumstances of a nuclear attack, prohibiting the act of "deliberately inflicting on the group conditions of life calculated to bring about its physical destruction in whole or in part." In the case of *Akayesu*, the ICTR held that:

> the means of deliberate inflicting on the group conditions of life calculated to bring about its physical destruction, in whole or part, include, *inter alia*, subjecting a group of people to a subsistence diet, systematic expulsion from homes and the reduction of essential medical services below minimum requirement.[136]

A nuclear attack could, in particular due to the radioactive fallout it generates, destroy the basis for agriculture, farming, and fishing for a considerable period of time and within a wide geographic area and, thus, make an entire region inhabitable. Moreover, as observed above,[137] it is more than doubtful whether survivors of nuclear explosions could be adequately assisted in the aftermath of such a blast. Therefore, Article 6(c) might be relevant as well. The "Elements of Crimes" for Article 6 (a) to (c) indicate that the conduct considered must have taken place "in the context of a manifest pattern of similar conduct directed against that group or [have been] conduct that could itself effect such destruction."[138] A detonation of a nuclear weapon is likely to be covered by the second part of that sentence.[139]

In light of its unmatched destructive power, it is suggested here that the use of nuclear weapons could constitute genocide, if denoting a specific intent to destroy, in whole or in part, one of the groups mentioned in Article 6 of the Rome Statute.

between the term 'killing' in the English version and '*meurtre*' in the French version" (§ 104). This view was confirmed by the Appeals Chamber noting "that if the word 'virtually' is interpreted in a manner that suggests a difference, thought minimal, between the two terms, it would construe them both as referring to intentional but not necessarily premeditated murder, this being, in its view, the meaning to be assigned to the word '*meurtre*'" (*Prosecutor v. Kayishema & Ruzindana*, Case No. ICTR-95-1-A, Judgment, Appeals Chamber, June 1, 2001, § 151).

135 See, in this regard, Schabas, *The International Criminal Court*, pp. 131–132.

136 *Prosecutor v. Akayesu*, Trial Chamber, Case No. ICTR-94-4-T, September 2, 1998, § 506.

137 This volume, inter alia, Chapter 7, section B.2.c).

138 ICC, "Elements of Crimes," published by the ICC, The Hague, 2011, pp. 2–3, https://www.icc-cpi.int/NR/rdonlyres/336923D8-A6AD-40EC-AD7B-45BF9DE73D56/0/ElementsOfCrimesEng.pdf (accessed March 1, 2017).

139 Casey-Maslen, "Use of Nuclear Weapons as Genocide," p. 196.

5. Conclusions

To sum up this subsection, it can be recalled that different war crime provisions under the ICC Statute might come into play if nuclear weapons are used as a means of warfare. Moreover, due to its particularly destructive impact on potential victims, such use could also amount to crimes against humanity or, provided *mens rea* of this crime can be proven, the crime of genocide.

General conclusions and proposals for progress toward a world without nuclear weapons

Each chapter of the present study has been summarized and the most important aspects of humanization of arms control identified. They do not have to be reiterated at length here. It is, however, appropriate to highlight where the added value of such a human-centered approach to arms control lies and how it can be used in the future on the path toward a world without nuclear weapons.

A. CONSIDERING THE HUMAN-CENTERED APPROACH TO NUCLEAR WEAPONS AS PART OF A GENERAL HUMANIZATION OF INTERNATIONAL LAW

In the introductory remarks to Part I of the present study, it has been indicated that the notion of "human security" would replace concepts of security which focus exclusively on the security of the State. The same has been observed in the field of development where there is a trend toward a socio-economic development, placing human beings at the center of the discourse, in the sense of a "sustainable" and "human" development. In the same line of thought, it certainly makes sense that arms control should be humanized too. The initial examples have been, as indicated, the Ottawa and Oslo Conventions and, more recently, the ATT. A certain humanization has already also taken place in the field of nuclear weapons, in particular through the adoption of the two treaties limiting and prohibiting nuclear testing (PTBT and CTBT), both heavily inspired by human-centered arguments, as well as by the five treaties establishing regional NWFZ. This trend has been confirmed more recently, inter alia, by the three conferences on the humanitarian impact of nuclear weapons, where new evidence for the devastating impact of nuclear weapons on human beings has been presented. Those efforts should be seen as part of a larger picture; in that spirit, Cançado Trindade claims that the whole international legal order is being humanized today.[1]

1 See the title of his book, *International Law for Humankind: Towards a New Jus Gentium*, 2nd edn, Leiden and Boston, 2013.

B. CONSIDERING THE HUMAN-CENTERED APPROACH TO NUCLEAR WEAPONS AS THE ONLY SUSTAINABLE SOLUTION FOR NUCLEAR DISARMAMENT

The traditional security-based debate, inspired by the logic of coexistence, as experienced in the Cold War, has not proven successful and can no longer serve as a model for the future. Therefore, the alternative solution consisting of placing the individual at the forefront of the debate has to be promoted. It is more democratic insofar as it involves civil society and considers all States on an equal footing, contrary to more traditional nuclear weapons or relevant fora, such as the NPT or the Conference on Disarmament (CD), overshadowed and dominated by the privileges enjoyed by the permanent members of the UN Security Council, all possessors of nuclear weapons with their own security agendas, and characterized by the consensus principle capable of blocking all progress. In order to be sustainable and credible in the long run, more participatory and open discussions must replace, or at least reinforce, such fora. The OEWG on nuclear disarmament, held in 2013 and 2016, is a good example for such a new type of institution. It is expected that the negotiations due to start in 2017 will also be of the "new" kind.

C. MAINSTREAMING THE HUMAN-CENTERED APPROACH TO NUCLEAR WEAPONS

It is noteworthy to mention that several human rights institutions have dealt with the inhuman effects of nuclear weapons or related activities, as outlined in the present study, such as the HRC in its General Comments Nos. 6 and 14, devoted to the right to life (Article 6 ICCPR), the CESCR in its General Comment No. 14 on the right to the highest standard of health and in its General Comment No. 15 on the right to water, the UN Special Rapporteur on the implication for human rights of the environmentally sound management and disposal of hazardous substances and wastes, Calin Georgescu, having visited the Marshall Islands, and the Special Rapporteur on the right of everyone to the enjoyment of the highest attainable standard of physical and mental health, Anand Grover, having examined the situation in Japan after the Fukushima accident.

It can be expected that the debate on nuclear weapons and related activities will be further "exported" to other human rights fora. The HRC is currently preparing a new General Comment on the right to life, hopefully giving due regard to nuclear weapons and other weapons of mass destruction (WMD), as it has done in the past.

D. APPLYING THE HUMAN-CENTERED APPROACH ON A DAILY BASIS: INTERPRETATION OF EXISTING ARMS CONTROL TREATIES IN LIGHT OF HUMANITARIAN PRINCIPLES AND HUMAN RIGHTS

In accordance with Article 31 § 3(c) of the VCLT, which is customary in nature,[2] "any relevant rules of international law applicable in the relations between the parties" must be taken into account in the interpretation of a treaty. In other words, a treaty cannot be interpreted in a vacuum, but must be considered as part of a wider legal system. Therefore, even if a tribunal may only have jurisdiction with regard to a particular instrument, it must always interpret and apply that instrument according to its relationship with its normative environment. Koskenniemi refers to this means of interpretation by the expression "systemic integration."[3] This kind of integration is facilitated, as far as principles of humanitarian law and human rights are concerned, by the fact that many of them are imposed on States Parties on customary grounds, without necessitating the ratification of the relevant instruments.

In other words, in the interpretation of a treaty imposing a disarmament obligation, in particular Article VI NPT, principles of humanitarian law and human rights law are taken into consideration.[4]

E. PURSUING THE REGIONAL APPROACH TO NUCLEAR DISARMAMENT

As stressed in the present study, the establishment of NWFZ has to be seen in light of the promotion of peace, considerations of humanity, and the aspirations of humankind to rid the world of the threat of nuclear weapons forever.[5] These can be seen as ideal examples for a human-centered approach to nuclear arms control.

Moreover, the potential for the establishment of NWFZ in further regions in the future has been discussed. The establishment of such a zone in the Middle

2 See, among others, *LaGrand (Germany v. United States of America)*, ICJ, Reports 2001, § 99; and *Avena and Other Mexican Nationals (Mexico v. United States of America)*, ICJ Reports 2004, § 83.

3 International Law Commission, "Fragmentation of International Law: Difficulties Arising from the Diversification and Expansion of International Law," Report of the Study Group of the International Law Commission, finalised by Marty Koskenniemi, A/CN.4/L.682, April 13, 2006, p. 206.

4 D. Rietiker, "The Meaning of Article VI of the Treaty on the Non-Proliferation of Nuclear Weapons: Analysis under the Rules of Treaty Interpretation," in J. L. Black-Branch and D. Fleck (eds.), *Nuclear Non-Proliferation in International Law*, The Hague, 2014, pp. 47–84, 68–77.

5 Cançado Trindade, *International Law for Humankind: Towards a New Jus Gentium*, 2nd edn., Leiden and Boston, 2013, pp. 405 et seq.

East has been seriously discussed for many years,[6] even though the process experienced a certain setback during the 2015 NPT Review Conference. It goes without saying that a legally binding instrument declaring this historically unstable and troubled region forever nuclear-free would constitute an important step in the peace process and give hope for further steps toward achieving a world free from nuclear weapons.

The regional approach, more modest but more realistic than the universal approach, might be promising. If an increasing number of regions can decide in favor of such treaties, including the conclusion of protocols by which the status of those zones is recognized by NWS and by which they undertake not to use nuclear weapons in those regions, the puzzle of global denuclearization will be complete sooner or later.

Moreover, it is generally asserted that, especially in the field of human rights, regional solutions, such as the regional courts (ECtHR, IACtHR, and ACtHR), are more efficient than universal mechanisms, in particular since they more easily take into account local specificities than a global treaty regime and because solidarities between the parties are supposed to be deeper. The same applies, without doubt, to the field of arms control.

F. LEARNING FROM THE OTTAWA AND OSLO CONVENTIONS (I): BANNING NUCLEAR WEAPONS AS SOON AS POSSIBLE

Much of the effort in the field of nuclear disarmament is made today toward the goal of a new treaty that would, at the very least, prohibit the use of nuclear weapons. The conviction that no use of these weapons would respect the basic principles of humanitarian and human rights law, as confirmed in the present analysis, is the driving force behind this objective. Moreover, the harm inflicted, in particular, to the civil population during and long after the actual attack, as a result of radioactive contamination, is even worse in the case of nuclear weapons than in that of anti-personnel mines or cluster munitions.

As things stand at the time of writing, the UN General Assembly has adopted Resolution L.41 (October 27, 2016), calling for negotiations for the conclusion of a new treaty banning nuclear weapons to start in 2017. It is likely that such a treaty has much in common with the Ottawa and Oslo Conventions, characterized, as explained in Part I of the present study, by the absolute, non-reciprocal duty ("never under any circumstances") to refrain from using such weapons, including as a means of retaliation. Other duties flowing from the general clauses of the Ottawa and Oslo Conventions (Articles 1) might also be included in a new treaty,

6 See, for a recent document on this topic, Resolution UNGA 66/25 of December 13, 2011 (Establishment of a nuclear-weapon free zone in the region of the Middle-East).

despite the fact that they are also already foreseen in other instruments, in particular the NPT. As it has proven impossible to secure the CTBT's entry into force, even after 20 years, the confirmation of an absolute prohibition on nuclear testing might also be of some use.

In view of the uncontrollable effects of nuclear weapons, a new treaty banning nuclear weapons should also reiterate the principles of humanitarian law and the Martens Clause, and include clauses on victim assistance. Accordingly, it should take on a broad definition of "victims," including persons who suffer from psychological harm, economic loss, or social marginalization or stigmatization.[7] Victim assistance should also be granted in a gender- and age-sensitive manner, taking into account the needs of particularly vulnerable groups, such as women, children, and indigenous peoples. These aspects have been clearly neglected, as indicated in the present study, both in the aftermath of the Fukushima accident and in the context of nuclear testing on the Marshall Islands and elsewhere.

Finally, considering the transboundary damage caused by a nuclear explosion and the *erga omnes* nature of many of the human rights that would be breached by a nuclear attack, a clause such as Article 21 §§ 1 and 2 of the Oslo Convention would be very useful, requiring the States Parties to encourage other States to join the new treaty and to discourage third States from using nuclear weapons.

G. LEARNING FROM THE OTTAWA AND OSLO CONVENTIONS (II): CIVIL SOCIETY'S SUCCESSFUL CAMPAIGNING

There is no doubt that the Ottawa and Oslo processes were only successful thanks to civil society's skillful strategic campaigning. Several elements that characterized those processes, described in Part I of the present study, are also ingredients in the ongoing debate on nuclear disarmament: first, the pursuit of a clear and rather simple first goal, namely, the ban on an entire category of weapons; second, the humanitarian ideals as the driving factor behind the conclusion of a new treaty; third, the advocating and campaigning efforts in favor of those humanitarian concerns made by civil society and other actors (international organizations, academia, etc.), which alerted the international community by presenting new evidence for the intolerable sufferings caused, in particular, to the civilian population in the event of a nuclear explosion; fourth, the new avenues that civil society has chosen, outside the traditional disarmament channels, in particular outside the CD, which has been blocked for many years due to the consensus principle; fifth, the essential role played by medical and other professional experts, from the ICRC and other organizations experienced in field missions, who, reiterating their experience in Hiroshima and Nagasaki, have demonstrated the

7 See, for instance, Article 2 § 1 of the Oslo Convention.

impossibility of an adequate humanitarian and medical response to a nuclear weapons explosion; sixth, the support for the activities of civil society in favor of the ban on nuclear weapons by a group of like-minded States; and, seventh, the involvement of the victims and survivors of nuclear weapons, in particular the "Hibakusha" and victims of nuclear testing, who have directed the attention of the international community to the disastrous humanitarian impact of the weapons concerned.

If history repeats itself, one can expect rather short negotiations on a new treaty outlawing nuclear weapons and its conclusion and entry into force in due course, as was the case for the Ottawa and Oslo Conventions.

H. LEARNING FROM THE CWC: PREPARING FOR NUCLEAR DISARMAMENT

Given the difficult international political environment, it seems unrealistic that NWS will in the near future commit themselves to a treaty banning nuclear weapons. From this author's point of view, such a treaty nevertheless has its added value, in particular since it is likely to create the necessary momentum to break the stalemate which has existed in multilateral nuclear disarmament for two decades. Moreover, it fortifies the international law norms against nuclear weapons by explicitly spelling out, for the first time in a universal treaty, an absolute prohibition on the use of nuclear weapons.

A treaty banning nuclear weapons can nevertheless only be regarded as a first step toward a world without nuclear weapons. Such a treaty has to be followed by measures imposing nuclear disarmament under strict and effective international control. But there also, States can rely on and learn from past experience. In fact, the example of chemical weapons demonstrates that a ban on the use of a given weapon (i.e. the 1925 Geneva Protocol) is sometimes the triggering factor for a more comprehensive ban on the same weapon category to be concluded in the future (i.e. the 1993 CWC), including a duty to destroy the weapons and devices possessed. Both treaties have been concluded, at least partly, for the sake of humanity, as indicated in Part I of the present study, and are therefore relevant examples for a new treaty banning nuclear weapons.

In an ideal situation, should a treaty banning nuclear weapons, or at least their use, be concluded among NNWS in the near future, a protocol thereto, or an independent treaty concluded exclusively among the NWS, could follow. It should impose a schedule for the destruction of nuclear weapons under strict and effective international control, as is the case for chemical weapons (OPCW) and, in addition, a guarantee not to use such weapons against NNWS having accepted the ban treaty, similar to the duties which flow from certain protocols to the five treaties establishing regional NWFZ.

I. PLEADING THE ABSOLUTE ILLEGALITY OF USE OF NUCLEAR WEAPONS GIVEN THE NEW EVIDENCE FOR THE DESTRUCTIVE IMPACT OF NUCLEAR WEAPONS (I): ASSESSMENT IN LIGHT OF HUMANITARIAN LAW

It has been advocated in Part II of the present study that the possibility of using nuclear weapons, including low-yield or tactical nuclear weapons, in a manner which is in compliance with international humanitarian law is unthinkable. The new evidence and information gathered since the 1996 Advisory Opinion of the ICJ, including very convincing studies analyzing hypothetical nuclear attacks on cities such as Rotterdam or Lyon, suggest that nuclear weapons cannot be used without violating basic rules of international humanitarian law due to the uncontrollability of their impact, in terms of space, but also in terms of time, since those weapons might endanger, due to the radiation causing cancer and other diseases, the survival of humankind. The uncontrollable effects of nuclear weapons have an influence on the assessment of the principles of discrimination and proportionality as well as that of the unnecessary suffering rule, in particular when considered widely, taking into consideration the well-being and health of present and future generations.

Moreover, apart from those general principles of humanitarian law, more specific rules of the laws of war have been cited which place considerable limits on States in having recourse to nuclear weapons as a means of warfare. Those rules impose on States a duty to respect, inter alia, works and installations containing dangerous forces as well as cultural property, or prohibit the use of starvation of the civilian population as a means of warfare. Another rule commands the States to respect and protect medical units and to guarantee and facilitate the passage of humanitarian relief for civilians in need. For the reasons outlined in the present study, those rules are very relevant in the case of use of nuclear weapons. Moreover, they are today considered to be of a customary nature and, as a result, applicable even to States that have not ratified the relevant international instruments.

In light of the foregoing, it has been concluded that there exists a presumption of illegality of the use of nuclear weapons under humanitarian law. States still relying on nuclear weapons, which have so far been very discrete in the recent humanitarian debate, would have to rebut that presumption with convincing and plausible arguments.

J. PLEADING THE ABSOLUTE ILLEGALITY OF THE USE OF NUCLEAR WEAPONS (PART II): ASSESSMENT IN LIGHT OF HUMAN RIGHTS LAW

In addition to humanitarian law, it has also been demonstrated that human rights law places important limits on States in their decision to use nuclear weapons. Civil and political rights would be affected as much as economic, social, and cultural ones.

It has been asserted that human rights law would be applicable to the use of nuclear weapons and that such an act would fall into the jurisdiction of an attacking State. Several scenarios have been drawn in Part II of the study: First, the actual attack with a nuclear weapon which would constitute a total denial of all civil and political rights of the immediate victims and, in particular, would amount to breaches of the right to life, the prohibition of inhuman and degrading treatment (including torture), the prohibition of genocide, the right to respect for private life and home, and the right to property. A particular convincing argument in favor of illegality of nuclear weapons flows from the *jus cogens* nature of some of these rights, in particular the prohibition of torture or genocide. Those rights cannot be derogated from, even in times of public emergency or war.

Another conclusion of the same Chapter is that, in the aftermath of a nuclear attack, it would be almost impossible to comply with the positive obligations, as imposed by the relevant human rights instruments, to avoid and minimize deaths in a life-endangering situation. The report of the Special Rapporteur on the right of everyone to the enjoyment of the highest attainable standard of physical and mental health, having visited Fukushima, confirms those findings. His conclusions are similar to those drawn by the ICRC regarding the humanitarian situation after nuclear weapons use – namely, the impossibility of guaranteeing adequate medical and humanitarian assistance.

It has also been concluded that a regional nuclear war would have significant effects on the enjoyment of economic, social, and cultural rights, even by people who live far away from where the actual nuclear explosions take place. Given the transboundary impact of nuclear weapons as a result of radioactive fallout, the importance of the extra-territorial application of these rights and their *erga omnes* nature has to be emphasized. It has also been stressed that the rural, often poorer population, engaged in agricultural activities, would suffer in a disproportionate manner since climate change and "nuclear winter" are likely to affect them more seriously than people living in urban centers.

Various rights are likely to be affected by a regional nuclear war, such as the rights to development, to the highest standard of health, to a healthy environment, and to an adequate standard of living, but particular attention has to be drawn to the right to food and to water, the latter being affected by contamination of lakes, watercourses, and groundwater. The dynamic jurisprudence of the ECtHR regarding the right to water illustrates the relevance of this – relatively embryonic – right in the eventuality of the use of nuclear weapons.

K. USING THE HUMAN-CENTERED APPROACH FOR DISARMAMENT (I): HUMANITARIAN LAW

If it is agreed upon that no use of nuclear weapons would be legal under humanitarian law, it is hard to defend the argument that development, manufacture, production, and acquisition, as well as possession, is compatible with this body of law. From this author's point of view, a duty to reduce and eliminate the stockpiles of those weapons can be deduced, in particular, from the following principles of humanitarian law, all having been addressed in the present study, imposing significant limits on the freedom of States in the choice of methods and means of warfare: first, from the Martens Clause, which requires the filling of a possible legal vacuum by principles of international law, principles of humanity, and the dictates of public conscience; second, from common Article 1 to the Geneva Conventions and Article 1 § 1 of Additional Protocol I, imposing an obligation to respect and ensure respect for international humanitarian law in all circumstances; and, third, from Article 36 of Additional Protocol I, which imposes the duty to determine whether a new weapon would be compatible with this Protocol and other rules of international law. Interpreted in good faith and in light of the conclusions drawn above, according to which the use of nuclear weapons cannot be legal under humanitarian law, those principles must be read as imposing on States an obligation not to develop, manufacture, produce, acquire, or possess such weapons.

L. USING THE HUMAN-CENTERED APPROACH FOR DISARMAMENT (II): HUMAN RIGHTS, THEIR SPECIAL NATURE, AND EFFECTIVE INSTITUTIONS

It has been shown throughout the present study that human rights law has its advantages: applicability in all circumstances, including in times of armed conflict; special nature of some rights (*jus cogens*) which do not allow any derogation; institutional support, inter alia, by regional courts which can render legally binding judgments that have to be executed by the States Parties having violated human rights; and positive obligations imposed on States Parties to take adequate measures to protect the individuals under their jurisdiction against harmful acts of other persons or private entities. It is this author's conviction that those added values of human rights law should be used for the cause of nuclear disarmament in light of the human-centered approach to nuclear weapons.

In this regard, it can be reiterated that human rights courts have been sensitive to situations that are relevant for nuclear weapons. For instance, regional human rights courts have repeatedly condemned indiscriminate attacks against the civilian population, the use of anti-personnel mines having caused death and serious injuries among the local populations, or the use of chemicals for law-enforcement and against terrorism. The States which have failed in their human rights duties have had to remedy the situation and pay compensation to the victims. In some instances, the particular vulnerability of certain groups of victims, such as indigenous peoples, children, and women, has explicitly been recognized.

In terms of strategic litigation in favor of nuclear disarmament, what seems particularly interesting to elaborate upon is the possibility to deduce, from positive obligations recognized by international courts, especially in the field of environment and health, a duty of NWS to dispose of their nuclear weapons due to the risks those weapons represent to the life and health of people by accidental detonation.

As a matter of fact, modern human rights treaties, in particular through the right to life and the right to security, impose a positive obligation on States to take appropriate steps to safeguard the lives of those within their jurisdiction, especially when dangerous activities are at stake, and there is no doubt that the possession of nuclear weapons is such a risk. It has also been stressed that States are furthermore obliged to prevent private actors from perpetrating human rights violations. As a result, violations of human rights caused by terrorists by the use of nuclear weapons would engage the responsibility of a State possessing nuclear weapons if it turns out that that State has not taken the precaution that could reasonably have been expected from it.

The risks inherent in the possession of nuclear weapons is moreover reinforced by the fact that many nuclear weapons are on a high state of alert and ready to be used within a few minutes, on the one hand, and that the desire of terrorist groups to acquire and use WMD is said to be growing, on the other. As a result, since a zero-risk possession of nuclear weapons cannot be guaranteed, it might be argued that there exists, under the right to life, a duty to dispose of nuclear weapons and other nuclear devices.

The population of a State possessing nuclear weapons should at least be granted the right to receive information, under the right to life or the freedom of opinion and expression, about the risks inherent in the possession of nuclear weapons stockpiles and the preventive measures taken against accidents and the acquisition by terrorists of nuclear weapons or similar devices from the States' stockpiles.

M. ADDRESSING THE PERPETRATORS: THE POTENTIAL ROLE OF THE ICC IN THE PROSECUTION OF CRIMES CAUSED BY THE USE OF NUCLEAR WEAPONS

The prosecution by the ICC of the use of chemical weapons in Syria has been seriously discussed for some time. Likewise, it has been shown in Part II of the present study that a use of nuclear weapons could amount to war crimes, crimes against humanity, and, provided *mens rea* can be proven, genocide. The fact that neither the Rome Conference nor the Kampala Review Conference could agree on the inclusion of a specific war crime for the use of nuclear weapons is, as explained above, irrelevant.

It is suggested here that the mere knowledge of the possibility of being prosecuted and punished by the ICC for the use of nuclear weapons might have a preventive effect. More should be done to provide for the imposition of criminal sanctions on the perpetrators of nuclear weapons use and a clause should be inserted in a potential treaty banning nuclear weapons providing for a legal basis for the prosecution and punishment of such use by the ICC.

N. LEARNING FROM VICTIMIZATION OF NUCLEAR TESTING AND NUCLEAR ACCIDENTS, ESPECIALLY OF PARTICULARLY VULNERABLE GROUPS

In Part II of the present study, it has been shown that, based on "real-life" experiences endured by victims and survivors of nuclear testing and nuclear accidents, such as those which occurred in Chernobyl and Fukushima, it is safe to claim that certain groups of people suffer more than others in such situations.

The protection of indigenous peoples raises very specific problems, in particular due to their particular relationship to their traditionally possessed lands. The example of the Marshall Islands shows that nuclear testing causes forced displacement and deprives such peoples of their cultural identity. Lessons can be drawn from the destiny of the Marshallese peoples, a fortiori, for potential nuclear weapons use which would certainly also result in resettlement of the surviving peoples.

Moreover, it is well established that children and women are generally more affected by nuclear testing than adult men. Infant and child mortality, as well as certain types of cancer and congenital deformations, have disproportionately risen among children in the Semipalatinsk area and around other nuclear test sites, as well as after the Chernobyl accident. Finally, it has also been indicated that nuclear testing and nuclear accidents have caused particularly serious problems for women's reproductive rights. Those aspects call for additional efforts in favor of the entry into force of the CTBT and naturally raise the question of the rights of future generations.

O. PROMOTING THE RIGHTS OF FUTURE GENERATIONS

As indicated above, the effects of nuclear weapons are uncontrollable in space and time. Regarding the time element, the use of nuclear weapons, due to their considerable impact on human health, environment, and development, would affect inter-generational justice and endanger the rights of future generations. The present and future generations may thereby be deprived of an equitable share of natural resources for their development and an adequate environment. As indicated above, the ICJ, in its 1996 Advisory Opinion, recognized that nuclear weapons have the potential to destroy civilization as a whole and, therefore, are a serious danger to future generations.[8]

In light of the foregoing, what could more pertinently summarize the idea of inter-generational justice and rights of future generations in respect of nuclear weapons than the following extract of the speech given by John F. Kennedy on July 26, 1963 on the PTBT:

> . . . the number of children and grandchildren with cancer in their bones, with leukemia in their blood, or with poison in their lungs might seem

8 ICJ Reports 1996, § 35.

statistically small to some, in comparison with natural health hazards. But this is not a natural health hazard – and it is not a statistical issue. The loss of even one human life, or the malformation of even one baby – who may be born long after we are gone – should be of concern to us all. Our children and grandchildren are not merely statistics toward which we can be indifferent.[9]

9 Radio and television address to the American People on the PTBT, July 26, 1963, https://www.jfklibrary.org/Research/Research-Aids/JFK-Speeches/Nuclear-Test-Ban-Treaty_19630726.aspx (accessed March 8, 2017).

Bibliography

BOOKS AND COLLECTED COURSES

Adeniji O., *The Treaty of Pelindaba on the African Nuclear-Weapon-Free-Zone*, UNIDIR, New York and Geneva, 2002.

Akiner S., *The Formation of Kazakh Identity, From Tribe to Nation-State*, London, 1995.

Beauchamp S., *Explosive Remnants of War and the Protection of Human Beings under Public International Law*, Geneva, 2008, pp. 335–354.

Birnie P., Boyle A., and Redgwell C., *International Law and the Environment*, 3rd edn., Oxford and New York, 2009.

Boisson de Chazournes L., *Fresh Water in International Law*, Oxford, 2013.

Borrie J. and Caughley T., *An Illusion of Safety: Challenges of Nuclear Weapon Detonations for United Nations Humanitarian Coordination and Response*, UNIDIR, New York and Geneva, 2014.

Breitegger A., *Cluster Munitions and International Law: Disarmament with a Human Face*, London and New York, 2012.

Brown Weiss E., *International Law for a Water-Scarce World*, The Hague Academy of International Law Monographs, vol. 7, Boston and Leiden, 2013.

Cançado Trindade A. A., *International Law for Humankind: Towards a New Jus Gentium*, 2nd edn., Leiden and Boston, 2013.

Cassese A., Gaeta P., and Jones J. (eds.), *The Rome Statute of the International Criminal Court: A Commentary*, vol. I, Oxford, 2002.

Den Dekker G., *The Law of Arms Control – International Supervision and Enforcement*, The Hague, Boston, and London, 2001.

Detrick S., *The United Nations Convention on the Rights of the Child, A Guide to the "Travaux Préparatoires,"* Dordrecht, Boston, and London, 1992.

Garcia D., *Disarmament Diplomacy and Human Security: Regimes, Norms and Moral Progress in International Relations*, New York, 2012.

García Robles A., "Mesures de désarmement dans des zones particulières: le Traité visant l'interdiction des armes nucléaires," *Collected Courses of The Hague Academy of International Law*, vol. 133, 1971, pp. 43–134.

Gautam-Ott B., *The Legality of Landmines and International Law*, PhD, Geneva, 2004.

Gillis M., *Le désarmement: Un guide de référence*, 3rd edn., New York, 2013.

Goldblat J. and Cox D., *Nuclear Weapons Tests: Prohibition or Limitation?*, Stockholm and Oxford, 1988.

Gondek M., *The Reach of Human Rights in a Globalising World: Extraterritorial Application of Human Rights Treaties*, Antwerp, 2009.

Hamel-Green M., *Regional Initiatives on Nuclear- and WMD-Free Zones: Cooperative Approaches to Arms Control and Non-Proliferation*, UNIDIR, 2005.

Hamel-Green M., *The South Pacific Nuclear Free Zone Treaty: A Critical Assessment*, Peace Research Centre, Research School of Pacific Studies, Australian National University, Sydney, Australian National University Press, 1990.

Harris D., O'Boyle M., and Warbrick C., *Law of the European Convention on Human Rights*, 3rd edn., Oxford, 2014.

Henckaerts J.-M. and Doswald-Beck L., *Customary International Humanitarian Law*, vol. I: *Rules*, Cambridge, 2005.

Joyner D. H., *Interpreting the Nuclear Non-Proliferation Treaty*, Oxford and New York, 2011.

Kälin W. and Gabriel L., *Human Rights in Times of Occupation: The Case of Kuwait*, Bern, 1994.

Kellman B. and Tanzman E. A., *Manual for National Implementation of the Chemical Weapons Convention*, Chicago IL, 2nd edn., International Criminal Justice and Weapons Control Center, 1998.

Kissling C., *Civil Society and Nuclear Non-Proliferation: How do States Respond?*, Aldershot, 2008.

Lavieille J. M., *Droit international du désarmement et de la maîtrise des armements*, Paris and Montreal, 1997.

Maiocchi R., *L'ère atomique*, Florence, 1993.

Maresca L. and Maslen S. (eds.), *The Banning of Anti-Personnel Landmines: The Work of the International Committee of the Red Cross (1955–1999)*, Cambridge, 2000.

Maslen S., *A View from the Vanishing Point, Anti-Personnel Mines on the Battlefield under International Humanitarian Law*, PhD thesis submitted to Tilburg University, the Netherlands, 2000.

Maslen S., *Commentaries on Arms Control Treaties*, vol. 1: *The Convention on the Prohibition of the Use, Stockpiling, Production, and Transfer of Anti-Personnel Mines and on Their Destruction*, 2nd edn., Oxford and New York, 2005.

McGoldrick D., *The Human Rights Committee: Its Role in the Development of the International Covenant on Civil and Political Rights*, Oxford and New York, 1991.

Milanović M., *Extraterritorial Application of Human Rights Treaties: Law, Principles and Policy*, Oxford, 2011.

Murillo Chávarro J., *The Human Right to Water: A Legal Comparative Perspective at the International, Regional and Domestic Level*, Cambridge, 2015.

Naciones Unidas, *Las Zonas Libres de Armas Nucleares en el Siglo XXI*, New York and Geneva, UN-OPAL/UNIDIR, 1997.

National Research Council of the United States and Royal Society of Canada, *The Great Lakes Water Quality Agreement: An Evolving Instrument for Ecosystem Management*, Washington, DC, National Academy Press, 1985.

Nowak M., *UN Covenant on Civil and Political Rights, CCPR Commentary*, Kehl, Strasbourg, and Arlington, 2nd edn., 2005.

Nystuen G. and Casey-Maslen S. (eds.), *The Convention on Cluster Munitions: A Commentary*, Oxford and New York, 2010.

Peterson D. J., *Troubled Lands: The Legacy of Soviet Environmental Destruction*, Boulder, San Francisco, and Oxford, 1993.

Provost R., *International Human Rights and Humanitarian Law*, Cambridge, 2002.

Reid K., *A Practitioner's Guide to the European Convention on Human Rights*, 4th edn., London, 2012.
Rietiker D., *Le régime juridique des traités de maîtrise des armements: Plaidoyer pour l'unité de l'ordre juridique international*, Berne and Brussels, 2010.
Rogers A. P. V., *Law on the Battlefield*, Manchester, 1996.
Rombouts S. J., *Having a Say, Indigenous Peoples, International Law and Free, Prior and Informed Consent*, Oisterwijk, 2014.
Ruedin X.-B., *L'exécution des arrêts de la Cour Européenne des Droits de l'Homme: Procédure, obligations des Etats, pratique et réforme*, Basel, Brussels, and Paris, 2009.
Rutherford K. R., *Disarming States: The International Movement to Ban Landmines*, Praeger Security International, 2011.
Sauer T., *Nuclear Inertia: US Nuclear Weapons Policy After the Cold War*, London and New York, 2005.
Schabas W. A., *The International Criminal Court: A Commentary on the Rome Statute*, Oxford and New York, 2010.
Schwartz S. (ed.), *Atomic Audit: The Costs and Consequences of U.S. Nuclear Weapons Since 1940*, Washington, DC, 1998.
Shaker M. I., "The Evolving International Regime of Nuclear Non-Proliferation," *Collected Courses of The Hague Academy of International Law*, vol. 321, pp. 9–202.
Soka Gakkai Hiroshima Peace Committee Hiroshima, *6 August 1945, A Silence Broken*, Tokyo, 2014.
Tobin J., *The Right to Health in International Law*, Oxford, 2012.
Van Bueren G., *The International Law on the Rights of the Child*, Dordrecht, Boston, and London, 1995.
Villiger M., *Commentary on the 1969 Convention on the Law of Treaties*, Leiden and Boston, 2009.
Willett S., *The Costs of Disarmament: The South Asian Arms Dynamic*, Geneva, 2004.
Wittner L. S., *One World or None: A History of the World Nuclear Disarmament Movement through 1953*, vol. I, Stanford, 1993.
Wittner L. S., *Resisting the Bomb: A History of the World Nuclear Disarmament Movement, 1954–1970*, vol. II, Stanford, 1997.
Wittner L. S., *Toward Nuclear Abolition: A History of the World Nuclear Disarmament Movement, 1971 to the Present*, vol. III, Stanford, 2003.
Zermatten J., *La Convention des droits de l'enfant vingt ans plus tard*, Essai d'un bilan, Sion, 2010.

ARTICLES

Abi-Saab G., "On Discretion: Reflections on the Nature of the Consultative Function of the International Court of Justice," in L. Boisson de Chazournes and P. Sands (eds.), *International Law, the International Court of Justice and Nuclear Weapons*, Cambridge, 1999, pp. 36–50.
Acheson R., "Wider Consequences – Impact on Development," in B. Fihn (ed.), *Unspeakable Suffering: The Humanitarian Impact of Nuclear Weapons*, Geneva, 2013, pp. 59–65.
Akande D., "Can the ICC Prosecute for Use of Chemical Weapons in Syria?", *EJIL: Talk!*, August 23, 2013, http://www.ejiltalk.org/can-the-icc-prosecute-for-use-of-chemical-weapons-in-syria/ (accessed February 20, 2017).

Anastassov A., "The Sovereign Right to Peaceful Use of Nuclear Energy and International Environmental Law," in J. L. Black-Branch and D. Fleck (eds.), *Nuclear Non-Proliferation in International Law*, The Hague, 2014, pp. 159–197.

Arnett E., "Science, Technology, and Arms Control," in R. D. Burns (ed.), *Encyclopedia of Arms Control and Disarmament*, vol. 1/II, New York, Toronto, Oxford, Singapore, and Sydney, 1993, pp. 477–490.

Arnold R. and Wehrenberg S., "Article 8 § 2(b)(v)," in O. Triffterer and K. Ambos (eds.), *Rome Statute of the International Criminal Court: A Commentary*, 3rd edn., Munich, Portland, and Oxford, 2016, pp. 380–382.

Asada M., "A Path to a Comprehensive Prohibition of the Use of Chemical Weapons under International Law: From The Hague to Damascus," *Journal of Conflict & Security Law*, 2015, pp. 1–55.

Atapattu S., "Sustainable Development and the Right to Health," in M.-C. Cordonier Segger and C. G. Weeramantry (eds.), *Sustainable Justice: Reconciling Economic, Social and Environmental Law*, Leiden, 2005, pp. 355–363.

Avenhaus R. and Kyriakopoulos N., "Conceptual Framework," in R. Avenhaus, N. Kyriakopoulos, M. Richard, and G. Stein (eds.), *Verifying Treaty Compliance: Limiting Weapons of Mass Destruction and Monitoring Kyoto Protocol Provisions*, Berlin, 2006, pp. 13–37.

Bagshaw S., "Responding to the Detonation of Nuclear Weapons: A United Nations Humanitarian Perspective," in J. Borrie and T. Caughley (eds.), *Viewing Nuclear Weapons through a Humanitarian Lens*, New York and Geneva, 2013, pp. 118–130.

Barelli M., "The Role of Soft Law in the International Legal System: The Case of the United Nations Declaration on the Rights of Indigenous Peoples," *ICLQ*, vol. 58, 2009, pp. 957–983.

Barkhuysen T. and Van Emmerik M., "A Comparative View on the Execution of the Judgments of the European Court of Human Rights," in T. A. Christou and J. P. Raymond (eds.), *European Court of Human Rights, Remedies and Execution of Judgments*, British Institute of International and Comparative Law, 2005, pp. 1–23.

Bauer S. and Bromley M., "Implementing the Arms Trade Treaty: Building on Available Guidelines and Assistance Activities," *SIPRI Background Paper*, May 2015, http://books.sipri.org/files/misc/SIPRIBP1505.pdf (accessed February 20, 2017).

Bauer S., Beijer P., and Bromley M., "The Arms Trade Treaty: Challenges for the First Conference of States Parties," *SIPRI Insights on Peace and Security*, no. 2014/2, September 2014, http://books.sipri.org/files/insight/SIPRIInsight1402.pdf (accessed February 20, 2017).

Bauer S., Gusev B. I., Pivina L. M., et al., "Radiation Exposure due to Local Fallout from Soviet Atmospheric Nuclear Weapons Testing in Kazakhstan: Solid Cancer Mortality in the Semipalatinsk Historical Cohort," 1960–1999, *Radiation Research*, vol. 164, 2005, pp. 409–419.

Bengs B. L., "Legal Constraints upon the Use of a Tactical Nuclear Weapon against the Natanz Nuclear Facility in Iran," *George Washington International Law Review*, vol. 40, 2008, pp. 323–399.

Blake J. and Mahmud A., "A Legal 'Red Line'? Syria and the Use of Chemical Weapons in Civil Conflict," *UCLA L. Rev. Disc.*, vol. 61, 2013, pp. 244–260, http://www.uclalawreview.org/pdf/discourse/61-16.pdf (accessed February 20, 2017).

Blondel J.-L., "The Meaning of the Word 'Humanitarian' in Relation to the Fundamental Principles of the Red Cross and Red Crescent," *International Review of the Red Cross*, no. 273, November–December 1989, pp. 507–515.

Bodansky D., "Non Liquet and the Incompleteness of International Law," in L. Boisson de Chazournes and P. Sands (eds.), *International Law, the International Court of Justice and Nuclear Weapons*, Cambridge, 1999, pp. 153–170.

Boer B., "Environmental Law and Human Rights in the Asia-Pacific," in B. Boer (ed.), *Environmental Law Dimensions of Human Rights*, Oxford, 2015, pp. 135–179.

Boisson de Chazournes, L. and Condorelli, L. "Common Article 1 of the Geneva Conventions Revisited: Protecting Collective Interests," *International Review of the Red Cross (IRRC)*, no. 837, vol. 82, 2000, pp. 67–87.

Boisson de Chazournes L. and Sands P., "Introduction," in L. Boisson de Chazournes and P. Sands (eds.), *International Law, the International Court of Justice and Nuclear Weapons*, Cambridge, 1999, pp. 1–24.

Born H., Gill B., and Hänggi H., "Introduction," in H. Born, B. Gill, and H. Hänggi (eds.), *Governing the Bomb: Civilian Control and Democratic Accountability of Nuclear Weapons*, Oxford and SIPRI, 2010, pp. 1–24.

Borrie J., "Rethinking Multilateral Negotiations: Disarmament as Humanitarian Action," in J. Borrie and Martin Randin (eds.), *Alternative Approaches in Multilateral Decision Making, Disarmament as Humanitarian Action*, Geneva, 2005, pp. 7–37.

Brandes M., "'All's Well that Ends Well' or 'Much Ado About Nothing'?: A Commentary on the Arms Trade Treaty," *Goettingen Journal of International Law*, vol. 5, 2013, pp. 399–429, http://www.gojil.eu/issues/52/52_article_brandes.pdf (accessed February 15, 2017).

Brehm M., "Whose Security Is It Anyway? Towards a Treaty Prohibition of Nuclear Weapons," *EJIL:Talk!*, May 31, 2016, http://www.ejiltalk.org/whose-security-is-it-anyway-towards-a-treaty-prohibition-ofnuclear- weapons/ (accessed February 28, 2017).

Bromet E. J., Parkinson, D. K., Schulberg, H. C., et al., "Mental Health of Residents Near the Three Mile Island Reactor: A Comparative Study of Selected Group," *Journal of Preventive Psychiatry*, vol. 1(3), 1982, 225–276.

Bromley M., Cooper N., and Holtom P., "The UN Arms Trade Treaty: Arms Export Controls, the Human Security Agenda and the Lessons of History," *International Affairs*, vol. 88, 2012, pp. 1029–1048.

Brown Weiss E., "Opening the Door to the Environment and to Future Generations," in L. Boisson de Chazournes and P. Sands (eds.), *International Law, the International Court of Justice and Nuclear Weapons*, Cambridge, 1999, pp. 338–353.

Buffard I. and Zemanek K., "The Object and Purpose of a Treaty: An Enigma?" *Austrian Review of International & European Law*, vol. 3, 1998, pp. 311–343.

Bugnion F., "The International Committee of the Red Cross and Nuclear Weapons: From Hiroshima to the Dawn of the 21st Century," *International Review of the Red Cross*, vol. 87, no. 859, 2005, pp. 511–524.

Burroughs J., "The Vancouver Declaration and the Humanitarian Imperative for Nuclear Disarmament," *Nuclear Abolition Forum*, issue no. 1, October 2011, pp. 1–6, https://www.worldfuturecouncil.org/file/2016/01/NAF_2011_International_humanitarian_Law_and_nuclear_Weapons.pdf (accessed February 23, 2017).

Burroughs J., "International Humanitarian Law," in B. Fihn (ed.), *Unspeakable Suffering: The Humanitarian Impact of Nuclear Weapons*, 2013, pp. 68–75.

Burroughs J., "Legal Gap or Compliance Gap?", *Arms Control Today*, October 2015, https://www.armscontrol.org/ACT/2015_10/Letter-to-the-Editor/Legal%20Gap%20or%20Compliance%20Gap (accessed February 27, 2017).

Cannizzaro E., "Contextualizing Proportionality: *Jus Ad Bellum* and *Jus in Bello* in the Libanese War," *International Review of the Red Cross*, no. 864, December 2006, pp. 779–792.

Carnahan B. M., "Unnecessary Suffering, The Red Cross and Tactical Laser Weapons," *Loyola of Los Angeles International and Comparative Law Journal*, vol. 18, September 1996, pp. 705–732.

Casey-Maslen S., "The Use of Nuclear Weapons under Rules Governing the Conduct of Hostilities," in G. Nystuen, S. Casey-Maslen, and A. Golden Bersagel (eds.), *Nuclear Weapons under International Law*, Cambridge, 2014, pp. 91–127.

Casey-Maslen S., "The Right to a Remedy and Reparation for the Use of Nuclear Weapons," in G. Nystuen, S. Casey-Maslen, and A. Golden Bersagel (eds.), *Nuclear Weapons under International Law*, Cambridge, 2014, pp. 461–480.

Casey-Maslen S., "The Principles," in S. Casey-Maslen, A. Clapham, G. Giacca, and S. Parker, *The Arms Trade Treaty: A Commentary*, Oxford, 2016, pp. 33–40.

Casey-Maslen S., "Introduction," in S. Casey-Maslen, A. Clapham, G. Giacca, and S. Parker, *The Arms Trade Treaty: A Commentary*, Oxford, 2016, pp. 1–13.

Casey-Maslen S., "Preamble," in S. Casey-Maslen, A. Clapham, G. Giacca, and S. Parker, *The Arms Trade Treaty: A Commentary*, Oxford, 2016, pp. 17–32.

Casey-Maslen S., "Use of Nuclear Weapons as Genocide, a Crime against Humanity or a War Crime," in G. Nystuen, S. Casey-Maslen, and A. Golden Bersagel (eds.), *Nuclear Weapons under International Law*, Cambridge, 2014, pp. 193–220.

Casey-Maslen S. and Giacca G., "Article 6, Prohibitions," in S. Casey-Maslen, A. Clapham, G. Giacca, and S. Parker, *The Arms Trade Treaty: A Commentary*, Oxford, 2016, pp. 177–192.

Cassese A., "Weapons Causing Unnecessary Suffering: Are They Prohibited?", *Rivista di Diritto Internazionale*, vol. LVIII, 1975, pp. 12–42.

Charters C., "The Road to the Adoption of the Declaration on the Rights of Indigenous Peoples," *New Zealand Yearbook of International Law*, vol. 4, 2007, pp. 121–133.

Clapham A., "Article 7, Export and Export Assessment," in S. Casey-Maslen, A. Clapham, G. Giacca, and S. Parker, *The Arms Trade Treaty: A Commentary*, Oxford, 2016, pp. 244–285.

Clapham A., "Preamble (12th paragraph)," in G. Nystuen and S. Casey-Maslen (eds.), *The Convention on Cluster Munitions: A Commentary*, Oxford and New York, 2010, pp. 64–65.

Cook D., "An Insider's View of Nuclear Weapons Modernization," *Arms Control Today*, October 2016, pp. 14–18.

Cook R. J. and Undurraga V., "Article 12," in M. A. Freeman, C. Chinkin, and B. Rudolf (eds.), *The UN Convention on the Elimination of All Forms of Discrimination against Women*, Oxford, 2012, pp. 311–333.

Corden P. S., "Historical Context and Steps to Implement the CTBT," in M. Melamud, P. Meerts, and I. W. Zartman (eds.), *Banning the Bang or the Bomb? Negotiating the Nuclear Test Ban Regime*, Cambridge, 2014, pp. 17–31.

Corsi J., "Towards Peace through Legal Innovation: The Process and the Promise of the 2008 Cluster Munitions Convention," *Harvard Human Rights Journal*, vol. 22, 2009, pp. 145–157.

Cottier M. and Krivánek D., "Article 8 b) (xx)," in O. Triffterer and K. Ambos (eds.), *Rome Statute of the International Criminal Court, A Commentary*, 3rd edn., Munich, Oxford, and Baden-Baden, 2016, pp. 454–468.

Cottier M. and Richard E., "Article 8 § 2(b)(xxv)," in O. Triffterer and K. Ambos (eds.), *Rome Statute of the International Criminal Court: A Commentary*, 3rd edn., Munich, Portland, and Oxford, 2016, pp. 508–519.

Coulée F., "Article 120," in J. Fernandez and X. Pacreau (eds.), *Statut de Rome de la Cour pénale internationale: Commentaire article par article*, vol. II, Paris, 2012, pp. 2103–2116.

Coupland R. M., "Abhorrent Weapons and 'Superfluous Injury or Unnecessary Suffering': From Field Surgery to Law," *British Medical Journal*, vol. 315, November 29, 1997, pp. 1450–1452.

Dave B., "Kazakhstan Staggers under Its Nuclear Burden," *Transition*, November 17, 1997, pp. 12–13.

Davenport K., "UN Acts on Mideast Zone Amid Doubts," *Arms Control Today*, December 2015, https://www.armscontrol.org/ACT/2015_12/News/UN-Acts-on-Mideast-Zone-Amid-Doubts (accessed February 23, 2017).

David E., "La Convention de 2008 sur les armes à sous-munitions," *Revue générale de droit international public*, vol. 113, 2009, pp. 785–806.

De Feyter K., "Indigenous peoples," in *Realizing the Right to Development, Essays in Commemoration of 25 years of the United Nations Declaration on the Right to Development*, United Nations, Office of the High Commissioner, New York and Geneva, 2013, pp. 159–168.

Dinstein Y., "The Right to Life, Physical Integrity, and Liberty," in L. Henkin (ed.), *The International Bill of Rights: The Covenant on Civil and Political Rights*, New York, 1981, pp. 114–137.

Di Ruzza T., "The Convention on Cluster Munitions: Towards a Balance between Humanitarian and Military Considerations?" *Revue du droit militaire et du droit de la guerre*, vol. 47, 2008, pp. 405–448.

Docherty B., "Ending Civilian Suffering: The Purpose, Provisions, and Promise of Humanitarian Disarmament Law," *Austrian Review of International and European Law*, vol. 15, 2010, pp. 7–44.

Docherty B., "Breaking New Ground: The Convention on Cluster Munitions and the Evolution of International Humanitarian Law," *Human Rights Quarterly*, vol. 31, 2009, pp. 934–963.

Docherty B., Maresca L., Moyes R., and Reiterer M., "Article 2," in G. Nystuen and S. Casey-Maslen (eds.), *The Convention on Cluster Munitions: A Commentary*, Oxford and New York 2010, pp. 144–245.

Dörmann K. and Serralvo J., "Common Article 1 to the Geneva Conventions and the Obligation to Prevent International Humanitarian Law," *International Review of the Red Cross (IRRC)*, no. 895/896, vol. 96, 2014, pp. 706–736.

Doswald-Beck L., "Human Rights Law and Nuclear Weapons," in G. Nystuen, S. Casey-Maslen, and A. Golden Bersagel (eds.), *Nuclear Weapons under International Law*, Cambridge, 2014, pp. 435–460.

Drell S., Jeanloz R., and Peurifoy B., "Bunkers, Bombs, Radiation," *Los Angeles Times*, March 17, 2002, http://articles.latimes.com/2002/mar/17/opinion/oe-drell17 (accessed February 27, 2017).

Droege C., "The Interplay between International Humanitarian Law and International Human Rights Law in Situations of Armed Conflict," *Israel Law Review*, vol. 40, 2007, pp. 310–355.

Dumas L. J. and Nelson T. D., "Estimating the Economic Consequences of a Nuclear Weapons Explosion: Critical Factors," in B. Fihn (ed.), *Unspeakable Suffering: The Humanitarian Impact of Nuclear Weapons*, Geneva, 2013, pp. 50–57.

Dupuy P.-M., "Between the Individual and the State: International Law at a Crossroads?", in L. Boisson de Chazournes and P. Sands (eds.), *International Law, the International Court of Justice and Nuclear Weapons*, Cambridge, 1999, pp. 449–461.

Edmunds T., "The Environmental Movement in Kazakstan: Ecology, Democracy and Nationalism," in S. Hussey and P. Thompson (eds.), *The Roots of Environmental Consciousness: Popular Tradition and Personal Experience*, London and New York, 2000, pp. 139–159.

Eide A., "Realization of Social and Economic Rights and the Minimum Threshold Approach," *Human Rights Law Journal*, vol. 10(1–2), 1989, pp. 35–51.

Elegant R., "Fallout," *The National Review*, September 2, 2002, pp. 30–32.

Fihn B., "A New Humanitarian Era: Prohibiting the Unacceptable," *Arms Control Today*, July/August 2015, https://www.armscontrol.org/ACT/2015_0708/Features/A-New-Humanitarian-Era-Prohibiting-the-Unacceptable (accessed February 27, 2017).

Forsythe D. P., "The UN Security Council and Human Rights, State Sovereignty and Human Dignity," *International Policy Analysis*, Friedrich Ebert Stiftung, May 2012, http://library.fes.de/pdf-files/iez/09069.pdf (accessed February 14, 2017).

Fraser M., "The Illegality of Nuclear Weapons," *Nuclear Abolition Forum*, issue no. 1, 2011, pp. 36–39.

Fujita H., "The Changing Role of International Law in the Nuclear Age: From Freedom of the High Seas to Nuclear-Free-Zones," in A. J. M. Delissen and G. J. Tanja (eds.), *Humanitarian Law of Armed Conflict: Challenges Ahead: Essays in Honour of F. Kalshoven*, Dordrecht, 1991, pp. 327–350.

Gautier P., "Article 2," in O. Corten and P. Klein (eds.), *The Vienna Convention on the Law of Treaties: A Commentary*, Oxford and New York, 2011, pp. 23–56.

Geiss R., "Asymmetric Conflict Structures," *International Review of the Red Cross*, vol. 864, December 2006, pp. 757–777.

Giacca G., "Article 1, Object and Purpose," in S. Casey-Maslen, A. Clapham, G. Giacca, and S. Parker, *The Arms Trade Treaty: A Commentary*, Oxford, 2016, pp. 41–57.

Göcke K., "Indigenous Peoples in the Nuclear Age: Uranium Mining on Indigenous' Lands," in J. L. Black-Branch and D. Fleck (eds.), *Nuclear Non-Proliferation in International Law*, vol. I, The Hague, 2014, pp. 199–223.

Goldblat J., "The 1993 Chemical Weapons Convention: A Significant Step in the Process of Multilateral Disarmament," in D. Bardonnet (ed.), *The Convention on the Prohibition and Elimination of Chemical Weapons: A Breakthrough in Multilateral Disarmament*, Workshop, The Hague, November 24–26, 1994, Dordrecht, Boston, and London, 1995, pp. 15–25.

Golden Bersagel A., "Use of Nuclear Weapons as an International Crime and the Rome Statute of the International Criminal Court," in G. Nystuen, S. Casey-Maslen, and A. Golden Bersagel (eds.), *Nuclear Weapons under International Law*, Cambridge, 2014, pp. 221–243.

Goodby J. E., "A World without Nuclear Weapons: Fantasy or Necessity?" *SIPRI Yearbook 2010*, pp. 17–34.

Gowlland-Debbas V., "The Right to Life and Genocide: The Court and an International Public Policy," in L. Boisson de Chazournes and P. Sands (eds.), *International Law, the International Court of Justice and Nuclear Weapons*, Cambridge, 1999, pp. 315–337.

Greenwood Ch., "*Jus Ad Bellum* and *Jus in Bello* in the Nuclear Weapons Advisory Opinion," in L. Boisson de Chazournes and P. Sands (eds.), *International Law, the International Court of Justice and Nuclear Weapons*, Cambridge, 1999, pp. 247–266.

Hague W., Fabius L., Westerwelle G., and Bjorling E., "Why This Arms Trade Treaty Is Essential," *The Guardian*, July 2, 2012.

Hamel-Green M., "The South Pacific – The Treaty of Rarotonga," in R. Thakur (ed.), *Nuclear Weapons-Free Zones*, London and New York, 1998, pp. 59–80.

Havenaar J., Rumyantzeva G. M., van den Brink W., et al., "Long-Term Mental Health Effects of the Chernobyl Disaster: An Epidemiologic Survey in Two Former Soviet Regions," *American Journal of Psychiatry*, vol. 154(11), 1997, pp. 1605–1607.

Hawkins D., "Now We Can: Civil Society and Governments Moving Towards a Ban on Nuclear Weapons," in K. Vignard and J. Linekar (eds.), *Civil Society and Nuclear Disarmament*, disarmament forum, UNIDIR, 4/2010, pp. 39–47.

Herrmann I. and Palmieri D., "Les nouveaux conflits: une modernité archaïque?" *International Review of the Red Cross*, vol. 849, March 2003, pp. 23–44.

Hersh S. M., "The Iran Plans: Would President Bush Go to War to Stop Tehran from Getting the Bomb?", *New Yorker*, April 17, 2006, http://www.newyorker.com/magazine/2006/04/17/the-iran-plans (accessed February 27, 2017).

Hinds A., "The Arms Race and Human Rights," *International Journal of Human Rights*, vol. 1, 1997, pp. 26–40.

Hitchcock R. K., "International Human Rights, the Environment, and Indigenous Peoples," *Colo. J. Int'l Envtl. L. & Pol'y*, vol. 5, 1994, pp. 1–22.

Holtom P. and Bromley M., "Implementing an Arms Trade Treaty: Mapping Assistance to Strengthen Arms Transfer Controls," *SIPRI Insights on Peace and Security*, no. 2012/2, July 2012, http://books.sipri.org/files/insight/SIPRIInsight1202.pdf (accessed March 1, 2017).

Hulme K., "The 2008 Cluster Munitions Convention: Stepping outside the CCW Framework (Again)," *International and Comparative Law Quarterly*, vol. 58, 2009, pp. 219–227.

Human Rights Watch (HRW) and Landmine Action, "Banning Cluster Munitions, Government Policy and Practice," *Mines Action Canada*, Canada, May 2009.

Hutchinson A., "Is Radioactive Water Worth Worrying About?", *The New Yorker*, April 30, 2015, http://www.newyorker.com/tech/elements/is-radioactive-water-from-fukushima-worth-worrying-about (accessed February 28, 2017).

Ihonvbere J. O., "Africa – The Treaty of Pelidaba," in R. Thakur (ed.), *Nuclear Weapons-Free Zones*, London and New York, 1998, pp. 93–120.

Isbister R. and Tricot O'Farrell K., "Lessons Learned: How NGOs Contributed to the ATT Success," *saferworld*, June 4, 2013, http://www.saferworld.org.uk/news-and-views/comment/97-lessons-learned-how-ngos-contributed-to-the-att-success (accessed February 15, 2017).

Johnson R., "Advocates and Activists: Conflicting Approaches on Nonproliferation and the Test Ban Treaty," in A. M. Florini (ed.), *The Third Force, The Rise of Transnational Civil Society*, Tokyo and Washington, 2000, pp. 49–81.

Johnson R., "The Role of Civil Society in Negotiating the CTBT," in M. Melamud, P. Meerts, and I. W. Zartman (eds.), *Banning the Bang or the Bomb? Negotiating the Nuclear Test Ban Regime*, Cambridge, 2014, pp. 96–119.

Johnson R., "Linking Humanitarian Law and Nuclear Disarmament Action: The Case for a Nuclear Weapons Convention," *Austrian Review of International and European Law*, vol. 15, 2010, pp. 173–196.

Jurovics Y., "Article 7," in J. Fernandez and X. Pacreau (eds.), *Statut de Rome de la Cour pénale internationale: Commentaire article par article*, vol. II, Paris, 2012, pp. 417–478.

Kahn P. W., "Imagining Warfare," *European Journal of International Law*, vol. 24, no. 1, pp. 199–226.

Kellman S., "Nuclear Fallout: Nevada Takes Hard Look at Contaminated Groundwater From Historic Testing Grounds," *Water News*, November 15, 2009, http://www.circleofblue.org/2009/world/news-nuclear-fallout-nevada-takes-hard-look-at-contaminated-groundwater-from-historic-testing-grounds/ (accessed February 28, 2017).

Kimball D. G., "The Debate over Banning the Bomb," *Arms Control Today*, October 2016, p. 3.

Klabbers J., "Strange Bedfellows: The 'Interim Obligations' and the 1993 Chemical Weapons Convention," in E. P. J. Myjer (ed.), *Issues of Arms Control Law and the Chemical Weapons Convention – Obligations Inter Se and Supervisory Mechanism*, The Hague, Boston, and London, 2001, pp. 11–29.

Kleffner J. K., "Scope of Application of International Humanitarian Law," in D. Fleck (ed.), *The Handbook of International Humanitarian Law*, 3rd edn., Oxford, 2013, pp. 43–78.

Kohen M. G., "The Notion of 'State Survival' in International Law," in L. Boisson de Chazournes and P. Sands (eds.), *International Law, the International Court of Justice and Nuclear Weapons*, Cambridge, 1999, pp. 293–314.

Krause K. and MacDonald M. K., "Regulating Arms Sales through World War II," in R. D. Burns (ed.), *Encyclopedia of Arms Control and Disarmament*, vol. 2, New York, 1993, pp. 707 et seq.

Krisch N., "Capitulation in The Hague: The Marshall Islands Cases," *EJIL: Talk!*, October 10, 2016, http://www.ejiltalk.org/capitulation-in-the-hague-the-marshall-islands-cases/ (accessed February 27, 2017).

Krüger-Spengel F., "Le concept de proportionalité dans le droit de la guerre," *Military Law and Law of War Review*, 1980, pp. 175–204.

Krutzsch W., "The Preamble to the Chemical Weapons Convention," in W. Krutzsch, E. Myjer, and R. Trapp (eds.), *The Chemical Weapons Convention – A Commentary*, Oxford, 2014, pp. 51–57.

Krutzsch W., "Article I: General Obligations," in W. Krutzsch, E. Myjer, and R. Trapp (eds.), *The Chemical Weapons Convention – A Commentary*, Oxford, 2014, pp. 61–72.

Krutzsch W., Myjer E., and Trapp R., "The Chemical Weapons Convention – Objectives, Principles and Implementation Practice," in W. Krutzsch, E. Myjer, and R. Trapp (eds.), *The Chemical Weapons Convention – A Commentary*, Oxford, 2014, pp. 3–16.

Kunz M. and Viñuales J. E., "Environmental Approaches to Nuclear Weapons," in G. Nystuen, S. Casey-Maslen, and A. Golden Bersagel (eds.), *Nuclear Weapons under International Law*, Cambridge, 2014, pp. 269–291.

Kurosawa M., "New Vision towards a World Free of Nuclear Weapons," *Osaka University Law Review*, vol. 55, 2008, pp. 1–14.

Lachowski Z., "The Ban on Anti-Personnel Mines," *SIPRI Yearbook*, 1998, pp. 546–558.

Laumulin M., "Kazakhstan's Nuclear Policy and the Control of Nuclear Weapons," in G. Quester (ed.), *The Nuclear Challenge in Russia and the New States of Eurasia*, New York and London, 1995, pp. 181–211.

Leggeri F. and Gouttefarde F., "La Conférence de révision," in J. Fernandez and X. Pacreau (eds.), *Statut de Rome de la Cour pénale internationale, Commentaire article par article*, vol. II, Paris, 2012, pp. 251–268.

Levy Guyer R., "Radioactivity and Rights – Clashes at Bikini Atoll," *American Journal of Public Health*, vol. 91(9), 2001, pp. 1371–1376, http://www.ncbi.nlm.nih.gov/pmc/articles/PMC1446783/pdf/0911371.pdf (accessed February 28, 2017).

Lord M. E., "Nongovernmental Organizations in Arms Control and Disarmament," in R. D. Burns (ed.), *Encyclopedia of Arms Control and Disarmament*, vol. 1/II, New York, Oxford, Singapore, and Sydney, 1993, pp. 405–424.

Lorthois Louembet S., "Vers un traité international réglementant les transferts d'armes classiques en 2012," *Revue générale de droit international public*, vol. 114, 2010, pp. 723–746.

Makhlouf Obermeyer C., "A Cross-Cultural Perspective on Reproductive Rights," *Human Rights Quarterly*, vol. 17, 1995, pp. 366–381.

Maresca L., "A New Protocol on Explosive Remnants of War: The History and Negotiation of Protocol V to the 1980 Convention on Certain Conventional Weapons," *International Review of the Red Cross*, vol. 86, no. 856, December 2004, pp. 815–835.

Maresca L., "The Catastrophic Humanitarian Consequences of Nuclear Weapons: The Key Issues and Perspective of the International Committee of the Red Cross," in J. Borrie and T. Caughley (eds.), *Viewing Nuclear Weapons through a Humanitarian Lens*, New York and Geneva, 2013, pp. 131–144.

Martin Randin V. and Borrie J., "A Comparison between Arms Control and Other Multilateral Negotiation Processes," in J. Borrie and V. Martin Randin (eds.), *Alternative Approaches in Multilateral Decision Making, Disarmament as Humanitarian Action*, UNIDIR, Geneva, 2005, pp. 67–129.

Maslen S., "The 1996 Landmines Protocol for Refugees and the Internally Displaced," *International Journal of Refugee Law*, vol. 8, 1996, pp. 383–396.

Mathews R. J. and McCormack T. L. H., "The Influence of Humanitarian Principles in the Negotiations of Arms Control Treaties," *International Review of the Red Cross*, vol. 81, no. 834, 1999, pp. 331–352.

McCarthy P., "Deconstructing Disarmament: The Challenge of Making the Disarmament and Arms Control Machinery Responsive to the Humanitarian Imperative," in J. Borrie and V. Martin Randin (eds.), *Alternative Approaches in Multilateral Decision Making, Disarmament as Humanitarian Action*, UNIDIR, Geneva, 2005, pp. 51–66.

McLeish C. and Lak M., "The Role of Civil Society and Industrial Non-State Actors in Relation to the Chemical Weapons Convention," in W. Krutzsch, E. Myjer, and R. Trapp (eds.), *The Chemical Weapons Convention – A Commentary*, Oxford, 2014, pp. 37–48.

Metcalf C., "Indigenous Rights and the Environment: Evolving International Law," *Ottawa L. Rev.*, vol. 35, 2003–2004, pp. 101–140.

Milanović M. and Papić T., "As Bad as It Gets: The European Court of Human Rights' *Behrami and Saramati* Decision and General International Law," *ICLQ*, vol. 58, 2009, pp. 267–296.

Mills M. J., Toon O. B., Turco R. P., et al., "Massive Global Ozone Loss Predicted Following Regional Nuclear Conflict," *Proceedings of the National Academy of Sciences*, vol. 105, no. 14, 2008, pp. 5307–5312.

Miyazaki S., "The Martens Clause and International Humanitarian Law," in C. Swinarski (ed.), *Studies and Essays on International Humanitarian Law and Red Cross Principles in Honour of Jean Pictet*, The Hague and Geneva, 1984, pp. 433–444.
Momtaz D., "The Use of Nuclear Weapons and the Protection of the Environment: The Contribution of the International Court of Justice," in L. Boisson de Chazournes and P. Sands (eds.), *International Law, the International Court of Justice and Nuclear Weapons*, Cambridge, 1999, pp. 354–374.
Moxley C. J. Jr., "The Unlawfulness of the Use or Threat of Use of Nuclear Weapons," *ILSA Journal of International & Comparative Law*, vol. 8, 2002, pp. 447–472.
Moxley C. J. Jr., Burroughs J., and Granoff J., "Nuclear Weapons and Compliance with International Humanitarian Law and the Nuclear Non-Proliferation Treaty," *Fordham International Law Journal*, vol. 34, no. 4, 2011, pp. 595–696.
Myjer E. P. J., "The Law of Arms Control, Military Security and the Issues: An Introduction," in Myjer E. P. J. (ed.), *Issues of Arms Control Law and the Chemical Weapons Convention, Obligation Inter Se and Supervisory Mechanism*, The Hague, Boston, and London, 2001, pp. 1–10.
Nash T., "Preamble (2nd Paragraph)," in G. Nystuen and S. Casey-Maslen (eds.), *The Convention on Cluster Munitions, A Commentary*, Oxford and New York, 2010, pp. 45–50.
Nelson R. W., "Low-Yield Earth-Penetrating Nuclear Weapons," *Science and Global Security*, 2002, no. 1, http://scienceandglobalsecurity.org/archive/sgs10nelson.pdf (accessed February 23, 2017).
Nelson R. W., "Low-Yield Earth-Penetrating Nuclear Weapons," *FAS Public Interest Report*, January/February 2001, https://fas.org/programs/ssp/nukes/newweapons/loyieldearthpenwpnrpt.html (accessed February 27, 2017).
Nystuen G., "Conclusions on the Status of Nuclear Weapons under International Law," in G. Nystuen, S. Casey-Maslen, and A. Golden Bersagel (eds.), *Nuclear Weapons under International Law*, Cambridge, 2014, pp. 483–486.
Nystuen G., "Threats of Use of Nuclear Weapons and International Humanitarian Law," in G. Nystuen, S. Casey-Maseln, and A. Golden Bersagel (eds.), *Nuclear Weapons under International Law*, Cambridge, 2014, pp. 148–170.
Nystuen G. and Egeland K., "A 'Legal Gap'? Nuclear Weapons under International Law," *Arms Control Today*, vol. 46, no. 2, March 2016, pp. 8–14.
O'Connor S., "Nuclear Weapons and the Unnecessary Suffering Rule," in G. Nystuen, S. Casey-Maslen, and A. Golden Bersagel (eds.), *Nuclear Weapons under International Law*, Cambridge, 2014, pp. 128–147.
Oeter S., "Methods and Means of Combat," in D. Fleck (ed.), *The Handbook of International Humanitarian Law*, 3rd edn., Oxford, 2013, pp. 115–228.
Ogata S. and Cels J., "Human Security – Protecting and Empowering the People," *Global Governance – A Review of Multilateralism and International Organizations*, vol. 9, 2003, pp. 273–282.
Ohonvbere J. O., "Africa – The Treaty of Pelindaba," in R. Thakur (ed.), *Nuclear Weapons-Free Zones*, London and New York, 1998, pp. 93–120.
Okafor O. C., "A Regional Perspective: Article 22 of the African Charter on Human Rights and Peoples' Rights," in *Realizing the Right to Development, Essays in Commemoration of 25 years of the United Nations Declaration on the Right to Development*, United Nations, Office of the High Commissioner, New York and Geneva, 2013, pp. 374–384.
Orlov Y. A. and Shaversky A. V., "Indices of Neuro-Oncological Morbidity Dynamics among Younger Children in Ukraine," *Int. J. Rad. Med.*, 2004 6(1–4), pp. 72–77.

Osmani S. R., "Human Rights and Poverty: Building on the Capability Approach," *Journal of Human Development*, vol. 6(2), 2006, pp. 205–219.

Özdoğan M., Robock A., and Kucharik C. J., "Impacts of a Nuclear War in South Asia on Soybean and Maize Production in the Midwest United States," *Climatic Change*, vol. 116, 2013, pp. 373–387.

Pevec D., "The Marshall Islands Nuclear Claims Tribunal: The Claims of the Enewetak People," *Denv. J. Int'l L. & Pol'y*, vol. 35, no. 1, 2006, pp. 221–239.

Pfanner T., "David gegen Goliath oder asymmetrische Kriegsführung," *Humanitäres Völkerrecht*, vol. 3, 2005, pp. 165–176.

Poucet A., "Arms Control and Non-Proliferation Treaties: An Ontology of Concepts and Characteristics," in R. Avenhaus, N. Kyriakopoulos, M. Richard, and G. Stein (eds.), *Verifying Treaty Compliance: Limiting Weapons of Mass Destruction and Monitoring Kyoto Protocol Provisions*, Berlin, 2006, pp. 41–60.

Prăvălie R., "Nuclear Weapons Tests and Environmental Consequences: A Global Perspective," *Ambio*, October 2014, http://www.ncbi.nlm.nih.gov/pmc/articles/PMC4165831/ (accessed February 28, 2017).

Ramana M. V., "Effects of a Nuclear Blast over Bombay," in B. Fihn (ed.), *Unspeakable Suffering: The Humanitarian Impact of Nuclear Weapons*, Geneva, 2013, pp. 94–97.

Ramcharan B. G., "The Concept and Dimensions of the Right to Life," in B. G. Ramcharan (ed.), *The Right to Life in International Law*, Dordrecht, Boston, and Lancaster, 1985, pp. 1–32.

Reif K., "NATO Highlights Role of Nuclear Weapons," *Arms Control Today*, September 2016, pp. 5–6.

Reiterer M., "Preamble (8th Paragraph)," in G. Nystuen and S. Casey-Maslen (eds.), *The Convention on Cluster Munitions: A Commentary*, Oxford and New York, 2010, pp. 57–58.

Reiterer M. and Leibowitz T., "Article 5," in G. Nystuen and S. Casey-Maslen (eds.), *The Convention on Cluster Munitions: A Commentary*, Oxford and New York, 2010, pp. 328–372.

Ress G., "The Effects of Decisions and Judgments of the European Court of Human Rights in the Domestic Legal Order," *Texas International Law Journal*, vol. 40, 2005, pp. 359–382.

Rieffer-Flanagan B. A., "Is Neutral Humanitarism Dead? Red Cross Neutrality Walking the Tightrope of Neutral Humanitarism," *Human Rights Quarterly*, vol. 31, no. 4 (November 2009), pp. 888–915.

Rietiker D., "The Principle of 'Effectiveness' in the Recent Jurisprudence of the European Court of Human Rights: Its Different Dimensions and Its Consistency with Public International Law – No Need for the Concept of Treaty *Sui Generis*," *Nordic Journal of International Law*, vol. 79, no. 2, 2010, pp. 245–277.

Rietiker D., "Entre sécurité et protection de l'individu: la Convention sur les armes à sous-munitions comme dernier exemple d'un nouveau type de traité – et un modèle pour l'avenir?" *Journal du droit international*, vol. 139, no. 4, 2012, pp. 1295–1322.

Rietiker D., "Strange Bedfellows? The Cross-Fertilization of Human Rights and Arms Control, The European Court of Human Rights on Cases Involving Chemical Weapons and Anti-Personnel Mines," *Cyprus Human Rights Law Review*, vol. 3, no. 2, 2014, pp. 130–159.

Rietiker D., "The Meaning of Article VI of the Treaty on the Non-Proliferation of Nuclear Weapons: Analysis under the Rules of Treaty Interpretation," in J. L. Black-

Branch and D. Fleck (eds.), *Nuclear Non-Proliferation in International Law*, The Hague, 2014, pp. 47–84.

Ritchie N., "The Story So Far: The Humanitarian Initiative on the Impacts of Nuclear Weapons," *ILPI-UNIDIR Vienna Conference Series*, no. 1, http://www.unidir.org/files/publications/pdfs/the-story-so-far-en-616.pdf (accessed February 28, 2017).

Robinson J. P., "The Negotiations on the Chemical Weapons Convention: A Historical Overview," in M. Bothe, N. Ronzitti, and A. Rosas (eds.), *The New Chemical Weapons Convention – Implementation and Prospects*, The Hague, 1998, pp. 17–36.

Robinson J. P., "The Impact of Pugwash on the Debates over Chemical and Biological Weapons," *Annals of the New York Academy of Science*, no. 866, 1998, pp. 224–252.

Robock A. and Toon O. B., "Self-Assured Destruction: The Climate Impacts of Nuclear War," *Bulletin of the Atomic Scientists*, vol. 68, no. 5, 2012, pp. 66–74.

Ronzitti N., "Relations between the Chemical Weapons Convention and Other Relevant International Norms," in D. Bardonnet (ed.), *The Convention on the Prohibition and Elimination of Chemical Weapons: A Breakthrough in Multilateral Disarmament*, Workshop, The Hague, November 24–26, 1994, Dordrecht, Boston, and London, 1995, pp. 167–185.

Rothmar Herrmann J., "Reproductive Health," in B. Toebes, M. Hartlev, A. Hendriks, and J. Rothmar Herrmann (eds.), *Health and Human Rights in Europe*, Cambridge, Antwerp, and Portland, 2012, pp. 145–176.

Rudesill D. S., "Regulating Tactical Nuclear Weapons," *The Georgetown Law Journal*, vol. 102, 2013, pp. 99–177.

Ruff T. A., "The Health Consequences of Nuclear Explosions," in B. Fihn (ed.), *Unspeakable Suffering: The Humanitarian Impact of Nuclear Weapons*, Geneva, 2013, pp. 14–27.

Rydell R., "The United Nations and a Humanitarian Approach to Nuclear Disarmament," *International Humanitarian Law and Nuclear Weapons, Nuclear Abolition Forum*, issue no. 1, 2011, pp. 25–35.

Salmon J., "Quels sont les destinataires des avis?" in L. Boisson de Chazournes and P. Sands (eds.), *International Law, the International Court of Justice and Nuclear Weapons*, Cambridge, 1999, pp. 27–35.

Sauer T. and Pretorius J., "Nuclear Weapons and the Humanitarian Approach," *Global Change, Peace & Security*, vol. 26, no. 3, pp. 233–250.

Schultz G., Perry W., Kissinger H., and Nunn S., "Toward a Nuclear Weapon Free World," *The Wall Street Journal*, January 4, 2007.

Sen A., "Human Rights and Development," in B. A. Andreassen and S. P. Marks (eds.), *Development as a Human Right: Legal, Political and Economic Dimensions*, 2nd edn., Intersentia, 2010.

Serrano M., "Latin America – The Treaty of Tlatelolco," in R. Thakur (ed.), *Nuclear Weapons-Free Zones*, London and New York, 1998, pp. 35–58.

Shelton D., "The Inter-American Human Rights Law of Indigenous Peoples," *U. Haw. L. Rev.*, vol. 35, 2013, pp. 937–982.

Shelton D., "Human Rights and the Environment: What Specific Environmental Rights Have Been Recognized?," *Denv. J. Int'l L. & Pol'y*, vol. 35, 2006, pp. 129–171.

Shigeta Y., "The Perspective of Japanese International Lawyers," in L. Boisson de Chazournes and P. Sands (eds.), *International Law, the International Court of Justice and Nuclear Weapons*, Cambridge, 1999, pp. 435–446.

Sidel V. W., Geiger H. J., Abrams H. L. et al., "The Threat of Low-Yield Earth-Penetrating Nuclear Weapons to Civilian Populations: Nuclear "Bunker Busters" and Their Medical Consequences," *IPPNW Special Report*, http://www.ippnw.org/pdf/IPPNWEPWReport.pdf (accessed March 8, 2017).

Sikkink K., "Transnational Advocacy Networks and the Social Construction of Legal Norms," in Y. Dezalay and B. G. Garth (eds.), *Global Prescriptions, The Production, Exportation, and Importation of a New Legal Orthodoxy*, Ann Arbor, 2002, pp. 37–64.

Sommaruga C., "Does the Nature of Mine Injuries Also Justify a Total Ban?" in United Nations, *Landmines*, 1.4, September 1996, p. 11.

Spiermann O., "Lotus and the Double Structure of International Legal Argument," in L. Boisson de Chazournes and P. Sands (eds.), *International Law, the International Court of Justice and Nuclear Weapons*, Cambridge, 1999, pp. 131–152.

Stein M. A., "Disability Human Rights," *California Law Review*, vol. 95, 2007, pp. 75–121.

Tabassi L. and Dhavle A., "Article VII: National Implementation Measures," in W. Krutzsch, E. Myjer, and R. Trapp (eds.), *The Chemical Weapons Convention – A Commentary*, Oxford, 2014, pp. 195–233.

Tams C., "No Dispute About Nuclear Weapons?", *EJIL: Talk!*, October 6, 2016, http://www.ejiltalk.org/no-dispute-about-nuclear-weapons/ (accessed February 27, 2017).

Thakur R., "Stepping Stones to a Nuclear-Weapon-Free World," in R. Thakur (ed.), *Nuclear Weapons-Free Zones*, London and New York, 1998, pp. 3–32.

Ticehurst R., "The Martens Clause and the Laws of Armed Conflict," *International Review of the Red Cross*, March–April 1997, no. 317, Geneva, pp. 125–134.

Toon O. B., Robock A., Turco R. P., et al., "Consequences of Regional-Scale Nuclear Conflicts," *Science*, vol. 315, 2007, pp. 1224–1225, http://climate.envsci.rutgers.edu/pdf/SciencePolicyForumNW.pdf (accessed February 27, 2017).

Tuerlings E. and Robinson J. P., "A Trisectoral Analysis of the Chemical Weapons Convention," in W. Reinicke and F. Deng (eds.), *Critical Choices: The United Nations, Networks and the Future of Global Governance*, International Development Research Centre, Ottawa, 1999.

Tyson R., "News in Review," *Reach Critical Will (RCW)*, no. 4, May 1, 2003, pp. 1 et seq.

Venturini G., "Test-Bans and the Comprehensive Test Ban Treaty Organization," in J. L. Black-Branch and D. Fleck (eds.), *Nuclear Non-Proliferation in International Law*, The Hague, 2014, pp. 133–158.

Vöneky S., "Implementation and Enforcement of International Humanitarian Law," in D. Fleck (ed.), *The Handbook of Humanitarian Law*, 3rd edn., Oxford, 2013, pp. 647–700.

Wareham M., "The Role of Landmine Monitor in Promoting and Monitoring Compliance with the 1997 Anti-Personnel Mine Ban Convention," in J. Borrie and V. Randin (eds.), *Disarmament as Humanitarian Action: From Perspective to Practice*, UNIDIR, Geneva, 2006, pp. 79–108.

Watters K., "Environmental NGOs and the Development of Civil Society in Central Asia," in M. H. Ruffin and D. C. Waugh (eds.), *Civil Society in Central Asia*, Seattle and London, 1999, pp. 85–108.

Weiss E., "Implementing Intergenerational Equity," in M. Fitzmaurice, D. Ong, and P. Merkouris (eds.), *Research Handbook on International Environmental Law*, Cheltenham, 2010, pp. 100–116.

White J., "Landmine Survivors Speak Out," *Disarmament Forum*, 1999, pp. 7–18.

Wiebe V., Borrie J., and Smyth D., "Introduction," in G. Nystuen and S. Casey-Maslen (eds.), *The Convention on Cluster Munitions: A Commentary*, Oxford, 2010, pp. 1–36.

Wittner L. S., "Where Is the Nuclear Abolition Movement Today?", in K. Vignard and J. Linekar (eds.), *Civil Society and Nuclear Disarmament*, disarmament forum, UNIDIR, 4/2010, pp. 3–13.

Wittner, L. S. and Cooper, S., "Transnational Peace Movements and Arms Control: The Nineteenth and Twentieth Centuries,", in R. D. Burns (ed.), *Encyclopedia of Arms Control and Disarmament*, New York, 1993, pp. 491–505.

Wright T., "Do Nuclear Weapons Violate the Right to Life under International Law?", *Australian Journal of Peace Studies*, vol. 3, 2008, pp. 99–119.

Xia L. and Robock A., "Impacts of a Nuclear War in South Asia on Rice Production in Mainland China," *Climatic Change*, vol. 116, 2013, pp. 357–372.

Zambelli M., "Putting People at the Centre of the International Agenda: The Human Security Approach," *Die Friedenswarte*, vol. 77, 2002, pp. 173–186.

PUBLICATIONS AVAILABLE ONLINE

Acronym Institute for Disarmament Diplomacy, "Security and Humanitarian Implications of Relying on Nuclear Weapons for Deterrence, and Effective Legal Alternatives," A/AC.286/NGO/22, May 9, 2016, http://www.reachingcriticalwill.org/images/documents/Disarmament-fora/OEWG/2016/Documents/NGO22.pdf (accessed March 1, 2017).

Action on Armed Violence (AOAV), "Rise in Child Suicide Bombings – International Community Must Take Action," London, October 9, 2015, http://counteriedreport.co.uk/news/rise-in-child-suicide-bombings-international-community-must-take-action (accessed February 16, 2017).

Amnesty International, "How to Apply Human Rights Standards to Arms Transfer Decisions," October 2008, http://www.amnesty.org.uk/sites/default/files/how_to_apply_human_rights_standards_to_arms_transfer_decisions.pdf (accessed February 20, 2017).

Arms Control Association, "Options for Moving Forward on Disarmament," A/AC.286/NGO/23, May 9, 2016, http://www.reachingcriticalwill.org/images/documents/Disarmament-fora/OEWG/2016/Documents/NGO23.pdf (accessed March 1, 2017).

Article 36, "Humanitarian Consequences: Short Case Study of the Direct Humanitarian Impacts from a Single Nuclear Weapon Detonation on Manchester," United Kingdom, 2013, http://www.article36.org/nuclear-weapons/humanitarian-impacts-from-a-single-nuclear-weapon-detonation-on-manchester/ (accessed February 27, 2017).

Article 36 and the Women's International League for Peace and Freedom, "A Treaty Banning Nuclear Weapons," A/AC.286/NGO/3, February 24, 2016, http://www.reachingcriticalwill.org/images/documents/Disarmament-fora/OEWG/2016/Documents/NGO3.pdf (accessed February 28, 2017).

Burroughs J., "The Lawfulness of 'Low-Yield,' Earth-Penetrating Nuclear Weapons," Lawyers' Committee on Nuclear Policy, January 20, 2003, http://lcnp.org/wcourt/nwlawfulness.htm (accessed February 27, 2017).

Eide E. B., "Chair's Summary: Humanitarian Impact of Nuclear Weapons," March 5, 2013, https://www.regjeringen.no/en/aktuelt/nuclear_summary/id716343/ (accessed February 27, 2017).

Geneva Academy of International Humanitarian Law and Human Rights, "What Amounts to 'a Serious Violation of International Human Rights Law'?", *Academy Briefing*, no. 6, August 2014, https://www.sipri.org/sites/default/files/research/disarmament/dualuse/pdf-archive-att/pdfs/20140800_ga_what-amounts-to-a-serious-violation-of-international-human-rights-law.pdf (accessed February 16, 2017).

Geneva Academy of International Humanitarian Law and Human Rights, "The Arms Trade Treaty (2013)," *Academy Briefing*, no. 3, June 2013, http://www.snis.ch/system/files/academy_briefing_3_2013_arms_trade_treaty.pdf (accessed February 15, 2017).

Geneva Declaration on Armed Violence and Development, "Global Burden of Armed Violence 2011," http://www.genevadeclaration.org/measurability/global-burden-of-armed-violence/global-burden-of-armed-violence-2011.html (accessed February 14, 2017).

Global Security Institute, "Respond to the Critical Moment," A/AC.286/NGO/11, Rev. 1, May 3, 2016, http://www.reachingcriticalwill.org/images/documents/Disarmament-fora/OEWG/2016/Documents/NGO11.pdf (accessed March 1, 2017).

Handicap International (HI), "Circle of Impact – the Fatal Footprint of Cluster Munitions on People and Communities," Brussels, 2007, http://reliefweb.int/sites/reliefweb.int/files/resources/948D323F9A5BA883852572DF00674624-HI_ClusterMunitions_2007.pdf (accessed February 16, 2017).

Helfand I., "Nuclear Famine: Two Billion People at Risk? Global Impacts of Limited Nuclear War on Agriculture, Food Supplies, and Human Nutrition," IPPNW and Physicians for Social Responsibility, 2nd edn., 2013, http://www.psr.org/assets/pdfs/two-billion-at-risk.pdf (accessed February 27, 2017).

Human Rights Watch, "Ticking Time Bombs: NATO's Use of Cluster Munitions in Yugoslavia," vol. 11, no. 6 (D), June 1999, https://www.hrw.org/reports/1999/nato2/ (accessed February 15, 2017).

Human Rights Watch, "Civilians under Assault: Hezbollah's Rocket Attacks on Israel in the 2006 War," vol. 19, no. 3(E), August 2007, pp. 44–48, https://www.hrw.org/reports/2007/iopt0807/iopt0807webwcover.pdf (accessed February 15, 2017).

Human Rights Watch, "Attacks on Ghouta," September 10, 2013, https://www.hrw.org/report/2013/09/10/attacks-ghouta/analysis-alleged-use-chemical-weapons-syria (accessed March 1, 2017).

Human Rights Watch, "Syria: New Chemical Attacks in Idlib, Security Council Should Urgently Determine Responsibility," June 3, 2015, https://www.hrw.org/news/2015/06/03/syria-new-chemical-attacks-idlib (accessed February 20, 2017).

Human Rights Watch, "Syria: Chemicals Used in Idlib Attacks," April 13, 2015, https://www.hrw.org/news/2015/04/13/syria-chemicals-used-idlib-attacks (accessed February 20, 2017).

Human Rights Watch, "Landmines in Ukraine," *Technical Briefing Note*, April 2015, https://www.hrw.org/sites/default/files/supporting_resources/lm_landmines_in_ukraine-technical_briefing_note_6april2015_final.pdf (accessed February 20, 2017).

Human Rights Watch, "Ukraine: Widespread Use of Cluster Munitions," October 20, 2014, http://www.hrw.org/news/2014/10/20/ukraine-widespread-use-cluster-munitions (accessed February 20, 2017).
Human Rights Watch, "Ukraine: More Civilians Killed in Cluster Munition Attacks," March 19, 2015, https://www.hrw.org/news/2015/03/19/ukraine-more-civilians-killed-cluster-munition-attacks (accessed February 20, 2017).
Human Rights Watch, "Cluster Munition Use in Ukraine," *Technical Briefing Note*, June 2015, https://www.hrw.org/sites/default/files/supporting_resources/ukraine_clusters_briefing_note_final.pdf (accessed March 1, 2017).
IAEA, "Generic Procedures for Medical Response during a Nuclear or Radiological Emergency, Emergency Preparedness and Response," Vienna, April 2005, http://www-pub.iaea.org/MTCD/Publications/PDF/EPR-MEDICAL-2005_web.pdf (accessed February 27, 2017).
IAEA, "Radiation, People and the Environment," Vienna, February 2004, https://www.iaea.org/sites/default/files/radiation0204.pdf (accessed March 1, 2017).
IALANA, "A Legal Instrument for the Prohibition and Elimination of Nuclear Weapons," A/AC.286/NGO/12, May 2, 2016, http://www.reachingcriticalwill.org/images/documents/Disarmament-fora/OEWG/2016/Documents/NGO12.pdf (accessed February 28, 2017).
International Campaign to Ban Landmines, "Troubling Reports of Landmines Seizures and Use in Eastern Ukraine," July 8, 2014, http://www.icbl.org/en-gb/news-and-events/news/2014/troubling-reports-of-landmine-seizures-and-use-in-eastern-ukraine.aspx (accessed February 20, 2017).
International Committee of the Red Cross (ICRC), "Arms Availability and the Situation of Civilians in Armed Conflict," Geneva, 1999, https://www.icrc.org/eng/assets/files/other/icrc_002_0734_arms_availability.pdf (accessed February 15, 2017).
ICRC, "Women protected under International Humanitarian Law, Overview," October 29, 2010, http://www.icrc.org/eng/war-and-law/protected-persons/women/overviewwomen-protected.htm (accessed February 16, 2017).
ICRC, "Protecting Civilians and Humanitarian Action through the Arms Trade Treaty," Geneva, 2013, p. 4, https://www.icrc.org/eng/assets/files/publications/icrc-002-4069.pdf (accessed February 16, 2017).
ICRC, "What Are 'Serious Violations of International Humanitarian Law'?" *Explanatory Note,* Geneva, 2012, https://www.icrc.org/eng/assets/files/2012/att-what-are-serious-violations-of-ihl-icrc.pdf (accessed February 16, 2017).
ICRC, "Arms Transfer Decisions, Applying International Humanitarian Law Criteria," *Practical Guide*, Geneva, June 2007, https://www.icrc.org/eng/assets/files/other/icrc_002_0916.pdf (accessed February 16, 2017).
ICRC, "Toxic Chemicals as Weapons for Law Enforcement: A Threat to Life and International Law?", Synthesis prepared by the ICRC, in *"Incapacitating Chemical Weapons," Law Enforcement, Human Rights and Policy Perspectives*, Expert Meeting, Montreux, April 24–26, 2012, pp. 151–160, http://www.icrc.org/eng/assets/files/publications/icrc-002-4121.pdf (accessed February 20, 2017).
ICRC, "Working Towards the Elimination of Nuclear Weapons," *Background document prepared by the ICRC*, Council of Delegates of the International Red Cross and Red Crescent Movement, November 26, 2011, no. CD/11/4.1, https://www.icrc.org/eng/resources/documents/report/nuclear-background-document-2011-11-26.htm (accessed February 27, 2017).
International Council of Nurses, the International Physicians for the Prevention of Nuclear War, the World Federation of Public Health Associations, and the World

Medical Association, "The Health and Humanitarian Case for Banning and Eliminating Nuclear Weapons," A/AC.286/NGO/18, May 4, 2016, https://ippnweupdate.files.wordpress.com/2016/04/health-and-humanitarian-case-for-banning-and-eliminating-nuclear-weapons_oewg-may-2016.pdf (accessed February 28, 2017).

International Peace Bureau, Parliamentarians for Nuclear Nonproliferation and Disarmament, and World Future Council, "Move the Nuclear Weapons Money: A Handbook for Civil Society and Legislators," 2016, https://www.worldfuturecouncil.org/time-move-nuclear-weapons-money-new-resource-launched-parliamentary-event-geneva/ (accessed February 28, 2017).

International Physicians for the Prevention of Nuclear War et al., "Critical Analysis of the UNSCEAR Report 'Levels and effects of radiation exposure due to the nuclear accident after the 2011 Great East-Japan Earthquake and tsunami,'" June 5, 2014, http://www.fukushima-disaster.de/fileadmin/user_upload/pdf/english/Akzente_Unscear2014.pdf (accessed February 27, 2017).

James Martin Center for Non-proliferation Studies at the Monterey Institute of International Studies, "Disarmament and Non-Proliferation Education," A/AC.286, Misc.1/Rev.1, April 17, 2016, http://www.reachingcriticalwill.org/images/documents/Disarmament-fora/OEWG/2016/Documents/MISC1Rev1.pdf (accessed February 28, 2017).

Kellenberger J., "Foreword," in *Convention on Cluster Munitions*, Geneva 2008, p. 5, http://www.icrc.org/eng/assets/files/other/icrc_002_0961.pdf (accessed February 15, 2017).

Kytömäki E., Holtom P., and Bromley M., "Implementing the Arms Trade Treaty: Reporting International Arms Transfers," *UNIDIR Resources, Ideas for Peace and Security*, http://www.unidir.org/files/medias/pdfs/background-paper-implementing-the-arms-trade-treaty-reporting-international-arms-transfers-elli-kytoemaeki-paul-holtom-and-mark-bromley-eng-0-258.pdf (accessed February 20, 2017).

Lalanne D., "And If a Nuclear Bomb Exploded in Lyon (France)?" ican and Observatoire des armements, February 2014, http://www.obsarm.org/IMG/pdf/Bombe_sur_Lyon.pdf (accessed February 27, 2017).

Lewis P., Unal B., and Aghlani S., "Nuclear Disarmament: The Missing Link in Multilateralism," Chatham House, October 2016, https://www.chathamhouse.org/publication/nuclear-disarmament-missing-link-multilateralism (accessed February 28, 2017).

Middle Powers Initiative, "Options for a Framework Agreement," A/AC.286/NGO/20, May 4, 2016, http://www.reachingcriticalwill.org/images/documents/Disarmament-fora/OEWG/2016/Documents/NGO20.pdf (accessed February 28, 2017).

Morris-Suzuki T., "Introduction," in Greenpeace, "Lessons from Fukushima," 2012, pp. 11–13, http://www.greenpeace.org/slovenia/Global/slovenia/Dokumenti/Lessons-from-Fukushima.pdf (accessed February 27, 2017).

National Cancer Institute, "Dose Estimation and Predicted Cancer Risk for Residents of the Marshall Islands Exposed to Radioactive Fallout from the U.S. Nuclear Weapons Testing at Bikini and Eniwetok," https://dceg.cancer.gov/research/how-we-study/exposure-assessment/nci-dose-estimation-predicted-cancer-risk-residents-marshall-islands#purpose (accessed February 28, 2017).

Oxfam International, "Practical Guide: Applying Sustainable Development to Arms-Transfer Decisions," *Oxfam International Technical Brief*, https://www.oxfam.org/sites/www.oxfam.org/files/tb-practical-guide-arms-trade-decisions-apr09.pdf (accessed February 20, 2017).

Paulitz H., Eisenberg W., and Thiel R., "Health Consequences Resulting from Fukushima," Berlin, March 6, 2013, http://www.ippnw.de/commonFiles/pdfs/Atomenergie/Fukushima/Health_consequences_Fukushima_en.pdf (accessed February 28, 2017).

Pflugbeil S., Paulitz H., Claussen A., and Schmitz-Feuerhake I., "Health Effects of Chernobyl: 25 Years after the Reactor Catastrophe," Berlin, April 8, 2011, http://www.ratical.org/radiation/Chernobyl/HEofC25yrsAC.html (accessed February 28, 2017).

Reuters, "Pakistan Builds Low Yield Nuclear Capability," May 15, 2011, http://www.reuters.com/article/2011/05/15/pakistan-nuclear-idAFL3E7GE02F20110515 (accessed February 27, 2017).

Rietiker D. and Burroughs J., "The Incompatibility of WMDs with the Right to Life (Article 6 ICCPR), A Submission to the HRC," *Swiss Lawyers for Nuclear Disarmament (SLND) and International Association of Lawyers Against Nuclear Arms (IALANA)*, September 7, 2016, https://safna.org/2016/09/08/the-incompatibility-of-wmd-to-the-right-to-life-article-6-iccpr-a-submission-to-the-un-human-rights-committee/ (accessed February 28, 2017).

Trapp R., "'Incapacitating Chemical Agents': Potential Policy Options, Background Paper," in *"Incapacitating Chemical Weapons," Law Enforcement, Human Rights and Policy Perspectives*, Expert Meeting, Montreux, April 24–26, 2012, Report, pp. 99–116, http://www.icrc.org/eng/assets/files/publications/icrc-002-4121.pdf (accessed February 20, 2017).

Van der Zeijden W. and Snyder S., "The Rotterdam Blast," *Pax*, 2014, http://www.paxchristi.net/news-media/resources-pax-christi-member-organisations (accessed February 27, 2017).

Vandova V., "The European Court of Human Rights's Judgment in the Case of *Finogenov and Others v. Russia*," in *"Incapacitating Chemical Weapons," Law Enforcement, Human Rights and Policy Perspectives*, Expert Meeting, Montreux, April 24–26, 2012, pp. 46–49, http://www.icrc.org/eng/assets/files/publications/icrc-002-4121.pdf (accessed February 20, 2017).

Women International League for Peace and Freedom, "Cluster Munitions and Gender – It Takes More than a Ban," 2008, http://reliefweb.int/sites/reliefweb.int/files/resources/C9A349A5ED559761C125751D0037C209-wilpf_nov08.pdf (accessed February 16, 2017).

Index

For Product Safety Concerns and Information please contact our EU representative GPSR@taylorandfrancis.com
Taylor & Francis Verlag GmbH, Kaufingerstraße 24, 80331 München, Germany

www.ingramcontent.com/pod-product-compliance
Ingram Content Group UK Ltd.
Pitfield, Milton Keynes, MK11 3LW, UK
UKHW022009180926
475701UK00003B/269
9780367267018